Your Project
Management Coach

Your Project Management Coach

Best Practices for Managing Projects in the Real World

Bonnie Biafore
Teresa Stover

John Wiley & Sons, Inc.

Your Project Management Coach: Best Practices for Managing Projects in the Real World

Published by
John Wiley & Sons, Inc.
10475 Crosspoint Boulevard
Indianapolis, IN 46256
www.wiley.com

Copyright © 2012 by John Wiley & Sons, Inc., Indianapolis, Indiana
Published simultaneously in Canada

ISBN: 978-1-118-14424-4
ISBN: 978-1-118-22560-8 (ebk)
ISBN: 978-1-118-23895-0 (ebk)
ISBN: 978-1-118-26368-6 (ebk)

Manufactured in the United States of America

10 9 8 7 6 5 4 3 2 1

For general information on our other products and services please contact our Customer Care Department within the United States at (877) 762-2974, outside the United States at (317) 572-3993 or fax (317) 572-4002.

Wiley publishes in a variety of print and electronic formats and by print-on-demand. Some material included with standard print versions of this book may not be included in e-books or in print-on-demand. If this book refers to media such as a CD or DVD that is not included in the version you purchased, you may download this material at http://booksupport.wiley.com. For more information about Wiley products, visit www.wiley.com.

Library of Congress Control Number: 2011945553

About the Authors

Bonnie Biafore is an only child, so learning to play well with others did not come until much later in life. However, she has always been an unrepentant organizing fool, which is obvious to anyone who examines the storage bins in her garage with their neatly segregated collections of nuts, bolts, screws, fuses, and other items of home maintenance.

Bonnie earned a Bachelor of Science in Architecture and a Master of Science in Structural Engineering, but neither of those fields quite did the trick. Through a number of fortunate coincidences, Bonnie ended up managing projects, which, with training and experience, turned out to be an appropriate and satisfying career for her. Project management helped her social skills immensely and fulfills her desire to get things done and keep things organized. In 2003, she earned a Project Management Professional (PMP) certification from the Project Management Institute.

When she isn't managing projects for clients, Bonnie writes about project management, personal finance, investing, and technology. She applies her incorrigible sense of humor to writing about those dry subjects in such a way that people might actually want to read about them.

Bonnie is the author of more than 20 books, including *Successful Project Management, Project 2010: The Missing Manual,* and several other award-winning books. When she isn't working, she hikes in the mountains with her dogs, cooks ethnic food, and works out. She is also wrapping up work on her first novel. You can learn more at her website, www.bonniebiafore.com or email Bonnie at bonnie.biafore@gmail.com.

Teresa Stover can't think without a pen or keyboard in hand and can't function without a task list, complete with work estimates and schedule. As supervisor of a technical publications department for a Silicon Valley startup in the late 1980s, Teresa came face to face with the art and science of project management. Desperate to know who needed to be working on what on any given day, she discovered Gantt and PERT charts and has never looked back.

Since then, Teresa has worked more than 20 years as a technical communication and project management consultant for software, manufacturing, business, and education. She specializes in project management for entrepreneurial startups, nonprofit organizations, and content development endeavors. Her clients have included Apple Computer, National Semiconductor, Boeing, MetLife, and the Puyallup School District. Her work passions are clarity, organization, and process.

Teresa conducts workshops on project management, business, and writing topics and has authored 15 books, including *Microsoft Project 2010 Inside Out.* Other recent achievements include recognition for her work in instructional design, web content, and nonprofit organizational development.

Teresa lives in southern Oregon with her husband, Craig, and her German Shepherd, Draco. With this book finished, she hopes for new opportunities for exploration and experience, conversation and creativity. She also plans to volunteer more for her favorite cause — Josephine Community Libraries, a nongovernmental organization that runs the member-supported, volunteer-run local public library system.

For more, visit Teresa's website, www.stoverwriting.com. Teresa welcomes emails from readers sent to teresa@stoverwriting.com.

About the Technical Editor

Bob McGannon, currently based in Canberra, Australia, is an author, speaker, trainer, and consultant and is the owner of three project management–related businesses in the United States and Australia. He has 27 years of project management and information technology management experience and has delivered project management services in eight different countries.

Bob is certified as a Project Management Professional (PMP) by the Project Management Institute. He is also a certified Prince2 Practitioner, a certified IBM Corporation Project Executive, a certified DMR-P project management mentor for the Boeing Aircraft Corporation, and a Certified Master Project Coach by the International Institute of Project Coaching.

Bob is the author of a blog entitled Intelligent Disobedience that can be accessed at `mindavation.com/IDBlog/`. He also can be heard on the In My Judgment weekly podcast which can be accessed at `www.mindavation.com`.

Credits

Executive Editor
Robert Elliott

Project Editor
Christina Haviland

Technical Editor
Bob McGannon

Production Editor
Rebecca Anderson

Copy Editor
Nancy Rapoport

Editorial Manager
Mary Beth Wakefield

Freelancer Editorial Manager
Rosemarie Graham

Associate Director of Marketing
David Mayhew

Marketing Manager
Ashley Zurcher

Business Manager
Amy Knies

Production Manager
Tim Tate

Vice President and Executive Group Publisher
Richard Swadley

Vice President and Executive Publisher
Neil Edde

Associate Publisher
Jim Minatel

Project Coordinator, Cover
Katie Crocker

Proofreader
Dawn Adams

Indexer
Johnna VanHoose Dinse

Cover Image
© Bruce Lonngren/iStockPhoto

Cover Designer
Ryan Sneed

Acknowledgments

Behind every book is a team that is responsible for turning the rough drafts of the authors into something wonderful. This book is no exception. Our thanks go to Christina Haviland, Nancy Rapoport, and the rest of the Wiley folks for their guidance, support, and patience as this book wound its way to publication.

It is hard to find the words appropriate to thank Bob McGannon, whose official role for this book was technical editor. He provided many of the helpful techniques you'll find in this book. He regaled us with project management stories and helped set the "Let's not take ourselves too seriously" tone for the book. Best of all, he brought us back on track when we strayed from reality with his signature "Whoa, Nellie!" comments.

Contents at a Glance

Introduction   xxix

Part I   Understanding Projects and Project Management   1
Chapter 1   Getting to Know Projects   3
Chapter 2   Getting to Know Project Management   11

Part II   Planning a Project   33
Chapter 3   Getting a Project Off the Ground   35
Chapter 4   Getting to Know a Project Plan   73
Chapter 5   Identifying the Work to Be Completed   85
Chapter 6   Estimating Work and Cost   105
Chapter 7   Planning Project Resources   121
Chapter 8   Building a Schedule   131
Chapter 9   Planning for Quality   155
Chapter 10   Setting Up a Communication Plan   169
Chapter 11   Setting Up a Change Management Plan   191
Chapter 12   Managing Risk   203

Part III   Executing a Project   225
Chapter 13   Kicking Off a Project   227
Chapter 14   Taming Processes, Problems, and Conflicts   239

Chapter 15   The Keys to Successful Meetings   251

Chapter 16   Transforming People into a Team   267

Part IV   Monitoring and Controlling   277

Chapter 17   Gathering Progress Information   279

Chapter 18   Evaluating Progress and Performance   289

Chapter 19   Getting a Plan Back on Track   303

Part V   Closing the Project   315

Chapter 20   Obtaining Acceptance and Other Wrap-Up Tasks   317

Chapter 21   Documenting a Project for Posterity   327

Chapter 22   Don't Forget Lessons Learned   337

Part VI   Taking the Next Steps in Project Management   355

Chapter 23   Running a Project Management Office   357

Chapter 24   Managing a Portfolio of Projects   369

Chapter 25   Selecting the Right Projects   379

Part VII   Reference   395

Appendix A Answers   397

Appendix B Forms   423

Glossary   439

Index   451

Contents

Introduction		**xxix**
Part I	**Understanding Projects and Project Management**	**1**
Chapter 1	**Getting to Know Projects**	**3**
	What Is a Project?	3
	A Project Is a Unique Endeavor	5
	A Project Has Clearly Defined Objectives and Deliverables	5
	A Project Has a Beginning and an End	7
	A Project Usually Has a Budget	8
	How Do Projects Differ from Other Work?	9
	Summary	10
	Coach's Review	10
	Test Your Knowledge	10
	Project Challenge	10
Chapter 2	**Getting to Know Project Management**	**11**
	What Is Project Management?	12
	Project Management Processes: Start to Finish	13
	Initiating a Project	14
	Planning a Project	15
	Executing a Project	17
	Monitoring and Controlling a Project	18
	Closing a Project	19
	Balancing Scope, Time, Cost, and Quality	20
	Project Management Methodologies	21
	Traditional Waterfall Project Management	21
	Iterative and Agile Project Management	22
	Project Management Knowledge Areas	23
	Scope Management	24
	Time Management	25

Cost Management   25
Human Resource Management   25
Procurement Management   26
Communication Management   26
Quality Management   26
Risk Management   27
Integration Management   27
Who Makes a Good Project Manager?   28
Business Savvy   28
Technical Skills   28
Soft Skills   29
Varying Viewpoints   29
Delegating   30
Leadership and Interpersonal Skills   30
Flexibility   30
Doing the Right Things for the Project   30
Summary   30
Coach's Review   31
Test Your Knowledge   31
Project Challenge   31

Part II   Planning a Project   33

Chapter 3   Getting a Project Off the Ground   35
From Idea to Project: An Overview of
  Project Initiation   36
Defining a Project   37
Discovering the Problem or Opportunity   40
Articulating the Project Goal and Objectives   44
Developing the Project Goal   44
Creating the Project Objectives   45
Deciding on the Project Strategy   46
Brainstorming Possibilities   46
Identifying Constraints   47
Choosing the Right Strategy   48
Gathering Requirements   49
Starting with Broad Requirements   49
Mining for Requirements   49
Differentiating and Prioritizing Requirements   50
What Constitutes Success?   51
Documenting Project Scope   52
Elements of the Scope Statement   53
Controlling Scope Creep   55
Specifying the Deliverables   57
Identifying Risks, Assumptions, and Constraints   58
Working with Risks   58
Working with Assumptions   59

Working with Constraints   59
Identifying the Project Stakeholders   60
Preparing the Project Proposal   62
Getting Approval or Sign-Off   65
Publicizing the Project Charter   66
    Preparing a Project Charter   67
    Distributing the Project Charter   68
Assembling the Project Notebook   68
    Using the Project Notebook for Approved Projects   69
    Using the Project Notebook for Tabled or
        Denied Projects   69
    Choosing the Form of the Project Notebook   69
Summary   71
Coach's Review   71
    Test Your Knowledge   71
    Project Challenge   72

Chapter 4   **Getting to Know a Project Plan**   **73**
What Work Has to Be Done?   74
    Identifying Work   74
    Organizing Work into Major Categories   74
How Much Will the Project Cost?   75
    Obtaining Early Cost Estimates   75
    Building a Budget   75
Who Will Do the Work?   76
    An Introduction to Project Resources   76
    Identifying Resources   77
When Will the Project Be Done?   77
    What You Need to Build a Schedule   78
    Brick Wall Deadlines Versus Soft Date Targets   80
How Will the Project Be Managed?   80
    The Project Manager and Managing Stakeholders   81
    Setting Ground Rules   81
    Defining Management Processes   81
    Remembrance of Projects Past   82
Summary   83
Coach's Review   83
    Test Your Knowledge   83
    Project Challenge   84

Chapter 5   **Identifying the Work to Be Completed**   **85**
Understanding the Work Breakdown Structure   86
    What Is a Work Breakdown Structure?   86
    Why Is the WBS Essential?   87
Identifying Work   88
    Who Helps Identify Work?   88
    Jump-Starting with Other Sources   88

Planning as a Group 89
Identifying Work from the Top Down 90
Identifying Work from the Bottom Up 92
How Much Is Enough? 93
Validating the WBS 95
Organizing Work in the WBS 96
Calling Out Deliverables 97
Formatting Your WBS 97
Naming Your WBS 99
Numbering Your WBS 99
Specifying Task Details 101
Summary 102
Coach's Review 102
Test Your Knowledge 102
Project Challenge 103

Chapter 6 **Estimating Work and Cost** **105**
Who Should Estimate a Project? 106
Using a Core Planning Team 106
Obtaining Estimates from Team Members 107
Managing the Uncertainty of Estimates 107
When to Use Different Levels of Estimates 108
Preventing Problems from Padded Estimates 109
Preparing Estimates 110
The Difference between Duration and Effort 110
Estimating Methods 111
Reusing Existing Information 112
Engaging Experts 112
Using a Parametric Model or Estimating Tool 112
Applying the Delphi Technique 113
Using Optimistic, Pessimistic, and Most Likely Estimates 114
Estimating from the Top Down 115
Estimating from the Bottom Up 115
Estimating Project Costs 115
What Goes into Labor Costs? 116
Material, Equipment, and Facility Costs 116
Estimating Other Costs 117
Building a Budget 117
Summary 118
Coach's Review 118
Test Your Knowledge 118
Project Challenge 118

Chapter 7 **Planning Project Resources** **121**
Documenting Roles and Responsibilities 122
Who's Involved with What 123

Levels of Involvement 124
Identifying Resource Needs 125
Types of Resources 125
Breaking Down Resource Needs 126
Building a Project Organization Chart 127
Preparing a Resource Plan 127
Summary 128
Coach's Review 128
Test Your Knowledge 129
Project Challenge 129

Chapter 8 **Building a Schedule** **131**
Tools for Building a Schedule 132
Sequencing with Dependencies 135
Setting Up Predecessors and Successors 135
Understanding the Dependency Types 136
Starting to Schedule 137
Understanding the Critical Path 138
Scheduling with Lead and Lag Time 139
Applying Date Constraints 140
Keeping Date Constraints Flexible 141
Scheduling Specific Dates 142
Marking Deadlines 142
Indicating Milestones 142
Assigning Resources to Tasks 143
Adding Generic Resources 143
Adding Specific Resources 144
Assigning Multiple Resources to One Task 144
Modeling a Realistic Schedule 145
Scheduling around Nonworking Time 146
Defining Non-Project Time 146
Adjusting Tasks for Resource Productivity 147
Managing Part-Timers and Multitaskers 147
Scheduling with the Critical Chain Method 148
Working Back from the Finish Date 148
Balancing Constrained Resources 149
Adding Buffers 149
Optimizing the Schedule 149
Shortening the Schedule 150
Reducing Project Costs 151
Balancing Resource Assignments 152
Summary 153
Coach's Review 154
Test Your Knowledge 154
Project Challenge 154

Chapter 9	**Planning for Quality**	**155**
	Defining Quality	156
	Quality and the Requirements Document	157
	Constraints on Quality	158
	Quality Standards and Methods	158
	Developing the Quality Plan	159
	Elements of the Quality Management Plan	160
	Understanding the Cost of Quality	161
	Integrating the Quality Management Plan	161
	Taking Responsibility for Quality	161
	Building in Excellence with QA	162
	Evaluating Quality Results	162
	Implementing Corrective Actions	163
	Verifying the Standards with QC	164
	Measuring and Recording Quality	165
	Finding Causes of Quality Problems	166
	Summary	166
	Coach's Review	167
	Test Your Knowledge	167
	Project Challenge	167
Chapter 10	**Setting Up a Communication Plan**	**169**
	Guidelines for Good Communication	170
	What Is Communication?	170
	How to Get Your Message Across	172
	The Importance of Listening	174
	The Components of a Communication Plan	175
	Who Are the Audiences?	176
	The Project Sponsor	177
	Management Stakeholders	177
	Team Members	177
	External Audiences	177
	What Do You Communicate?	178
	What Information Do Audiences Need?	178
	Information for Management Stakeholders	178
	Functional Managers	180
	Team Members	180
	Status Reporting	180
	Status from and to Team Members	181
	Status for Management	183
	What's the Best Communication Method?	184
	In-Person Meetings	184
	Videoconferencing and Conference Calls	184
	Email	185
	Telephone	187
	Written Documentation	187

	Who's Responsible?	187
	Frequency and Timing	188
	Summary	188
	Coach's Review	189
	Test Your Knowledge	189
	Project Challenge	189
Chapter 11	**Setting Up a Change Management Plan**	**191**
	When to Manage Changes	192
	When You Don't Manage Changes	192
	When You Do Manage Changes	193
	Who Sits on a Change Review Board	193
	The Anatomy of a Change Management Process	194
	Defining the Baseline Documents	195
	Documenting a Change Request	195
	Using a Change Request Form	195
	Tracking a Change Request	197
	Evaluating a Change Request	198
	Making Decisions about Change Requests	199
	Updating the Baseline Documents	200
	Monitoring Change Requests	201
	Summary	201
	Coach's Review	201
	Test Your Knowledge	201
	Project Challenge	202
Chapter 12	**Managing Risk**	**203**
	Identifying Risks to a Project	204
	Analyzing the Risks	208
	Rating Risks as Low, Medium, or High	208
	Rating Risks Numerically	209
	Recording the Risk Ratings and Scores	210
	Choosing the Risks to Manage	210
	Planning Risk Responses	211
	Planning Responses to Negative Risks	212
	Planning Responses to Positive Risks	214
	Compiling the Risk Management Plan	215
	Establishing Contingencies	216
	Building in a Schedule Buffer	217
	Setting Up Contingency Funds	218
	Tracking Risks	218
	When a Risk Becomes Reality	220
	Tracking Issues	221
	Summary	222
	Coach's Review	222
	Test Your Knowledge	222
	Project Challenge	223

Part III	**Executing a Project**	**225**
Chapter 13	**Kicking Off a Project**	**227**
	Preparing to Execute the Project	228
	Obtaining Approval	228
	Saving Project Baselines	229
	Updating the Project Notebook	230
	Obtaining Resources	231
	Obtaining In-House Resources	231
	Procuring Resources from Vendors	232
	Soliciting Vendors	232
	Selecting Vendors	233
	Contracting	233
	Next Steps	234
	Holding a Kickoff Meeting	235
	Implementing Your Plans	235
	Summary	236
	Coach's Review	236
	Test Your Knowledge	236
	Project Challenge	237
Chapter 14	**Taming Processes, Problems, and Conflicts**	**239**
	Defining Project Processes	240
	What Makes a Good Process?	240
	Making Processes a Success	241
	Defeating Poor Processes	243
	Guidelines for Effectiveness	244
	Making Decisions and Solving Problems	244
	Focus on What's Important	244
	Define the Problem	246
	Prioritize	246
	Consider Your Options	246
	Ask for Help	247
	Making Things Happen	247
	How to Resolve Conflicts	248
	Summary	250
	Coach's Review	250
	Test Your Knowledge	250
	Project Challenge	250
Chapter 15	**The Keys to Successful Meetings**	**251**
	Running Effective Meetings	252
	Planning a Meeting	252
	Setting the Agenda	253
	Inviting Participants	254
	Preparing for the Meeting	255
	Starting on Time	256

Setting Expectations   256
Facilitating the Meeting   257
Ending on Time   258
Types of Project Meetings   258
Kickoff Meetings   258
Project Status Meetings   259
Management Meetings   260
Brainstorming Meetings   261
Planning Meetings   262
Following Up after Meetings   263
Documenting Decisions and Action Items   264
Adjusting the Project Plan   264
Summary   264
Coach's Review   265
Test Your Knowledge   265
Project Challenge   265

Chapter 16   Transforming People into a Team   267
Developing a Team   267
Turning Individuals into a Team   268
Building Relationships with Your People   269
Increasing Your Influence   272
Evaluating People's Performance   273
Finding Out What's Going On   273
Working with Line Managers   274
Handling People Problems   275
Summary   275
Coach's Review   276
Test Your Knowledge   276
Project Challenge   276

Part IV   Monitoring and Controlling   277

Chapter 17   Gathering Progress Information   279
Choosing the Data to Collect   280
Schedule and Cost Data   280
Quality Data   282
Issues and Risks   282
Determining the Level of Detail   283
Obtaining Time and Status   283
Choosing the Frequency   283
Sources of Data   284
Summary   286
Coach's Review   287
Test Your Knowledge   287
Project Challenge   287

Chapter 18	**Evaluating Progress and Performance**	**289**
	Evaluating Progress and Variance	290
	Reviewing Milestones	290
	Evaluating Variances	291
	Earned Value Analysis	293
	Understanding Earned Value Measures	293
	Planned Value	293
	Earned Value	294
	Actual Cost	294
	Analyzing Performance with Earned Value	295
	Evaluating Earned Value Measures in a Graph	295
	Using Additional Earned Value Indicators	296
	Evaluating Financials	297
	Determining the Payback Period	297
	Identifying the Net Present Value	298
	Calculating the Internal Rate of Return	300
	Summary	300
	Coach's Review	301
	Test Your Knowledge	301
	Project Challenge	301
Chapter 19	**Getting a Plan Back on Track**	**303**
	Ways to Correct Course	304
	Fast-Tracking a Project Schedule	304
	Which Tasks Should You Fast-Track?	304
	Fast-Tracking Options	305
	Crashing a Schedule	305
	Which Tasks Should You Crash?	306
	Other Crashing Considerations	307
	Using Different Resources	308
	Asking People to Work Overtime	308
	Reducing Scope	309
	Who Approves Course Corrections	310
	Getting a Project Out of Trouble	311
	Recognizing the Problem	311
	Evaluating the Situation	312
	Preparing a Recovery Plan	312
	Monitoring the Recovery	313
	Summary	313
	Coach's Review	314
	Test Your Knowledge	314
	Project Challenge	314
Part V	**Closing the Project**	**315**
Chapter 20	**Obtaining Acceptance and Other Wrap-Up Tasks**	**317**
	Determining Whether the Project Is a Success	318
	Developing Acceptance Tests	318
	Running Acceptance Tests	319

Obtaining Sign-Off 320
Documenting the Project: The Project Closeout Report 320
Summarizing the Project 321
Quantifying Results 321
Financial, Legal, and Administrative Closeout 323
Project Transitions 324
Handing Off Information 324
Transitioning Resources 325
Summary 325
Coach's Review 326
Test Your Knowledge 326
Project Challenge 326

Chapter 21 Documenting a Project for Posterity 327
Gathering Information 328
Organizing the Project Archives 330
Beware of Too Much Information 331
Categorize Wisely 331
Do It Today 331
Offer a Roadmap 332
Storing the Project Archives 333
Summary 334
Coach's Review 334
Test Your Knowledge 334
Project Challenge 335

Chapter 22 Don't Forget Lessons Learned 337
How Lessons Learned Help 338
Gathering Lessons Learned 340
Collecting Feedback 341
Preparing for Lessons Learned Meetings 342
Conducting Lessons Learned Meetings 344
Minimizing the Fear of Lessons Learned 346
Documenting Lessons Learned 348
Deciding on the Information to Include 349
Presenting Lessons Learned 350
Disseminating Lessons Learned 352
Using Past Lessons Learned 352
Summary 353
Coach's Review 353
Test Your Knowledge 353
Project Challenge 354

Part VI Taking the Next Steps in Project Management 355

Chapter 23 Running a Project Management Office 357
Defining PMO Functions 357
Facilitating Standards and Best Practices 358
Ensuring Compliance Requirements 360
Supporting Project Methodologies 360

Providing Project Management Tools 360

Managing Resources and Communication 361

Mentoring and Training Project Managers 362

Setting Up a PMO 362

When Do You Need a PMO? 363

Understanding PMO Types 364

Specifying PMO Objectives and Services 365

Summary 366

Coach's Review 367

Test Your Knowledge 367

Project Challenge 367

Chapter 24 Managing a Portfolio of Projects 369

What Is Project Portfolio Management? 370

Evaluating and Prioritizing Projects for
the Portfolio 372

Tracking and Managing the Project Portfolio 374

Tracking Portfolio Projects 375

Conducting Checkpoint Evaluations 375

Reporting on Portfolio Projects 377

Managing Portfolio Details 377

Summary 378

Coach's Review 378

Test Your Knowledge 378

Project Challenge 378

Chapter 25 Selecting the Right Projects 379

Capturing Ideas for Projects 380

Mining the Organization's Strategic Goals 380

Documenting a Project Idea 382

Tracking Project Ideas 384

Selecting Projects 385

Developing a Selection Process 385

Criteria for Selecting Projects 386

What Benefits? 387

What Cost? 387

Can It Be Done? 388

Scoring and Prioritizing Project Ideas 389

Exceptions to Selection Criteria 390

Succeeding with a Project Review Board 391

Summary 392

Coach's Review 392

Test Your Knowledge 393

Project Challenge 393

Part VII	Reference	395
Appendix A	Answers	397
Appendix B	Forms	423
	Glossary	439
	Index	451

Introduction

Projects come in all shapes and sizes — from monumental undertakings, such as building the Great Wall of China, to less grand endeavors such as developing a new product for your company, to smaller projects that can be just as satisfying, such as helping your beloved only child get into college and out of your hair. In days of old, when pharaohs and emperors could direct thousands of minions to do their bidding, managing budgets, meeting delivery dates, and using resources effectively might not have been as important as they are today. On the other hand, the consequences of failing to achieve objectives were probably grim.

Today, projects are more abundant than ever. But the business climate has changed and continues to evolve. Organizations want more work done more quickly or more benefits delivered for less money. Change is the only constant, but even the pace of change has accelerated. A haphazard approach to projects just won't do.

Common sense goes a long way toward getting things done in projects, even if you don't have formal training in project management. But, add in good project management practices and your projects will run more smoothly and deliver objectives more dependably. As you work on larger and more complex projects, project management processes become even more important. How else can you hope to achieve project goals while staying on top of thousands of tasks performed by hundreds of team members over several years?

Sometimes, a project might throw you an unexpected curve that has you wondering what to do. Maybe the pressure is on to "get something done" and you need to choose the most important action you can take to make your project a success. Perhaps your new project management assignment takes you into aspects of project management you've never dabbled in before.

At times like these, you probably wish you had a project management expert in the next office to coach you and give you sage advice. If you aren't so fortunate, this book can help. The authors of this book have managed their fair share of projects and learned techniques for resolving problems and getting things done more effectively. Most important, they have learned that the most helpful information doesn't come from academic textbooks but from the real world of projects and from other project managers. With that principle in mind, the authors have written this book to help both beginning and experienced project managers take their project management skills to the next level.

If you are new to project management, you will learn the processes that make up project management from start to finish. Each chapter describes the processes you utilize, explains the benefits of performing those project management activities, and warns you about the potential pitfalls of skipping them. More experienced project managers will appreciate the advice and tools in each chapter that help tame challenging project management situations.

Overview of the Book

Whether you want to learn about project management from the beginning or get guidance on a project problem, your time is precious. The goal of this book is to help you get up to speed quickly or find the specific nugget of knowledge you need — not waste your time with dense, dry dissertations on all things project management.

If you're managing a project for the first time, this book acts as your mentor by explaining the fundamentals of project management in an easy-to-swallow, engaging style. You can learn which activities are essential, which are optional, and which are needed only in specific situations. The book uses stories and examples to make concepts and techniques easier to understand.

If you're already managing projects, the book regularly dishes out handy advice for managing projects more successfully, avoiding the more common project management mistakes, and dealing with the realities of managing projects.

How This Book Is Organized

Your Project Management Coach is a resource for beginning and experienced project managers. If you're just starting to manage projects, this book explains the basics so you will be able to avoid common project management mistakes and start off on the right foot managing your projects.

Managing a project isn't a linear progression from start to finish. Before your project is done, you'll revisit various aspects, sometimes several times, for example, as you gradually fine-tune your project plan to satisfy all the project objectives. The chapters in this book introduce project management activities in the order in which you typically perform them from the beginning of a project. You will learn which processes you might revisit and repeat, or perform simultaneously with others.

For experienced project managers, there's no need to read the book cover to cover. Simply jump to the topic you need to prepare for your next project management activity or resolve the latest project situation.

The book is organized in parts that map to the project management process groups outlined in the Project Management Institute's Project Management Body of Knowledge (PMBOK). That way, readers who are new to project management can start by learning how to prepare a project for success with the activities performed in the initiating process group. The remaining parts describe what you do as a project manager to plan, execute, monitor and control, and finally close a project.

The following is a brief summary of what each chapter covers. The book builds on topics from previous chapters, so you'll find cross-references to related topics. In addition, the chapters include handy advice in tips, notes, and warnings. If you're preparing to take the Project Management Institute's Project Management Professional Examination, take note of the cross-references that map material in chapters to the corresponding domains and tasks in the examination outline.

To help beginning project managers get started, Part I provides some background on projects and project management. Chapter 1 describes what makes a project a project and also shows how to differentiate project work from other types of work. Chapter 2 is a high-level introduction to project management. It covers a lot of ground but it provides a solid orientation before you learn all the specifics in later chapters.

Part II discusses the processes for planning projects. Chapter 3 details the steps in the initiating processes that take a project from a mere idea to a plan. Chapter 4 provides an overview of all the essential elements of a project plan, including scope, cost, and schedule. In Chapter 5, you learn how to identify the work to be done in the project and how to create the work breakdown structure. Chapter 6 introduces estimating, including who should prepare estimates, when to use different levels of estimate accuracy, what you estimate, and which methods to use in different situations. Once you estimate the project, you can turn to Chapter 7 to learn how to plan for the resources you'll need to perform the project work. Chapter 8 brings together the work breakdown structure, the estimates, and the resource plan to build the project schedule. Here you set the task sequence, apply dates, and assign resources to tasks. You also optimize the project plan, balancing scope, time, and cost, along with resources, quality, and risk.

In addition to the project schedule, a project plan has several additional subplans that describe how you will run the project. Chapter 9 explains how you create the quality plan, including the complementary roles of quality assurance and quality control in the project. Communication is a huge part of project management, so Chapter 10 begins by describing techniques for communicating effectively. Then, it explains how to build a communication plan to make sure that everyone involved in the project receives the information they need in the most effective way. Chapter 11 covers setting up a change management plan, which describes how you will manage the inevitable change requests that arise in every project. In Chapter 12, you learn how to work with your team to identify and analyze project risks, plan responses to the most dangerous risks, and track risks and issues.

Part III covers the processes for executing a project. Chapter 13 describes the initial activities, such as obtaining formal approval to begin work and saving a baseline for the plan. This chapter also discusses obtaining resources, whether they come from within your organization or from vendors. Chapter 14 provides an overview of techniques for handling a variety of situations: defining good processes that team members will use, making decisions, solving problems, making things happen, and resolving conflicts. Chapter 15 includes tips and techniques for running effective project meetings, whether it's a weekly status meeting, a management presentation about a proposed project, or a brainstorming session. Chapter 16 returns to the topic of team members, this time to discuss how to transform individual team members into a functioning team and also how to evaluate team members' performance.

Part IV includes monitoring and controlling projects. Chapter 17 describes the data to collect about a project, including time, status, quality, cost, and other information. Chapter 18 introduces several methods for evaluating progress and performance. Then, if you find that your project is off course, Chapter 19 describes methods for bringing the project back on track.

Part V covers processes for closing a project and wrapping up all the loose ends. Chapter 20 covers how to determine whether the project was a success and how to obtain sign-off that the project is complete. It also describes other activities you must perform to close a project. Chapter 21 explains methods for documenting the history of your project for the archives. Chapter 22 details the importance of collecting and recording lessons learned throughout the project or at the end.

Part VI takes project management further with methods for an organization to expand its effectiveness while managing multiple projects. Chapter 23 describes the services and advantages a project management office can bring to an organization that implements many projects. Chapter 24 explains how project portfolio management can help an organization meet its business objectives. Coming full circle, Chapter 25 covers techniques for capturing and evaluating project ideas to determine which of them merit approval and support as a project that will help fulfill the organization's strategic goals.

The book includes three appendixes. Appendix A provides the answers to the questions in the "Test Your Knowledge" sections at the end of each chapter. Appendix B includes sample project management forms used throughout this book and that are also available for download from the companion website. The third appendix is a Glossary of project management terms.

Who Should Read this Book

This book can help project managers at several stages of experience advance to a deeper level of experience, applied skills, and understanding. For example, if you're graduating from supervising a few tasks with a few team members to managing larger projects and teams, you can learn project management basics from project initiation to final closure by reading this book from start to finish. Reading the chapters in sequence is also helpful for experienced project managers who want to prepare to manage larger, more complex projects.

On the other hand, if you want to increase your understanding and skill in specific aspects of project management or learn about a knowledge area unfamiliar to you, such as risk management or managing a portfolio of projects, you can jump right to the corresponding chapter.

Tools You Will Need

You don't need specific software or technology to learn the concepts and soft skills described in this book. However, for all but the tiniest projects, you will need a few programs to manage projects effectively. Here are the basic types of programs to consider:

- **A project scheduling program:** To plan and manage more than a couple of tasks and resources, you need a program to help you build a project schedule and track progress. Microsoft Project and Primavera are two of the more commonly used programs.

- **A word processing program:** Documents are a natural result of running and managing projects, so a word processing program is a must.

- **A spreadsheet program:** Some aspects of project management, such as risk and quality management, benefit from the numerical processing and analysis that a spreadsheet program, such as Excel or OpenOffice Calc, can provide.

- **A presentation program:** Communication is a huge part of project management and the work that team members do. Depending on the size of your project, you might need a presentation program, such as PowerPoint, to communicate information to your team members or stakeholders.

What's On The Book's Website

The web page for this book can be found at `www.wiley.com/go/ProjMgmtCoach`. It includes files for the sample project management documents referenced in the chapters in the book, such as a cost estimate spreadsheet, communication matrix, change request form, and lessons learned questionnaire. These files are set up so you can use them as the basis for your own project management document templates.

The web page also includes a link to our blog, where we'll periodically post thoughts on a wide range of project management topics. We invite you to visit the blog and join in on the discussion.

Where To Go From Here

What we enjoy most about projects is that each one is unique so they are always interesting. They provide us with the opportunity to learn about new industries, new technologies, new people, and new ways of doing things. At the same time, project management provides an ongoing opportunity to learn and grow for as long as we're up to the challenge. We hope that you'll find projects and project management to be as engaging and captivating as we do. Most of all, we hope that the information in this book helps as you manage your projects. If you care to share your project management experiences, we'd love to hear about them.

Understanding Projects and Project Management

Chapter 1: Getting to Know Projects
Chapter 2: Getting to Know Project Management

Getting to Know Projects

If your boss walks into your cubicle one day and says "I've got a little project for you to do," you probably don't even think twice. You've tackled your share of projects at home and at the office so you already know that quite often they're simple, short-term assignments. When you're finished, you wipe your hands and go back to what you normally do.

At some point, you probably think about taking a more structured approach to handling them. Perhaps you want to try your hand at bigger projects, increase your success rate on the projects you perform, or simply get them done with less drama and fewer surprises. The first thing you want to know is what makes a project a project. They come in all shapes and sizes, but projects share a few characteristics that differentiate them from day-to-day work. This chapter provides a definition of a project and describes each characteristic. It also discusses how projects differ from other types of work.

What Is a Project?

It's tough to get through a week without working on some kind of project, at work, at home, or both. Projects span a broad range of endeavors and so you'll meet them regardless of what line of work you're in. If you've built a deck in your backyard, thrown a party, bought a house, or remodeled your kitchen, you've worked on projects. In the work world, producing a new marketing brochure or website, developing new products, building a new corporate campus, and landing on the moon all represent projects. What do all these undertakings have in common? The following is one definition of a project:

> A project is a unique endeavor with clearly defined objectives and deliverables, clear-cut starting and ending dates, and, most of the time, a budget.

Figure 1-1 shows how all the pieces of the project definition fit together. But what do all the components of that definition really mean? What is a unique endeavor? What are clearly defined objectives and deliverables? What are clear-cut starting and ending dates? And how does a budget fit in? The following sections discuss the various aspects of a project in more detail and provide several examples so you can identify projects when you see them.

A Unique Endeavor

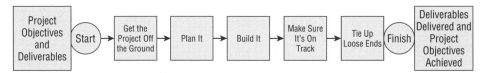

Figure 1-1: Elements of a project

EXAMPLE PROJECTS

This book uses four different projects as examples. The sections in this chapter explain why each of these examples meets the criteria for a project.

▪ **Backyard deck construction**

Almost everyone has worked on a simple construction project, so this example acts as a link between what you're learning about project management and your experience with projects so far. Building a deck in the backyard is a simple example of a construction project.

▪ **New product development**

Companies develop new products and services all the time, so you may run into a project like this at work. Later in this chapter, you learn how a project to develop a new product is different than actually manufacturing or providing the product to customers.

▪ **Exhibiting at a trade show**

A trade show is like a lot of other types of events, such as parties or conferences. They require a lot of planning and preparation up front in order to make the big finale a success.

▪ **Training program development**

Whether you want to teach your kids about money or have an assignment to develop training for your company, the development of a training program is a good example of a project.

A Project Is a Unique Endeavor

Every project is unique, although the differences can be large or small. Some projects are performed more than once, so you might mistake them for ongoing work. For example, a landscaping contractor might build dozens of backyard decks each summer, but each deck has aspects that make it unique. The variations from project to project are what make managing projects so special and interesting. Not only is every project different, but every day that you manage one is different, too. Here are some examples of how projects are unique:

- **Backyard deck construction:** Your idea of the perfect size and shape of a deck can be different than your neighbor's. You can choose from a variety of materials. The types of supports you use depend on whether the backyard is soft dirt, sand, or solid rock. The schedule could be affected by a long string of bad weather or whether you hire kids or a professional contractor.

- **New product development:** Every product is a little different from every other product, even the previous version of a product your company already sells. For example, your company's new product, the in-town hover-scooter, requires different designs, different components, and different testing procedures from a traditional scooter that has wheels on the ground.

- **Exhibiting at a trade show:** The audiences for trade shows can vary from the do-it-yourself construction crowd to professional contractors. Trade shows take place in different locations. The procedures you must follow to ship materials to the show or the crews that you use on site vary depending on the trade show organizers.

- **Training program development:** The topic of a training program can affect the way you teach and the tools you use. The materials for a course vary depending on whether it's taught in a classroom, online, or through video. Courses for adults are designed differently than those for school-age children. The duration of courses vary.

A Project Has Clearly Defined Objectives and Deliverables

Projects have a point. Otherwise, you or your organization wouldn't spend time, effort, and money doing them. Projects are run in order to achieve a goal — a problem to solve or an opportunity to take advantage of. Although you might be able to sum up the purpose of a project in a single sentence, that purpose usually represents a number of specific objectives that the project must achieve and deliverables that you must hand over to call the project complete.

Clearly defined objectives and deliverables are important because you use them to tell when a project is done. Otherwise, a project can seem to go on forever because it's never quite finished. Similarly, clearly defined objectives and deliverables help you determine whether a project has been completed successfully. When you spell out objectives and deliverables, it's easier for everyone involved to tell whether the objectives have been met and the deliverables match the description you started with.

WHO'S RESPONSIBLE FOR ACHIEVING BUSINESS GOALS?

As a project manager, you are rarely responsible for achieving the business goals that led to your project being started. Typically, your project is defined to produce deliverables and achieve intermediate objectives that business managers can use to drive the business results they want.

Vaguely defined or missing objectives lead to the demise of many a project. Without clearly defined objectives, you can end up working on a project long past its due date because you can't tell whether you're done. Or you can work longer and spend a lot more money because you didn't accomplish what you were supposed to. Yogi Berra famously said, "You've got to be very careful if you don't know where you are going because you might not get there." The same could be said for projects with poorly defined objectives.

The following are some possible objectives and deliverables for the four example projects in this book:

- **Backyard deck construction:** Your primary deliverable is a constructed stable platform for your deluxe gas grill and outdoor dining set. You might have other deliverables, such as a building permit to construct the deck and a signed inspection report confirming that the jewel you built is ready for action. But you might also have an objective for a deck built with low-maintenance materials so you can entertain more and maintain the deck less. Maybe you want to save money so you choose a simple off-the-shelf design so you can build the deck yourself over a few weekends. And you also want the deck completed in time for your annual end-of-summer barbecue.

  Your objectives and deliverables enable you to assess whether the deck is done and meets your requirements. If the gas grill and furniture don't tip over, you've obtained a stable platform for your outdoor meals. The design you picked includes a list of materials and instructions, so you know you're done when you've used up the materials you purchased and the deck looks like the last picture in the how-to guide. If you don't have to sand and stain the deck, you've achieved your low-maintenance nirvana. And you completed the deck in time for your barbecue, so you met your schedule.

▪ **New product development:** You might develop a new product to enter a new market, increase revenue, or to keep up with new technology. If returns or high levels of customer support have been a problem in the past, your objective might be to develop a product that's easier to maintain or more dependable. Or you could design a product to decrease manufacturing costs so you can reduce the selling price or increase your profit margin. Those business objectives drive the specifications for the product. Your project's deliverables could include a prototype that the customer and executive team approve along with the documentation that tells the manufacturing team how to build the products your organization will then sell.

▪ **Exhibiting at a trade show:** Vendors usually attend trade shows to reach potential new customers. You might have an ancillary objective to see what your competition is up to or find out what customers think about your new products and services. The deliverables for this project might include the booth you set up at the show and the marketing materials you pass out. You might also have an objective to spiff up the booth and marketing materials to bring them up-to-date with your company's offerings and make them look fresh.

▪ **Training program development:** If you work for a training organization, the deliverable could be a new course to offer to students. In a corporation, you might develop a training program to improve customer service, increase productivity, or increase quality. Another project objective might include development of new training features that improve students' comprehension of the material.

A Project Has a Beginning and an End

Projects are temporary, so they have a clear-cut beginning and a clear-cut end. Usually, the end of the project is the primary focus for the people involved in a project. The people who initiate a project want to enjoy the benefits that come when the project objectives are achieved. In addition, you, as the project manager, and the rest of the people working on the project, will be able to add it to your list of accomplishments and move on to something else.

As you learned in the previous section, the project goal and clearly defined objectives are essential to identifying the end of a project. When you've spelled out a project's objectives clearly, you can tell when you're done and bring the project to an end.

NOTE In addition to the final date for a project, you usually have a passel of intermediate deadlines to meet, whether you're trying to enclose a structure before cold weather sets in or your contract includes specific dates for milestones, which in turn trigger payments from the customer.

The following are examples of clear-cut ends to projects:

- **Backyard deck construction:** The end of the backyard deck project comes when you move the grill and dining set onto to the deck for your first barbecue. However, you might have other deadlines such as obtaining an inspection certificate from the county.

- **New product development:** The project to develop a new product is complete when you turn the product over to manufacturing.

- **Exhibiting at a trade show:** A trade show isn't over when the last attendee leaves. As a vendor, your trade show project is complete when you get your gear back to the office and wrap up the action items from the event, such as turning the list of new leads over to the sales team.

- **Training program development:** A training program is complete when the course materials are ready and the program is ready to schedule.

A Project Usually Has a Budget

Most projects don't have the luxury of a blank check for the cost or unlimited resources to get the work done. Projects usually have a financial budget that must be met, similar to the budget you follow for your personal spending. And they almost always have to work with a limited amount of resources or a finite number of hours from the people who do the work.

Here are examples of project budgets:

- **Backyard deck construction:** You decide to use this year's bonus to build a deck in the backyard, so you have $5,000 to get the job done.

- **New product development:** The executive team in your organization determines that developing a new product has to cost less than $200,000 in order to achieve the company's required annual return on investment of 15 percent.

- **Exhibiting at a trade show:** The director of sales has allocated $30,000 to cover the cost of attending a trade show based on the estimated sales that will result from the event. In addition, two sales people and two marketing people have been assigned to handle all aspects of preparing for and attending the trade show.

- **Training program development:** The training program is forecast to save the company $50,000 by the end of the first two years of training employees. Your boss has given you a budget of $15,000 to develop the training program.

TIP Once in a blue moon, you might manage a project that doesn't have a budget, but that doesn't mean your options are unlimited. For example, a project is essential to the survival of your company so the CEO has told you to do whatever it takes to make the customer happy. You might ask the CEO for more people or submit expense requisitions for approval. However, at some point, other alternatives might make more business sense. Even if you aren't asked to work within a budget, it's a good idea to build your own budget and aim to meet it. Chapter 6, "Estimating Work and Cost," discusses building a budget.

How Do Projects Differ from Other Work?

Work that remains the same day after day, that is ongoing work or operations, is not a project. For example, delivering the mail to mailboxes on a route is ongoing. If you work in the accounting department, you might spend your days recording payments or paying bills.

Some projects might appear to represent recurring work. However, small differences make each project and the work it entails unique. The following list describes ongoing work that is similar to the four example projects:

- **Backyard deck construction:** Each deck project is a little different. The terrain of your yard, the ground you build on, and the weather can affect your project. So, you could go to your local building supply store and work with a designer to come up with the deck of your dreams. Then, you get drawings and the building materials you need to construct the deck in your backyard. On the other hand, the building supply store that stocks the building materials you use or the company that manufactures the deck components performs the same work day after day.

- **New product development:** A new product development project does just that — it develops a new product and delivers documentation about how to manufacture that product. The project also includes tasks to turn over information to manufacturing so that that team knows how to build the products correctly. But once the product is in the hands of manufacturing, the production line does the same thing every day to pump out products to sell.

- **Exhibiting at a trade show:** If your organization attends trade show after trade show, your marketing department might have a team assigned to prepare standard materials for the shows. Some members of the team spend their days gathering copies of marketing collateral and then ship the materials to their destination.

- **Training program development:** Although developing a training program is a project, teaching a course can become ongoing work. Although each class of students might be different, the overall work in presenting a class is the same. Or, if you offer online training, the ongoing work is keeping the website operational and up-to-date.

Summary

A project is work you undertake that is both unique and temporary. A project has specific goals and objectives. The good news is that a project ends when you achieve those goals and objectives. Most of the time, a project must be finished using a fixed amount of money or resources. It's important to be able to differentiate projects from ongoing, repetitive work, because projects require different management techniques.

Coach's Review

Use this section to assess what you've learned in this chapter and to apply it to a real-life project you're currently working on.

Test Your Knowledge

Test your knowledge of the material in this chapter by answering the following questions. See Appendix A for the answers.

1. What is the key characteristic that differentiates projects from other types of work?

2. Describe two ways that clearly defined objectives help a team complete a project successfully.

Project Challenge

Describe work you have done in the past or are working on now and explain why that work is or is not a project.

Getting to Know Project Management

You have projects to do and you want to complete them successfully — without making yourself or the people on your team miserable. Projects can present challenges. They may be incredibly complex or they might have to be finished in record time or with only a tiny budget. At the same time, customers could change their minds or not know exactly what they want to begin with.

To conquer the challenges your projects face and achieve the desired results, you and the people on your team have to work smart. That's what project management is all about. What you do to manage projects should help you achieve the results the project is supposed to deliver or prevent problems that get in the way. If it doesn't, you shouldn't waste time or resources on it.

Getting projects done right boils down to knowing what you're trying to do, figuring out how you're going to do it, and then making sure you did it. This chapter introduces you to the five project management processes that help you address those areas. You'll also learn about several areas of expertise a project manager needs to master to make things happen the way they're supposed to.

Project management isn't one size fits all. You can use different approaches depending on the project size and complexity, and how clear the solution is, how tough your constraints are, and so on. In this chapter, you meet a few different methodologies and learn the pros and cons of each one.

Project managers have to master a diverse set of skills (although, fortunately, you don't have to do everything yourself). You tackle technical tasks such as building schedules, evaluating variances, and calculating financial results. At the same time, you need a host of soft skills including effective communication, good people skills, business savvy, leadership, and more. This chapter summarizes what it takes to be a good project manager. The rest of this book digs into these topics in detail.

What Is Project Management?

You don't need jargon or technical concepts to understand the basics of project management. It boils down to answering several questions about your project:

- **Why are you doing the project?** The reason you're doing a project is one of the most important keys to making your project a success. A project is often about solving a problem, but projects are also launched to take advantage of opportunities. For example, your company might run a project to develop a training program because your company is growing quickly and it's taking too long for new employees to become productive. On the other hand, a lucrative and untapped market might move your organization to develop a new product.

- **How are you going to solve the problem?** Once you have a problem or opportunity to tackle, you need to figure out the solution you're going to employ. Most problems can be solved in a variety of ways, so you can consider different strategies. Then, you have to define what the solution looks like. The most common method for describing a solution is to document requirements and deliverables. (Deliverables are the tangible results the project is supposed to deliver.)

NOTE As you learn in later chapters, defining the solution can be quite a challenge, particularly at the beginning of the project. During the process of project definition, you might consider which project management methodology is most appropriate. If your solution is clear-cut, you can use a traditional approach to managing your project, as described in the section "Traditional Waterfall Project Management." For murkier solutions, in which you know the overall context of the solution, but not the details, you have to tease them out over time. That's when the agile approach, described in the section "Iterative and Agile Project Management," comes in handy. You

make several iterations through the project, each time getting closer to the final solution.

- **How are you going to get the project done?** You answer this question by developing a plan for performing the project. You define the work that needs to be done, the people who will do the work, how long it will take, and how much it will cost. You also define other processes, such as how people communicate about the project, how you manage risks, and so on.

- **How will you know you're done?** After you define your project's objectives, requirements, and deliverables, you need clear-cut methods of measuring that you've achieved those goals. Most of the time, success isn't black and white. By defining quantifiable success criteria up front, you'll have an easier time identifying whether or not you're done at the end.

- **How did the project go?** When you evaluate how a project went, you actually look at two different things. First, you look at the quality of the solution. Did it meet the requirements and achieve its objectives? What does the business look like now that the project is done? For example, are business processes easier, are people more productive, and so on. You also have to evaluate how well your project management processes worked. Did the processes you put in place work well with the project? How well did you and your team apply those processes? And did the processes help you produce the results you wanted?

Project Management Processes: Start to Finish

The previous section provided a commonsense look at what project management is about. If you want a more structured take on managing projects, you can turn to a standard definition of project management. This book follows the Project Management Institute's (PMI) Guide to the Project Management Body of Knowledge (PMBOK), which breaks down project management into five process groups: Initiating, Planning, Executing, Monitoring and Controlling, and Closing.

Every project management methodology uses these five process groups. How and when you use them can vary. For example, with simple and clearly defined projects, you might work your way through the five groups, as shown in Figure 2-1. For more complex or less clearly defined projects, you can repeat the processes several times. This section describes what each process group represents and when you use it.

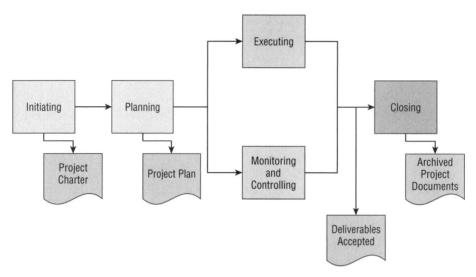

Figure 2-1: The five project management process groups and the deliverables they produce

Initiating a Project

The *initiating* process group takes care of answering the questions "Why are you doing the project?" "How are you going to solve the problem?" and "How will you know you're done?" from the previous section. Initiating a project is like starting your day off right by eating a nutritious breakfast. You identify what the project is about and the definition of success.

The first thing you accomplish with this process group is to ensure that everyone interested in and involved with the project agrees on what the project is all about. Then, at the end of the process, you obtain approval to plan the project. More than a few projects have gone astray because various stakeholders held different perceptions of the project's goals and approved the projects based on those perceptions. The PMBOK lists only two processes: Develop Project Charter and Identify Stakeholders. However, the initiating process group includes several activities:

- **Appoint the project manager:** The first step in initiating a project is to assign the project manager.

TIP Sometimes a project gets through the initiating phase without a project manager. If you're assigned to manage a project and the initiating process is already complete, it's a good idea to review the work that's been done and fill in any holes.

- **Describe the business case for the project:** This is another name for why you're doing the project. You want to make sure that the project is worth the investment that will be made in it.

- **Identify stakeholders:** The project manager identifies the project stakeholders, who are people involved in the project or who have an interest in its outcome. By lining up the stakeholders in the beginning, you can identify their expectations for the project and build support for it.

- **Prepare an initial project definition:** The project definition includes an initial draft of the objectives, requirements, success criteria, risks, assumptions, and constraints for the project.

- **Prepare the project charter:** The project charter, described in the section "Preparing a Project Charter" in Chapter 3, is like the daily sheets at the races. Signing the project charter is like the starter's gun going off to start the race, or, in this case, the project.

- **Obtain approval:** The initiating phase is complete when the customer and senior management give their approval to move to the planning phase.

CROSS-REFERENCE Initiating the Project is Domain I in the PMP Exam. Chapter 3 of this book, "Getting a Project Off the Ground," describes the initiating process in detail.

Planning a Project

The *planning* process group represents all the activities that go into answering the question "How are you going to get the project done?" Most project managers find their vocation because they love to plan ahead. Planning a project is like putting together a nutrition plan to achieve your personal objectives, whether you want to improve your health, lose weight, or run a marathon. You identify what you're going to do to run the project and achieve its objectives.

TIP Planning before you begin work pays off. Stakeholders may be anxious to start work, but it's a good idea to request the time you need to plan up front. Otherwise, you'll spend a lot more time later on putting out fires or listening to the customer say, "Love the new deck, but it was supposed to be on the back of the house."

During the planning process, you define the work you have to do to complete the project and how you're going to do it:

- **Fine-tune requirements:** As you learn more about the project, you're likely to identify additional requirements or clarify the existing ones.

- **Define the work that must be done:** You identify all the work that must be done to complete the project. You build a *work breakdown structure* of the project tasks, which shows the project work in manageable pieces that you can assign to your team.

- **Estimate the resources you need to complete the work:** After you identify the project work, you determine the resources you need to perform the work and how many.

- **Estimate the time the project will take:** You also estimate how many hours the work will take.

CROSS-REFERENCE To understand the difference between duration and the number of hours of work, see the section "The Difference Between Duration and Effort" in Chapter 6.

- **Estimate the cost of the project:** The cost of the project depends on the labor costs for performing the work and the cost of other resources you need, such as equipment and materials.

- **Build a schedule for the project:** To build a project schedule, you need to know the work that must be done, the resources you need, and the time it will take to complete the work. The final piece to the puzzle is the sequence in which the tasks must be performed.

- **Fine-tune the plan:** Projects usually have constraints, such as a specific timeframe, a budget, or limited resources. Your initial schedule and cost might not meet the constraints you have. During planning, you iterate through your planning tasks until you come up with a plan that works.

- **Develop ancillary plans, including a communication plan, risk management plan, quality management plan, and change management plan:** Part of project planning is defining the processes you'll use to run the project and how you'll manage the project to achieve success. A communication plan describes guidelines and processes for communicating with stakeholders and team members. A risk management plan identifies the risks the project faces and your plan for controlling the negative risks and capitalizing on the positive ones. A quality management plan describes the processes you will use to produce the level of quality desired. A change management plan describes the processes you will use to address change requests that are made.

- **Assemble the complete project plan:** Because so much goes into a project plan, you have to put all the pieces together to present to the customer and senior management.

- **Obtain approval to launch the project:** The planning phase is complete when the customer and senior management give their approval to launch the project and start work.

CROSS-REFERENCE In the PMP Exam's outline, Planning the Project is Domain II, which represents 24 percent of the examination's questions. Part II of this book, "Planning a Project," includes several chapters that cover each part of this process group in detail.

Executing a Project

The *executing* process group represents the activities you perform to launch the project work. You bring your project team on board and explain the rules to follow. And you put all your plans to work. Think of this as your trip to the grocery store to stock up on celery, protein powder, and whatever else is in your nutrition plan. You call your friends to ask them for moral support when Belgian chocolate ice cream sings its siren song; and then you start following your plan.

The executing process group includes the following processes:

- **Procure and manage project resources:** Before you can start work, you have to procure the people and other resources you need. Once you have people on board, you have to turn them into a team. The project launch might be the first time your team members meet. You must work with the individuals and the entire group — training, mentoring, motivating, and leading — to get the best they have to offer.

- **Communicate project rules:** This is a good time to communicate the rules that everyone on the project is supposed to follow.

- **Perform the tasks identified in the WBS:** Now that you have your project resources, you start the tasks you identified during planning.

CROSS-REFERENCE Executing the Project is Domain III of the PMP Exam and represents 30 percent of the exam's questions. Part III of this book, "Executing a Project," describes the executing activities in detail.

Monitoring and Controlling a Project

The *monitoring and controlling* process group is a combination of art and science. As project manager, you get to show off all your skills. Monitoring the project tells you how well your plan is working, much like you count your calories and hop on the scale to see where you are on your weight loss plan. You don your problem-solving hat to control the results and get the project back on track, if necessary. At the same time, you use your soft skills to deal with the customer, senior management, and the rest of the team.

The monitoring and controlling process group includes the following activities:

- **Implement quality, risk, and change management plans:** For example, as change requests come in, you push them into the change management process you set up. You initiate some of your planned risk responses before events occur to reduce their impact or probability of occurring. You plan responses for new risks you identify as the project progresses. You also monitor the remaining risks and initiate responses if necessary. And you measure quality to determine whether the project is delivering the required level of quality.

- **Monitor project performance:** As your team performs work on the project, you keep track of what's going on and measure results — the schedule, cost, scope, resource assignments, and so on. You compare the actual performance to your plan to identify and measure any variances, which help you determine whether corrective actions are needed.

- **Report performance and status:** You communicate project performance and status to the relevant audiences, such as stakeholders and team members.

- **Manage procurements:** If you used a procurement process to obtain resources, you manage those procurements, including paying invoices and communicating with vendors.

- **Solve problems:** Issues and obstacles are a fact of life and a fact of projects. As they arise, you evaluate them and decide what you're going to do to solve them.

- **Control scope, schedule, and cost:** If your performance monitoring identifies variances from your plan, you determine the root cause and then the corrective actions you're going to use and put them into motion.

CROSS-REFERENCE Domain IV of the PMP Exam is Monitoring and Controlling the Project, which represents 25 percent of the examination. Part IV of this book, "Monitoring and Controlling," describes the activities in this group in detail.

Closing a Project

The *closing* process group is the time to tie up all the loose ends when the project work is complete. It includes officially accepting the project as complete, documenting the final performance and lessons learned, closing any contracts, and releasing the resources to work on other endeavors. Are the success criteria satisfied or do you have checkpoints in the near future to determine whether they are? Does everyone involved agree that the project is a success and have they officially signed off on acceptance?

Similar to the initiating process group, the PMBOK's closing process group contains only two processes: Close Project or Phase and Close Procurements. However, you must perform several activities to make sure your project is truly finished:

- **Obtain approval from the customer:** This is the milestone everyone is waiting for. You work with the customer to obtain final acceptance of the project deliverables.

- **Transfer ownership of the deliverables:** Acceptance is really the first step. Once deliverables are accepted, you have to install them and transfer ownership to the customer.

- **Close contracts and accounts:** If you opened contracts for the project — for example, for third-party vendors or contractors — you perform the steps to close those contracts. In addition, you close most if not all of the billing accounts you used to track charges to the project. You might keep a few accounts open, for instance, to track the cost of support.

- **Conduct a closing audit:** A thorough review of the project, including what went well and what could use improvement, is a huge help for improving future projects.

- **Prepare a final project report:** At the end of the project, you write a final report that sums up the project status.

- **Archive project documents:** When the last document is complete, you're finally ready to archive everything about the project — not to gather dust. These documents might be a project requirement, but they can also provide background for future projects.

CROSS-REFERENCE Closing the Project is the final domain of the PMP Exam. Part V of this book, "Closing the Project," describes what you do to finish your project management work for a project.

Balancing Scope, Time, Cost, and Quality

Projects are balancing acts, in which you have to juggle project scope along with the constraints you have on time, cost, and quality. If you change any of these project factors, the others have to adjust to bring the project back into equilibrium.

The relationships between project constraints are a fact of project life, so they've earned several names over the years: the project triangle, the scope triangle, and the triple constraint. The names emphasize the number three, but, as you can see, you actually have to balance four, sometimes more, aspects of your project. For example, if you can't adjust time or cost, you can consider changing the scope or level of quality.

Think about it this way: you can decide which aspects of your project you want to keep as is and which ones to cut back on. For example, you can approach a project to build a deck in your back yard in several ways:

- You can build the deck really fast with very little money, but it won't be very good.
- You can build a high-quality deck, but it will take longer and might cost more.
- You can build a larger deck with more features (increased scope), but it will cost more and take more time.

The project triangle has been depicted graphically in many ways. The interpretation in Figure 2-2 shows scope as the area within the triangle. That's because the project scope can affect all the other aspects of the project. If the scope increases or decreases, the time and cost are likely to increase or decrease in response.

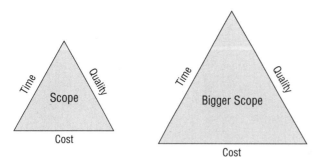

Figure 2-2: Changes in any aspect of a project affect the other constraints.

NOTE Resource availability is another common constraint, so you might see a project triangle drawn with resource availability as one of the sides of the triangle. For example, you could have your project scope, time, cost, and quality nicely balanced, but a lack of resources with the appropriate skills could push the schedule longer, require a reduction in scope, and require more money to hire more people.

Project Management Methodologies

Project management comes in a variety of flavors. Traditional waterfall project management and agile project management are two of the most commonly used methodologies. Some large companies actually develop their own in-house project management approaches to fit the company culture and the types of projects they run. Regardless which approach you choose, you'll still work through the five process groups described in the section "Project Management Processes: Start to Finish" earlier in this chapter. This section provides an introduction to a few standard methodologies and how they differ from one another.

NOTE You don't have to design your own project management methodology. Many companies, organizations, and universities have developed methodologies that you can use — or borrow from. For example, the PMBOK documents PMI's principles, which companies have used to develop methodologies. PRINCE2 (an acronym for Projects in Controlled Environments) is a methodology developed in the United Kingdom. TenStep is a consulting and training company that offers the TenStep methodology.

Traditional Waterfall Project Management

The traditional approach to project management earned the name "waterfall" because the process groups you use mostly flow one after the other, as shown previously in Figure 2-1. You step through initiating and planning to produce your project plan. Then, the executing and monitoring and controlling groups take over until the work is complete. And finally, you finish up with the closing process group.

The waterfall approach works well when your project goal and solution are clearly defined. You know what needs to be done, so you can take one pass through each project management process group from start to finish. Unfortunately, projects such as these don't appear very often these days.

The more information you have about the project, the better waterfall project management will work. Here are several other characteristics that help you decide whether waterfall is the answer:

- **Simplicity:** Projects that are simple or familiar are good candidates for the waterfall approach because you know most of what you need to get the project done.

- **Low risk:** Risk is about uncertainty, so less risk means more certainty. For example, if you've run similar projects, you can be reasonably sure that the requirements are complete. You also know the risks and mistakes to watch for and how to handle them if they arise.

- **Familiar technology:** You know the technical glitches and the workarounds to solve them. Your team members are productive because they've worked with the technology before.

- **Experienced resources:** If team members have worked on similar projects in the past, they're familiar with the work and the technology, so they will be more productive. They also know problems that can occur and how to prevent them.

NOTE Critical chain project management is a variation of the waterfall approach. Resources are usually in short supply, so one of the critical chain techniques is to eliminate resource overallocations starting with the ones that are most in demand. This approach also adds shared time buffers to the project and to sequences of tasks to help keep the project on schedule. The section "Modeling a Realistic Schedule" in Chapter 8 explains the techniques for critical chain project management.

Iterative and Agile Project Management

Projects in which the solution isn't clearly defined, which is true of as many as 80 percent of all projects, require a different approach. If you don't know the solution, you can't build a plan for the entire project. You have to identify the solution as you go, bringing it into focus over time. Iterative, rolling wave, and agile project management methodologies use iterations to gradually uncover the solution.

With an iterative approach, you plan what you're going to deliver for each iteration, as shown in Figure 2-3. In effect, the project delivers a partial but production-quality solution every few months. The customer receives business value sooner. At the same time, the customer provides feedback on the solution so far, which helps enhance the solution.

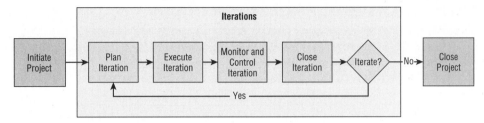

Figure 2-3: An iterative approach helps identify the solution over time.

Iterative and agile methodologies also call for more interaction between all the players. The customer has to be more closely involved than in traditional projects, because the solution evolves over time. The project needs the customer's feedback to get to the solution the customer wants. Project teams tend to be smaller, highly skilled, and work closely together without much supervision.

Because of the iterations shown in Figure 2-3, some of the project management process groups work a little differently than in traditional project management:

- **Planning:** You can develop a high-level plan for the project, although it won't have the level of detail that a traditional project plan would. You develop more detailed plans for the work in each iteration.

- **Executing:** The project team is smaller and more autonomous. You execute the work for a single iteration.

- **Monitoring and Controlling:** You still monitor progress and make course corrections if needed. However, you typically distribute reports more often because of the short length of the iterations.

- **Closing:** With iterations, you perform a closing process for each iteration and then another closing process for the entire project.

Project Management Knowledge Areas

A lot of different types of management make up managing a project. In the PMBOK, these specialized management skills are called *knowledge areas* and they're present in every project management life cycle. This section introduces each of the knowledge areas, why they're important, and when they occur during the project life cycle.

The knowledge areas and process groups are inextricably linked. Each knowledge area pops up in at least two of the process groups. As its name implies, integration management is a part of every process group. Table 2-1 maps the knowledge areas to the process groups.

Table 2-1: The Links between Process Groups and Knowledge Areas

KNOWLEDGE AREAS	INITIAT-ING	PLAN-NING	EXECUT-ING	CONTROL-LING AND MONITORING	CLOS-ING
Scope		X		X	
Time		X		X	
Cost		X		X	
Quality		X	X	X	
Communi-cation	X	X	X	X	
Human Resources		X	X		
Risk		X		X	
Procurement		X	X	X	X
Integration	X	X	X	X	X

CROSS-REFERENCE   As you can see from Table 2-1, the planning process group employs all nine knowledge areas. The information in this section applies to Domain II of the Project Management Professional Examination, "Planning the Project."

ETHICS AND THE PROJECT MANAGER

Ethical behavior is increasingly important. At the same time, newspaper head-lines seem to indicate that it's growing rarer every day. Ethics is not one of the project management knowledge areas. However, project managers frequently run into ethical dilemmas and the correct path may not be obvious.

A code of conduct, such as the PMI Code of Ethics and Professional Conduct, can help you make good decisions even in the face of sticky situ-ations. For example, the PMI code describes a standard of behavior for the project manager, including taking responsibility, respecting others, and being fair and honest.

Scope Management

The project scope defines the boundaries of your project — what work you will do and what work you won't do. Scope management revolves around making sure that you do all the work that's required to complete the project scope without doing anything extra.

The first part of managing scope is identifying and documenting the requirements that the project must satisfy in order to achieve its objectives. You can choose from several approaches for obtaining requirements, as you'll learn in the section "Gathering Requirements" in Chapter 3. Once you define the requirements, you can then document the project scope in a scope statement (see the section "Documenting Project Scope" in Chapter 3).

With the requirements and scope in hand, you're ready to identify the work for the project. Scope management includes building a work breakdown structure, which is covered in Chapter 5 "Identifying the Work to Be Completed." In addition, you also have to manage changes to the scope as work on the project progresses.

Time Management

For individuals, time management means working efficiently and keeping track of appointments. Time management for projects relates to getting them done on time.

During planning, you put time management into practice when you build the project schedule. First, you define project tasks. Then, you put them into sequence (see Chapter 8, "Building a Schedule") and estimate the effort and resources you need to complete them (see Chapter 7 "Estimating Work and Cost.") And voilà! You have your project schedule.

Once the project is underway, you monitor progress and take action, if necessary, to control the schedule. Time management includes managing changes to the baseline schedule.

Cost Management

Cost management also shows up during planning as well as during monitoring and controlling. During planning, you estimate the cost of project work including labor costs, materials, and other resources. From those costs, you build a budget for the project. Then, as work progresses, you monitor the status of the project and evaluate how much has been spent.

Human Resource Management

Projects need people to perform the work that's required. The people who work on your project probably have line managers back in their departments. However, as project manager, you also have to manage these people in their roles on your project.

During planning, you identify the skills and roles you need to perform your project work. You build a staffing plan for your project, as described in Chapter 7, "Planning Project Resources." The next step is to acquire the people you need.

Once people are on board, you have to help them become a team, rather than a group of individuals, so they're more productive and autonomous as a team. You also manage people as individuals, performing tasks similar to the ones that line managers do. For example, you track people's performance, provide feedback to help them improve, and step in to resolve issues, if necessary. Chapter 16, "Transforming People into a Team," discusses all these activities.

Procurement Management

If you need resources or services from outside your organization, you use a procurement process to acquire them. You begin by identifying what you need. Part of procurement is obtaining bids or proposals from vendors or other organizations and choosing who you will use. The next step is awarding a contract. While work is underway, you have to manage those contracts and track the vendors' performance. When the work is done, you perform the steps to close the contracts you opened. The section, "Procuring Resources from Vendors," in Chapter 13 describes the activities in a procurement process.

Communication Management

In the project world, communication is one of the keys to project success. Whether you manage the expectations of stakeholders or guide team members while they do their work, your job as project manager involves a lot of communicating.

You start by identifying the stakeholders for your project, as described in "Identifying the Project Stakeholders" in Chapter 3. You need to understand how they're connected to your project so you can determine what information they need and want.

During planning, you develop your plan for communicating on your project, which is covered in Chapter 10, "Setting Up a Communication Plan." You identify the information you communicate, methods of communication, and how often you stay in touch. For the remainder of the project life cycle, you implement your communication plan, reporting status, performance, and other information to your audiences.

Quality Management

The goal of a project is to *meet* its objectives. (Contrary to many people's beliefs, quality does not mean exceeding the objectives or specifications of the project.)

Managing quality begins with planning. You identify the quality standards required for the project and deliverables, such as the specifications for a product or tolerances for dimensions. You also document how you will demonstrate that the project meets those standards.

Quality control represents measuring and recording the results of quality activities that you use to test your deliverables, such as testing and sampling. One aspect of quality assurance is ensuring that the quality of your project complies with the standards you defined. You analyze the results of tests to see whether they meet the variances or tolerances you set. But quality assurance does more than that. You can also evaluate your quality processes and procedures to identify ways to improve. For example, if you find the underlying cause of a problem that occurs frequently, you can implement new approaches to prevent that problem in the future. Chapter 9, "Planning for Quality," describes all three quality processes.

Risk Management

Risks are events that have some probability of occurring in the future. They also can affect your project, either positively or negatively, although most people think of risks as potential losses. Risk management comprises four processes, which are described in detail in Chapter 12, "Managing Risk":

- Identifying the risks that the project could face.
- Assessing the probability that each risk might occur and its impact on the project if it does.
- Developing risk responses. There are many ways to respond to risks, such as accepting the consequences, avoiding the risk, transferring the risk (like insurance), mitigating the impact of the risk, and planning for contingencies.
- Monitoring risks. If risks occur, you implement the response you planned and then track the results. For some risks, you implement your response ahead of time to reduce the impact or probability of the event occurring.

Integration Management

You need some way to tie all the other knowledge areas together. The activities you perform to do that fall under the heading "integration management." For example, developing your project charter and project plan are part of integrating all your project management pieces. Integration management also spans the work you do to execute, monitor, and control the project as it proceeds. Change management is part of this knowledge area because you use it to control the scope, schedule, and cost of your project. Finally, the tasks you perform to close a project, a phase, or an iteration also fall under integration management.

Who Makes a Good Project Manager?

Project managers tend to be organized and they thrive on the satisfaction of getting things done. But that's just the start. As you've seen so far in this chapter, managing projects covers a lot of ground. And project managers have to master a host of skills. This section breaks down the skills a project manager needs into three categories: business, technical, and soft skills.

TIP The best project managers acknowledge their strengths and weaknesses and ask for help in the areas in which they're weak or don't have enough experience.

Business Savvy

Projects are performed for a reason. Your job as project manager boils down to making sure that the project achieves its objectives. To do that, you need to understand the business side of your organization. What is its business model? What business objectives is it trying to achieve? What challenges does it face? How do the finances work? What do the executives care about? When you know the answers to those questions, you know what to focus on in your projects and can make better decisions about how to solve issues that arise.

Technical Skills

You'll learn all sorts of technical skills specific to project management. For example, you have to understand task dependencies and resource assignments to build a project schedule. To measure progress, you learn how to use techniques such as earned value analysis. Quality management is rife with applications of statistical analysis, such as the statistical mean, standard deviation, and sample populations.

Project managers need at least some technical knowledge of the project's subject matter. That knowledge helps you speak your team members' language and understand their issues.

SO YOU WANT TO BE A PROJECT MANAGER?

If you've read this far and still think project management sounds like something you want to do, you might wonder how to launch your project management career. In many cases, people are asked to manage projects before they even know what that means. If you haven't been so fortunate, don't worry. It's not too hard to kickstart your career. Here are a few techniques you can use to snag your first project management assignment:

- Take project management courses at a nearby school. Many universities offer degrees or certificates in project management. You can also build your skills by attending meetings, courses, or conferences offered by organizations such as PMI.

- Ask for the opportunity to manage a project. Don't be shy. Tell your manager what you've learned about project management and ask for a small project to manage.

- Volunteer to manage a project. If you can't coax your manager into giving you a chance, join a volunteer organization and offer to manage one of its projects. These organizations are always looking for people to get things done. In addition to honing your project management skills, you can add project management to your resume.

Soft Skills

Project managers use a lot of soft skills, such as effective communication and motivating people. As it turns out, project managers have to be flexible, because they also have to be able to act in different ways at different times. This section provides some examples.

Varying Viewpoints

Business savvy is important. A project manager has to keep the overarching goal of the project in the forefront. Without that high-level perspective, the project could lose its way and not deliver the value it's supposed to. You also have to make sure that the project team understands the big picture, so they stay focused.

At the same time, managing a project means keeping track of thousands of small details. You have to make sure that all the work is getting done the way it's supposed to, while solving problems, resolving issues, answering questions, and keeping the stakeholders happy.

Delegating

You have to delegate project tasks to your team members. You have a lot to do as project manager, so you need your team to work with minimal supervision. You also have to be able to take charge if there's a crisis.

Leadership and Interpersonal Skills

You lead a team comprising people from different departments and even different companies. You have to help individuals become productive members of a team. And you have to motivate individuals and the team to do what it takes.

The challenge is that the people on your team usually report to managers in another department or company. You don't have the influence on their jobs and compensation that line managers do. Yet, you need them to be productive on your project and get up to speed quickly.

TIP One way to motivate team members is by giving them the credit for success. You get your acknowledgements indirectly from the success of the team and the project.

Flexibility

If you love to plan, you probably don't like when your plans change. And yet, that's exactly what happens in projects. Your plan is just a guideline. Every day brings something new to deal with. As the project progresses, you will have to adapt the plan to incorporate changes and resolve problems.

Doing the Right Things for the Project

Although you answer to the project customer and management team, sometimes you have to disobey and not do what you're told. Maybe the management team has presented an insurmountable obstacle and you need to convince them to take a different direction. Or the customer asks for features that don't add business value but do add significant risk. As a project manager, you have to be willing to stand up for what you think is right.

Summary

Project management is made up of five process groups that help you define what your project is about, plan how you're going to get it done, and then follow through until it's complete. These process groups can fit together in different ways depending on the needs of your project. For example, traditional project management steps through the groups one after another, while iterative and agile project management cycle through several of the processes.

As a project manager, you have to have business savvy and be able to handle all the aspects of project management from managing scope to managing people. You also have to learn technical skills and master all sorts of soft skills.

Coach's Review

Use this section to assess what you've learned in this chapter and to apply it to a real-life project you're currently working on.

Test Your Knowledge

Test your knowledge of the material in this chapter by answering the following questions. See Appendix A for the answers.

1. What are the five process groups?

2. Which process group uses all nine knowledge areas?

3. Which knowledge area spans all five process groups?

4. When would you want to use an iterative approach to project management?

Project Challenge

Think about projects you have worked on in the past and the challenges you experienced on those projects. How could you have used the project management process groups and knowledge areas to complete those projects more effectively?

Part

II

Planning a Project

Chapter 3: Getting a Project Off the Ground
Chapter 4: Getting to Know a Project Plan
Chapter 5: Identifying the Work to Be Completed
Chapter 6: Estimating Work and Cost
Chapter 7: Planning Project Resources
Chapter 8: Building a Schedule
Chapter 9: Planning for Quality
Chapter 10: Setting Up a Communication Plan
Chapter 11: Setting Up a Change Management Plan
Chapter 12: Managing Risk

Getting a Project Off the Ground

Let's say your boss has assigned you as project manager to shepherd the company's exciting new mobile Web eyeglasses product through the design phase. You want to make your mark as a successful project manager with this prestigious, high-visibility project.

To ensure that the project fulfills your company's high hopes, you want to get the project on the right track from the beginning, which means doing the legwork and establishing the foundation to properly define the project and getting the necessary approval to continue.

This chapter covers the *project initiation processes*. Project initiating is also known as scoping or preplanning. After a discussion about where these new projects come from, you'll learn how to define the project and discover the driving forces for the project's existence and success. You'll understand how to identify the project stakeholders and prepare the project proposal. You'll also learn the importance of obtaining formal approval or sign-off to move ahead with project planning. By the time you distribute the project charter to publicize its existence and assemble the project notebook, you'll have a solid foundation from which to start the detailed project planning.

> **PRE-PLANNING FOR DIFFERENT PM METHODOLOGIES**
>
> Whether you're using the traditional waterfall, critical chain, agile, or some other project management methodology, your project initiation outcomes are the same. You still need to carefully define what your project is seeking to accomplish, you still need approvals to move forward, and you still need to publicize the project charter.

From Idea to Project: An Overview of Project Initiation

New projects rarely spring forth from your CEO's head fully formed. A project can start its life as a co-worker's casual musing, a customer's question, or a sketch on a bar napkin. In a more formal setting such as a departmental brainstorming session or off-site design meeting, new ideas are consciously coaxed into being, but even at that point, they are still just ideas.

So how does the germ of an idea grow into a full-fledged project?

In your workplace, you've probably seen the generation of a million ideas. Most ideas are quickly dismissed or even ignored. But some ideas seem to "have legs" and warrant further attention, because they're clearly advantageous. Other ideas see the light of day because they have a highly placed sponsor — such as an executive or customer — who wants to investigate this idea further.

The natural progression is to develop an idea into a proposal. In very broad strokes, someone determines the worthiness of the idea. Developing the proposal is part of the project initiating process, in which the problem, goal and objectives, success criteria, requirements, and scope are identified. In some cases, your project proposal might also need to include financial information such as a rough budget estimate or preliminary return on investment. Executives examining the proposal might ask about potential risks or the availability of resources to carry out the project.

The project proposal helps an organization determine which projects to do and which ones to say "no" to. The proposal succinctly demonstrates whether a project is worthwhile, given the organization's strategic goals and other measures of value.

To make sure the right projects are chosen to proceed to planning, an organization needs to devise and follow an unequivocal method for vetting and approving proposals. The next step is to maintain the necessary discipline and focus to deny proposals that don't make the grade. In fact, saying "yes" when they should say "no" is a big problem for many organizations. The proposals that receive approval from the managing stakeholders can then move on to the planning processes of project development.

CROSS-REFERENCE For more information about possible formats for a project proposal, see "Preparing the Project Proposal" later in this chapter. For more information about creating a process for evaluating and approving proposals, see "Selecting Projects" in Chapter 25.

Even after a proposal is approved for further planning, it's ideal to include additional checkpoints during project planning to ensure that resources, money, and energy are spent only on the right projects.

In addition to proposals that don't make it to projects, some projects in the midst of execution no longer support the organization's goals or fall short of their promised benefits. Evaluations at various stages of the project life cycle can identify the projects that should be canceled.

CROSS-REFERENCE The information in this section relates to the PMP Exam's Domain I: Initiating the Project, Task 1, "Perform project assessment based upon available information and meetings with the sponsor, customer, and other subject matter experts, in order to evaluate the feasibility of new products or services within the given assumptions and/or constraints."

THE CANDID COACH: THIS ISN'T A PRESCRIPTION

Although the elements for preplanning a project are discussed in a certain order in this chapter, this isn't necessarily a prescription for initiating all projects. While certain principles apply to all projects, the uniqueness of each project makes it nearly impossible to set down a universal formula for initiating. Small projects have different needs than big projects. Projects performed by fewer resources have different needs than projects carried out by huge teams.

This chapter describes the elements commonly included in project initiation, but you should look at each one to discern whether it applies to your situation. You might work on elements in a different order than described here or combine two elements into one.

The order you follow is not as vital as the fact that you've done the thinking, questioning, researching, developing, and documenting that's needed to build a strong foundation for a successful project.

Defining a Project

Whether you're proposing a project idea or you've been assigned to manage an approved project, defining the project is one of the most important things you can do to ensure success. If you want to build a house to last, you start with a good foundation. In the same way, a good project definition, which includes many or all of the elements described in Table 3-1, is the foundation on which to build and execute your project.

Table 3-1: Asking the Right Questions

PROJECT DEFINITION ELEMENT	QUESTIONS TO ANSWER
Problem statement	What is the problem? Why is that a problem?
Project goal	What is the purpose of this project?
Project objectives	How do we break down the goal into specific, measurable, and actionable components?
Project strategy	How are we going to solve the problem? How are we going to take advantage of the opportunity?
Requirements	What are the detailed results being produced by the project?
Success criteria	What needs to happen for the sponsor, customer, and stakeholders to say this project was a success? What business value are we gaining from this project?
Project scope	What will the project do? What will the project not do?
Deliverables	What tangible items are we producing that prove that the scope is being fulfilled?
Risks	What might happen that can affect the success of the project? How likely is it? What would the impact be? How might we respond?
Assumptions	What don't we know yet and what do we have to assume to allow planning to move forward?
Constraints	What limitations are imposed on undertaking this project?

BOGGED DOWN IN SEMANTICS

Maybe you've spent more than a few days with clients wrangling over the definition of terms: Is it a tactic or a strategy? One woman's goal is another man's purpose. You say "business case" and I say "success criteria." Let's call the whole thing off.

Although this chapter neatly lists a series of elements that are a part of project definition, please don't get hung up on the terminology.

Instead, think about the questions that you're trying to answer. Your answers will keep you on track as you work through your project definition.

> You'll probably need to assign a term to those questions or answers, but as long as you're all using the same names to describe the same things, it doesn't really matter what you call them.
>
> That said, this chapter uses a certain set of terms. But again, focus on the questions and answers, and adapt the elements and their names to the needs of your organization and your project.

In today's quick-turnaround "get 'er done" world, you're likely to encounter intense pressure to just start planning, or worse yet, start building without a plan. The project sponsor or the customer might want to plunge in and start "working," rather than articulating everything.

But project definition ensures that the picture so clear in the sponsor's mind is accurately and completely conveyed to you. Without the proper project definition, the project is like that house without a foundation. At the first sign of trouble, the project falls apart and comes tumbling down around you.

FROM THE FIELD: THE PROJECT THAT SKIPPED ITS INITIATION

The human resources department at a large corporation that does business and has employees in more than a dozen countries had been struggling with inconsistencies in its processes. This wasn't the biggest problem it faced, and it wasn't its highest priority.

However, one of the chief executives got hyped up about implementing a centralized human resources system for all sites. There was some initial consultation with HR, but as it turns out, not nearly enough.

Without looking at alternative solutions or researching requirements, the executive made a headlong commitment into selecting a particular system and rolling it out to all sites worldwide. The project was planned and the execution processes began.

However, the stakeholders, especially the users of the system, had not been consulted. The right people were not on board with the project, and the right questions were not asked. Too many assumptions were made. There was no analysis or buy-in. Project initiation wasn't performed properly. In effect, the project went from an idea straight into planning and execution.

The further the project proceeded, the worse it got. Originally planned as a multimillion-dollar project, the cost more than doubled and then increased yet again by another 40 percent.

Regardless of the cost, the HR community throughout the corporation was dead set against the new system and maintained they would not use it if it were implemented.

This project should have been killed at several points for several reasons, but the executive didn't want to give it up. The company spent so much money that it was overcommitted.

Continued

> **FROM THE FIELD: THE PROJECT THAT SKIPPED ITS INITIATION** *(continued)*
>
> This is a classic case of a project jumping ahead to planning and execution without project initiation. The problem or opportunity wasn't clearly identified. The business case wasn't clear. The plan was that the users would fit to the system, rather than the other way around. The project might have completed, but it was a failure.

The amount of time and the level of detail involved with defining a project depend on the size and complexity of the project. A lot also depends on the culture and politics of your organization.

If you're proposing the project, many of the elements of the project definition will be part of the project proposal that you present for approval or sign-off. After the project is approved, the elements of the project definition become part of the project plan. They guide the project during the planning and execution processes as the inevitable changes occur.

> **REALITY CHECK: VALIDATE AN INHERITED PROJECT**
>
> You might be assigned to manage a project that has already been defined. It might have even gone through all the project initiation processes and been approved.
>
> However, this doesn't mean you're off the hook and you can plunge in and start creating the work breakdown structure. Rather, your first job is to validate the project definition. Make sure that all the elements are complete and that you fully understand them.
>
> You might find that a scope statement was written, but the requirements need more detail. Or, you might discover that the project goal, objectives, and strategy are complete, but there is no problem statement.
>
> Take the time to fill in the gaps, whether in actual project definition elements or in your knowledge and understanding. The time spent will more than pay off in preventing problems down the road.

Discovering the Problem or Opportunity

Your first all-important task in initiating the project is to dig deep enough to discover the problem the project is trying to solve. You need to get to the point where you can state the problem clearly and unambiguously. The articulation of the problem becomes the project problem statement.

Unfortunately, stating the problem (or opportunity) is not as easy as it sounds. When faced with a situation, it's just human nature for people to propose solutions. When asked to describe a problem, people often answer with a solution instead, based on solutions from their past experience. Furthermore, it's often easier to describe a solution than it is to describe a problem.

However, in the rush to get to a solution, people often don't fully understand the problem to be solved or the opportunity to be developed. And if the problem or opportunity is not properly understood, an inordinate amount of time and money can be spent devising a solution that doesn't solve the problem at all.

For example, suppose your television suddenly stops working. You push buttons in vain and finally call for a technician to make a house call. You assumed that there's a problem with the microprocessor only to find out, expensively, that the dog had somehow managed to unplug the television from the electrical socket.

Don't fall into the trap of believing that the problem the project must solve is self-evident. Be like the four-year-old, and keep asking "Why?" "Why is that a problem?" "Why is this an opportunity for us?" "What will happen if we don't do this project?" or "So what?" and other related questions until you drill down to the heart of the problem or opportunity. This is referred to as the "5-why analysis" or the "Why why analysis."

FROM THE FIELD: THE CUSTOMER TRACKING SYSTEM

The following is a conversation that started with a project strategy and ended with the definitive problem identification:

"We need to develop a customer tracking system."

"Why is this system needed?"

"Isn't it obvious? We don't have any way to capture customer complaints."

"Why can't you just handle complaints as they come up and be done with it?"

"It'll help us see how many customer complaints we're getting and if there's any correlation between the issues."

"Why do you need to see the correlation?"

"We need to be able to track trends and identify and resolve systemic problems, of course."

"What will that do for you?"

"We'd be able to increase our repair and maintenance efficiency and reduce customer complaints over time if we can analyze the problems and their sources."

"I can see how that would be valuable. Why can't this be done under the current way of doing business?"

"We have no historical data on our customer complaints."

"Ah."

Continued

FROM THE FIELD: THE CUSTOMER TRACKING SYSTEM   *(continued)*

If the project manager had stopped at the solution statement of "We need a customer tracking system," a misguided project goal, objectives, and strategy might have been proposed that tracked customer contact information or customer purchasing habits. With the appropriate problem statement of "We need historical data on customer complaints so we can identify and resolve systemic problems," the team can develop the right solution that addresses the actual problem.

Another advantage of digging for the real problem is that you can unearth conflicting goals held by different key stakeholders. One stakeholder can interpret the nature of the project in a wildly divergent manner from another stakeholder. Or, they might have different agendas for what they want the project to accomplish for them. The sooner you're aware of any political headwinds, the better you can navigate around them. Even if you can't resolve an issue, awareness can help you manage the conflict.

While you can give yourself a lot of latitude in developing your project problem/opportunity statement, you might consider some guidelines. It's most effective if your statement:

- Is phrased as a problem to be solved or an opportunity to be leveraged.

- Does not include or suggest the solution.

- Describes what the outcome will look like when the problem is solved or opportunity is leveraged.

- Is open to multiple possible solutions.

THE CANDID COACH: IT'S NOT ALWAYS A PROBLEM

Sometimes an opportunity, rather than a problem, triggers a project. Even so, the wise project manager still does the necessary investigative work, asking questions to get to the root of why this opportunity is a good thing for the organization.

For example, perhaps a market window is discovered for a product your company can readily produce. You want to examine the opportunity and ask questions such as:

- Why would we want to do this?

- Why is this opportunity a good thing for us?

As with problems, keep asking "Why?" until you get to the point where the answer really is self-evident, such as, "We'll reduce our costs," "We'll gain and retain more customers," or "We'll make more profit."

There are a number of problem analysis techniques you can use to get down to the real problem. One of the most popular is the root cause analysis. Other techniques and tools associated with problem analysis include the *fault tree analysis* or *cause and effect diagram* (see Figure 3-1), *Ishikawa diagram* or *fishbone diagram* (see Figure 3-2), and Pareto analysis.

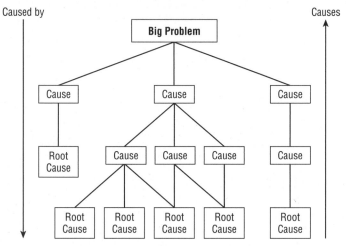

Figure 3-1: Cause and effect diagram

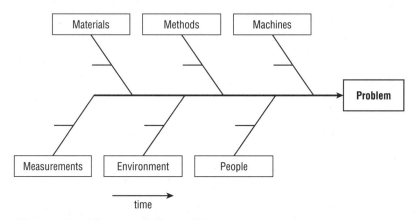

Figure 3-2: Ishikawa or fishbone diagram

PROBLEM STATEMENT EXAMPLES

The following are examples of good problem statements.

- "The kitchen is outdated, looks unattractive, and has an awkward work flow."

- "The market share for our mobile Web eyeglasses product is too low."

- "Software developers are not aware of our mobile Web eyeglasses and our need for applications."

- "We are not providing information to our customers fast enough, and the information is often inaccurate, causing dissatisfaction among our customers and frustration among our staff."

Upon articulating the real problem, you have the cornerstone from which you can continue the project initiation processes. From the problem, you can determine the project goal and objectives. From the goal and objectives, you and your team can brainstorm possible solutions and develop the strategy. From the selected strategy, you can research the project requirements, and so on.

Articulating the Project Goal and Objectives

Now that you've identified the problem or opportunity, you can develop the project goal and the objectives that will help the project achieve that goal.

Developing the Project Goal

The *project goal* is the broad description of what the project intends to achieve. The goal expresses the desired state of affairs. When you put the problem statement next to the goal, the gap between the two becomes apparent, and you can select the strategy that bridges that gap.

Returning to the kitchen example, you can see how you build from problem statement to goal statement:

- **Problem:** The kitchen is outdated, looks unattractive, and has an awkward work flow.
- **Goal:** Create a kitchen that's modern, attractive, and easy for two people to work simultaneously.

Here are some guidelines for writing your goal statement:

- Describe the desired state, typically in a positive fashion.
- Paint a picture of the desired state, perhaps even being a bit inspirational.
- If the project will help achieve a specific business goal, such as improved customer service or increased profits, consider speaking to that.
- Keep the goal statement short and more general (but not vague). The objectives will do the heavy lifting with respect to the appropriate level of specifics.

Think of the project goal as a kind of vision or mission statement for the project. It's your guiding light. Because of this, the goal statement will have lots of visibility throughout the life of the project. Some project managers like to print and frame the goal statement for all team members.

You might include the goal statement at the top of your meeting agendas and other project documents.

Table 3-2 contains examples of project goal statements.

Table 3-2: Problem Statements and Resulting Goal Statements

PROBLEM STATEMENT	RESULTING GOAL STATEMENTS
The kitchen is outdated, looks unattractive, and has an awkward work flow.	Create a kitchen that is modern, attractive, and easy for two people to work in simultaneously.
The market share for our mobile Web eyeglasses product is too low.	Increase the availability of popular high-quality apps developed for the mobile Web eyeglasses in order to increase our share of the mobile device market.
We are not providing information to our customers fast enough, and the information is often inaccurate, causing dissatisfaction among our customers and frustration among our staff.	Modify the current environment to provide accurate real-time information.
Our current manufacturing capacity can't keep up with the demand of our customers' orders.	Fulfill customer orders in a timely and cost-effective manner.

Creating the Project Objectives

The project objectives are a deconstruction of the goal — they are explicit statements that indicate the details or increments in which the project goal can be accomplished. When the objectives are fulfilled, the goal is achieved.

While the project goal tends to be broad and general, objectives need to be very specific and measurable. In fact, the best objectives are "SMART" objectives, as follows:

- **Specific:** The objective should be detailed enough to know what exactly is to be done. Objectives should never be vague.
- **Measureable:** The objective should be verifiable by some metric, such as a percentage of increase, number of dollars, number of hours, and so on.
- **Assignable:** The objective should be something that can be assigned to a person or group of persons to be completed.

- **Realistic:** The objective is not a "pie in the sky." It's something that is doable by the project team.
- **Time-based:** The objective has a deadline or timeframe within which it is to be done.

Objectives might also speak to any business goals that are being achieved by the project.

Deciding on the Project Strategy

In the drive to get to your problem statement and develop the project goal, you've been careful not to state, suggest, or imply solutions. Your focus has been to drill down to the actual problem and identify the project goal. You should now have succinct and accurate problem and goal statements from which to build your project strategy.

Brainstorming Possibilities

At this point, you are free to start looking at possible solutions to the problem that can fulfill the stated goal. You might work on your own, with a management team, with a potential project team, or a group of relevant experts to arrive at the best solution.

Various brainstorming techniques can help encourage creativity in a group situation. Some include mind-mapping and the SWOT (strengths, weaknesses, opportunities, and threats) analysis.

CROSS-REFERENCE For more information about brainstorming, see "Brainstorming Meetings" in Chapter 15.

Whatever your technique, keep an open mind about all possible alternatives. Later on, you determine the best option for your circumstances. Table 3-3 lists problem statements, their associated goal statements, and several possible strategies for each.

REALITY CHECK: CYCLE BACK TO THE PROBLEM IF NECESSARY

When looking at possible solutions to the stated problem, you might discover that the problem statement still has you wondering why it's a problem. If this is the case, revisit that problem statement and continue to drill down until you're satisfied that the problem is crystal clear.

You might also find that the problem statement has already suggested or even mandated a single solution. Again, return to the problem statement and change its focus until it's truly stating the problem, and not the solution.

Table 3-3: Project Problem Statements and Possible Strategies

PROBLEM STATEMENT	GOAL STATEMENT	POSSIBLE STRATEGIES
The kitchen is outdated, looks unattractive, and has an awkward work flow.	Create a kitchen that is modern, attractive, and easy for two people to work in simultaneously.	Completely remodel the kitchen.
		Put in a work island that includes a stove and position it across from the refrigerator and sink.
		Move the location of the refrigerator.
We have no historical data on customer complaints, so we have no way to identify and resolve systemic problems.	Develop a system for tracking and analyzing customer complaints.	Create a paper form for each customer complaint and maintain those forms in the customer filing cabinet.
		Create a computer form that's completed for each customer complaint. Print the form and file it in the customer filing cabinet.
		Create a computerized customer database that includes a data entry form and includes fields for complaints.
		Add complaint fields to the existing customer tracking system.
Our current manufacturing capacity can't keep up with the demand of our customers' orders.	Increase manufacturing capacity so we can fulfill customer orders more quickly.	Build a new manufacturing building with the square footage and facilities necessary to accommodate the needed capacity.
		Outsource the manufacturing to another local provider.
		Outsource the manufacturing to an offshore provider.

Identifying Constraints

In some situations, you might need to identify constraints on the project. You can do this before or after identifying many possible solutions. If you're brainstorming with a team, and you don't want to squelch the free flow of creative ideas, you might choose not to apply constraints until after all the ideas are captured.

With other methods for developing alternative solutions, it might be more efficient to identify any constraints ahead of time. Suppose the problem is that software developers are not aware of the existence of your mobile Web eyeglasses product. If you consider the constraints that the project must cost less than $15,000 and use a team of no more than three people within the company, you now have the boundaries you need to arrive at feasible solutions more quickly.

Constraints can involve budget, space, resources, time, regulatory require-ments, environmental limitations, customer preferences, and so on. Certainly, the organization's strategic goals should always be a strong consideration.

CROSS-REFERENCE Constraints typically become part of the scope statement. Read more about constraints in the scope statement later in this chapter in "Working with Constraints."

Choosing the Right Strategy

Once you've developed a list of possible strategies that could solve the stated problem within the given constraints, it's time to choose. Sometimes the right solution almost immediately suggests itself. Other times you end up with a long list of solutions that seem more or less equally good (or equally bad). Consider rating and ranking the solutions to determine a fairly objective score, as shown in Figure 3-3. While you don't necessarily have to take the solution with the best score, it will help you and your team clarify your thinking and determine the best course of action.

	A	B	C	D	E	F	G	H	I	J
1	**Solution Rating Matrix**									
2										
3	Problem: We have no historical data on customer complaints, so we have no way to identify and resolve systemic problems.									
4	Goal: Develop a system for tracking and analyzing customer complaints.									
5										
6				Solution rating: How well does the solution satisfy the criteria? (0=not at all, 5=very well)						
7										
8	Criteria	Weight: How important is the criteria? 5=required	Solution 1 rating: Paper form with hardcopy file	Solution 1 score	Solution 2 rating: Computer form with hardcopy file	Solution 2 score	Solution 3 rating: Customer database including complaint fields	Solution 3 score	Solution 4 rating: Add complaint fields to existing customer tracking system	Solution 4 score
9	Track customer complaints.	5	5	25	5	25	5	25	5	25
10	Compile customer complaint	4	5	20	5	20	5	20	5	20
11	Easy to record complaints.	4	4	16	5	20	5	20	5	20
12	Easy to compile complaints.	3	1	3	1	3	4	12	4	12
13	Generates reports.	2	0	0	0	0	5	10	3	6
14	Quick to develop.	2	5	10	5	10	2	4	4	8
15	Inexpensive.	2	5	10	5	10	1	2	4	8
16										
17	TOTAL SCORE			84		88		93		99
18										

Figure 3-3: Solution rating tool

CROSS-REFERENCE A solution matrix for rating possible solutions is available in the companion files for this book. You can download it at `www.wiley.com/go/ProjMgmtCoach.`

Another thing to consider is the level of complexity of a solution. Often the simplest solution is the best. But be sure to consider whom the solution is simple for. For example, in software development, what might be simple for the programmer often makes the program complex for the user. Making a software solution easy and intuitive for the user often makes more work for the programmers.

Keep in mind that you might find that a combination of several suggested solutions turns out to be the best. This solution, and the extent to which you apply it, becomes your project strategy.

Gathering Requirements

Requirements are the detailed specifications for the product, service, or other result that the project will produce, given the overall project goal, the objectives, and the chosen strategy. These specifications are developed from an analysis of the needs and expectations of the sponsor, customer, and other stakeholders. The more completely the requirements are defined, the better the chances are for project success.

You've already seen how tempting it is to bypass the problem definition and jump straight to a solution, the peril being that the solution might not be right for the problem (or opportunity) at hand. In a similar way, costly mistakes are often made in project planning regarding requirements. Too often, the planners make sweeping assumptions about the requirements without consulting the stakeholders. This section covers methods for discovering, prioritizing, and validating project requirements so you can avoid the pitfall of misguided requirements.

Starting with Broad Requirements

When you don't yet know whether the project will be approved for planning, it's wise to spend as little time and money on gathering requirements as you can get away with. Develop a broad set of requirements that provide enough information to develop the scope and then the project proposal.

The broad requirements will also serve as a sanity check with the customer or project sponsor, making sure you're on the right track. And just like problem definition, the process of gathering requirements can go a long way toward uncovering political agendas and conflicting expectations among stakeholders.

After you gain approval to move ahead with project planning, you then revisit the broad requirements and drill down until you have the right level of detail for a successful project outcome. The resulting detailed requirements will in turn refine the project and product scope, and those in turn will drive the tasks for the nitty-gritty work.

Mining for Requirements

So where do requirements come from? If you're gathering broad requirements to start with, or if it's a small or simple project with which you have a fair amount of expertise, it might be enough for you to simply interview one or more of the key stakeholders.

If you're gathering definitive and detailed requirements, and it's a larger or more complex project, consider one or more of the following techniques for uncovering requirements:

- **Interview:** Interview the project sponsor, the customer(s), key representatives of the end user group, subject matter experts, and other stakeholders as appropriate.

- **Reuse:** Adapt existing requirements from previous similar projects. If available, use these requirements as a starting point and build from there. You'll be ahead of the game and will likely be able to improve on what was done before.

- **Facilitate:** Conduct a group requirements meeting, focus group, or workshop. In such a group setting, bring together the key stakeholders, and use a structured approach to identify requirements. Consider using group creativity and decision-making techniques to bring requirements to light and engender stakeholder buy-in at the same time.

- **Model:** Use a structured technique such as business process modeling or use cases. Such methods help define and describe processes and results, and therefore help to identify requirements.

- **Observe:** Witness the existing system or process that the project's result will replace or interact with. Job-shadow end users of the existing system or process. Later on, go back and confirm the assumptions you've made about your observations by talking with the users.

- **Prototype:** Build prototypes. Provide something tangible for the stakeholders to work with and learn what is needed, what is wanted, and what is not essential.

When you have researched the requirements, document them. Confirm the findings from your requirements research by having your stakeholders review and validate the documented requirements. Remember that the managing stakeholders will need to sign off on these requirements before you can proceed with planning.

Differentiating and Prioritizing Requirements

Even when you consult stakeholders on requirements, another common mistake is to not identify the true needs or to not differentiate between the wants and needs of customers or end users. If you overlook true requirements, the customer won't be satisfied with the results. If you include requirements that weren't really needed, you may be faced with a more expensive or time-consuming project than necessary.

It's best to gather all requirements, and then prioritize them. This can be especially helpful if the project needs to be completed within a certain time frame or budget. Include the highest priority requirements in the first phase. Then, if there is time or money remaining, you can propose a second phase to complete the lower priority requirements.

FROM THE FIELD: THE CASE OF THE OVERWHELMED CUSTOMER

The owner of a growing software company, Hannah, consulted with a vendor's representative, Max, to develop an online help system. Her original objective was a simple system she could implement quickly and rather cheaply.

As Max asked questions about what Hannah wanted in the system, she saw a bigger vision with new possibilities beyond the original basic system. Inspired, she explored several new ideas with Max. They had a great discussion about various features.

However, when Max presented Hannah with the proposal including all the items they had discussed, she nearly fell out of her chair. What she had thought was a basic online help system was four times more expensive and would take three times longer than she had expected.

Max had lumped everything that Hannah said she wanted all together into a single timeline and cost without differentiating between her original requirements and the new ideas spawned by their conversation.

"Thank you for your time, but we won't be able to implement a help system at this time," Hannah murmured and showed Max to the door without opportunity for any further conversation.

The next time Max spoke with a customer about possible projects, he made sure that his proposal included phases, which differentiated feature priorities, with a cost and time associated with each phase.

With that approach, he got approvals for these projects every time. In fact, he usually got approval to go for the entire project with all phases.

When the requirements are differentiated between needs and wants, the customers are in control and can decide what is important to them.

What Constitutes Success?

An important part of project initiation is to articulate the *success criteria*, which are specific unequivocal statements of how and when the project results are satisfied. You might think a project is successful if it's delivered on time, achieves its budget, and fulfills its requirements. However, as challenging as those items are to achieve, project success is far more than that. When the project is complete, how will you (and the customer or sponsor) know that it achieved what it was supposed to?

The best success criteria are quantifiable and can reflect strategic business goals such as increased revenue, reduced costs, or improved service. Take the new product, for example. The goal is to increase share of the mobile device market. For this goal, the success criteria might be to increase the company's share in the mobile device market by 25 percent or to achieve $5 million in revenue from that product in the next two years.

On the call center training project, the goal is to increase customer satisfaction. The success criteria might be to increase customer satisfaction by 35 percent in the next six months as measured by customer surveys.

If success criteria speak to strategic business goals, it becomes very clear why you're doing the project and whether the project is worth doing. They become the selling points for a project proposal. If the success criteria are quantified, there can be no debate or qualifying shades of gray over whether the project is a success; it's clear whether it is or not. Either you've achieved $5 million in revenue for the product over the ensuing two years or you didn't.

With a project that is selected on the strength of its success criteria, the project team understands that those criteria are the driving forces for their work. The team builds the product or develops the service accordingly and tests the qualities and capabilities to meet those criteria throughout the project life cycle.

Another way to think of success criteria is that they are the project outcomes or *benefits realization*. Rather than looking at completion of objectives or fulfillment of requirements, benefits realization typically happens a while after the project is completed and closed out. For the mobile Web eyeglasses, it won't be known if $5 million in revenue was achieved until two years after the project was completed. You won't start measuring customer satisfaction until the call center training project is complete, and you won't know whether you met your success criteria until six months after that.

At project closure, the customer bases acceptance on the fulfillment of the project requirements for the deliverables. If satisfaction of the success criteria can be ascertained at that time, that also becomes part of the acceptance process. However, if the project includes success criteria that cannot be measured for a period of time, often a *post-implementation review* is scheduled for that time.

Documenting Project Scope

You might not believe how often organizations try to stuff ten pounds of potatoes into a five-pound bag in terms of their projects. Ensuring that you limit yourself to five pounds of potatoes for a five-pound bag — that is, doing the tasks that are appropriate to the time and resources available for this project — is all about establishing and managing the project scope.

Project scope is the definition of the work to be done as part of a particular project. The project scope identifies the boundaries of a project, indicating not only what will be done to deliver a product, service, or other result, but what will not be done.

Project scope is not the same as *product scope*, which summarizes the features and functions of the product or service. For example, the project scope for the kitchen project might be "to remodel the kitchen from design through installation to décor." The product scope that characterizes the features and functions of the remodeled kitchen might be that "the remodeled kitchen will contain updated appliances, attractive cabinetry and countertops, and an efficient work flow."

The product (actually, service) scope for the training program, is "an ongoing training program that keeps our customer service specialists continually updated with the latest information." The project scope to achieve this might be "to develop curriculum, conduct the training to a pilot group, and then train the trainers."

Again, while the product scope describes the features and functions that characterize the product, service, or result, the project scope describes the work that must be done to deliver that product, service, or other result with the specified features and functions.

CROSS-REFERENCE The information in this section relates to the PMP Exam's Domain I: Initiating the Project, Task 2, "Define the high-level scope of the project based on the business and compliance requirements, in order to meet the customer's project expectations."

Elements of the Scope Statement

Everything you've done as part of the project definition process feeds the project scope. The project scope closely reflects the problem, goal, strategy, and success criteria (see Figure 3-4).

Project Name:
Scope Statement

Scope Description
The characteristics of the product, service, or result that the project is to achieve.

User Acceptance Criteria
The process and criteria for accepting completed products, services, or other results.

Success Criteria
The business goal(s) to be achieved by the project: what, how much, by when.

Project Deliverables
The tangible items being produced through the execution of the project.

Project Boundaries
What is being excluded from the project.

Project Constraints
Limitations on the project that constrain project options, such as time, budget, etc.

Project Assumptions
Identification of any information that is unknown at the time.

Figure 3-4: Scope statement template

CROSS-REFERENCE A scope statement template is available in the companion files for this book. You can download it at `www.wiley.com/go/ ProjMgmtCoach.`

A good scope statement includes the following:

- **Scope description:** The scope description details the work that must be done to deliver a product, service, or other result according to the features and functions described in the product scope.

- **User acceptance criteria:** The process and criteria for accepting completed products, services, or other results that come out of the execution of the project.

- **Success criteria:** The unequivocal statement of how and when the project result is satisfied, typically supporting strategic goals of the organization.

- **Project deliverables:** The tangible items, such as specifications, prototypes, and documented processes being produced that prove that the project is being fulfilled. Deliverables are discussed later in this section.

- **Project boundaries:** What is excluded from the project, as contrasted with the scope description, which indicates what is included.

- **Project constraints:** Limitations on the project — for example, an imposed finish date, a not-to-exceed budget amount, or contractual conditions. Constraints are discussed later in this section.

- **Project assumptions:** Factors that are as yet unknown but must be understood to be true or certain to move forward with planning. Assumptions are discussed later in this section.

EXAMPLE SCOPE STATEMENT

Scope: The scope of this project is to develop curriculum, conduct training to a pilot group, and then train the trainers. This will result in an ongoing training program that keeps our customer service specialists continually knowledgeable of the latest information.

Success Criteria: Through this project, we expect to increase customer satisfaction by 35 percent as measured by customer surveys over the six months after the completion of training, with incremental increases beyond that period.

Deliverables: Deliverables will include elements of the training curriculum, including the participant workbook, instructor workbook, written and skills demonstration certification exams, pilot training class list, pilot training evaluation, train-the-trainers class list, train-the-trainers evaluation, and handoff of all materials.

Project Boundaries: Items beyond the scope of this project include the printing of curriculum materials and the delivery of training to the general population of customer service specialists.

> **Constraints:** This project must begin within one month and must be completed within five months from the start date. The project will not exceed a budget of $50,000. The pilot training and train-the-trainers sessions must take place at the customer site.
>
> **Assumptions:** It is assumed that trainees will be made available from their everyday tasks to participate in the training program when scheduled.

CROSS-REFERENCE Other items that could be part of the scope statement might be more appropriate for the project charter. Such items might include the project purpose or justification, project objectives, high-level requirements, and project approval requirements. As always, include the elements in the scope statement that seem most appropriate for your project and the way your organization does business.

For more information about the project charter, see the section "Preparing a Project Charter" later in this chapter.

Controlling Scope Creep

Documenting the project scope is important for the successful management of the project throughout its life cycle. Particularly in the planning and execution processes, the project scope will be tested in a big way because there will be constant pressures to expand that scope, to do more in the project. Some of the expansions will be big and obvious, such as adding a greenhouse off the side of the remodeled kitchen. Other requests will seem trivial and easy to accomplish, such as installing an appliance caddy, pull-out drawers in the pantry, and a wine cooler, but they can add up to a large change in scope — which leads to the discussion of scope creep.

Scope creep is the addition of tasks to the project scope — typically reflecting functions and features — without examining the effects of those additions on the project schedule, budget, or resources and without obtaining approval from the customer. Although scope creep is often caused by seemingly small tasks or trivial additions, scope creep is a huge problem — so huge, in fact that it's the reason why many projects run late or over budget or fail altogether (see Figure 3-5).

A well-defined project scope that supports the project goal and success criteria and is agreed on by the stakeholders stands a good chance of remaining under control throughout the project. In fact, it's those managing stakeholders who are often the ones asking to increase scope, so the well-documented project scope provides the defense you need when this happens.

Notice the phrase "under control" rather than "intact" or "unchanged." Having the exact same project scope at project closure that you had at project initiation is very rare. New information is always discovered during the project planning and execution processes. New ideas arise that are recognized as an improvement to the project. Other activities can leverage activities taking place in the project, with a little adjustment. Even the nature of the business the project is working within can change, and the project needs to respond to remain viable.

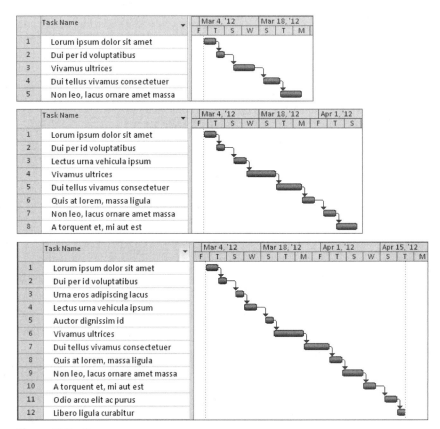

Figure 3-5: Scope creep

The best way to manage changes to project scope is to implement a change review board. An effective change review board is typically made up of the project manager, the project customer or sponsor, key project team members, and others as appropriate. The board reviews requested changes to the project and decides which changes can improve the project and its chances for success, and which changes should be tabled or rejected for now.

The challenge is to manage the scope and changes to that scope throughout the project in such a way that:

- You can still meet or renegotiate the project finish date.
- You can still meet or renegotiate the project budget.

- Resources are still well-balanced.
- You don't sacrifice quality.
- You don't increase risk, or you're willing to manage increased risk.
- You still meet the overall project goal.
- You still can achieve the project's success criteria.

CROSS-REFERENCE For more information about managing scope changes and the work of the change review board, see Chapter 11, "Setting Up a Change Management Plan."

Specifying the Deliverables

The project *deliverables* are those tangible outcomes of a task or series of tasks. Deliverables answer the question "What are we producing that proves that the project and product scope are being fulfilled?" In other words, deliverables are proof that the project is being executed. Deliverables are verifiable and complete a process, phase, or project. They are often subject to approval by the customer or project sponsor.

What the deliverables are depends on the nature of the project. In a construction project, deliverables might include architectural drawings and permits or acceptance of the actual building. In a product development project, deliverables might include specifications and prototypes. In a trade show project, deliverables might include the exhibitor contract, booth layout drawings, or a banner. In a training program project, deliverables might include the curriculum outline and the first draft of the student workbook.

Deliverables are typically identified as part of the development of the scope statement, or they can be identified soon after the scope is defined. During these project initiating processes, it's more likely that your deliverables will be defined at a higher level, as associated with your higher-level objectives. When the project is approved to move forward into project planning, you'll refine and add detailed deliverables as you create the work breakdown structure process and more information is uncovered.

TIP If you find you or other stakeholders are starting to identify deliverables very early in the project initiation process, put the brakes on. This might mean that a solution, in the form of deliverables, is being proposed before the problem is clearly understood. As discussed earlier in this section, too many projects fail because solutions are proposed and accepted before fully understanding the problem, success criteria, and scope.

CROSS-REFERENCE The information in this section relates to the PMP Exam's Domain II: Planning the Project, Task 1, "Assess detailed project requirements, constraints, and assumptions with stakeholders based on the project charter, lessons learned from previous projects, and the use of requirements-gathering techniques (e.g., planning sessions, brainstorming, focus groups), in order to establish the project deliverables."

Identifying Risks, Assumptions, and Constraints

Project management, similar to stock trading, is a form of structured soothsaying. You're trying to do the impossible — plan and predict the future. More specifically, as the project manager, you are trying to plan around events and conditions you don't know will or will not happen.

As part of your fortune-telling bag of tricks, you address three important items:

- Risks
- Assumptions
- Constraints

CROSS-REFERENCE The information in this section relates to the PMP Exam's Domain I: Initiating the Project, Task 4, "Identify and document high-level risks, assumptions, and constraints based on current environment, historical data, and/or expert judgment, in order to identify project limitations and propose an implementation approach."

Working with Risks

A *risk* is an uncertain event or condition that has a possibility of occurring in the future, which if it occurs, can affect the success of a task, a phase, a deliverable, or even the entire project. Risks are typically occurrences beyond the control of your project that could muck up the works. For example, on a construction project, weather and the availability of equipment and building materials are common risks. On a product development project, there might be risks of a competitor getting to the market sooner or investors pulling out because of an economic downturn.

A good risk management plan identifies risks, indicates the likelihood of each risk, specifies the severity of the impact if the risk should come to pass, and outlines a plan for responding to the higher priority risks. Often, risk likelihood and severity are quantified with numerical scores to help prioritize which risks you will track in your plan.

TIP Most people think of risks as negative occurrences. However, some risks have a positive outcome. For example, your construction project might plan for an average number of days of rain, but what if the season is drier than usual and you're able to finish the project sooner with less cost? Your risk management plan could therefore also anticipate instances of positive risk and describe how you might take advantage of such fortuitous occurrences.

The project initiation processes generally occur too early to enable you to create a full-blown risk management plan. However, key stakeholders need to be aware of any high-level risks when approving or signing off on a new project. Project initiation is also a good time to address risks that have plagued projects in the past. This ensures that the key stakeholders have the facts necessary to make a sound decision about moving on to the next steps.

CROSS-REFERENCE For more information about identifying risks and creating the risk management plan, see Chapter 12, "Managing Risk."

Working with Assumptions

An *assumption* is a condition you're certain is part of the project or will affect the project, but for which specifics are as yet unknown. To move forward with planning, you must make assumptions about those specifics. Those assumptions might prove true or false, and that's a risk you have to take.

For example, if you're planning a trade show exhibit project, you might need to make an assumption as to how many people will attend and how many people will stop by for a demonstration and promotional gifts. Those assumptions affect how many data sheets you print and how many gift items you order, which, in turn, affect the project cost.

Assumptions are typically included as part of the scope statement, either integrated with the scope description or called out as a separate section. There should be a provision for what happens if the assumption turns out to be false. The provision might be that a false assumption is one of the risks identified in the risk management plan. If a false assumption creates the need for more funding, it can be part of the contract that the customer would automatically provide that funding.

Working with Constraints

A *constraint* is any limitation that places boundaries on the project. Common examples include a finish date or budget imposed by the project sponsor or contractual conditions imposed by the customer.

For example, in a training program project, you might wish to develop an interactive video component in addition to the printed training workbooks. One constraint might be that the training program must cover all the topics for a specific certification exam. Another constraint might be that the interactive components must be developed using software that is already available in-house.

Like assumptions, constraints are typically included as part of the scope statement, either integrated with the scope description or called out as a separate section. With constraints as part of the scope statement, managing stakeholders see the limitations of the project and understand the factors that can affect finish dates, cost, and other factors.

Unlike assumptions or risks, constraints are not educated guesses or possibilities; they're either points for negotiation with the customer or facts for which provision must be made in the project. The project manager should clarify the business implications of adding or changing a constraint.

Identifying the Project Stakeholders

For a kitchen remodel, there are a number of individuals who control, influence the outcome of, or are affected positively or negatively by the project. These are the project stakeholders. The person who is asking for the kitchen remodel may or may not be the same person paying for it. The kitchen designer and building contractor will be doing the work. Members of the family who use the kitchen will be negatively affected by the disruption during the remodel, and they are also the end users who you hope will be positively affected and even delighted by the finished product.

A project *stakeholder* is anyone who has a vested interest in the project. This is everyone from the project sponsor to the last project team member and end user.

CROSS-REFERENCE The information in this section relates to the PMP Exam's Domain I: Initiating the Project, Task 3, "Perform key stakeholder analysis using brainstorming, interviewing, and other data-gathering techniques, in order to ensure expectation alignment and gain support for the project."

You can categorize your stakeholders into four groups, as follows:

- **Managing stakeholders:** These include the project sponsor or customer, the portfolio manager, and the project manager. The project sponsor or customer is the person or group paying for the project. These managing stakeholders have influence throughout the organization and significant decision-making authority over the project.

- **Team members:** These are the project resources that perform the project tasks.

■ **Representatives of support functions:** These include various groups throughout the organization who are affected by the work of the project — for example, accounting, human resources, purchasing, or facilities. In some situations, they have review or approval responsibilities.

■ **Representatives of customers or end users:** These are the people who will use the product, service, or other result that the project will be producing. Consultation and buy-in from these stakeholders are essential to your project.

THE CANDID COACH: INVOLVEMENT OF SUPPORT FUNCTIONS

Consider including representatives of support functions in the decision-making process for the project proposal. The person who proposes the project, and even the project manager, tends to be largely focused on the core mission of the project. While this is appropriate, a consequence is that he or she can forget or neglect to give enough thought to how that core mission can impact these other functions.

The project sponsor and project manager can make assumptions about what those functions need to do for the project, but they might not be aware of issues internal to those groups that can affect project success. For example:

■ Other projects taking place at the same time

■ Resource issues during the time of the proposed project

■ Special considerations for this type of project

■ Operational cycles that can affect the project

During project initiation, especially when you're working on a project proposal, you think in terms of *potential* project stakeholders. Even so, the input of those potential stakeholders is vital. The project will affect them if it is approved, so they must be informed and their input must be considered.

Still, at this early point in the game, the most critical stakeholders are the project sponsor, the managing stakeholders who will decide whether or not the project should move forward into planning, and you, the project manager.

THE CANDID COACH: BEWARE OF "PERCEIVED" STAKEHOLDERS

Many projects are plagued by an influential person who mistakenly thinks he or she is going to be responsible for or benefit from a project.

It can take a lot of back-pedaling and angst-ridden project reviews to remove this person from the stakeholder list.

To prevent "perceived" stakeholders, consider who might believe herself to be a stakeholder. Who might see this project as a platform for launching a different agenda?

Consider creating a preliminary list of stakeholders to include in the project notebook. You can use actual names, generic titles, department names, or a mixture of all three. The stakeholder registry and project organization chart will be fleshed out if and when the project makes it to the planning processes. But this list can provide the nucleus you need to get through the initiation processes.

CROSS-REFERENCE For more information about creating the responsibility matrix, see Chapter 7, "Planning Project Resources." For information about appropriate communication with different types of stakeholders, see "Who Are the Audiences?" in Chapter 10.

Preparing the Project Proposal

Congratulations! You have completed a lot of hard work. You've excavated and built the foundation for a project that clearly identifies the problem to be solved, the project goal and objectives, the recommended solution, the requirements, and the success criteria. You've also developed the project scope, including the deliverables, risks, assumptions, and constraints.

If your project must be approved before it can move on to the project planning, you need to prepare a project proposal that provides the information necessary for the powers that be to make an informed decision about moving forward.

WORKING TOWARD APPROVAL VERSUS SIGN-OFF

Most of the time, the project sponsor assigns the project manager to complete the project proposal. This means the project is essentially already approved. As project manager, you still must do all the project initiation work described in this chapter. You need to document and confirm an understanding of the requirements and scope, which will still be reviewed and signed off by key stakeholders.

In a handful of other cases, one department, such as IT or marketing, proposes a project for another department — for example, accounting or product development — to sponsor. In such a situation, the originator of the project proposal is trying to sell a concept to another group.

In another handful of cases, someone wants to investigate the feasibility of an idea for a project. The proposal looks at alternatives to solve a particular problem or exploit a specific opportunity. Many of these projects are indeed approved to move forward, but many also die on the vine after project initiation as being too difficult, too risky, or not an appropriate use of resources at that time.

> Be cognizant of which category of project you're initiating, and tailor your effort accordingly. If you're working toward sign-off, you don't need to convince the stakeholders of the need for the project. If you're selling the idea to another group, you do. If you're researching feasibility, you might need to present more data, but you might not necessarily "sell" the idea; you're presenting the facts from which the stakeholders can draw their conclusion.

Even if the project is already approved, you need sign-off on the proposal. The managing stakeholders must be in agreement for everything from the problem to the scope. If you don't have this agreement, there's more work to be done. If that work isn't done, you're just asking for trouble when planning and execution get under way.

As a rule of thumb, keep your project proposal as simple and as inexpensive as possible. (See Figure 3-6 for an example.) You don't want to spend a lot of money doing analysis for a project proposal that may be killed. Adapt this rule as necessary to fit your organization's requirements and culture, as well as the needs of the project being proposed. Consider who will review the proposal and what they need to know to make an informed decision. If your organization has a specific protocol for submitting and assessing project proposals, be sure to follow it.

Project Proposal for _____

Problem or Opportunity Statement
Scope Statement, Project Description, or Statement of Work
Project Goal
Project Objectives
Success Criteria
Risks
Assumptions
Constraints
High-Level Project Costs

Figure 3-6: Project proposal template

CROSS-REFERENCE A project proposal template is available in the companion files for this book. You can download it at www.wiley.com/go/ ProjMgmtCoach.

THE CANDID COACH: THE QUICK AND DIRTY PROPOSAL

According to Bob McGannon, director of Mindavation, "You want the project proposal to be as *cheap* as possible."

At the same time, he stresses that you should do the right amount of research and validation. Don't take shortcuts but know when enough is enough. At that point, stop, write the proposal, and move forward.

"Keep it simple," he says. "Avoid the 'measure with a micrometer, mark with a crayon, cut with an axe' syndrome!"

If you're creating a simpler proposal, try to fit the necessary information on one or two pages. Such a proposal could include the following:

- Problem or opportunity statement
- The scope statement or the statement of work, essentially the project summary
- Goal and high-level objectives
- Success criteria
- Risks, assumptions, and constraints
- High-level project costs

FIGURING A PRELIMINARY COST ESTIMATE

You can't create a detailed or accurate cost estimate until you are planning the project. At this point, with the development of the work breakdown structure, identification of the project resources, and work estimates, the costs become more and more clear.

But at the proposal stage, you still need some kind of rough cost estimate. For this purpose, you can create a "quick and dirty" cost estimate, also known as a *rough order of magnitude (ROM)* estimate. Just like the proposal itself, you don't want to put too much effort into developing a cost estimate only to learn the project doesn't make sense financially and won't be approved.

With an order of magnitude estimate, you're basically guessing whether a project will be in the neighborhood of a number like $1,000, $10,000, $100,000, or $1,000,000 — that is, an order of magnitude for costs. Typically, you arrive at such estimates based on the cost for similar projects in the past.

When using an order of magnitude estimate, be sure to call it out as such in your proposal so you're not held to it as an exact figure later when you develop the "real" budget.

CROSS-REFERENCE   For more information on estimating costs for a project, see Chapter 6, "Estimating Work and Cost."

The proposal boils all this information down to an executive summary of the project initiation, no more than one or two pages. You might also include the risks, assumptions, and constraints on a separate page and the project costs on yet another page.

Whatever you do, remember that the folks reviewing the proposal are busy executives. They largely need to see the 30,000-foot view, but they also need sufficient detail to make an informed decision. If you're a proponent of the project, remember that this proposal is essentially a sales pitch, and you're trying to get them to say "yes."

If you're really trying to sell the proposal to the deciding management team, keep the following suggestions in mind as you finalize your proposal:

- Know the team's project approval criteria.

- Be well-versed in your organization's strategic goals, and make a business case that shows how this project helps achieve one or more of those goals.

- Understand any bias of the members of the deciding management team.

- Lobby the members of the management team as appropriate.

- Develop a thorough and compelling proposal that essentially proves how this project will solve the problem at hand or take advantage of a promising opportunity.

- Be aware of prevailing political winds.

Getting Approval or Sign-Off

With the project proposal completed, it's now time to submit it and see whether it gets approved. If the project is already approved, you need confirmation and sign-off from the key stakeholders. Remember that this is just the first review to assess the broad outlines of the project idea. This review determines whether the project can move forward with planning, which is a more extensive and detailed process and takes far more time and resources than these initiation processes.

Most projects have a second approval, which takes place after planning is complete to determine whether the project can move forward with the actual execution of the project.

CROSS-REFERENCE For more information about approval of the project plan before the start of project launch and execution, see the section "Obtaining Approval" in Chapter 13.

In some projects, the management team might include additional checkpoints to see whether they want to continue work on the project. For example, they might review the project deliverables, schedule, budget, and other characteristics at the end of a project phase. If the project has fallen significantly short, the project might be re-evaluated or even canceled.

According to your organization's process, the project proposal is vetted against agreed-upon criteria by specific stakeholders in a management team. These stakeholders might include the project sponsor or customer, the project management office or project portfolio manager, and other executives.

It's best if the criteria used to approve or deny the project proposal are in line with the organization's strategic goals. But whatever the measuring stick, the decision should determine whether the project is worth doing given the cost in money, time, and resources for the organization. The decision should also take into account that if this project is approved, it might exclude the opportunity to implement another, possibly more worthwhile, project.

The outcome of this review process is that the project proposal is approved, denied, or tabled. It might be sent back for rework or to provide additional information.

If a project proposal is approved, communicate the news immediately to the stakeholders closest to the project — the ones you worked with to develop the proposal and who will be involved with the project. Do the same if the proposal was denied or tabled. These individuals need to be removed from the holding pattern for a project that won't be happening after all.

CROSS-REFERENCE For more information about an ideal project selection process and a project review board, see Chapter 25, "Selecting the Right Projects."

Publicizing the Project Charter

The first thing that must be done after a project is approved is to make sure a project manager is assigned to the project. If you're reading this section, there's a good chance that project manager is you.

If there's a project management office, ask about the project standards and processes you need to follow as you proceed with planning. Likewise, follow any other protocols as appropriate when a project is approved in your organization. Then move on to the important business of preparing and publicizing the project charter.

CROSS-REFERENCE The information in this section relates to the PMP Exam's Domain I: Initiating the Project, Task 5, "Develop the project charter by further gathering and analyzing stakeholder requirements, in order to document project scope, milestones, and deliverables."

Preparing a Project Charter

The *project charter* is a document that officially announces and authorizes the existence of the project. Over the signature of the project sponsor, the charter names the project manager and indicates the extent of the project manager's authority over the project and its resources. The project charter is prepared as part of your initiation work, so it's ready to distribute once the project is approved.

CROSS-REFERENCE The information in this section relates to the PMP Exam's Domain I: Initiating the Project, Task 6, "Obtain approval for the project charter from the sponsor and customer (if required), in order to formalize the authority assigned to the project manager and gain commitment and acceptance for the project."

The project charter should contain at least the following elements:

- Project description and characteristics of the product, service, or result
- Name, responsibility, and authority level of the assigned project manager
- Name and responsibility of the person or persons authorizing the project charter

Your project charter can also include the following items:

- Project purpose or justification
- Measurable project objectives
- Summary milestone schedule (these could be the same as the project objectives at this point)
- Success criteria
- High-level requirements
- Summary budget (this would be the rough order of magnitude cost estimate)
- Project approval requirements, including the success criteria, who determines whether those criteria have been met, and who signs off for project approval

Sometimes the project charter and scope statement are the same or include overlapping information.

Distributing the Project Charter

After the project charter has been written and approved by the project sponsor, send it to everyone in the organization who needs to know about it. This should include the following:

- All managing stakeholders
- Any potential project team members
- Representatives of any support functions affected by the project
- Peripheral stakeholders, including those who are positively or negatively impacted by the project
- Anyone else who should be informed for courtesy or political reasons

In the old days, you might have distributed the charter as a memo. But these days, the most standard practice is to distribute it as an email. To give it more authority and make it known as the heavyweight document that it is, consider marking the email as a high-priority message. Including a graphic of the organization's logo at the top of the message can also make the recipients pay closer attention. And although you might have written the charter, be sure that it is sent from the project sponsor's email account.

As with anything, be sure to adhere to your organization's culture and politics as it relates to communicating and publicizing something this important.

CROSS-REFERENCE Publicizing the project charter marks the beginning of your project communication strategy. For more information about project communications, see Chapter 10, "Setting Up a Communication Plan."

Assembling the Project Notebook

After the project is approved, you need to assemble the elements you've developed through the project initiation processes into a central location — the project notebook. The project notebook includes everything from the problem/opportunity statement to the scope statement. This is true whether the project is approved, tabled, or denied.

The project notebook itself can take the form of a manual binder, an electronic notebook, a shared website, or even a project situation room.

Using the Project Notebook for Approved Projects

If the project is approved, you'll certainly need all the initiating elements as you develop the schedule, plan the resources, detail costs, and develop your plans for communication, change management, and risk management. You'll add the planning elements to the project notebook as you and your team develop them.

When the project moves to the project execution processes, the project notebook will contain schedule and cost tracking information and progress reports. You'll also need to keep an eye on the scope, requirements, deliverables, and more, while adding necessary detail as you move deeper into the project or adjusting scope in accordance with direction from your change review board.

When the project moves to the project closure processes, the project notebook contains the requirements instrumental to project sign-off. The closure documents, project closeout report, and lessons learned report or knowledge base are added to the project notebook. Finally, the project notebook is archived as a resource for future projects.

Using the Project Notebook for Tabled or Denied Projects

If the project is not approved, don't toss out all your work in disgust or despair. That work is not wasted.

Project ideas have a way of cropping up again, especially when there's a change in the cast of characters. Rather than just saying, "We looked into that before and decided not to do it," you can dust off the project notebook for a rejected idea and have another look. That might help new players see why the idea is not feasible, without making the old players look like uncooperative sticks-in-the-mud.

Also, circumstances can change. An idea that seemed ridiculous two years ago might suddenly seem very doable. Maybe market conditions have changed, people with the needed skills are available, or special funding for exactly this kind of project has surfaced.

Sometimes a rejected project idea can benefit from a new perspective. With all the groundwork you did with the original proposal, the new idea takes on new life. Because of your previous work, project initiation won't take as much time.

Choosing the Form of the Project Notebook

Although an ever-expanding three-ring binder might be the image that comes to mind when you think of a project notebook, the term is just a euphemism for the collection of project documents. The project notebook can actually take a variety of different forms:

- An actual three-ring binder with tabs for the different processes and different documents that define the project.

- A bookshelf of multiple binders for all the various documents and plans.

- A set of electronic documents in a folder on your hard drive or a public folder on the network accessible by all project stakeholders.

- A secure website accessible by all project stakeholders, whether it's a free collaborative group website, a wiki site, a Microsoft SharePoint site, or other means for online collaboration.

- A "situation room" that's used exclusively to house project information and to host project meetings. The project schedule might eventually be posted on the wall, and all the project documents are available in the room.

Regardless of the form you adopt for the project notebook, the important thing is that all the elements are together in one place for easy reference by everyone who needs it.

THE CANDID COACH: A COLLABORATIVE PROJECT SITE

If your project is sizable and many stakeholders need to refer to project documents, consider creating a project website. With your choice of many document management and Web-based collaboration tools, you can:

- Keep all your project documents in a document library. Any stakeholders with permission to access the site can view the documents. You can allow editing of documents if you want, and use a check-out/check-in system and version history feature. You can also control which stakeholders can view or edit which documents.

- Hold online discussions among project team members and other stakeholders.

- Maintain a calendar, which can include project meetings and milestones.

- Track risks, with a description of the risk, a score of the risk's likelihood and impact, a mitigation plan, and the person responsible.

- Track issues, with a description of the issue, the person responsible, the deadline, and the resolution.

Summary

Project initiation is a vital, but sometimes overlooked, process in the project management life cycle. It is essential to the success of the project that a solid foundation is laid through proper project initiation.

The major component of the initiation processes is project definition. This is where you discern the root problem or opportunity, identify the project goal and objectives, decide on the right strategy, gather project requirements, define the success criteria, and document the project scope including high-level deliverables, risks, assumptions, and constraints.

Also part of the initiation processes is the preliminary identification of project stakeholders, submittal and approval (or denial) of the project proposal, development and dissemination of the project charter, and assembly of the project notebook.

Coach's Review

Use this section to assess what you've learned in this chapter and to apply it to a real-life project you're currently working on.

Test Your Knowledge

Test your knowledge of the material in this chapter by answering the following questions. See Appendix A for the answers.

1. Name at least three factors that can figure into whether an idea or project proposal is appropriate for your organization.
2. List at least five elements that should be part of a solid project definition.
3. Describe at least two negative results that can happen if the project definition processes are skipped.
4. What is the 5-why analysis and how is it helpful in problem definition?
5. Define project goal.
6. What is a "SMART" objective?
7. Name at least three techniques for gathering project requirements.
8. What's the difference between project scope and product scope?

9. Define stakeholder.

10. What is the purpose of the project charter?

Project Challenge

Practice the knowledge you've gained in this chapter by working through one or more of the following challenges using a real-life project you're working on, or one similar to the types of projects you might work on.

1. With your own project in mind, identify the problem that the project is solving. Use the 5-why analysis to trace back to the root problem that the project is solving. Write the problem statement.

2. Write the project goal for your project.

3. Write the objectives for your project, keeping the "SMART" guidelines in mind.

4. Draft the project's requirements as you know them. Use one or more of the requirements-gathering techniques to go out and learn the requirements of the project to the level that's necessary for project initiation. Document the requirements.

5. Considering your organization's strategic goals and your project, write the success criteria for your project. How will you know your project is a success? When will you know this? What business value is being gained from doing this project?

6. Write a *product* scope description for the result of your project. Then write the *project* scope description.

7. Write the full scope statement for your project.

8. List the high-level deliverables, as you know them now, that you expect your project to produce.

9. List risks, assumptions, and constraints associated with your project.

10. List the names and titles or functions of your project's stakeholders. Identify any possible perceived stakeholders and consider what you might do about them.

11. Using the information you have prepared up to this point, prepare a one- or two-page project proposal.

12. Write the project charter for your project.

13. Determine the form you want your project notebook to take, assemble the elements, and create that notebook.

Getting to Know a Project Plan

Up until this point in the life of a project, the big question has been "Will they approve the project?" Now that the project has gotten past that huge hurdle, a multitude of new questions beg to be answered: Who? What? When? How? How much?

The answers to these new questions address how you plan to implement the project and accomplish what it's supposed to do. When you put all the detailed answers together, you have a project plan that you can use to manage the project to its conclusion.

The project plan is a detailed definition of the work to be done, how much it will cost, who will do the work, and when the project will be done. It isn't a single document. It's actually a repository for all plans, charts, and other documents you need to define, track, and manage the project.

In addition, the project plan contains the scope and requirements documents, the project charter, risk management plan, and more. It provides information about the project stakeholders, not the least of which is the person at the helm — you, the project manager — who keeps the ship sailing toward its goal.

This chapter introduces the components of a project plan and how they contribute to completing a project successfully. Subsequent chapters in Part III of this book cover the components in detail.

What Work Has to Be Done?

After you've obtained approval for a proposed project, the first thing to do is get your brain around what actually has to be done to accomplish that project. The project scope, introduced in "Scope Management" in Chapter 2 and "Documenting Project Scope" in Chapter 3, describes what the project will and will not do. A list of activities details that project scope and gives it substance and reality. Here, you identify the work that must be performed so you don't leave anything out. And you organize it so that it's easier to plan and manage.

Identifying Work

You can use any number of techniques to brainstorm the work that has to be done. This is where you start to develop the *work breakdown structure* (WBS), which forms the framework, or skeleton if you will, of your project plan. As its name makes obvious, the WBS breaks the work of a project down into bite-sized pieces that are easy to define, estimate, schedule, assign, track, and manage.

For example, suppose you've been assigned as project manager for the development of a training program. You might deconstruct the project into phases such as determining needs, creating the student workbook, and doing the actual training. Then, you break the workbook phase into its logical parts — research, writing, review, and testing.

At this point in the project, the work breakdown structure shows manageable tasks that are easy to explain and assign to the folks who will perform them. As you learn in Chapter 5, "Identifying the Work to Be Completed," you decide what level of decomposition makes sense for the type of project you're planning.

Organizing Work into Major Categories

After you have a broad list of work to be done, you categorize that work into logical chunks, such as phases or functions or some other organizational scheme. Most often, you start with the project objectives identified in your scope statement and break down those objectives into smaller chunks until you have a hierarchy that starts with the overall project at the top and spells out specific tasks that can be easily assigned and tracked at the bottom.

CROSS-REFERENCE You learn techniques for identifying and organizing project tasks in Chapter 5, "Identifying the Work to Be Completed."

How Much Will the Project Cost?

Money is the engine that drives projects. As the project manager, you might be asked to propose the project budget or you simply might be told to keep the budget below a specific limit. In some projects, you don't have to deal with a budget at all.

CROSS-REFERENCE Developing and tracking a project budget is introduced in "Cost Management" in Chapter 2.

Obtaining Early Cost Estimates

Even at the project proposal stage, you usually have to estimate the cost of a project. By necessity, these broad "ballpark" estimates are based on preliminary task and work estimates and can be plus or minus 50 or even 75 percent of what will become the final cost.

At the project proposal stage described in Chapter 3, "Getting a Project Off the Ground," an initial high-level cost estimate helps determine whether a project is worth doing. Providing what amounts to a "quick and dirty" estimate makes sense because you wouldn't want to spend an inordinate amount of time in detailed project cost analysis only to find that the project doesn't make sense financially. An early cost estimate that doesn't need to be very accurate (yet) is a good tool at the project proposal and selection stage. Such an early cost estimate is called a *rough order of magnitude (ROM) estimate*. With a rough order of magnitude estimate, you're approximating whether a project price tag is in the ballpark of a number like $5,000, $50,000, or $500,000. Typically, you arrive at these estimates based on the cost for similar projects in the past.

After the project is approved, the work breakdown structure is defined, and resources and their costs are identified, you can refine your cost estimate to an accuracy tolerance of plus or minus 25 percent. Then, as you develop more detailed work estimates and assign specific resources, you can arrive at your final project cost estimate to an accuracy of plus or minus 10 percent.

Building a Budget

With an accurate and detailed cost estimate, you can build a reliable budget that you can commit to. A detailed cost estimate is based largely on your work estimates. For most projects, the largest cost is the cost of the people needed to complete task work. So when you have estimated the amount of work, identified the resources needed to do that work, and determined how much those people cost, you can estimate the labor cost for your project. Add in estimates for the equipment, materials, and any other costs, such as travel, and your overall project budget emerges.

If you're able to set the budget based on this estimate, your budget work is done for now. However, if the project customer or management team sets the project budget, you must check whether this cost estimate meets your target. If it doesn't, you have to revisit your project plan. You might adjust the plan in a way that affects the project's scope and finish date — that is, the other two sides of the project triangle. Or, you might need to have a heart-to-heart discussion with your customer or management team regarding the budget expectations in relation to the anticipated scope and finish date.

CROSS-REFERENCE For more information on estimating costs for a project, see Chapter 6, "Estimating Work and Cost."

Who Will Do the Work?

A list of project tasks is just a sketch of what the project should do. What gives your project forward movement and drives it to completion are the actions and effort that your project resources provide.

CROSS-REFERENCE Obtaining resources from within your organization is part of the human resource management processes (see the section "Human Resource Management" in Chapter 2). Engaging the services of vendors and purchasing equipment and supplies are part of the procurement processes (see the section "Procurement Management" in Chapter 2).

An Introduction to Project Resources

Resources are the people and things you need to complete the tasks in your project plan. In addition to the folks who perform work, projects often require equipment, such as bulldozers or computers; consumable materials, such as lumber or reams of paper; and a universal favorite, money, for things like airfare or training costs.

The following are types of resources you might need for your project:

- *People resources* are the individuals who perform the tasks in your project. They make up your project team. These people might be employees within a single department, individuals from several departments within your organization, contingency staff, vendors, contractors, consultants, or a combination of these.

- An *equipment resource* is a machine, device, tool, or vehicle that helps accomplish project tasks. For example, you might need a computer-aided manufacturing system to create parts for a new product design project or a backhoe to excavate a foundation.

- *Material resources* are goods or supplies consumed as you perform tasks, such as lumber and screws for a deck or paper and binders for a training course.

- Additional resources might include *work space facilities* and *money* for expenses such as travel or training.

Each type of resource contributes to the cost of a project. People and equipment can also affect the timing of a project — for example, delaying a project until the giant crane or expert programmers you need are available. Materials and money aren't scheduled by the hour or day, but they can affect the schedule if you don't have enough of them when you need them.

Identifying Resources

In the initial stages of the project planning processes, you can identify in generic terms the people resources you need — for example, by job title or skill set. You also identify the equipment, materials, and other resources needed for the project. Early on, it's important to identify all the resources you need so you can estimate how much the project will cost and determine whether you can get the resources you need when you need them.

As you move along in project planning, you can become more and more specific. Eventually, you replace job titles or skill sets with the names of real people or vendors enlisted for the project. With this level of detail, you know how much time you need resources for, you know each person's availability for work on your project, and you know their skill level. This information is essential, first for creating a realistic schedule and then for projecting and tracking the budget.

CROSS-REFERENCE You learn more about specifying the people, equipment, and materials needed for your project in Chapter 7, "Planning Project Resources."

When Will the Project Be Done?

On time and on budget. If you can say that about your project, you are most of the way to achieving success. Of course, there are other success criteria, but time and budget are typically at the top of the list. The project schedule tells you when the project should finish, but it also shows when tasks are supposed to start and finish throughout the course of the project.

The schedule tells team members when their tasks are due. It can flag tasks you need to pay special attention to, what's late, what's on time, or where you can take advantage of any slack in the schedule to deliver the project earlier. All the schedule factors together tell you whether you're on track to deliver project completion on time.

CROSS-REFERENCE Developing the project timeline is part of the schedule management processes, as introduced in "Time Management" in Chapter 2.

What You Need to Build a Schedule

To develop a schedule, you need several pieces of information for each task: work estimates, task dependencies, and deadlines.

The first key scheduling element is the *work estimate*. In most cases, it's best to estimate the effort or hours of work for each task. You can then determine the duration of the task based on the resources that are available. For example, if you estimate that a task will take 80 hours, you might set the task duration at 80 hours for a single person. Or, you can compress the duration to 40 hours and assign two people.

An alternative, albeit a more risky one, is to just estimate duration. In such cases, you have to assign enough people to complete the task within that duration. This method works well only if you already have a dedicated project team in place — for example, a department of people waiting for the project to start . . . which is somewhat rare.

CROSS-REFERENCE You learn more about how duration and work estimates affect each other in Chapter 6, "Estimating Work and Cost."

Task dependencies are a second key scheduling element. A *task dependency*, also known as a *task relationship*, shows how tasks depend on each other. The most common dependency is the finish-to-start relationship, as shown in Figure 4-1. In a finish-to-start dependency, a preceding task (or *predecessor*) must finish before a succeeding task (*successor*) can start. For example, in a backyard deck project, the concrete pads have to be poured and hardened before you can build the deck supports. And the deck supports must be constructed before you can put the decking on top.

Other task dependencies are start-to-start, finish-to-finish, and start-to-finish, as shown in Figure 4-2.

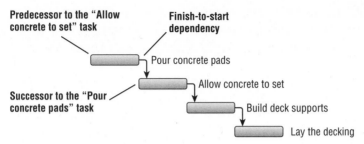

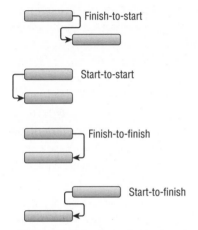

Figure 4-1: Task dependency

Figure 4-2: The four dependency types

CROSS-REFERENCE You learn the details of task dependencies in "Sequencing with Dependencies" in Chapter 8.

A third major element for building your schedule is the availability of project resources. Based on your work estimates and task dependencies, your schedule might show that the project will be completed by January 2013. But if you discover that a crucial person can't start on the project until a month later than you had hoped and another indispensible resource is available only half time, you might find that the project won't finish until March 2013.

Resource availability doesn't always have a detrimental effect on your schedule. You might find that three skilled designers are available when you thought you could get only one. In this case, you can assign more resources to shorten the duration of your design tasks and possibly shorten the overall length of the project.

CROSS-REFERENCE You learn how resource availability affects scheduling in "Assigning Multiple Resources to One Task" and "Managing Part-Timers and Multitaskers" in Chapter 8.

Brick Wall Deadlines Versus Soft Date Targets

You might have some dates floating around in your head — dates that are simply nice-to-achieve targets for an ideal schedule. But some dates might be in big red letters on a sticky note on your computer monitor, because they're unmovable.

There are deadlines, and then there are *DEADLINES*. Brick wall deadlines are dates that your project must meet, such as the date that the trade show starts whether or not your vendor booth is set up. Perhaps upper management has set a product release date and announced it to the general public. If a missed date would result in significant embarrassment, a flood of criticism, or financial penalties to your organization, that date is probably a hard deadline to schedule for.

On the other hand, setting intermediate targets for dates can help you determine whether you're going to meet your brick wall deadlines. But not meeting such a target isn't the end of the world in the way that not meeting a brick wall deadline would be. For example, you can set targets to complete a module of a software system every two weeks, but some modules might take more or less time.

CROSS-REFERENCE You learn the details of building a schedule and working with durations, dependencies, and deadlines in Chapter 8, "Building a Schedule."

How Will the Project Be Managed?

As the project manager, you integrate all aspects of the project plan — the work definition, work and cost estimates, resources, and the schedule. You also need to specify how you will orchestrate the myriad of project elements.

You, as the project manager, must define your own role in the project and also identify the roles and responsibilities of the other managing stakeholders. Then you can spell out the project's ground rules and the management processes you will use. You'll also determine how lessons learned from past projects inform your current project.

CROSS-REFERENCE The integration management processes comprise all the processes of a project, including scope management, time management, cost management, human resource management, and procurement management. These are described in "Integration Management" in Chapter 2.

The Project Manager and Managing Stakeholders

Even before resources are all on board, you can start to develop the project responsibility matrix and project organization chart. Early on, you can use these to show how you and the other managing stakeholders relate to one another.

At this stage, the project organization chart might include team leaders, resource managers, functional managers, portfolio managers, project sponsors, customers, and so on. Use the responsibility matrix to specify roles, responsibilities, and relationships.

Start with yourself as the project manager. You have to decide and document whether you will be part of the team with your own tasks assigned, or whether you will devote all your time to managing the project. If you manage multiple projects, specify the amount of time you will be able to devote to managing this project.

Clarify the roles and responsibilities of each managing stakeholder. You might also consider specifying the nature of communication flow between the project manager and the stakeholder.

CROSS-REFERENCE For more information, see "Identifying the Project Stakeholders" in Chapter 3, "Documenting Roles and Responsibilities" and "Building a Project Organization Chart" in Chapter 7, and Chapter 10, "Setting Up a Communication Plan."

Setting Ground Rules

A project's ground rules reflect your leadership style and the culture of your organization. The ground rules define the project processes you will use through the life of the project. In this way, you specify the guidelines within which the project team works and, in effect, set the culture for the project. For example, ground rules establish how the team will communicate, track issues, solve problems, make decisions, and resolve conflicts.

CROSS-REFERENCE For more details on setting ground rules for the project, see Chapter 14, "Taming Processes, Problems, and Conflicts."

Defining Management Processes

The management processes outline how you intend to manage project quality, communication, and risk. In short, your management processes specify how you and your team will operate in the project on a day-to-day basis.

The quality plan can specify any quality standards your project must adhere to. It can also indicate how you will monitor quality throughout the project, whether you use quality checkpoint milestones or deliver periodic audit reports. You learn more in Chapter 9, "Planning for Quality."

A successful project depends heavily on good communication throughout the life of the project. The communication plan outlines how this communication will take place. It specifies who needs what kind of information and when. The communication plan also indicates the methods of communication to be used for different purposes. You can find details in Chapter 10, "Setting Up a Communication Plan."

Many experienced project managers maintain that project management is essentially risk management. *Risk management* is the process of identifying potential negative impacts to your project, analyzing the likelihood and impact of those risks, and creating a plan for handling risks should they become reality. The risk management plan also includes methods for preventing risks and for tracking risks throughout the project lifecycle. The risk management plan can also address ways to increase the likelihood of possible positive impacts, or *positive risk*, coming to fruition. You explore this further in Chapter 12, "Managing Risk."

In addition to developing plans for quality, communication, and risk management, your management processes also deal with the initial task assignments, status reporting, issues tracking, change management, cost control, and so on. Detailed information about handling changes to a project is in Chapter 11, "Setting Up a Change Management Plan."

Remembrance of Projects Past

As you create your new project plan, be sure to peruse the "lessons learned" or "post mortem" reports or knowledge base from past projects performed by your organization. That way, you can see what has worked well and what could have gone better. You can apply the suggestions and solutions from past projects to head off problems you hadn't even thought about.

Referencing projects similar to your current project is helpful, but not absolutely necessary. Suppose you're planning your company's presence at a high-profile trade show, but the only lessons learned information available from your organization is one having to do with the development and delivery of a training program. Perhaps the report discusses issues with communication with accounting, scope creep from the project sponsor, and motivation from a group of resources. If your new project involves the same accounting department, sponsor, and resources, you might experience those same issues in your trade show project.

Don't neglect the positive aspects of a lessons learned report or knowledge base. You might find that issues that were causing you sleepless nights are probably not going to be a problem. You also want to pay attention to methods and processes that worked particularly well in other projects so you can adapt them for your new project.

TIP If you can get your hands on them, lessons learned from another organization doing the same kind of project can be helpful. For example, if you're part of a fledgling nonprofit organization about to host your first major fundraising gala, you have none of your own lessons learned. If you have a buddy at another nonprofit who's willing to share their lessons learned for your edification, and if that information is not confidential, by all means take advantage of that.

When you're finished with your current project, you will be conducting your own lessons learned session. Learn more about gathering feedback on your finished project in Chapter 22, "Don't Forget Lessons Learned."

Summary

After you obtain approval for a project, you are free to start planning the project. A project plan includes the work definition, the resource list, the cost estimate, the schedule, and information about how you will be managing the project.

In this chapter, you got a general orientation to each of these components of the project plan. In Chapter 5, you will plunge into the details of defining the work, building a work breakdown structure, and specifying task details.

Coach's Review

Use this section to assess what you've learned in this chapter and to apply it to a real-life project you're currently working on.

Test Your Knowledge

Test your knowledge of the material in this chapter by answering the following questions. See Appendix A for the answers.

1. Name five components of a typical project plan.
2. Name the knowledge areas associated with the five components of a typical project plan.
3. Name three categories of project resources that could be assigned in any typical project.
4. What is a rough order of magnitude (ROM) estimate?
5. What information is a detailed cost estimate based on?
6. Name four items that help establish your project schedule.
7. Define task dependency and give an example.

8. How can you prevent problems that have been encountered in the past or take advantage of tips and techniques that worked particularly well?

9. What project processes could be part of your project plan?

Project Challenge

Practice the knowledge you've gained in Chapter 4 by working through one or more of the following challenges using a real-life project you're working on, or one similar to the types of projects you might work on.

1. With your own project in mind, jot down notes about what you know so far about the work to be done. Consider any information you might already have about tasks, milestones, deliverables, phases, task sequencing, and task hierarchy. Keep these notes handy for work to be done in Chapter 5, "Identifying the Work to Be Completed" as you continue to develop your project plan.

2. In your notes, indicate any task durations, task relationships, resource schedules, and fixed deadlines you're already aware of. Specify whether this project should be scheduled from the start date or finish date and indicate why.

3. In your project workbook, jot down notes regarding costs associated with your project. Include what you know so far about resource costs. Consider additional types of costs as well. Your cost estimates will be refined in Chapter 6, "Estimating Work and Cost."

4. In your project workbook, sketch a rough preliminary project organization chart for your project. Be sure to include resource names or resource types you know will need to be a part of the project. Also include managing stakeholders and other functional departments as appropriate. This will be refined in Chapter 7, "Planning Project Resources."

5. In your project workbook, draw a line down the middle of the blank page to create two columns. Title the left column "Successes." Title the right column "Challenges." Going from memory or even speculation, think about past projects done by the same organization that will be implementing your new project. Jot down aspects of the project that went particularly well in the "Successes" column. Jot down aspects of the project that were struggles and could be improved in the "Challenges" column. Also in the Challenges column, consider how you might prevent or resolve those problems in your own project.

Identifying the Work to Be Completed

The project is approved and you've been assigned as project manager. The project charter has been distributed, making everything official. Time to roll the sleeves up and really get to work. Or rather, figure out just what the work is.

You have the broad directive — the project goal: build a bridge across the Tacoma Narrows, go to the moon by the end of the decade, or invent the first eyeglasses that double as a mobile Web device. Any of these sound like an impossible undertaking unless you break it down. In fact, you break work down into smaller and smaller components until you arrive at pieces that everyone can wrap their brains around, and those pieces can actually be assigned to someone to accomplish.

The framework in which the project goal is deconstructed into task-sized details is called the *work breakdown structure*, or *WBS*. This chapter details the processes of identifying the work, building the work breakdown structure, and fleshing out the task details. The finished WBS forms the core of your project plan. With the WBS in hand, you can estimate your resource requirements, figure an accurate budget, and build the project schedule.

CROSS-REFERENCE Creating the work breakdown structure is part of the project scope knowledge area described in the section "Scope Management" in Chapter 2.

Understanding the Work Breakdown Structure

You break down work every day without even realizing you're doing it. You decide to go out for an evening, and you think, where are we going, what are we doing, and what are we wearing? Your boss asks you to give a short presentation on next year's work plan to the company's department heads, and you break it down by preparing your notes, handouts, and slides. You decide to take a vacation, and your mind starts clicking away on categories such as destination choices, flight reservations, and pet-sitting arrangements.

It is a natural part of our thought process to break any everyday activity into its components. The automatic breakdown makes it easier to get organized and quickly get the thing done. If you instead take a scattershot approach and dive in without much thought, you run the risk of forgetting something, and you end up scrambling to create a couple of coherent slides just before the meeting, or racing to the gate to make your flight.

The rational alternative is to break down a daunting project goal into its component pieces. A kitchen remodel project can be broken down into design, construction, and installation. A new product development project can be broken down into research, development, pilot, and commercialization.

The larger or more complex a project is, the further it needs to be broken down. Such a project has more levels, or needs to drill down further, before you get to the manageable piece that can be assigned to someone to actually do.

CROSS-REFERENCE The information in this chapter relates to the PMP Exam's Domain II: Planning the Project, Task 2, "Create the work breakdown structure with the team by deconstructing the scope, in order to manage the scope of the project."

What Is a Work Breakdown Structure?

The work breakdown structure helps model the breakdown of a project goal into its actionable, assignable pieces. As shown in Figure 5-1, the WBS is a hierarchical chart that progressively subdivides or decomposes project work into smaller, more manageable components.

The lowest level is the planned work, or *work package*. This work package is the project component that's finite enough to be scheduled, assigned to a resource for implementation, budgeted, managed, monitored, and tracked.

NOTE Some organizations assign and track tasks at the work package level but do cost tracking at one level above for ease of administration.

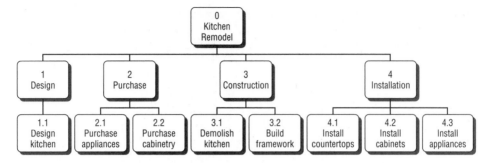

Figure 5-1: One example of a work breakdown structure

As the project manager, you lead the effort to translate the goal and objectives, requirements, and scope statement into the WBS.

Why Is the WBS Essential?

The work breakdown structure is the nucleus of the project plan. From that core radiates the resource, budget, and schedule planning. Specifically, the WBS does all of the following:

- **Helps plan the project:** The WBS helps you determine how to organize the project, as well as estimate and schedule the project.

- **Details the work:** The WBS itemizes the work to be done to fulfill the project scope. This work can be assigned to resources in understandable and manageable "chunks" with sufficient detail.

- **Shows gaps:** The WBS prevents the omission of tasks that might have otherwise slipped through the cracks and been forgotten. In this way, the WBS is also a first test of the requirements and scope definition.

- **Enables cost estimates:** By providing the detail needed to estimate resource requirements and costs, the WBS helps you create the resource plan, calculate the final project budget, and then make any necessary adjustments as a result.

- **Enables work estimates:** The WBS facilitates your ability to estimate how long it will take to do smaller bits of work, that is, the work packages. When you know how long the work packages will take to do, you can arrive at an overall project finish date.

- **Shows the big picture:** With its logical, graphical layout, the WBS helps the team members and other stakeholders visualize the project, whether it's the project's full scope or the details of a particular phase.

- **Helps track progress:** Because the smaller work packages provide visibility into where progress is really happening, you know when work is started, when it's in progress, and when it's complete.

- **Helps manage change:** The WBS helps you manage and document changes as they happen. As part of your change management process, when new tasks are approved and added (or deleted) after the project plan is baselined, those tasks can be called out as such. This can help you see more clearly the impact of changes to the scope.

Identifying Work

The best way to identify the work and build the WBS is to herd members of your project team and other key stakeholders into a room and start planning the WBS. As guided by your requirements document and scope statement, you work together or in specialized teams to itemize the activities that need to be done, either from the high-level activities down to the nitty-gritty tasks, from the tasks up to the high-level activities, or both.

Who Helps Identify Work?

Your project team is probably not formed yet, but there might be potential project team members around, especially if you will be working with in-house resources. Track down subject matter experts who can help, whether or not they are likely to eventually become team members. Consider asking for input from consultants or vendors you might engage for the team.

The more participation you have from your potential project team and other experts, the more grounded in reality your WBS will be. If these potential team members end up joining your team, they'll be ahead of the game, having already contributed to the intensive exercise of planning the WBS. The team members will also be further along in the team-building life cycle in the context of this project. In addition, remember that team members who helped identify their own work will have more ownership and buy-in to the project overall.

Jump-Starting with Other Sources

Gathering potential team members and key stakeholders to identify the work to be done suggests you're starting from scratch. Lucky for everyone involved, that's not the case.

You start with the requirements document that you created as part of the initiating processes. You also use the scope statement. In fact, everything in your project notebook can be useful in orienting the planning team.

CROSS-REFERENCE For more information or a refresher about the initiating processes, see the sections "Gathering Requirements," "Documenting
Project Scope," and "Assembling the Project Notebook," all in Chapter 3.

If one is handy, the WBS of an archived project plan of a similar type can be
helpful as you start. You might also find an industry-standard WBS for your
project type. Either of these can save you a great deal of time while still providing exactly the work definition you need for your unique project.

Planning as a Group

Just as brainstorming helps a group dream up potential strategies for a particular problem and gather project requirements, working together as a group in a
project planning session is a great technique to develop a solid work breakdown
structure. In such as session, you can capture all pertinent work for what will
become all levels of the WBS.

A group planning session works best with everyone together in a room.
However, you might need to adapt variations on this because of the realities
of your group.

In whatever way you manage your planning session, be sure that the right
skills are represented in the room for whatever aspect of the project you're
working on. People can sometimes get caught up with guessing about areas
outside their expertise, and this can produce inefficiencies and conflicts that
will hamper your progress.

Depending on what has been developed so far, and what level you're working at, you can have categories on one or more white boards or flip chart sheets
around the room. Those categories can be the already-identified top level of the
WBS — for example, the phases, subsystems, disciplines, or deliverables. If the
group is small enough (or the conference room large enough), you can have a
free-for-all. Participants armed with sticky-note pads and marking pens write
and affix suggested activities and tasks to the right place.

After all the suggestions are in place, you can work together to group items
that appear to address the same thing. Determine whether you need to break
it down further and run through the process again to uncover the necessary
detail for the WBS.

A variation on this, which often works well, is to break into small groups,
with each group charged with developing the activities and tasks for a particular top-level WBS item. The small group brainstorms, records, and affixes
their sticky notes for the branch from just the one item. Then the small groups
rotate to another top-level item. The new group reviews and validates the work
of the previous group.

With the participants working the room with their sticky notes, you — as
the project manager and facilitator — maintain sufficient control and achieve

overall coverage of the WBS. Such processes are also preferable to more formal facilitation techniques using a scribe or recorder, in which ideas can be unconsciously suppressed or incorrectly expressed.

This said, if the group is too large (or the room too small) for everyone to mill about the room setting down their ideas, you might need a more facilitated session with a recorder. In such a session, you follow a similar process but use a recorder or gatekeeper to handle the sticky notes. As the group suggests activities and tasks, the recorder writes them on the sticky note and affixes them to the board or flip chart sheet.

After all the activities and tasks are identified and validated to everyone's satisfaction, the discussion can progress to the organization of the activities and tasks. Is everything in the right place in the hierarchy? The sticky notes can be moved to different levels or branches as appropriate.

With your project scope at the top center, you organize the work statements vertically in increasingly decomposed levels of work. You'll repeat this in separate vertical branches reflecting the different subprojects or phases or other groupings the team has identified. Your resulting WBS will therefore show multiple levels vertically, and multiple branches horizontally, as shown in Figure 5-2.

NOTE In certain types of project management methodologies, such as rolling wave planning or agile, the entire WBS cannot be specified until earlier phases of the WBS are complete. In such projects, where the execution of the project is in itself a process of discovery, you revisit the WBS at planned checkpoints and develop the next phase in multiple iterations.

Identifying Work from the Top Down

Whether planning the work breakdown structure with a large group, with three or four key stakeholders, or all by your lonesome, you can choose whether to identify work from the top down, the bottom up, or in both directions.

When planning work from the top down, you start with the requirements document, scope statement, and deliverables identified in the initiating processes. Place the project goal, scope summary, or the overall deliverable (such as a building or a product) at the top center of the workspace where you are creating your WBS.

Your first task as a group is to determine what categories go into the first level. Deriving them from the requirements document and scope statement, determine the categories and subcategories of activities that branch off that first level until you wind your way down to the bottom level that contains the assignable work packages.

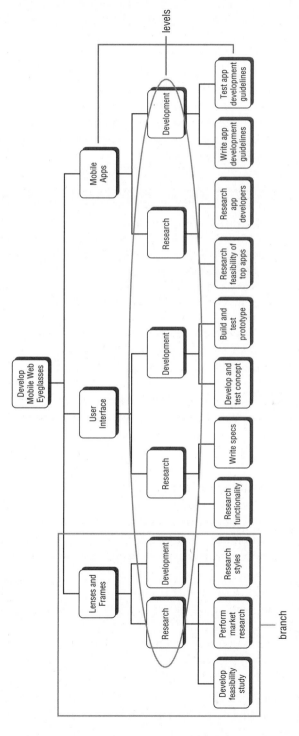

Figure 5-2: WBS with multiple levels and multiple branches

Identifying work from the top down is often effective on larger projects using multiple specialized teams. In one planning session, the team works on the higher levels of the WBS — that is, whatever broad categories and subcategories are appropriate under the project scope and deliverables. These broad categories can be project phases, subsystems, subprojects, or whatever makes sense for the project. Then specific branches of the WBS are handed off to a team of experts to create the detailed breakdown to the work package level.

Remember that you're still at the group planning stage in which your focus is to identify all the work activities. The actual organization of the WBS — with the choice of format, naming, and numbering — is covered in the section "Organizing Work in the WBS" later in this chapter.

THE CANDID COACH: DON'T THINK ABOUT SEQUENCE OR SCHEDULE

When developing your work breakdown structure, don't tie yourself into knots worrying about the sequence in which activities must be done, or any dependencies between activities. This just makes the WBS exercise more difficult, and frankly, it's not the right time for that.

Furthermore, many of the activities can be done in parallel by different teams with their different specialties. This is especially true on the larger, more complex projects.

You'll develop the sequence, establish dependencies, and deal with other date-related issues when you build the schedule.

CROSS-REFERENCE Sequencing, dependencies, date constraints, and resource assignments are all covered in Chapter 8, "Building a Schedule."

Identifying Work from the Bottom Up

An alternative for identifying work is to start at the bottom and work your way up. This is often effective for smaller projects using smaller teams. Bottom-up planning is also a good technique for projects in which most team members are familiar with most of the work details, possibly because they've all done this kind of project before or because the project doesn't call for widely different specialties.

You start the WBS planning session by stating the project goal, scope summary, or the final project deliverable. Then you start at the bottom level — identifying the work packages — and work up from there. When you start with the work packages, you categorize them. You put similar categories together and create a summary for those categories. Keep doing this until you've reached the top level.

Be aware that when planning work from the bottom up, the results can be uneven and the team can lose its sense of proportion. You might have more detail than needed in one area and less than needed in another area. It can be easy to forget entire areas.

However, because your objective is to capture as many of the necessary work activities as possible, this inconsistency is okay for now. You'll later organize all the great information you get from the process into the WBS.

Bottom-up planning is more prone to bringing out sequencing tendencies. Considering task sequence when you're trying to develop the WBS only bogs down the process. The facilitator needs to focus participants on just capturing the tasks and activities, and assure them that sequencing will come later when the schedule is being built.

THE CANDID COACH: TOP-DOWN VERSUS BOTTOM-UP THINKERS

People have a tendency to be either *top-down thinkers* or *bottom-up thinkers*. The top-down thinker tends to be most comfortable assessing the big picture first and then systematically drilling down from there to the details.

Conversely, the bottom-up thinker tends to be most comfortable, and therefore more productive, thinking out the details. After the details are in place, they group the details into categories, working their way up toward the overall project goal.

Consider dividing the project planning team into top-down versus bottom-up thinkers and let them have their own planning sessions. The top-down thinkers can identify the high-level structure while the bottom-up thinkers can identify the tasks without regard as to where they will go in the WBS. You can organize the tasks as a group exercise later.

"I find this technique works well," says Bob McGannon, director of Mindavation. "And it's great for mitigating the possibility for fist fights while deriving the WBS!"

How Much Is Enough?

So you see that building the WBS is the craft of deconstructing each work activity down and down further until you reach the work package level for each branch. But knowing when you've "arrived" is the debatable question. How detailed should work packages be? How short or long a time should work packages represent? When do you say "when"? The rule of thumb is that work packages should be manageable, trackable, and assignable to a team member (or several team members).

NOTE Remember that different branches will get to the work package level sooner than others. For example, the design phase might have six levels between the project goal and the work package, while the pilot phase in the same project might have only three.

If the task still seems too vague and too large to be assigned to a team member and effectively tracked, deconstruct to the next level. On the other hand, if the activity seems specific, but painfully trivial, then whoa, Nellie! You've probably gone too far. If a task is too small, it feels like too much trouble to schedule, assign, track, and manage so much minutiae. The assigned resources might feel micromanaged, and you as the project manager, might end up ignoring those tasks. Look at the level above the tiny activity to see if that instead is the right level of detail.

NOTE While the identified work at the upper levels is often referred to as *activities*, "work package" is typically synonymous with *task*.

This isn't an inviolable law, however; sometimes the two terms are used the opposite way, and in some environments, the two terms are synonymous.

Use the following criteria as a checklist to see if your work packages have the appropriate level of detail. Make sure each work package:

- **Has definite start and finish boundaries:** It's easy to identify the beginning and ending points for the work package. This will make it easy to schedule with start and finish dates when you get to that stage.

- **Can have time and cost estimated:** If the work package is still too large to consider estimating the work effort and cost, you might need to break it down to at least another level.

- **Appears to have a reasonable level of effort:** You're not estimating work effort at this point, but you should be able to see whether the effort seems somewhat consistent with other work packages and proportional to the project as a whole.

- **Is measurable as to progress and completion:** The work package should be specific enough to know whether you're moving along and when it's finished.

- **Is at a level of detail you can and will manage:** The work package is not too large or too vague to track, and it's not so small that it feels too trivial to bother with.

THE CANDID COACH: MAKE THE WORK PACKAGES PROPORTIONAL

In your WBS, be sure to break the work down far enough to allow for recovery if a task deadline is missed.

For example, if you have a year-long project, breaking the tasks into roughly 2-week or 80-hour increments is probably fine. If a team member misses a task deadline, you have time to adjust and recover.

On the other hand, if you have a two-month project, and a team member misses the deadline on a two-week task, you could be in a heap of trouble! You have 25 percent of the total project time to make up somehow, and it's unlikely you'll be able to do it. Big "uh-oh!" that you want to avoid.

Keep in mind that different types of tasks can require different levels of detail. Some tasks or phases require more granular detail, perhaps because of their degree of difficulty or their relative importance. Other tasks can be broader than the others, maybe because they're easily executed or because they're something your team can do in its sleep.

With all these guidelines, just remember that it's your project and your WBS. There are no hard and fast rules — you and your team will know what's right, what you can live with throughout the project, and what will help the project be effective and successful.

Validating the WBS

Whether you use the top-down or bottom-up approach to identifying work, you can use the opposite direction to validate the WBS and make sure that all work that needs to be there is indeed present. If you used the top-down approach in your group, do the validation also as a group. Start at the work package level at the bottom, look at the next level, and up and up. If you find that anything has been missed, this is your opportunity to add it.

Likewise, if you used the bottom-up approach in your group, start at the top level and work your way down. Insert additional activities as needed.

In fact, the most successful teams and project managers use both the top-down and bottom-up approaches at the same time with great results. The project manager and team leaders create the overall structure at a high level, and then the teams work from the bottom up adding the necessary details. The plan is then reconciled to be sure that all activities are covered and there is no duplication.

THE CANDID COACH: UPDATE REQUIREMENTS IF NECESSARY

It's likely that the construction of the WBS has uncovered details that need to be updated in the requirements document or the scope statement. Don't be afraid to add the necessary information to those documents. When you developed those documents as part of the initiating processes, it was with the understanding that they would be refined as you discovered information during planning.

The nature of the revisions you make at this point often do not warrant re-approval by the managing stakeholders who originally signed off on the project proposal. You can usually make them aware of any large changes to the requirements or scope statement when you submit the WBS and other planning documents for approval to actually launch the project.

But if the changes indicate a significant shift in direction, let the managing stakeholders know now, and let them determine how to proceed.

Organizing Work in the WBS

By now, you and your team have energetically identified a robust collection of statements that reflects the project work. If you paid no mind to WBS organization or structure, chances are you have what amounts to a rather stormy sea of identified project activities that have little to no relation to one another. At least, not yet.

Now your mission is to shape this chaotic mass into something that makes sense, an organized grouping and subgrouping of project work to be done — the work breakdown structure.

If you have already applied some kind of structure as part of your group project planning sessions, you might be well on your way. For example, you might have already divided the project scope or final deliverable into phases or subprojects and identified work for each segment individually.

In any case, this is the point where you reflect and refine the WBS to be sure that its structure makes sense for your company. Consider issues such as how teams and departments operate, risks that exist from previous projects, or points of emphasis that need to be highlighted for managing stakeholders.

You can organize the branches of your WBS in a variety of ways. Figure 5-3 shows a project organized by process phase. Figure 5-4 shows the same project organized by subproject or subsystem. Either of these can work just fine. You might have other ways to organize the project, for example, by departmental responsibility. You're going to be living with this WBS for a long time so make sure it's really workable for your project.

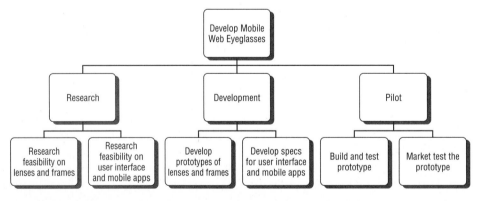

Figure 5-3: WBS for product development project organized by phase

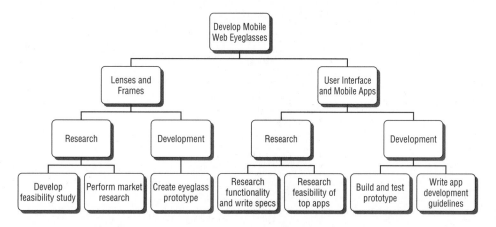

Figure 5-4: WBS for product development project organized by subsystem

Calling Out Deliverables

As discussed in "Specifying the Deliverables" in Chapter 3, *project deliverables* are those unique, tangible, and verifiable outcomes of a task or series of tasks. Whether it's a product, result, or capability, a deliverable proves that the project and product scope are being fulfilled, that the project is being executed. A deliverable often completes a process, phase, or the entire project. Deliverables are often subject to approval by the project customer or sponsor.

Deliverables often drive the construction of the WBS; in fact, they are often in the first or second level. So deliverables almost always figure prominently in your WBS.

> **NOTE** In the initiating processes of the project lifecycle, you typically need to describe the deliverables more generally, or at a higher level. After you get approval for the project to move on to planning, however, you must detail the deliverables. These details emerge as you research the project and work through the processes involved in project planning. Be sure the deliverables are well understood and well documented by the time you start building the WBS.

Formatting Your WBS

Work breakdown structures are typically formatted as a hierarchical flowchart, a kind of organization chart. The project goal or scope summary is in the top box, at what's usually considered "Level 0." The deliverables, phases, subprojects, or other activities in the boxes at the next level, are then considered "Level 1." As shown in Figure 5-5, the decomposed boxes drop down from there in succeeding levels until they end with the work packages at the bottom. Such a flowchart can be created with programs such as Microsoft Visio or Microsoft Project, or mind-mapping software. The organization or hierarchy chart feature in Microsoft Word can work nicely. You can also create a simple flowchart in any drawing program.

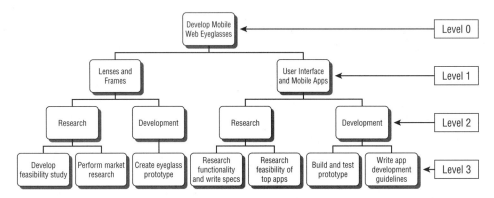

Figure 5-5: WBS in organization chart format

A WBS can also be represented in outline format, as shown in Figure 5-6. In the outline format, the project goal appears in the upper-left corner. The Level 1 activities are listed vertically down the page, with their deconstructed activities successively indented below them. The work packages appear furthest to the right. The outline format is more compact and can be easier to create than the often large and unwieldy flowchart format. You can use programs such as Microsoft Excel, Microsoft Word, or Microsoft Project to create an outlined WBS.

	A	B	C	D	E	F
1	Develop Mobile Web Eyeglasses					
2						
3	Lenses and Frames					
4		Research				
5			Develop feasibility study			
6			Perform market research			
7		Development				
8			Create prototype of eyeglasses			
9	User Interface and Mobile Apps					
10		Research				
11			Research functionality and write specs			
12			Research feasibility of top apps			
13		Development				
14			Build and test prototype			
15			Write app development guidelines			
16						

Figure 5-6: WBS in outline format

Naming Your WBS

When building your WBS, it pays to give thought to the naming of each activity and develop a convention that works for the project. If you decide to organize your WBS by deliverables, subsystems, functionality, or other physical aspects, you might prefer a noun-based naming convention for your breakdown. For example, if you're developing a new product (such as the mobile Web eyeglasses) and the WBS breaks the project down by the product's systems as detailed in the requirements document, you might have WBS boxes named "Lenses," "Frames," "User Interface," "Mobile Apps," and "Integration."

If you organize your WBS according to a particular methodology or process, a verb-based naming convention might be more appropriate. For developing that same new product, your verb-based naming convention might have you creating WBS boxes named "Design," "Build," "Test," and "Implement."

However, by the time you get down to the work package level, it's best to have a verb-noun combination — for example, "Develop feasibility study" or "Build prototype." This is essential for clarity as you assign the work package to team members. A verb-noun combination makes it crystal clear what's they're supposed to do with the feasibility study: Develop it or review it? For the prototype, they'll understand whether they're being charged to write the specifications, build it, or test it.

Whatever naming convention you choose for your WBS, create concise statements that say as much as possible and be consistent in your scheme.

Numbering Your WBS

WBS numbering is a convention that gives you a good shorthand for the activity and where it's placed in the overall structure. Each WBS activity has its own unique number. The numbers are like map coordinates that indicate the branch and the level of the activity's location in the WBS. The shorter the number, the higher the level. The longer the number, the lower and more detailed the level.

As shown in Figure 5-7, the typical WBS numbering scheme works as follows:

- The project goal or scope summary is placed at the top of the WBS, as Level 0.

- The deliverables, phases, subprojects, or whatever activities are in the top series of boxes are Level 1. Those boxes are numbered 1, 2, 3, and 4.

- Boxes at the next level under WBS 1 are numbered 1.1, 1.2, 1.3, and so on.

- Boxes under WBS 2 are numbered 2.1, 2.2, and so on.

- Boxes at the third level might look like 2.1.1, 2.1.2, and 2.1.3.
- Each level adds another digit until you get finish at the work package level.

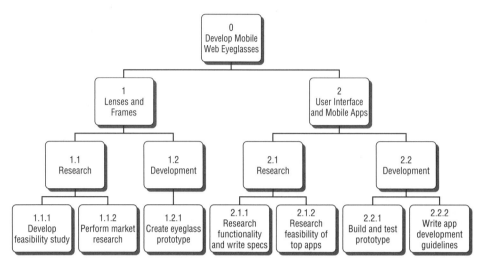

Figure 5-7: WBS numbering scheme

Some organizations like to have a prefix for the WBS that indicates the project code, for example, "MWE 3.2.3." Some organizations might use a combination of letters with the numbers ("3.b.3"), or other punctuation besides periods ("3-2-3"). Like the naming conventions, know what your numbering convention is, communicate it to your team members and other stakeholders so they understand it, and be consistent in its use. The point of the numbering scheme is to clarify, not to confuse.

> **TIP** At this point, the WBS is complete, and you're ready to move on to the next steps in the planning processes. Before you do, however, it's a good idea to have the WBS reviewed with a fresh set of eyes by an expert in the field. Typically, your managing stakeholders will not have the time or inclination to review the amount of detail a WBS entails. However, they might benefit from an overview or a look into the upper layer structure of the WBS.
>
> You will soon use the WBS to identify project resources, estimate work, build a budget, and schedule the project. This is why it's wise to have the WBS validated and approved before moving on to these other crucial pieces of planning.

Specifying Task Details

With the WBS complete, you have work packages, or tasks, identified for the entire project. But with the concise nature of the WBS names, there often isn't enough detail for assigned team members to effectively carry out those tasks.

The solution is to create a *work package document*, also known as the *WBS dictionary* (which, incidentally, is the term used by the Project Management Institute (PMI) in its Project Management Body of Knowledge (PMBOK)). This document identifies the work the assigned resources are to perform and how they'll know when it's done correctly. The work package document might reference other documents such as specifications, blueprints, checklists, or guidelines.

At the simplest end of the spectrum, this document might be as simple as a to-do list or assignment sheet. At the other end of the spectrum, a single work package can require a whole page of notes, including the description, notes, predecessors, successors, and links to supporting documents.

CROSS-REFERENCE Of course, no resources are assigned to the work packages just yet; that will happen when you start creating the schedule, as described in Chapter 8, "Building a Schedule." It's still a good idea to create the work package document now and add detail to it as you work through the planning processes.

However simple or detailed your work package document needs to be, remember that its purpose is to provide the information the resources will need to carry out the work package. It can also serve as a backup or as risk mitigation — if assigned resources cannot carry out their assigned tasks after all, replacement resources can review the work package document and carry on.

When you complete the WBS development, the work package document can contain the name of the work package, any details from the requirements document, any references to supporting documents, and any notes that have come out of the WBS planning sessions.

THE CANDID COACH: NEED A WORK PACKAGE DOCUMENT?

It can be overkill to create a work package document for every last work package on every project. For some projects, work package documents are not needed at all; for other projects, they're essential, especially when much integration is involved or a new product is being developed. In still other projects, you might provide work package documents for only a handful of the work packages.

This is a project manager judgment call. If you're not sure, err on the side of providing more detail.

As you continue to work through the planning processes, additional details will be added to the work package document. These details include work estimates, cost estimates, scheduling (duration, dependencies, deadlines, start and finish dates), and assigned resources.

CROSS-REFERENCE For more information about the next steps in the planning processes, see Chapter 6, "Estimating Work and Cost," Chapter 7, "Planning Project Resources," and Chapter 8, "Building a Schedule."

Summary

The first step in the planning processes is to identify the work activities and create the work breakdown structure. In the WBS, you and your team deconstruct the broad project goal or scope summary into successively smaller increments until you arrive at the work packages — the tasks that can be assigned to resources and tracked as part of the executing processes. Once you and the team have identified the work activities, you can organize and format the WBS in a way that's most suitable for your team, this project, and your organization.

The WBS forms the core of the project plan. When the WBS is complete and validated, you can move on with the next steps in the planning processes: specifying task details and creating the work package document, estimating resource requirements, calculating the project budget, and building the schedule.

Coach's Review

Use this section to assess what you've learned in this chapter and to apply it to a real-life project you're currently working on.

Test Your Knowledge

Test your knowledge of the material in this chapter by answering the following questions. See Appendix A for the answers.

1. What is the primary purpose of the work breakdown structure?
2. What is the ideal method for identifying the work and building the work breakdown structure?
3. What documents are the key inputs to the WBS?
4. Explain the top-down method for identifying work.
5. How do you know you have a good work package with the right level of detail?

6. Name the two typically used WBS formats.

7. What does the WBS number 3.1.2 signify?

8. What is the purpose of the work package document?

Project Challenge

Practice the knowledge you've gained in this chapter by working through one or more of the following challenges using a real-life project you're working on, or one similar to the types of projects you might work on.

1. In your project notebook or file, find your project goal, the project requirements, and the scope statement you developed from Chapter 3. With these items and the other information in your project notebook, work with a potential project team or on your own to identify all work activities needed to fulfill the project goal or scope summary.

2. Organize the work activities into a work breakdown structure, with successive deconstruction of the project goal until you arrive at the work packages.

3. Format the work breakdown structure using a computer program of your choice. Also choose the format you prefer, along with the activity naming conventions and the WBS numbering scheme.

4. Create a preliminary work package document with the task information you have so far.

Estimating Work and Cost

Estimating is almost always a challenge because estimates by definition have some level of uncertainty. With work that's familiar, you can use past experience to build estimates that are close to the actual results. However, even estimating something as familiar as the time it takes to drive from home to the office can be tough if you have to take into account construction, rush hour traffic, weather, and a car that's emitting its last exhaust.

Estimates of project work and cost are challenging in other ways, too. Some people optimistically estimate getting a ton of work done each day. Others deliver high estimates to make sure that the work is completed before the dates they estimated. Estimators don't wear "Optimist" and "Pessimist" name tags, so you won't know which type of estimates you're getting unless you've worked with these people before. And because projects bring people together temporarily, you may work with people you don't know.

Early in a project life cycle, estimates can be rough. As you learn more about a project, you can develop better estimates. In this chapter, you learn how to obtain estimates with the level of precision you need. Getting the right people to estimate goes a long way toward obtaining realistic numbers. There are many estimating methods from which to choose. You learn about several different methods and the best time to use each one.

This chapter also describes what you estimate for a project. You'll learn why estimating hours of effort is better than estimating duration. Although work hours contribute to the cost of a project, you have to estimate other project costs to complete the budget picture. Finally, you learn how to start building a budget for your project based on the costs you identify.

CROSS-REFERENCE The information in this chapter relates to the PMP Exam's Domain II: Planning the Project, Task 3, "Develop a budget plan based on the project scope using estimating techniques, in order to manage project cost."

Who Should Estimate a Project?

The people who estimate project work and cost must have experience with the work that's being done. If someone has never remodeled a house, developed a website, or organized a big event, she won't know what it takes to complete the project: the tasks that have to be performed, how many hours those tasks will take, the types of resources needed, issues that could arise, and so on.

You might turn to different people for estimates as your project proceeds from initiating to planning into executing. This section describes the resources who might contribute to project estimates and the benefits of working with each one.

TIP As you will learn throughout this chapter, one of the best techniques to obtain dependable estimates is to ask several people to provide them. This approach helps you identify optimistic and pessimistic estimates, and zero in on a realistic value.

Using a Core Planning Team

When you're defining and planning a project, you work with a core planning team that usually sticks with the project from start to finish. The people on the core team are usually familiar with most, if not all, aspects of the project. Their experience makes them prime candidates for preparing rough estimates of effort and cost.

The core team knows what the project is all about so the members can develop rough estimates of effort and cost in a relatively short period of time. For example, based on the core team's work on similar projects in the past, they might estimate 1,000 hours of development work and a project cost of $1,800,000.

NOTE For smaller projects, the core team may represent a significant percentage of the project team. If that's the case, these team members can produce estimates for individual tasks, as described in the next section.

Obtaining Estimates from Team Members

The people assigned to do work can provide the best estimates, because they develop their estimates based on their skills, capabilities, and typical productivity. However, your entire team won't be on board until after planning is complete. In the meantime, you can work with the people who are available to fine-tune your estimates.

More of the project team might join the festivities during planning — for example, team leads who head up major portions of a project or specific deliverables. These people can produce estimates for the portions of the project for which they're responsible. Even at this level, estimators don't know the specific people who will be assigned to tasks, so they have to estimate assuming resources with average capabilities.

TIP Team leads often estimate effort based on their own capabilities and skill levels. If you ask team leads to estimate effort, remind them to prepare their estimates assuming people with average skill levels.

Once the project is under way and you have your entire team on board, you can turn to team members for estimates for their assignments — or for new estimates based on the progress that's been made so far. Individual team members should be able to produce closer estimates of the hours it will take them to complete their assignments. They know their strengths and weaknesses, and have a good idea how much they usually get done. In addition, individuals often are more committed to meeting the estimates they provide.

NOTE Team members can commit to delivering based on estimates that others make — as long as they feel the estimates are realistic. However, it's a good idea to find out what team members think about the estimates you have. Many people will strive to meet a challenge. But if they consider estimates unrealistic, they might work at their customary pace regardless of the impact on the schedule or give up. In the worst case, resources might work at a slower pace to "prove" that the estimates aren't achievable.

Managing the Uncertainty of Estimates

Estimates can be a balancing act with accuracy of the estimate on one hand and the time and expense of developing the estimate on the other. Estimates can be uncertain if a project isn't fully defined when you need to prepare them. Estimates improve as you learn more about your project and the work it entails.

The people who prepare estimates can introduce another source of uncertainty. As described in the previous section, people may estimate high or low for a variety of reasons. This section explains methods for managing the inherent inaccuracy of estimated values.

When to Use Different Levels of Estimates

Spend only a few minutes thinking about the project and the resulting estimate will be rough at best. However, taking time to research the project itself and other similar projects can lead to an estimate closer to what eventually occurs. Rough estimates, accurate estimates, and those somewhere in between all have their place. The key is to pick the right level of estimate for the job. Figure 6-1 shows how estimates improve as a project moves through project management processes. Here are typical levels of estimates and when you might use them:

- **Order of magnitude:** This estimate level is very rough; it estimates values to an order of magnitude, such as $20,000, $200,000, or $2,000,000. These estimates don't require a lot of time or money to prepare. For example, if the initial rough estimate to remodel your house is $400,000 and you were budgeting closer to $40,000, you'll stop the plans right there. You might use a feasibility study to determine the price tag for a very large project within an order of magnitude to see whether the project makes sense to pursue further.

- **Plus or minus 50 to 75 percent:** Project selection requires more accurate estimates because you're deciding which projects deliver the most value. A low estimate could lead you to choose the wrong project. The project doesn't deliver the financial benefits it promised and it prevented other, more worthy, projects from seeing the light of day.

- **Plus or minus 25 percent:** Projects that pass the initial selection hurdle often go through a more detailed evaluation. During this evaluation, a team researches the project to understand it better and to prepare an estimate within the range of plus or minus 25 percent.

- **Plus or minus 10 percent:** During planning, you learn more about the project and document the details. With this knowledge, you can fine-tune your estimates. Ideally, you would like an estimate to be within 10 percent of the final numbers. However, some projects, such as research and development projects, are simply too uncertain for that level of accuracy. In these situations, it's important that you communicate the variance in the estimate and possibly your level of confidence regarding the estimate to the customer, management, and other key stakeholders. In addition, you will revisit these estimates as the project progresses to fine-tune the estimates as you go.

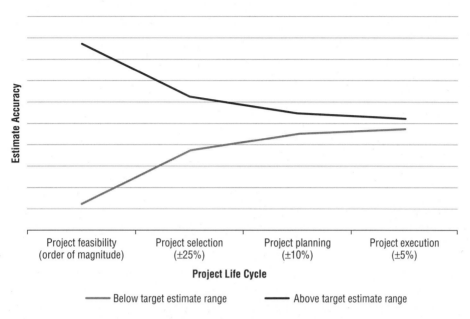

Figure 6-1: The accuracy of estimates improves as you learn more about a project.

Preventing Problems from Padded Estimates

Some people add a little extra to their estimates to make sure they deliver on time and within budget. Having a margin of safety doesn't sound like such a bad idea. The problem arises when estimates receive a bit more padding as they work their way up the management chain. The person assigned to a task adds a few extra hours to the estimate. The team lead adds a few more. The development lead adds hours to the entire development estimate. And you, as project manager, are tempted to add some hours to the whole project. The original 8-hour task could end up at 16 hours or more. There's a simple solution. Instead of keeping padding a secret, make it public.

Public padding has two main advantages:

1. You eliminate multiple levels of padding on each task in the project.

   Your estimates will be closer to reality. In addition, you can prevent the padding games that many organizations play. Team members add padding. Managers cut numbers assuming they're padded. The size of the padding and cuts increases, while the relationship between team members and managers deteriorates.

   TIP High estimates are no better than low ones. When estimates are too high, your organization might turn down projects because it thinks the funding and resources are fully allocated. Those passed-over projects mean the organization doesn't obtain all the benefits it could from worthwhile projects.

2. A smaller amount of padding is shared across tasks and it's allocated only to the tasks that need extra time (or money).

    Shared padding goes by several names. *Contingency funds* represent money that's set aside to resolve issues. You can also add a buffer of time at the end of a project so the finish date is protected even if delays occur. For example, critical chain project management uses the term *buffer* for shared padding. Each sequence of tasks has a time buffer at the end. That way, if any task in that sequence is delayed, it consumes part of the sequence buffer without affecting the rest of the project. In addition, critical chain scheduling includes a project buffer at the end of a project.

    Management reserve is an additional buffer that isn't part of individual project plans. It represents time and money that management can hand out, for example, should an unanticipated problem arise.

TIP Even with public padding, arbitrary buffers that you include as a generic safety margin may be cut by management. However, if you document that you are reserving funds or including a time buffer in case a specific risk comes to fruition, the management team is more likely to keep that padding in place. In fact, they might even commend you for your smart planning.

Preparing Estimates

As you learned earlier in this chapter, estimating takes place many times during the life of a project. Because you will request various types of estimates from a variety of people involved with your projects, it's important to understand how estimates are prepared. The goal is to obtain the best possible estimates at every stage of a project. This section begins by explaining the difference between duration and effort and why estimating effort is preferable. You also learn several techniques for producing better estimates.

The Difference between Duration and Effort

Some people make the mistake of equating duration with effort (hours of work). And that error can lead to big discrepancies in your time and cost estimates. Duration and effort are both measured in units of time, but they are not the same.

■ *Effort* represents the hours someone spends to complete work. If a team member works unwaveringly for 4 hours to prepare a lesson for a training course, the effort is 4 hours.

   One factor that can affect estimates of effort is individuals' skill levels. A person's experience and other characteristics, such as ability to focus, affect how much he or she can achieve in a specific amount of time. Typically, you base your estimates on workers with average skill levels. When you know who has been assigned to your project and their skill levels, you can adjust your estimates to match your team members' productivity.

- *Duration* is the elapsed work time (not including weekends, holidays, and other nonwork time) between the start and finish of a task. For example, if filing papers is your least favorite task, you might file papers for 15 minutes each day. Using the 2-hour example, it would require an 8-day duration to complete your 2 hours of filing effort.

A variety of factors affect the amount of effort that's expended within a specific duration. (The section "Modeling a Realistic Schedule" in Chapter 8 explains these factors in more detail.)

- **Non-project work** consumes part of each work day. The percentage of time that people spend on non-project work can be as much as 50 percent of each work day. Frequently, the percentage of time that people have available for project work is between 50 and 75 percent of each work day.

- **Multitasking** results in a duration that's longer than the effort. Most resources work on more than one task or project at a time, so they can't devote all their time to each assignment.

- **Interruptions** not only take time away from project work, but also affect people's productivity. It takes a significant amount of time to switch gears and focus on the next task at hand.

- **Assigning more than one person to a task** shortens the duration, although this approach works only up to a point. Too many people on the same assignment can increase the duration. In addition, some tasks can't be shortened by adding resources, such as having a baby, driving a truck route, or holding a meeting.

Estimating Methods

There is no shortage of methods for estimating. The approach you choose depends to some extent on the type of project and how familiar you are with the work. For example, existing information, parametric models, and estimating tools are all helpful when the project you're working on is similar to many others in the same industry. When the work that needs to be done isn't as clear, the Delphi technique and Program Evaluation and Review Technique might be more appropriate.

RECORDING ESTIMATED VALUES

As you develop estimates for project effort and cost, you need somewhere to store that information. If you use a project management software program to build a task list and work breakdown structure, you can add the estimates you obtain directly to the file for the project. The fields that you use to store work hours, labor rates, and other costs depend on the program.

For small projects that you manage without project management software, you can create a spreadsheet to keep track of estimates. This spreadsheet might list the tasks in rows and the work hours and different types of costs in columns. Then, you can total the values in each row and each column to obtain estimates for the entire project. Figure 6-2 provides an example of a spreadsheet that calculates costs for a project's higher-level summary tasks.

Reusing Existing Information

You can base estimates on similar work performed in the past. If your organization creates project notebooks for projects, you can peruse that documentation to obtain actual values from past projects. Then, if necessary, you can adjust your estimates to make up for any differences between the past and current project.

NOTE If you don't have written documentation about the results from past projects, you can interview people who worked on those projects about how long they took. Memory isn't as reliable as hard copy, but it's better than nothing.

Engaging Experts

A particular type of project might be a first for your organization, but that doesn't mean it's uncharted territory. You can seek out people with the necessary experience outside your organization. For example, vendors or consultants can help you develop your estimates. Or you can interview other organizations (that don't compete with yours) that are knowledgeable in the project arena.

Using a Parametric Model or Estimating Tool

Some industries have a long history with thousands of completed projects on record, such as construction. With so much data available, the construction industry has estimating programs and databases that provide guidelines for construction work and cost estimates. These tools often use parametric models to calculate estimated values. A parametric model combines the parameters or characteristics of a project, such as the square footage of a building, the construction materials used, and the geographical location with work and cost factors to calculate estimated effort and cost.

Off-the-shelf tools are convenient. However, you might consider building your own parametric model, especially if your organization has performed many projects over the years. That way, you apply the effort and cost that are typical for your company's projects.

> **TIP** Many computer programs are available to help you estimate different types of work. Try performing an online search for estimating tools that focus on your industry, the type of project you're managing, and so on.

Applying the Delphi Technique

This estimation approach relies on the opinions of a small group of five or six experts to produce a consensus of estimated values. The Delphi technique is an iterative estimating approach that surveys experts and employs anonymity in the hopes of removing bias from the results. Here is how the original model for the Delphi technique works:

1. Identify a small group of experts knowledgeable about the project. Brief each participant about the project.

2. Ask the experts to produce estimates anonymously and independently of one another. That way, the estimators can produce estimates without worrying about negative consequences or being influenced by others. The individuals don't collaborate with one another on their estimates.

3. Average the first round of estimates from each person in the group. For example, suppose the individual estimates of work hours are 100, 80, 210, 170, and 120. The resulting average is 136.

4. Share the first-round average values with the individuals. In the original Delphi technique, the estimators don't discuss the results.

5. Ask each person for a second estimate. Average the second round results and share them with the group. Say the second round results are 100, 100, 170, 150, and 110. The second-round average is 126.

6. Ask for a third estimate.

7. Use the average of the third round as your final estimate.

One variation on the Delphi technique adds discussion to the mix. For example, you can hold a meeting with all the participants and present the average values from the round. You might ask the individuals who submitted the highest and lowest estimates to explain their reasoning, so that the other members of the group can consider those ideas before the next round of estimates.

Using Optimistic, Pessimistic, and Most Likely Estimates

The Program Evaluation and Review Technique (PERT) is a statistical approach to estimating that uses three estimated values in acknowledgement of the fact that you can never forecast results with 100 percent certainty. If you perform the same work under the same conditions, it won't take exactly the same amount of time. In addition, the duration of tasks can be affected by many variables. To account for the inherent variability of results, PERT uses three estimates: optimistic, pessimistic, and most likely. This method is effective when a project includes a significant amount of uncertainty and risk. You can apply PERT to individual work packages or to higher-level portions of the project.

Another advantage of asking for optimistic, pessimistic, and most likely estimates is that the nature of the request makes people think about what could go wrong or what might reduce the amount of time required. Here is an example of how PERT works using an estimate of how long it will take to construct a building foundation:

- The **optimistic estimate** is 2 weeks. It is based on the assumption that the equipment is available immediately and that the weather cooperates. The optimistic estimate also assumes that all the members of the construction team are highly skilled.

- The **most likely estimate** is 2.8 weeks. It assumes that it takes a few days to get the equipment onsite and that a few days will be rainy. It also assumes that the crew has average skills.

- The **pessimistic estimate** comes in at 3 weeks because it includes the possibility of bad weather and delays in getting equipment on site.

The resulting **PERT estimate** is a *weighted average* of the three values with the most likely estimate receiving the heaviest weighting. The calculation for the weighted average estimate is:

$(2 + (4 \times 2.8) + 3) \div 6 = 2.7$ weeks

SIMULATING RESULTS WITH THE MONTE CARLO METHOD

You can develop project schedules based on the optimistic, pessimistic, and most likely durations. However, it's highly unlikely that all the tasks will complete in the optimistic durations you estimated, just as they are unlikely to all complete in the pessimistic, or most likely. The Monte Carlo method takes into account the variability of task durations when calculating the overall project schedule. This method is named after the Monte Carlo casino because the method is based on random outcomes as are games of chance.

> The Monte Carlo method is typically implemented with computer simulations because it runs hundreds or even thousands of simulations. It relies on the availability of PERT optimistic, most likely, and pessimistic estimates for each task in the project being simulated. Each simulation calculates an overall project duration based on randomly selected durations for each task (with the values somewhere between the optimistic and pessimistic ranges for the task). The final result is a distribution of possible outcomes. Using this method, you can determine the probability that the project will take 8 to 10 months to complete. Off-the-shelf computer programs are available to apply the Monte Carlo method to projects.

Estimating from the Top Down

In addition to the estimating methods described in the previous sections, you might approach your estimates from different directions depending on the information that's available about the project. Early in the project life cycle when you don't have many details, you might develop estimates for major portions of the project. Then, you allocate those time and cost estimates to smaller segments of work, similar to building a work breakdown structure.

TIP One way to validate estimates is to estimate from the top down and the bottom up, similar to validating a work breakdown structure as described in the section "Validating the WBS" in Chapter 5.

Estimating from the Bottom Up

Estimating from the bottom up starts with the project's work packages. You estimate the effort and cost for each one. Then, you total the work package estimates to obtain estimated values for portions of the project. You keep rolling the values up until you reach the top of the WBS, which represents the effort and cost for the entire project.

Estimates for individual work packages are usually easier to prepare because you consider the details of the work while you put your number together. What you might forget to include is additional time for collaboration, communication, and integrating pieces of the project into a whole. You can estimate single values for work packages or use PERT and estimate optimistic, most likely, and pessimistic values for each work package.

Estimating Project Costs

In addition to the hours it will take to perform a project's tasks, you also need an estimate of project cost. Although labor costs are usually a big part of the cost picture, materials, equipment, and facilities could contribute substantially to the cost of some projects. Depending on the project, you also might need to account for other types of costs, such as travel, training, and fees.

What Goes into Labor Costs?

An estimate of work hours isn't enough to figure out the labor cost for a project. You also need to know how much each work hour will cost. But hourly rates are estimates in their own right. During planning, you don't know who will be assigned to your project, so you don't know how much you will have to pay for resources.

The solution is to use an average hourly rate for each type of resource you need. Whether you get rates from vendors or from your human resources department, you build your cost estimates based on the average cost for resources with the skill sets you need: business analysts, developers, testers, and so on.

With rates from vendors, you're probably good to go. You pay the rate, whether it is a fixed price for a deliverable or an hourly rate, and the vendor handles the details.

For team members you obtain from within your organization, you need to consider overhead costs, such as the cost of office space, support personnel, utilities, and equipment that isn't dedicated to your project. Most organizations cover overhead costs by billing employees out using burdened labor rates — that is, the average amount someone costs including their salary, benefits, and some allocation of overhead costs. For example, suppose a business analyst earns an annual salary of $100,000. Benefits are 40 percent of salary, so you add another $40,000 to the annual total. And the allocation of overhead expenses is another $60,000. The annual cost of the analyst is $200,000. With approximately 2,000 work hours in a year, the burdened rate for the analyst is $100 per hour. You can obtain burdened labor rates from the human resources department or possibly the accounting team.

NOTE Consider whether you have to account for overtime. Salaried employees usually don't receive overtime pay, so you can use the same burdened labor rate for hours worked beyond the standard work day. However, if you plan to use resources who are paid overtime and you anticipate some overtime hours, be sure to calculate those hours at the overtime rates.

Material, Equipment, and Facility Costs

Depending on the project, you might need resources other than people. For example, construction projects also consume materials, such as concrete, lumber, and screws. The project might require equipment, such as a crane, backhoe, or a computer server. In some cases, you might also need additional facilities, such as office space for the people you hire for the project. In addition to estimating the number of human resources you need, you also have to estimate the quantity and cost of the materials, equipment, and facilities your project requires.

Estimating Other Costs

Finally, you also need to estimate any other costs that the project might incur. Travel costs are the most common type of cost in this last category. However, additional costs could include tuition for training classes, shipping, or fees, such as the fee for exhibiting at a trade show.

Building a Budget

When project work gets underway, you compare your actual costs to what you had planned. Before you can do that, you need a budget for your project. A project budget is the culmination of your estimating work and risk management planning. You use the estimated hours and cost to obtain the total estimated cost of the project. Then, you add in contingency funds and management reserves to produce the final budget, as shown in Figure 6-2.

CROSS-REFERENCE To learn about risk management, contingency funds, and management reserve, refer to Chapter 12, "Managing Risk."

144244 F0602.xlsx

	A	B	C	D	E	F
1		Hours	Labor cost	Materials, equipment, and facilities	Other costs	Total cost
2	Mobile web eyeglasses project	1885	$232,500	$55,000	$25,500	$313,000
3						
4	Lenses and frames	830	$100,500	$27,000	$10,000	$137,500
5						
6	Develop feasibility study	200	$20,000	$1,000	$1,000	$22,000
7	Perform market research	280	$28,000	$1,000	$3,000	$32,000
8	Create eyeglass prototype	350	$52,500	$25,000	$6,000	$83,500
9						
10	User Interface and mobile apps	1055	$132,000	$28,000	$15,500	$175,500
11						
12	Research functionality and write specs	325	$32,500	$2,000	$3,000	$37,500
13	Research feasibility of top apps	200	$20,000	$1,000	$4,000	$25,000
14	Build and test prototype	350	$52,500	$25,000	$8,000	$85,500
15	Write app development guidelines	180	$27,000	$0	$500	$27,500
16						
17						
18	Total mobile web eyeglasses estimate					$313,000
19						
20	Contingency funds (15%)					$46,950
21						
22	Project cost					$359,950
23						
24	Management reserve (5%)					$15,650
25						
26	Project budget					$375,600
27						

Sheet1 / Sheet2 / Sheet3

Figure 6-2: When you estimate hours and cost for work packages, you can tally up the individual estimates into an estimate for the entire project.

Summary

You need estimates of the time and cost for a project to build a project schedule and budget. But you can't determine these values with absolute accuracy until the project is complete. However, several techniques help you develop estimated values you can use for planning. Some of these techniques also help eliminate some of the biases that can arise in estimates — for example, when people tend to over- or underestimate.

You begin by estimating the hours of effort that the work will take. Then, you can estimate the labor costs for those hours. But cost estimates also include cost for other elements, such as materials required, equipment, facilities, and other costs, such as travel. Finally, the project budget represents the estimated cost of the project with the addition of safety margins, such as contingency funds and management reserves from your risk management plan.

Coach's Review

Use this section to assess what you've learned in this chapter and to apply it to a real-life project you're currently working on.

Test Your Knowledge

Test your knowledge of the material in this chapter by answering the following questions. See Appendix A for the answers.

1. What is the advantage to estimating the hours of effort rather than task duration?

2. How does the Delphi technique help eliminate bias in estimates?

3. How do you estimate labor costs when you don't know who will be assigned to your project?

4. What numbers do you include in the project budget?

Project Challenge

Apply the knowledge you've gained in this chapter by estimating a real-life project you're working on. Use the Delphi technique to prepare an estimate for a portion of the project that hasn't been started.

1. Ask several team members to estimate the hours of effort for the tasks you've selected. Average the results and share them with the team members. Repeat these steps for three rounds.

2. Evaluate the results. How did the average estimate change for each round? What is your opinion of the final estimate you obtained?

3. Hold a meeting with the team members and share the results with them as a group. Ask the participants to share their reasoning for their estimates.

4. Ask team members to provide one last round of estimates. How do these estimates differ from the ones you obtained before the discussion? Do you think these estimates are more realistic?

5. Take the estimates that you obtained from this exercise and add them to a spreadsheet or a project file created with a project management software program.

CHAPTER 7

Planning Project Resources

For very small projects, resource planning can be fairly informal. A handful of resources is all it takes, so you can identify which resources you need, stop those people in the hallway, and sign them up. However, when the project team grows to hundreds or thousands of people, an informal resource plan won't do. This chapter describes methods and documents you can use to flesh out larger teams.

A resource plan doesn't emerge fully formed. It blossoms over time as planning uncovers more about your project. Early on, you identify which groups are involved in the project, which portions of the project they participate in, and the level to which they're engaged in goings-on. This chapter describes the responsibility matrix — a grid that spells out how groups or individuals are connected to your project.

After you identify the project work that needs to be done and estimate the effort that work will take, you can delve deeper into resource planning. With the resource plan, you identify the skills you need for each task (along with other resources such as materials, facilities, equipment, and money). You see the types and quantities of resources you need, which brings the picture of your team into better focus. Because a project pulls people together temporarily, you also need a project organization chart to show the reporting structure within your team.

CROSS-REFERENCE The information in this chapter relates to the PMP Exam's Domain II: Planning the Project, Task 5, "Develop a human resource management plan by defining the roles and responsibilities of the project team members in order to create an effective project organization structure and provide guidance regarding how resources will be utilized and managed."

Documenting Roles and Responsibilities

In the beginning, when you're defining the project, you need to figure out who the stakeholders are (see the section "Identifying the Project Stakeholders" in Chapter 3) so you know who should be involved in that definition process as well as the planning that follows soon after. Over the entire project life cycle, you need owners for each part of the project, such as a phase or the tasks that produce a project deliverable. Without someone accountable, it's unlikely that project work will get done correctly or at all. But having too many owners can create problems, too.

A responsibility matrix shows the groups or individuals involved with each part of the project and their level of involvement. By correcting any gaps or overabundance in ownership, you can avoid a "who's on first?" scenario. A responsibility matrix helps you achieve the following benefits:

- **Ensure every part of the project has an owner:** When no one takes ownership of a piece of a project, the work will be at risk. If the research folks and the development team look at each other when you ask when the mobile Web frames and lenses are due to arrive, you know your project is going to be delayed. If you find sections in your responsibility matrix without owners, you can track down who should be responsible.

- **Eliminate ownership conflicts:** Suppose there's an important decision to be made and several would-be owners step up to make it. The atmosphere could get tense as groups try to mark their territory. All the while, the decision is up in the air until the group in charge is sorted out. You can prevent this type of turf turmoil by scanning your responsibility matrix for sections with multiple owners and identifying the true owner.

- **Improving communication between stakeholder groups:** A responsibility matrix delineates the different ways that groups are involved in a project. It documents who is responsible for doing the work for a portion of the project, who should be consulted, who makes decisions, and who should be informed of results. Clear roles and communication also help avoid the ownership conflicts mentioned in the previous bullet point.

Consider the mobile Web eyeglasses project. The software development team might come up with a new approach for the user interface. However, the eyeglass development team has to be consulted to make sure the approach will work; the customer has the authority to approve the change; the pilot team is responsible for turning the whole thing into real-life mobile Web eyeglasses; and the marketing team needs to know about the features in order to develop an advertising campaign.

Who's Involved with What

A *responsibility matrix* (sometimes called a *responsibility assignment matrix*) documents which groups are involved with different parts of a project. This document keeps groups from stepping on each other's toes and improves communication because it spells out who's responsible, who needs to consulted, who is authorized to make and approve decisions, and who needs to be kept informed. It also identifies the boundaries for what each team on the project produces so the teams don't duplicate effort.

Because the responsibility matrix focuses on groups and major segments of a project, you can start it while you're defining the project. As your plan takes shape, you can fill out the matrix to the level of detail you want — even to the point of identifying roles and responsibilities for individual tasks.

A responsibility matrix, shown in Figure 7-1, is just that — a matrix with rows and columns, and cells at the intersections of each row and column. Here's how you use this layout to document roles and responsibilities:

- **Project sections or activities:** Add the major sections or activities to cells in the first column of the matrix. For example, a high-level matrix might include the items from your project scope statement. Then, once the work breakdown structure is built, you can flesh out a matrix using summary tasks at whichever level of detail you want to use.

- **Groups or teams:** Fill in the cells in the first row of the matrix with the names of the people heading up the groups involved with the project. If you want to add more detail to the matrix, you can break stakeholder groups down into the teams that work on the project.

- **Involvement:** Each cell within the body of the matrix represents a combination of a project section and a group. That's where you specify the ways that the group is involved in that part of the project. A group can have more than one role within a project section so you fill in the corresponding cell with every type of involvement that applies. The next section describes the common notation used to identify involvement.

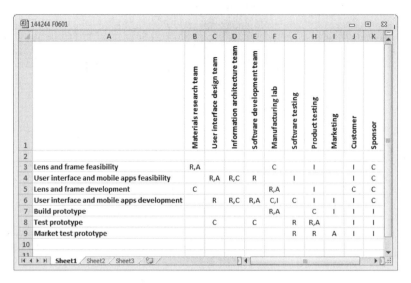

144244 F0601	Materials research team	User interface design team	Information architecture team	Software development team	Manufacturing lab	Software testing	Product testing	Marketing	Customer	Sponsor
	B	C	D	E	F	G	H	I	J	K
3 Lens and frame feasibility	R,A				C		I		I	C
4 User interface and mobile apps feasibility		R,A	R,C	R		I			I	C
5 Lens and frame development	C				R,A		I		C	C
6 User interface and mobile apps development		R	R,C	R,A	C,I	C	I	I	I	C
7 Build prototype					R,A		C	I	I	I
8 Test prototype		C		C		R	R,A		I	I
9 Market test prototype						R	R	A	I	I

Figure 7-1: A responsibility matrix shows the types of involvement each group has with each project section.

Levels of Involvement

A responsibility matrix typically includes four levels of involvement, abbreviated as *RACI*:

- *R* stands for *responsible*, which means that the group is responsible for performing the work in the corresponding part of the project. For example, the software development team is responsible for developing the interface and mobile apps for the eyeglasses, while the software testing team is responsible for verifying that the mobile apps do what they're supposed to.

- *A* represents *accountable*, which means the group is in charge of making sure that the project section is completed successfully. A group that's accountable can make or approve decisions, delegate work, and approve deliverables. While several groups may participate at the other levels of involvement, only one group is accountable for each part of a project. The manufacturing lab is accountable for the actual construction of the mobile Web eyeglasses. The product testing team is accountable for the testing of the assembled prototype.

- *C* means that a group is *consulted* regarding decisions. For example, the software development team might consult the system architecture folks to determine the best way to design the applications. Or the manufacturing lab takes part in discussions about the software but isn't accountable for decisions that are made.

- *I* stands for *inform*, which means that a group needs information. The testing teams are informed of progress so they're ready when it's time to test the prototype.

Identifying Resource Needs

You've identified the work that needs to be done (see Chapter 5, "Identifying the Work to Be Completed") and you've put together some estimates on the effort and cost it will take to get that completed (see Chapter 6, "Estimating Effort and Cost). With that information available, it's time to start figuring out the resources you'll need.

NOTE Identifying resources will launch you into a cycle of planning itera- tions. As you identify the types and quantities of resources you need, you might discover that you have to obtain resources outside your organiza- tion, which could result in higher or lower resource costs. Or the costs could demand a schedule change or introduce any number of other changes to your project plan, which, in turn, has an effect on the resources you need. Don't fret. Just start identifying resources and plan to fine-tune the project until everything balances out.

Types of Resources

You need people to perform project work. However, depending on the type of project, you may need other types of resources, too. When you start identify- ing resources, be sure to consider whether the following resources apply to your project:

- **People:** People (also called human resources in business and PMI-speak) are the toughest resources to identify because you might require a com- plex blend of skills and expertise for the work you assign. Although each person brings a unique amalgam of skills, people's assignments eventually boil down to how much time you need from them. This time factor can complicate scheduling if people aren't available when you need them or don't have as much time available as you need. In addition, people can affect your schedule and budget in other ways, such as when resources work faster or slower than you anticipated or cost more or less than you estimated.
- **Equipment:** Depending on the project, you might also require equip- ment to complete tasks, such as a giant construction crane, a monster earth mover, or perhaps a room full of computer servers and networking

equipment to support all the people toiling on your project. If you don't plan ahead for equipment, your schedule and costs will be at risk. For example, construction cranes are in demand, so you have to plan ahead and account for lead time to get one on site. Server rooms take time to install and troubleshoot. Equipment costs come in a variety of flavors. You might purchase equipment, rent it by the day or by the hour, or pay one-time fees, for example, to get that crane on site.

■ **Facilities:** If the people working on your project all sit at their desks doing their work, you might not need additional facilities. However, if you bring in people temporarily or the project requires specialized space (such as a server room), you'll have to plan for the type of space you need.

■ **Materials:** With construction projects, materials are easy to understand. The process of building consumes things like lumber, concrete, steel, pipes, wallboard, and so on. Other projects require different types of materials, such as reams of paper to print handouts, ID cards with clip-on holders, or disposable Hazmat suits.

■ **Other resources:** Like so many other things, some resources don't fit into the other categories, but they still affect the project cost and might impact the schedule. For example, with geographically dispersed teams, you might have to include travel expenses or videoconferencing services in your plans. Other examples include inspection fees and training costs.

Breaking Down Resource Needs

The same people who helped you identify the work your project involves can provide the details about the resources you need. You don't just name resource names and pin them to your schedule like butterflies in a natural history exhibit. Think about job postings you've seen or the list of components for the last computer you purchased. Whether you're identifying human resources or those made of more substantial stuff, you need to know the specifics.

The most effective way to get to the nitty-gritty of resources is to use the work packages at the lowest level of your WBS (see "Specifying Task Details" in Chapter 5). Because work packages spell out the details of what has to be done, you and your planning team can figure out the skills people need to do the work and the other resources that are required. Similar to a WBS, a resource breakdown structure, shown in Figure 7-2, rolls up work by resource type to give you an idea of staffing and other procurements.

TIP Depending on your organization, you might gradually add resource details. For example, you could start at higher levels of the WBS to identify broader categories of skills — the software portion of the project requires developers, whereas the testing phase needs testers and developers. Or you might tackle the project's needs by the departments in your organization. For example, from your responsibility matrix, you can leave it to the line managers in departments involved in the project to figure out the resource details. Your project plan merely identifies the number of people from each department, the skills required, and the average pay scale.

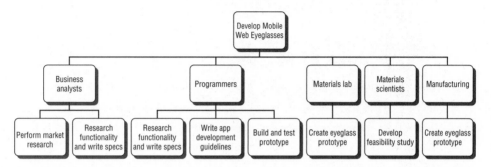

Figure 7-2: A resource breakdown structure breaks work down by types of resources.

For many tasks, a generic resource name that represents the required skill set might do: carpenter, crane operator, developer, graphic designer, technical writer, or social media guru. If you start with work packages, you'll probably have some specialized resources, such as a Java developer with experience in geospatial applications.

As you progress to building a schedule (see Chapter 8), you use these generic resources to rough out how long tasks will take, when tasks will occur, and how many resources you need at any given time. For example, you know that too many people on the same task can actually make the work take longer, so you begin with the ideal number of team members.

Building a Project Organization Chart

Because a project is a temporary endeavor, the everyday organizational chain of command doesn't apply. So you also need a *project organization chart* so people know who reports to whom, where status reports go, and whom to ask if a question comes up or a decision needs to be made. For that reason, a project organization chart looks a lot like the typical business organization chart.

If you work with vendors or other organizations, you might include some of the reporting structure within those groups. That way you know who to go to if deliverables are late or aren't what you expected.

Preparing a Resource Plan

When you need a large number of people for your project, you need a formal process for managing resources. That's where a resource plan comes into play.

With a resource plan, you identify how you bring team members on board — and when. You also plan how you will manage them and release them from the project when their assignments are over. A resource plan starts with the responsibility matrix and organization chart. However, the resource plan isn't complete without a detailed staffing plan, which includes the following:

- A plan for where you will obtain resources (for example, in-house or from vendors, as described in Chapter 13)
- Resource schedules, which include information about when people are available and when you need them
- Training requirements for the resources you obtain
- Release plans that show when resources will be finished and no longer work on the project
- Human resource processes for rewards, regulatory compliance, and so on

As you can see, a staffing plan comes together over time. Initially, you can define staffing processes and determine potential sources for resources. However, the rest of the staffing plan has to wait until you complete your project schedule and size up the budget. Only then will you know when you need the resources you've identified.

Once the schedule and cost look good, you'll initiate your quest for commitments. You provide the draft resource plan to line managers, team leads, vendors, and so on, and ask them to commit the resources under their control. That's when you begin to adjust your resource plan to include the people assigned to your project, when they are available, their levels of expertise, and the training they require.

Summary

As you plan a project, you inexorably home in on the resources you need. The responsibility matrix starts with the groups involved in the project so you know who's responsible for what. That way, the project is more likely to proceed smoothly because each part of the project has a group accountable for the results. You also have to put together a resource plan. That plan spells out the types of resources you need, when you need them, and for how long. You use this plan to obtain commitments from the people in charge of resources. The project organization chart shows the hierarchical reporting structure specific to your project.

Coach's Review

Use this section to assess what you've learned in this chapter and to apply it to a real-life project you're currently working on.

Test Your Knowledge

Test your knowledge of the material in this chapter by answering the following questions. See Appendix A for the answers.

1. Why is it important to have one group (and a specific person from within that group) accountable for each portion of a project?
2. How can you use the WBS to determine the resources you need?
3. What are three components you might include in a resource plan?
4. How does a project organization chart differ from a regular organization chart?

Project Challenge

Practice the knowledge you've gained in this chapter by working through this resource challenge. You can use a real-life project you're working on, or invent a project to practice resourcing using your organization's resource environment.

1. For the project you've selected, build a responsibility matrix that shows the major sections of the project. Using your organization and outside vendors if necessary, identify groups involved in the project. For each group and each section of the project, use the RACI categories to identify which groups are involved in the project. Come up with examples to back up your choices.
2. From the WBS you've developed for your project, select several work packages and identify the skill sets and other resources you need to complete the work. Based on how your organization manages resources, put together the initial resource plan you can present to line managers to obtain commitments for resources.
3. Prepare a list of types of adjustments you might have to make to your project plan if you don't get the commitments you want.
4. Construct a project organization chart to show the reporting structure you would use in your project.

CHAPTER 8

Building a Schedule

By now, you and your team have identified the project work to be done in the work breakdown structure (WBS). You've estimated how much time each work package or task will take. You've identified the types and numbers of resources you need to carry out those tasks and how much they'll cost for the project.

When you build the project schedule, you take these ingredients and put them all together. Using a Gantt chart or network diagram, you link and sequence related tasks from the beginning to the end of the project and identify when tasks should start and finish. If you have any date constraints, you add those to the schedule and make the necessary adjustments. When you assign resources — either specific or generic — to tasks, you adjust the schedule further to account for resource availability in a normal workday.

Finally, you review the resulting schedule and see if it meets the expectations of the project sponsor, customer, and other stakeholders in terms of the project finish date, cost, and other objectives. If necessary, you can optimize the schedule with a variety of techniques to achieve targets for finish date, cost, and resource allocation. While optimizing in this way, you work with the inevitable trade-offs among scope, time, and cost, as well as resource usage, quality, and risk.

NOTE This chapter covers the basics of building a project schedule that apply to many scheduling methods, including critical path method (CPM), critical chain method, and others. However, the specific variations and techniques of these methods are beyond the scope of this book.

CROSS-REFERENCE The information in this chapter relates to the PMP Exam's Domain II: Planning the Project, Task 4, "Develop a project schedule based on the project timeline, scope, and resource plan, in order to manage timely completion of the project."

Tools for Building a Schedule

You can represent your project schedule as a network diagram or a Gantt chart. A *network diagram* represents each task as a box, or node. The box includes the task name, start and finish dates, work amount, assigned resources, and other schedule information. If tasks are linked to one another, a connecting line appears between the two tasks in the diagram, as shown in Figure 8-1. Although the boxes display the dates, a network diagram doesn't show task scheduling along a graphical timeline.

CROSS-REFERENCE You learn about links between tasks in the next section of this chapter, "Sequencing with Dependencies."

On the other hand, a *Gantt chart* represents each task as a horizontal bar along a timeline. The position of the bar along the timeline indicates the task's start and finish date. The length of the bar indicates the task duration. In most scheduling programs, the bar can also display progress information, names of assigned resources, and other schedule information. Connecting lines between the bars represent the links between tasks (see Figure 8-2).

In addition, the Gantt chart includes a table area that shows the corresponding task name and often other task information as well, such as duration, status information, notes, and more. Variations on these two charts include milestone charts and summary schedules, which show a subset of the full detailed schedule. You can draw a network diagram or Gantt chart using software such as Microsoft Visio or other drawing or charting applications. You can also represent a Gantt chart with a spreadsheet program.

A smarter alternative, however, is to use an interactive project scheduling application that's designed to calculate your data dynamically as you work on the schedule and use that data to draw the charts. You can assign resources to tasks and the schedule for those tasks can be adjusted to accommodate the resources' working times. Such a program can also help you track progress and recalculate your schedule based on status updates as well as the other changes inevitable to all projects.

Examples of scheduling applications include Microsoft Project, Open Workbench, Primavera, and many others. These tools vary widely in their capabilities and associated complexity. Figure 8-3 provides a glimpse into two different applications.

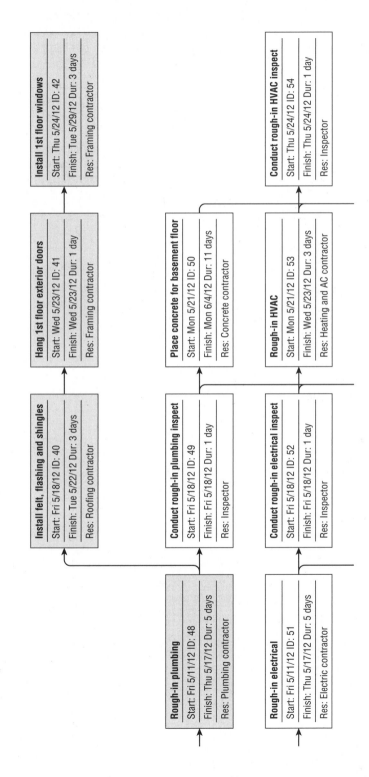

Figure 8-1: Network diagram of a project schedule

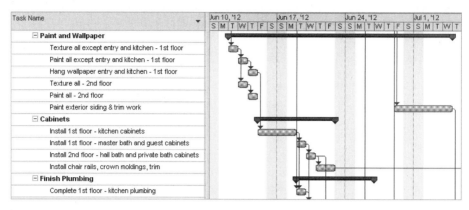

Figure 8-2: Gantt chart

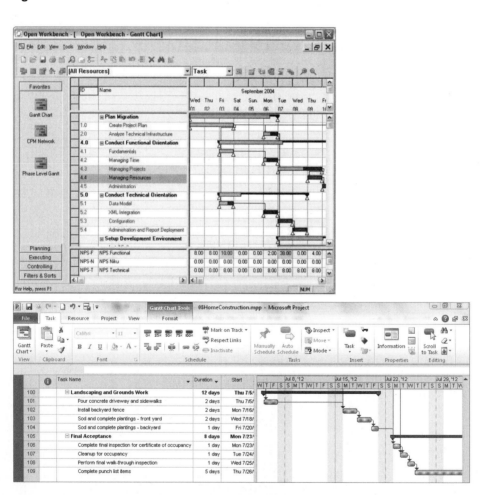

Figure 8-3: Open Workbench and Microsoft Project

Consider your project management needs when exploring the various applications. How do you want to build and view the schedule? How important is resource scheduling? Do you need the tool to respond dynamically as you enter progress information? What do you need in terms of budgeting and cost tracking? What kinds of reports do you want? Does the application need to allow input and collaboration among team members?

You can obtain a free trial of most project scheduling software applications. Some are completely free. Experiment, get recommendations, and consider what your organization needs and is willing to fund.

Sequencing with Dependencies

Suppose you're planning a kitchen remodel and trying to work out the sequence of activities. You need to demolish the old kitchen before you can rough in the plumbing and electrical lines. Those lines need to be installed before you can complete the insulation, drywall, and flooring. You need to complete the walls and floor before you start to hang cabinets and install appliances. The countertops must be installed before you set the backsplash tile.

This example illustrates that a sequence of events is often driven by *task dependencies* — relationships or links between tasks. Most tasks in a project depend upon at least one other task. That is, one task cannot begin or end until another task ends or begins.

Setting Up Predecessors and Successors

A task that must finish or start before another one can start or finish is called the *predecessor* to the other task. That other task waiting for the predecessor to finish or start is called the *successor*, much like an impatient prince waiting for his royal mother or father to step down from the throne (see Figure 8-4). Most tasks serve as both a successor and a predecessor to at least one other task.

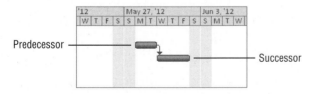

Figure 8-4: Predecessor and successor Gantt bars

One task can have several predecessors. In addition, one task can be a predecessor to several different successors (see Figure 8-5).

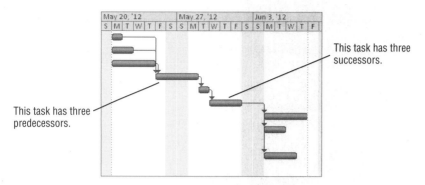

Figure 8-5: Multiple predecessors and successors

TO LINK OR NOT TO LINK

You only want to establish dependencies between tasks that are truly dependent. While the dependencies help create the sequence and schedule, they also impose restrictions, and it's in your best interest to avoid unnecessary scheduling restrictions.

For example, in your kitchen remodel plan, you might be tempted to link the faucet and appliance installation to the lighting installation. But the two do not depend on each other. One person can connect the faucet, another can install appliances, and yet another can hang the lighting, all at the same time.

But maybe there's only one resource to do all three things, and therefore you think the three tasks are dependent in that way. Such a case should not be handled with task dependencies. Only link the tasks that truly depend on each other for task-oriented issues and not for resources. Deal with adjusting the schedule for resource availability later, after you assign those resources. This will give you more flexibility with your schedule in the long run, and you'll be grateful for that flexibility.

Understanding the Dependency Types

Knowing the differences between the four types of task dependencies will ensure that the relationships you create between tasks accurately reflect how those tasks depend on one another.

- **Finish-to-start:** The FS dependency is by far the most common type of task relationship. As soon as the predecessor finishes, the successor can start. For example, as soon as the kitchen floor is finished, you can start installing the appliances.

- **Start-to-start:** In the SS dependency, the successor can start when the predecessor starts, although the SS dependency is typically associated with at least a short period of lag time so the successor starts a short while after the predecessor. For example, when registration for a training course starts, students can start signing up to take the course.

- **Finish-to-finish:** In the FF dependency, the successor cannot finish until its predecessor also finishes. The predecessor's finish triggers the successor's finish, although the FF dependency is typically associated with at least a short period of lag time. For example, suppose you have two tasks, "Complete wall" and "Inspect electrical." The "Complete wall" task cannot be finished until the "Inspect electrical" task is finished.

- **Start-to-finish:** The SF task dependency is more complex and the most rare because it flips "normal" sequencing around. The start of the predecessor triggers the finish of the successor. For example, if you ask vendors for proposals, the task to receive proposals finishes when the task to evaluate proposals start.

Figure 8-6 shows how tasks are linked using each of the four dependency types.

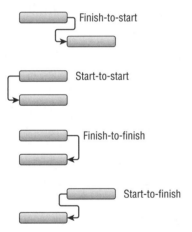

Figure 8-6: The four dependency types

Starting to Schedule

When you identify the relationships between the tasks in your project plan, the sequence starts to emerge. Linked tasks create a path of related tasks. If you're scheduling from the project start date forward, the first task is scheduled to start on the project start date. Task dependencies determine when the next tasks start, and so on throughout the path of related tasks.

Projects typically have multiple task sequences happening in parallel throughout the schedule, as shown in Figure 8-7. Different phases of subsystems associated with the project might start at the same time, if they're not connected with one another. For example, the kitchen remodel might happen at the same time as a bathroom remodel and a new deck construction. The three can conceivably start at the same time and make progress independently of one another; yet they're all part of the same home improvement project. These paths of tasks are also called chains, branches, or clusters.

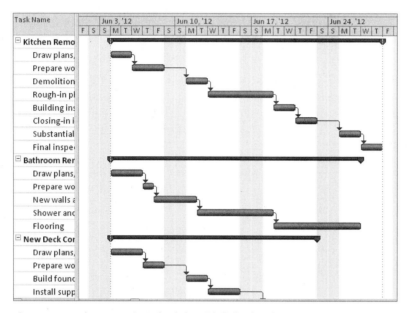

Figure 8-7: The start of a schedule with linked tasks

So although you still need to assign resources to see a meaningful schedule, you now have a set of task sequences.

Understanding the Critical Path

When tasks are connected by dependencies, they can make each other late (or early) depending on when the assigned resources start and finish. If any task along the path starts late, takes longer than planned, stalls, or is delayed for any other reason, that lateness cascades along all of its successors, which, in turn, delays the finish date for the entire path.

Delaying the end of a task sequence can have serious consequences if it happens to be the longest task sequence through the schedule. The longest path is known as the *critical path*. Each task along the critical path is called a *critical task*. They're critical because a delay of any critical task also delays the project finish date.

Similarly, if a critical task finishes early, that earliness might also cascade along the task's successors. If the resources on the successor tasks are available to start their assignments early, the critical path — and therefore the project finish date — could occur sooner.

Because the critical path affects the finish date of the entire project, the critical path enjoys a lot of attention, as do the resources assigned to critical tasks.

CROSS-REFERENCE **For more information about adjusting the critical path to shorten the schedule, see "Shortening the Schedule" later in this chapter.**

Scheduling with Lead and Lag Time

Lead and lag time can be used to refine the scheduling of tasks with dependencies. *Lead time* is like a head start for a successor task so it can start a little earlier. Suppose two tasks are linked with a finish-to-start dependency. With three days of lead time, the successor can start three days before the finish of the predecessor.

Using lead time means you can use your resources more efficiently because they're not waiting around when they don't need to. For example, you might start washing dishes before your spouse is finished cooking dinner — whether you just want the task out of the way or you need clean bowls for another round of culinary magic.

Because lead time overlaps two tasks, adding lead time is also a technique for accelerating or "fast-tracking" the schedule. With 3 days of lead time between a schedule's two tasks, the task finishes 3 days earlier than it would have without lead time (see Figure 8-8).

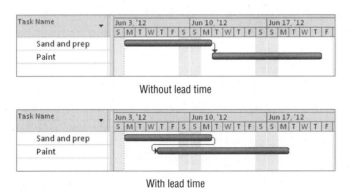

Without lead time

With lead time

Figure 8-8: Lead time

Conversely, *lag time* is a delay between two dependent tasks, such as waiting 2 days for paint to dry before you begin installing trim. If two tasks such as these are linked with a finish-to-start dependency and 2 days of lag time, the successor (installing trim) cannot start until 2 days after the predecessor (painting) is complete (see Figure 8-9).

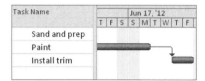

Figure 8-9: Successor task with 2 days lag time

SCHEDULING FROM THE PROJECT START DATE OR PROJECT FINISH DATE

An important aspect of your schedule is whether you're building it from the project start date or the project finish date. Scheduling from the start date shows the earliest date that the project can finish because you set the start date and schedule forward until the work is done.

However, you can schedule from the finish date when you want to work backwards from an imposed finish date. The schedule then indicates when you must start the project in order to finish by that date. One disadvantage to this approach becomes very apparent if the start date that the schedule produces is earlier than today's date. Another potential problem occurs if you don't include any buffers in the schedule to allow for the inevitable bumps in the road.

Scheduling from the finish date is a characteristic of critical chain project management, as you learn later in this chapter. The critical chain method includes buffers in the schedule that can be used if issues arise.

Applying Date Constraints

During the early stages of initiating and planning your project, dates invariably become part of the discussion. The project sponsor or customer might ask for a milestone to be completed by the end of a fiscal quarter or suggest a ballpark finish date. Before you agree, investigate the validity of these dates. They might be true requirements. On the other hand, they might only be guidelines or even wishful thinking. Don't bind up your schedule with unnecessary date constraints.

A fixed *date constraint* is a fixed, imposed date that specifies when a project task can be scheduled. These are dates you absolutely have to make. For example, perhaps your kitchen remodel has to be completely finished before the Monday of Thanksgiving week, when family starts arriving and you start cooking. That Monday is your fixed date constraint for project completion.

Or, perhaps your company CEO is planning to announce and demonstrate the new mobile Web eyeglasses as part of an industry conference keynote speech to be given on March 15. The date of the keynote speech is absolute and unchangeable. Therefore, you must have a working prototype before March 15.

Keeping Date Constraints Flexible

In every project schedule, you'll find at least a few date goals or soft deadlines. On the schedule, you can mark suggested deadlines for deliverables, milestones, or the project finish date and monitor how close the schedule comes to hitting those deadlines. In some cases, you must constrain the dates when tasks can occur — for example, to schedule them when the assigned resources will be available.

Strive to have as few date constraints as possible. Date constraints limit your ability to manipulate the schedule, dependencies, resource assignments, and even scope. In addition, date constraints increase risk because your project has more deadlines to meet.

The fewer date constraints you impose on your schedule, the more choices you have in planning the project and resolving issues. By keeping your schedule as flexible as possible, it's easier for you (or your scheduling program) to make the necessary adjustments to figure out what happens when.

The following are the three types of date constraints, with three levels of decreasing flexibility:

- **As Soon As Possible or As Late As Possible:** These are the most flexible date constraints because they don't actually limit a task's date in any way. The scheduling of these tasks is controlled by the work estimate, any dependencies, and the schedules of assigned resources. These flexible tasks should make up the great majority of the tasks in your project.

- **No Earlier Than or No Later Than:** The task can start or finish no earlier than or later than the specified date. This date constraint is somewhat flexible. The task can be scheduled either any time before the specified date or after the specified date. For example, a task that can't start until funding is released at the start of the new fiscal year could have a No Earlier Than constraint applied. The completion of the kitchen remodel by the Monday before Thanksgiving and the completion of the mobile Web eyeglasses before the industry trade show are both examples of the No Later Than constraint.

- **On This Date:** The task must start or finish on a particular day — no earlier or later. This is the least flexible of the date constraints. The keynote speech at the industry trade show is an example of an On This Date constraint.

Scheduling Specific Dates

When scheduling a fixed date, first choose the most flexible constraint type possible. Indicate the date prominently in your schedule. See how it works with any dependencies and resource scheduling, and make adjustments from there.

If you're using a project scheduling application, you can specify the fixed date and the constraint type. The application reschedules the project accordingly. Sometimes the application will also tell you where the constraint has caused scheduling conflicts you need to resolve.

CROSS-REFERENCE Learn techniques for optimizing your project plan to hit a certain date in "Shortening the Schedule" later in this chapter.

Marking Deadlines

If you want to be reminded of an important date without making it a date constraint, flag it as a deadline in your schedule. Such dates can be targets for deliverables or milestones, and you and your team can strive to meet those dates. But with the deadlines flagged instead of set in stone, you have more flexibility with how to meet them.

Indicating Milestones

A *milestone* is any significant event within the schedule that you want to recognize. You might mark a milestone at the completion of a deliverable, the beginning or ending of a phase, a decision point, or a handoff to another team. Milestones can also be a billing trigger to your customer and a celebration point with your team.

Rather than controlling the schedule, a milestone indicates progress. In your schedule, a milestone typically does not have time associated with it — that is, it's usually a task with "0 hours" or "0 days." You often link a milestone to a predecessor to show when the sequence of tasks is complete. As soon as the last task in the sequence is complete, the milestone is instantaneously complete as well. Likewise, a milestone can be the launching point to a series of successors.

Some project managers like to create a high-level milestone Gantt chart or network diagram. Such a chart helps the managing stakeholders understand the progress being made. It can also help team members keep an eye on the big picture of the overall project.

THE CANDID COACH: USE A MILESTONE TO CELEBRATE PROGRESS

Projects with lengthy timelines, or ones that are distributed around the globe, can sometimes make team members feel like they've been sailing in a vast ocean for months with no sign of land.

Consider using milestones to mark significant progress — for example, the end of a phase, the halfway point in a project, or an achievement of some significance. Milestones are great motivators for the team to see that they are indeed making progress and will be coming ashore soon.

Assigning Resources to Tasks

In Chapter 7, "Planning Project Resources," you identified the types of resources you need and developed the resource plan. Now you also have task sequences indicating which tasks have to start or finish before other tasks.

At this point, you can put the two together and assign resources to project tasks to build a true project schedule. Because you're still planning the project, most of your identified resources may be little more than job titles or skill sets. However, you might have a core team of people who have been helping you plan the project and who are expecting to become a part of the project when it moves into the executing processes.

REMEMBER EQUIPMENT AND MATERIAL RESOURCES

This section focuses on assigning human resources to tasks. However, if your project requires equipment and material resources to execute the task, be sure to assign those as well.

As with human resources, update the resource plan as needed so you know what equipment must be obtained and for what period of time. When summarizing material requirements in the resource plan, include the types, quantities, and deadlines for needed materials.

When the project plan is approved and you're kicking off the project, you can provide this information to your organization's procurement department.

For more information about equipment and material resources, see the section "Types of Resources" in Chapter 7.

Adding Generic Resources

Generic resources are placeholders indicating the types of resources you need — for example, "Engineer," "Trainer," or "Plumber." By assigning generic resources to tasks, your resource requirements are more sharply focused. You not only know the skill sets needed and how many resources you need of each type, you also know when you need them on the project and for how long. As you fine-tune your schedule, you can update your resource plan with the necessary detail.

When you've finished with the project planning processes and are obtaining approval to kick off project execution, you'll have a solid resource plan for hiring, borrowing, or procuring exactly the resources you need.

CROSS-REFERENCE For more information about identifying resource requirements, see the section "Preparing a Resource Plan" in Chapter 7.

Adding Specific Resources

If you already know some of the people who will work on your project, such as the members of your core planning team, you can assign them to their tasks by name. Even though these resources are already working on the project, you still need key information. As with the generic resources, add these resources' job titles and skill sets if you don't have them already, when each resource is needed to start, and when they can be released from the project. You also need to know each person's availability. Don't assume that they're yours for the entirety of the project, and don't assume you get them full time. Just as you did with generic resources, update your resource plan with this information.

CROSS-REFERENCE For more information about acquiring in-house employees as well as contractors and vendors, see the section "Obtaining Resources" in Chapter 13.

Assigning Multiple Resources to One Task

Having multiple resources assigned to a single task makes it possible for the work to be completed in a shorter time frame, which might be just what you need to complete the project by the date the stakeholders request. Some tasks naturally lend themselves to multiple resources. You might plan for three instructional designers to develop training lessons or five carpenters to frame a building.

When you assign one resource to a task, you schedule the resource to work the estimated number of hours. If the resource works full time, the length of the task and the estimated hours are equivalent. For example, if the task is estimated to take 40 hours, the resource would work 40 hours on the task.

However, if you add a second resource to the same task, you can reduce the task duration. For example, suppose a task is estimated to take one person 20 hours to complete. If you assign two resources to it and the task is a simple one, such as stacking firewood, you shorten the duration to half the time:

10 hours. If you assign four resources, it might finish in 5 hours. Of course, at some point, you get diminishing returns, where the addition of resources actually increases rather than reduces duration because the wood stackers begin to run into one another or squabble over logs.

WORK ESTIMATES ARE DIFFERENT FROM TASK DURATIONS

It can be tempting to think of work estimates and task durations as the same thing; but they're actually quite different. The *work estimate* indicates the amount of time (such as work hours) the task will take, regardless of the number of resources assigned. The work estimate is also known as effort.

Duration, on the other hand, is the time span of the task, from start to finish, and often (although not always) depends on the number of resources assigned.

For more information, see the section "The Difference between Duration and Effort" in Chapter 6.

For some types of tasks, dividing the work between the two resources doesn't cut the duration in half. For example, suppose you assign one programmer to write code and the estimate is 24 hours of work. If you assign two programmers to write code, they might have to plan how to design the software modules and then integrate their code. The new estimate might increase to 28 work hours.

CROSS-REFERENCE For more information about the implications and limitations of adding resources to a task, see the section "Crashing a Schedule" in Chapter 19.

Modeling a Realistic Schedule

Anyone can pencil out a pipe dream. But when your schedule more accurately considers the impact of resources, you have a better chance for staying within your project constraints of scope, schedule, and budget. A realistic schedule also ensures that the resource work is balanced, the quality meets the requirements, and the risks are appropriately managed.

Assigning resources to tasks ensures that you are building accountability in to your schedule, by identifying the people, equipment, and materials that will actual carry out the tasks. In this way, assigning resources helps you refine your schedule and make it more concrete. However, resources impose another layer of constraints. When you assign resources, examine the following factors and adjust the schedule as necessary so it accurately reflects the reality of your project:

- What days or times are your resources not available for work? Nights? Weekends? Holidays? Vacations?

- Is a resource available full time or part time to your project?

- How many hours can you reasonably expect team members to devote to project work each day?

- How much faster or slower might an assigned resource work than the average reflected in your work estimate?

Scheduling around Nonworking Time

Be sure your schedule accounts for the nonworking days and times throughout the project. Start with organizational nonworking days and times, such as nights, weekends, holidays, and so on. If the organization has any seasonal shutdowns, such as a two-week furlough for factory maintenance at the end of the calendar year, account for those as well.

As you assign resources, you must choose how to schedule individuals' nonworking times. For significant planned time off, such as someone's vacation, you might build that nonworking time into the schedule. However, the people who work on your project have other non-project commitments such as administrative work, and unplanned nonworking time such as sick days. Rather than trying to build unknowable details into the schedule, you're better off assuming shorter workdays. For example, if non-project work eats up 2 hours of each day, you can assign resources to work on tasks no more than 6 hours a day.

CROSS-REFERENCE Risk management is the science of planning for the unplannable. For more information, see Chapter 12, "Managing Risk."

Defining Non-Project Time

It's unrealistic to expect you and your team members to devote eight hours of every day to project tasks. You all need time to deal with non-project email, paperwork and other administrative tasks, department and company meetings, and more.

Non-project time often consumes 2 hours a day, which means a full-time resource committed to your project has only 6 hours a day for project work. Some studies have even reduced that figure to 4 to 5 hours.

Determine what you mean by a day of project work — whether it's 5 or 6 hours. If necessary, you might want to define a project week as 25 or 30 hours of project work. Then you can adjust the project schedule accordingly to account for that time. When you give your resources their task lists, they'll know that you're firmly grounded in reality when they see a 16-hour task scheduled across three days, for example.

Adjusting Tasks for Resource Productivity

Although you have work estimates for the tasks in the schedule, you base those estimates on average workers. You might need to adjust those estimates when you obtain your resources. Here are some typical scenarios:

- Resources with less experience have a longer learning curve and may take longer to complete tasks.
- Resources with more experience can dive right in and do the work in less time.
- Some resources naturally work at a faster or slower pace than their peers, either due to a natural energy level or a propensity for perfectionism.

This means that in the hands of a faster, more productive resource, a 30-hour task might take 25 hours. In the hands of a slower, less productive resource, that same task might take 35 hours. It's a good idea to annotate such adjustments. If you need to replace the slower or faster resource, you can return to your original estimate for the new resource.

Managing Part-Timers and Multitaskers

You might have part-time resources who work for only 20 or 30 hours each week. You might also have resources on loan to your project part time. In either case, you need to adjust your schedule to reflect the amount of time these resources can devote to your project. If you don't, your schedule will become inaccurate within a week or two.

If you're using a project scheduling application, you can designate the availability for resources. For example, someone designated at 50 percent availability is available 50 percent of the norm you've set for full-time resources. Depending on the scheduling program you use, you might be able to adjust a resource's working time to reflect the team member's availability. That way, the tasks are scheduled based on when and how much the assigned resource is available.

REALITY CHECK: PART-TIMER PERFORMANCE AND PRODUCTIVITY

In addition to recalculating the schedule for part-time availability, consider the performance and productivity of part-time resources. There can be a problem with focus and momentum when they join the project for the day or week. The time it takes to switch gears is a real issue for many multitaskers.

On the other hand, part-timers and multitaskers can actually be more productive because they aren't burnt out with the same old grind. Some multitaskers might be in that position because their proficiency and productivity have put them in great demand, and they have proven to be up to the challenge.

Scheduling with the Critical Chain Method

The scheduling described so far follows the precepts of traditional project management, or *critical path method (CPM)*, in which the critical path is based on the sequence of tasks through the project as determined by the work estimates, task dependencies, and date constraints.

However, many project managers believe that the critical path method doesn't do enough to account for the impact that resources have on a schedule. Instead, they use the critical chain method to create a more realistic and reliable schedule.

The critical chain method or *critical chain project management (CCPM)* focuses on the ways that assigned resources — particularly overallocated resources — affect the schedule's critical path. This approach also adds shared time buffers to the project and task sequences. The three major characteristics of the critical chain method are:

- Scheduling from the finish date
- Balancing the most constrained resources
- Adding time buffers and resource flags

Working Back from the Finish Date

In most traditionally scheduled projects, the schedule is calculated as soon as possible, working from the start date forward. By contrast, in critical chain project management, the schedule is typically calculated working back from the target finish date, or as late as possible.

By scheduling as late as possible, you can incur project costs later and you can reduce the number of resource overallocations. By using time buffers, you can reduce the risk you might otherwise face from scheduling from the finish date.

Balancing Constrained Resources

Resource impact on the schedule is not necessarily a driving force in projects scheduled according to the critical path method, although resources are assigned first to the critical path in hopes of protecting and possibly shortening the critical path. However, paying special attention to how assigned resources affect the schedule, particularly the critical path, is a key element of the critical chain method.

In fact, the *critical chain* is the resource-constrained critical path that results when resource availability is applied to the schedule. That is, the critical chain is the result of reducing or eliminating resource overallocations. Because of this and the built-in time buffers, the critical chain is often longer than the critical path.

CROSS-REFERENCE For information about adjusting the schedule for constrained resources, see "Balancing Resource Assignments" later in this chapter.

Adding Buffers

Another key characteristic of the critical chain method is the use of time buffers to protect the schedule. The buffers are as follows:

- **Project buffer:** A period of time added to the end of the critical chain to protect the target finish date from slippage.

- **Feeding buffer:** A period of time added to the end of a sequence of tasks that lead into the critical chain. This feeding buffer protects the critical chain from slippage by protecting the finish date of the sequence of tasks.

- **Resource buffer:** A flag, usually placed on the critical chain, to alert a resource that he or she will soon be needed for an upcoming task along the critical chain.

CROSS-REFERENCE For more information about adding time buffers to the schedule, see the sections "Managing the Uncertainty of Estimates" in Chapter 6 and "Building in a Schedule Buffer" in Chapter 12.

Optimizing the Schedule

After you build the schedule and refine it to reflect the reality of day-to-day work, it's time to look at your overall results. Is the finish date reasonable? Is it hitting the target your customer expects? Is the cost within the budget? Are any resources assigned beyond their available time?

If any of your answers are "no," you can revisit the schedule and make changes as necessary to achieve the schedule, budget, and resource targets. To make such adjustments, you artfully sculpt the project triangle to rebalance the scope, schedule, budget, resources, quality, and risk.

Shortening the Schedule

One of the primary reasons that you might need to shorten a schedule is that the finish date is projected to be later than it should be. Perhaps the finish date for a new product is set to fit a market window, such as the holiday season, or for a training program to coincide with a new system rollout. If your schedule shows the project finish date happening later than that market window or system rollout, you need to bring in the finish date. To do this, focus on the critical path and see if you can shorten any critical tasks.

Another reason to shorten the schedule is that an interim date constraint, such as the availability of a prototype for an all-important industry trade show, needs to be met. When you need to make an interim date constraint, focus on the sequence that includes the task associated with the interim date, and shorten tasks leading up to that date.

The following are strategies for adjusting the schedule to bring in dates:

- **Overlap tasks:** Also known as *fast-tracking*, review the schedule for opportunities to overlap tasks or execute them in parallel rather than in sequence. While this typically does not increase cost, it can increase risk because you begin one task before its predecessor is complete.

- **Add money and resources:** Because you're still in project planning, you can choose to add resources to the plan to accelerate the schedule, which is referred to as *crashing* the schedule.

- **Use different resources:** Revise the plan to replace slower resources with faster or more experienced ones. Outsource work or use resources provided by the customer.

- **Plan and budget for overtime:** Adjust the schedule and budget to allow for overtime. When the project is approved and you're kicking off the project, plan to ask your team members to work overtime, at least for certain critical tasks. Note that this strategy increases cost and should not be used for an extended period of time.

- **Cut scope:** If there was any scope buffer — that is, tasks or activities that are considered "nice to have" but not an essential requirement — this is a good time to cut them.

CROSS-REFERENCE For details about these schedule-shortening strategies, see the section "Ways to Correct Course" in Chapter 19.

THE SHIFTING CRITICAL PATH

If you shorten tasks on the critical path enough, they could actually cease to be on the critical path. Other tasks could take their place in the longest path through the project, dictating the project finish date.

Because of this, it's a good idea to re-evaluate the critical path after each schedule-shortening modification you make. That way, you can be sure that you're focusing your attention on the tasks that directly affect the project finish date.

Reducing Project Costs

After building your schedule and assigning resources, you get a clearer look at the resource costs, which determine the largest part of your budget. Task-related costs also come to light, for example, travel costs and conference room rentals. If the resulting project costs overshoot your estimates or the not-to-exceed amount that the customer has dictated, you need to find ways to decrease costs.

Here are strategies for adjusting the schedule to reduce project costs:

- **Check schedule and cost assumptions:** The easiest approach is to make sure cost data is entered properly. Confirm the resource costs, the tasks to which resources are assigned, and the work amounts for those assignments. Check that costs are not being double-counted and that no costs are in the wrong place.

- **Use different, less expensive resources:** Because the largest project costs are resource costs, this is where you can potentially find cost savings. However, using cheaper resources can increase risk. In terms of people, less expensive resources can mean less experienced resources who might cause schedule delays. Choosing cheaper equipment and materials might carry the risk of lower quality, which might not meet customer requirements.

- **Cut scope:** Again, cut any tasks or activities that were considered optional. Besides the scope buffer of any optional activities, see where you can save money. Another strategy is to focus on the tasks that are assigned to the most expensive resources as well as the tasks that have the longest work estimates.

CROSS-REFERENCE For more information about the project budget, see the section "Estimating Project Costs" in Chapter 6.

Balancing Resource Assignments

Another aspect of optimizing your schedule and reflecting reality is to check that the resources — even generic placeholder resources — are allocated properly in their task assignments. Are any resources scheduled to multiple tasks during the same time period? Are any resources scheduled beyond what their availability will allow? Resources who are overscheduled like this are said to be *overallocated*.

Also check to see whether any resources are underallocated. Underallocated resources waste project money and can potentially interfere with other resources performing their assignments.

Because you're still in project planning, you have time to rebalance resource assignments with the following strategies:

- **Check resource assignments.** Make sure the resources are assigned properly. Confirm the work amounts for those assignments. Check that resources are not double-assigned, for example, to a task and also to the parent summary task.

- **Level overallocated resources.** *Resource leveling* is a technique that moves tasks to when the assigned resources are available to work on them. Resource leveling often uses available slack between tasks. However, because critical tasks by their nature have no slack, resource leveling can lead to a longer project duration and a later project finish date.

- **Add, rearrange, or redistribute resource assignments.** If possible, reassign underallocated resources to replace or assist overallocated resources. If you can obtain additional resources, reassign work from overallocated resources to new ones.

- **Cut scope.** If overallocated resources are assigned to any tasks that are considered optional, consider cutting those tasks.

UNDERSTANDING FREE SLACK AND TOTAL SLACK

Slack, also known as *float*, is the amount of time a task can be delayed without delaying other tasks. Similar to the slack in a length of string, project slack represents flexibility — in this case, within the project schedule.

More specifically, *free slack* (or *free float*) is the amount of time a task can be delayed without delaying the start of any successors.

Total slack (or *total float*) is the amount of time a task can be delayed without also delaying the finish date of the project.

A characteristic of critical tasks is that they have no slack. Any delay to a critical task will not only delay their successors but also delay the project finish date.

The slack associated with noncritical paths in your schedule might provide opportunities to bring in the finish dates of those paths or to shorten the overall project. If tasks have slack, you can reschedule tasks assigned to over-allocated resources and use the slack to alleviate the overallocation. Or you might reassign resources from noncritical to critical tasks to shorten the project duration.

SETTING SCHEDULE CONTINGENCIES

After your optimizing efforts are complete, you might feel your schedule has an accuracy of +/–10 percent. That's a pretty good tolerance considering you're trying to forecast the future.

As realistic and optimized as the schedule might be, however, there are still risks. What happens if the schedule indeed slips by 10 percent?

It might not sound like much, but suppose a ten-month project slips by 10 percent — that's an entire month. Consider the impact on budget and resources a one-month slip could have. Whether the project is a new product, a new building, or a training program, a month can be huge.

A solution to this is to adopt the practice of using schedule contingencies when estimating work and managing risk. A schedule contingency is an amount of time you build in to the schedule in case the schedule slips.

For more information about schedule contingencies, see the sections "Managing the Uncertainty of Estimates" in Chapter 6 and "Building in a Schedule Buffer" in Chapter 12.

Summary

In building a schedule, you combine the work breakdown structure, work and cost estimates, and resource planning to develop the timeline of project tasks in a Gantt chart or network diagram. You link related tasks with dependencies, thereby creating sequences or paths of tasks throughout the project schedule. You also incorporate any date constraints into the schedule — for example, for tasks that must occur within specific dates — although you strive to keep these to a minimum.

When you assign specific or generic resources to tasks, the schedule finally starts to take shape. You adjust the schedule further to account for resource availability.

Finally, you review and optimize the schedule to be sure it meets the finish date and cost expectations of the project sponsor or customer. You also review resource allocation and adjust the resource plan to ensure that resources are not overallocated or underutilized.

Coach's Review

Use this section to assess what you've learned in this chapter and to apply it to a real-life project you're currently working on.

Test Your Knowledge

Test your knowledge of the material in this chapter by answering the following questions. See Appendix A for the answers.

1. What's the difference between a Gantt chart and a network diagram?
2. Why would you create a task dependency between tasks?
3. What is the most commonly used task dependency?
4. What makes the critical path so critical?
5. Why is it important to avoid date constraints?
6. Why is there a distinction between the work estimate and task duration?
7. Name at least two ways that assigned resources can affect the project schedule.

Project Challenge

Practice the knowledge you've gained in this chapter with the following challenge. Use the real or practice project you're planning as you work through the chapters in this book.

1. Using the WBS, work estimates, and resource plan you've developed in Chapters 5–7, use either a Gantt chart or network diagram to build your project schedule. Create the chart using any tool or application you wish.
2. Use dependencies to link and sequence tasks. Apply any necessary date constraints and mark any other date targets or deadlines.
3. Assign generic and specific resources to your schedule. Decide how you're going to reflect nonworking time, non-project time, and part-time resources in the schedule.
4. Review and optimize the schedule for a targeted finish date and budget. Make sure that resource assignments are balanced and adjust the resource plan as necessary.

CHAPTER 9

Planning for Quality

As you plan and execute your project, often what's topmost in your mind are the schedule and the cost. But quality is also a huge factor in making a project successful. So in addition to constantly monitoring and answering the questions "When?" and "How much?" quality demands that you answer the question "How well?"

Managing quality in a project has to do with ensuring that the product, service, or other project result meets the standards specified in the scope statement or requirements document. Project quality management emphasizes customer satisfaction, prevention of quality problems, continuous improvement, and management responsibility.

During project planning, you create the quality management plan that defines how you will implement quality standards. When you move on to project execution, your team performs quality assurance, ensuring that quality is built into the project results and that defects are prevented every step along the way. As part of project monitoring and controlling, quality control efforts include testing and inspecting the results and making sure they're within established specifications.

This chapter covers how quality is defined, implemented, and validated in a project. You get an overview of some of the most widely used quality standards and methodologies. You learn how to develop the quality plan for your project, and see how to use quality assurance and quality control techniques to ensure that your customer's quality specifications are being met.

Defining Quality

You've probably heard the saying (or seen the sign at a print shop or auto repair shop) "Fast, cheap, or good—pick two." While these are relative terms, you can easily define what you mean by "fast" or "cheap" as it relates to a project. But what do you mean by "good"? Translating the idea of quality from a hazy notion to something tangible, even measurable, starts at the project scope statement or requirements document. That's where the project sponsor or customer starts to define the standard against which the result of the project is to be measured.

Definition of the quality standard can challenge the constraints of the project triangle. You try to fulfill the scope of the project within a certain finish date and budget maximum, while upholding the quality standard for the results being produced. Any changes to the project's scope, time, or money constraints can directly affect the level of quality the project can achieve.

TALK THE QUALITY TALK

Quality management is arguably as sizable and as specialized a field as project management. Like so many other intersecting disciplines, you need to become familiar, if not expert, with the basics of quality management. Here are some concepts to get you on your way toward a good working vocabulary of quality management:

- **Defect:** Any process output that does not meet customer specifications. Related terms are error, failure, mistake, and nonconformance.

- **Inspection:** Evaluating results in order to keep defects or errors out of the hands of the customers. Inspection is a major focus of quality control and is the means for validating that a product or service meets the customer's requirements.

- **Prevention:** Keeping defects or errors out of the process to begin with. Prevention is a major focus of quality assurance and, in fact, most quality management methodologies.

- **Quality assurance (QA):** The practice of improving, auditing, and stabilizing a product, service, or other result based on quality requirements and the results of quality control measurements. The focus of QA is to avoid or minimize defects or errors.

- **Quality control (QC):** The practice of testing or measuring and recording results at checkpoints to assess performance and ensure that it's meeting the standard within appropriate parameters (such as product dimension tolerances). If results do not meet the standard, QC recommends changes as necessary.

- **Quality management:** The ongoing process of assessing, anticipating, and fulfilling stated and implied needs, with an emphasis on customer satisfaction, defect or error prevention, continuous improvement, and management responsibility.

Quality and the Requirements Document

The level of quality for the project's results is defined in the objectives, the requirements document, or the scope statement. These are drafted during the initiating processes when the project is being defined and finalized during the planning processes.

CROSS-REFERENCE   For information about defining the project with the objectives, requirements document, and scope statement, see Chapter 3, "Getting a Project Off the Ground."

Project objectives can define quality because they're broken down into its actionable and measurable components. A measurable objective is one that can be proven or verified by some quantitative metric. Although many measures represent "how much" or "how many," for objectives related to quality, the standard that you include helps define "how well."

IDENTIFY AND SPECIFY THE QUALITY REQUIREMENTS

As the project manager, you (along with any early team members) are often the one in charge of gathering and documenting the requirements. You work with the customer or sponsor to tease out the product specifications. While gathering all these facts, be sure to get the information you need about quality standards.

For example, if the customer says, "We need the new mobile Web eyeglasses to be as fast as other current mobile devices," ask for more detail. Is there a particular benchmark of speed that must be met? What are the details of that benchmark? Perhaps there's a set of commonly performed mobile tasks that the mobile Web eyeglasses must complete faster than the five primary competing mobile devices.

The customer might also say, "The new mobile Web eyeglasses must conform to the Mobile Web Initiative established by the W3C (World Wide Web Consortium)." This indicates a specific industry standard to which the product must conform.

Suppose the project is a trade show booth at a high-profile expo, and your sponsor says, "We want the booth to be eye-catching yet sophisticated." This is a subjective statement of quality. You need to work with the sponsor to define the look of the booth further until your picture of "eye-catching yet sophisticated" matches the sponsor's picture.

The requirements might have been broadly defined at the project initiating processes. But now you're well into project planning, so the requirements are becoming more and more specific.

As part of fleshing out the requirements document, add the concrete quality standards that your customer is expecting. That way, you can ensure that you and the stakeholders have the same result in mind and you'll know when you've achieved those quality standards.

The scope statement can offer clues to the quality standards because it includes characteristics of the product or service being produced. However, because thorough requirements definition is so central to the success of a project, quality standards are most often spelled out in the requirements document. This document is based on the needs and expectations of the project sponsor, customer, and other key stakeholders and enumerates the detailed specifications for the project results.

Constraints on Quality

The trouble with defining quality standards and measurements is that it throws another plate in the air for you to juggle, along with the other plates of project scope, time, budget, resources, and risk. What's more, they're all interrelated. An adjustment to scope, time, or budget changes your ability to meet quality standards. That change can make you scramble if scope is increased, or if time or budget is cut back. Sometimes, however, you get lucky. An unexpected windfall of time or money can allow you to accommodate increased scope.

Quality Standards and Methods

Often the customer identifies the specific quality standards; other times your organization specifies it. Sometimes you and your team commit to a quality standard because you believe it to be right for the project and for the organization.

Many standards are developed by international or national standards organizations whose primary activities consist of producing technical standards for certain industries. The following are examples of standards organizations that have developed widely accepted standards for various purposes:

- American National Standards Institute (ANSI)
- ASTM International (formerly the American Society for Testing and Materials)
- Institute of Electrical and Electronic Engineers (IEEE)
- International Organization for Standardization (ISO)
- National Institute of Standards and Technology (NIST)
- United States Military Standard (MIL-SPEC)
- World Wide Web Consortium (W3C)

Standards developed by these and other organizations can have very specific applications to specific industries—for example, standards for water quality, software quality, housing quality, architectural woodwork, government auditing, and so on.

In addition to standards, your organization, or your customer's organization, might commit to using a particular quality methodology for all its projects. Examples of various approaches to improving quality in an organization include the following:

- **Continuous Improvement (CI):** The ongoing effort to improve products, services, or processes in every facet of an organization's operations, thereby increasing competitiveness. Improvements are based on many small changes that tend be generated by the existing workforce who take ownership for their work and their performance. CI is characterized by involvement of the entire organization at all levels, often in teams. CI is also known as *Kaizen.*

- **ISO 9000 Quality Management:** The set of standardized requirements and recommendations for an organization's quality management system, based on conformance to specifications and prevention of defects. The standards include fundamentals and vocabulary, performance improvements, documentation, training, and financial and economic aspects. ISO 9000 is among the most widely used management tools in the world.

- **Six Sigma:** A set of practices designed to improve manufacturing and business processes to reduce and eliminate defects. It uses a set of quality management methods, including statistical methods, and creates specialists within the organization who are experts in these methods. Each Six Sigma project follows a defined sequence of steps and has quantified financial targets such as cost reduction or profit increase.

- **Total Quality Management (TQM):** A management philosophy based on the premise that the quality of products and processes can be continuously improved. The nine common TQM practices are cross-functional product design, process management, supplier quality management, customer involvement, information and feedback, committed leadership, strategic planning, cross-functional training, and employee involvement.

The standards specified for your project, as well as the quality methodology used, are the foundation for your project's quality plan.

Developing the Quality Plan

The quality management plan identifies quality requirements and standards for the project and its results. This plan documents the procedures and processes that will be applied and how the project will demonstrate compliance with the requirements and standards.

You and your team develop and maintain the quality management plan. In fact, your project team members should all feel empowered to make or suggest continuous improvements within their realms of responsibility. You also need support for the quality standards from the managing stakeholders. Achieving the desired quality standards is the responsibility of everyone involved, and it can't just be lip service.

CROSS-REFERENCE The information in this section relates to the PMP Exam's Domain II: Planning the Project, Task 8, "Develop a quality management plan based on the project scope and requirements, in order to prevent the occurrence of defects and reduce the cost of quality."

Elements of the Quality Management Plan

Your quality management plan specifies how your project will implement the identified quality standards and requirements throughout the project life cycle. Your quality management plan can include the following elements:

- **Quality standard:** This can be a formal standard such as the W3C Mobile Web Initiative. If you're not using a formal standard, work with appropriate team members to define your own ad hoc standard for the purposes of this project. Start with the quality-oriented specifications that you've already defined in the requirements document. For example, indicate that the mobile Web eyeglasses will have fewer than three bugs per 1,000 lines of code and at least a 99 percent uptime rate. If the objectives or scope statement include additional quality specifications, be sure to include them as well.

- **Quality methodology:** This can be a formal methodology such as TQM or ISO 9000. But if you're not using a formal methodology, work with a subset of your team to identify the processes and procedures you will use throughout the project to implement your quality standard and demonstrate compliance.

- **Quality assurance (QA):** Specify the procedures and checklists that you and your team have developed to prevent defects or errors and to build quality into the product, service, or other project results. As appropriate, indicate how and when audits will take place and how audit responses will be handled.

- **Quality control (QC):** Specify the checkpoints, sampling, metrics, measurement tolerances, logs, and charts your team have decided to use to inspect the product, service, or other result of the project to ensure that defects or errors don't find their way to the customer. Indicate the process for handling out-of-range conditions and validating deliverables.

Understanding the Cost of Quality

While you develop the quality management plan, keep in mind that quality truly is its own reward. Preventing errors and making continuous improvements save your project money and time. And meeting your customer's needs? Well, that's just priceless.

In fact, you can quantify the quality with a cost-benefit analysis and include this in the quality management plan as well. For each quality activity you add, consider the cost savings in less rework and lower costs. Also consider the gain in terms of higher productivity and increased customer satisfaction within the boundaries of their requirements.

A concept related to the cost-benefit analysis is *cost of quality (COQ)*. Cost of quality considers the costs for meeting quality requirements against the costs for dealing with nonconformance to requirements. In other words, the cost of quality is money spent during the project to avoid failures, and it includes prevention and testing costs. The cost of nonconformance is money spent during and after the project because of failures. This includes failures found by the project team resulting in rework and scrap. This also includes failures found by the customer, which results in liabilities, warranty work, and lost business.

Integrating the Quality Management Plan

Don't expect the quality management plan to exist in a vacuum. Revisit the work breakdown structure (WBS) and the project schedule to add and assign tasks and checkpoints that have to do with the quality standards, the methodology you're using, QC, and QA. Additional tasks and resource assignments will certainly affect the project finish date and cost. You might need to bring on additional resources. Your quality management plan almost certainly affects your risk management plan. The risk identification process often brings up quality issues, and the quality management plan details actions to reduce those risks.

Your quality management plan becomes part of your project notebook. And like everything else in your project notebook, the quality management plan is a living document. As you discover more details in the planning and executing processes, you might need to update aspects of the quality management plan.

Taking Responsibility for Quality

The different quality methodologies appear to speak with one voice regarding who is responsible for quality—it's everyone at all levels of the organization, in this case, all levels of the project. The commitment to quality starts with the managing stakeholders. They define the standards of quality the project is to achieve. They provide the guidance as well as the resources for implementing the quality standards in the project. They might decide on a particular methodology and make sure that the organization follows through with it. They make decisions regarding time and budget, which are directly related to quality.

If a quality manager is associated with the project, this person can help the project manager put the quality management plan together and make sure its processes are implemented. Even if the quality manager is not part of the project team, he or she can certainly provide invaluable guidance about the standards and methodology.

As the project manager, you build the standards into your project plan. You have to take the initiative, create the plan, and assign the quality-related tasks. You make sure that the right tasks are present in the WBS, that time is built in to the schedule, and that there is sufficient budget to carry out the quality management plan. You follow through to create a culture of quality in your project organization.

If your organization has a quality assurance department and a quality control department, they can help fulfill the QA and QC functions in your project. Project team members are responsible for carrying out quality-related tasks. Furthermore, all team members, whether they're assigned to quality-related tasks or not, are empowered to be always on the lookout within their realm for process improvement and error prevention; in short, anything ensures that customer expectations are met.

Building in Excellence with QA

Quality assurance (QA) is the continuous process of improving a product or service with a focus on minimizing defects or errors. In QA, the emphasis is on "doing it right the first time." Everyone is involved and the process is ongoing.

QA is part of the project executing processes. The product or service is audited against the quality requirements as well as quality control (QC) results to ensure that appropriate quality standards are used.

CROSS-REFERENCE The information in this section relates to the PMP Exam's Domain III: Executing the Project, Task 3, "Implement the quality management plan using the appropriate tools and techniques, in order to ensure that work is being performed according to required quality standards."

Evaluating Quality Results

Although QA and QC are distinct from one another, QA uses the test and measurement results from QC to analyze and evaluate the quality results of the project.

Quality audits are also a key component of QA. A *quality audit* is a structured, independent review of the project to determine whether and how well the project is adhering to organizational and project policies, processes, and procedures. The audit might be scheduled or random. Because a quality audit is an independent review, the ideal is for it to be done by the organization's QA department or by the QA department of the customer's organization.

A quality audit identifies good practices being implemented as well as any shortcomings in the project process. The shortcomings can help you identify how to improve processes with the goal of reducing errors, enhancing productivity, or meeting customer requirements.

The quality audit can not only uncover a systemic problem, but also help you identify the underlying cause of the problem. With this knowledge, you can develop process improvements to prevent the problem in the future.

Implementing Corrective Actions

The QA auditor documents any shortcomings found in the quality audit in the form of corrective actions, including defect repairs and preventive actions. As the project manager, you review the corrective actions. The following are possible responses to the corrective actions:

- If a corrective action constitutes an issue that can be handled through your issues tracking system, assign the corrective action to the appropriate team member and make sure that the necessary information is recorded in the issues log.

- If a corrective action constitutes a project scope change, work it through your project's change control process.

- If a corrective action has to do with your project management processes— for example, an action having to do with running your status meetings or submitting reports to upper management—you can make the appropriate adjustments.

The QA auditor provides a certain amount of time to respond to the audit and implement the corrective actions. You need to document the corrective action taken, and the auditor checks the corrective action to make sure it meets the standard. If it does, the auditor validates, resolves, and closes the corrective action. The outcome of a corrected shortcoming is a reduced cost of quality and an increase in the customer acceptance of the product or service.

The QA auditor also documents good practices being implemented. These practices are shared with others in the organization, and they're added to the lessons learned knowledge base for the project.

CROSS-REFERENCE For information about change control, see Chapter 11, "Setting Up a Change Management Plan." For information about documenting and assigning issues, see the section "Tracking Issues" in Chapter 12. For information about the lessons learned knowledge base, see Chapter 22, "Don't Forget Lessons Learned."

Verifying the Standards with QC

Quality control (QC) is the process of testing or measuring and recording specific aspects of the product or service at identified checkpoints. The purpose of QC is to

- Assess performance, for example, the speed of a mobile device.
- Check that the project results meet the quality standard within identified parameters or tolerances—for example, that a software product has less than the specified bug rate or system failure rate.
- Recommend changes as needed to help the product or service meet the standard.

The emphasis of QC is inspection, which strives to ensure that defects do not make their way into the hands of the customer. QC is part of the project monitoring and controlling processes. The product or other result of the project is inspected against the quality requirements, and those inspection results are recorded in logs, trend charts, control charts, or other such documentation.

The QC testing might be done by the project's QC team or by the QC team of your organization or the customer's QC department. The QC testers inspect the results at identified checkpoints throughout the project to ensure their alignment with the quality standards as outlined in the product scope and requirements document.

QC testing identifies substandard processes or deficient product quality. QC activities can also help identify the root causes of these problems and can recommend actions to eliminate these causes. QC testing also determines how and whether deliverables are successfully verified and validated against the customer's requirements. If a deliverable does not meet the quality standard, QC reports this to the managing stakeholders, who then decide on next steps.

CROSS-REFERENCE The information in this section relates to the PMP Exam's Domain IV: Monitoring and Controlling the Project, Task 3, "Ensure that project deliverables conform to the quality standards established in the quality management plan by using appropriate tools and techniques (e.g. testing, inspection, control charts), in order to satisfy customer requirements."

Measuring and Recording Quality

The quality checkpoints and the types of measurements are determined by the customer requirements and outlined in the quality management plan. The results of a measurement or test are recorded on an appropriate log or chart. The following are examples of such charts:

- **Control chart:** A control chart is a line graph showing the upper and lower tolerance limits, as defined in the requirements document. Data collected over time about the process is plotted on the control chart. The chart shows whether the process trends and fluctuating values are within the acceptable tolerance. If a data point is outside the tolerance limits, the process is said to be out of control. In some cases, prescribed adjustments to the process can bring the process back into control.

- **Run chart:** Like a control chart, a run chart is another line graph. Unlike a control chart, however, a run chart does not show any upper or lower tolerance limits. Data collected over time about the process is plotted on the run chart, showing trends, for example, that the number of errors are decreasing over time. A trend analysis can be done using the data from run charts. Run charts are also known as *trend charts*.

- **Scatter diagram:** A scatter diagram shows the relationship between pairs of graphed data points. One variable is graphed on the x axis and the other is graphed on the y axis. This helps show whether there's a relationship or correlation between the two variables. If the variables are correlated, the points will fall along a line or curve. The closer the points are to the line, the closer the variables are correlated. Such a diagram can help with problem identification—for example, examining whether there's a correlation between speed of processing and number of errors.

- **Statistical sampling:** Samples of the identified product are selected and tested, typically at random. The sample frequency and sizes are specified in the quality management plan. The testing of a proper number or percentage in the sample is a statistically reliable predictor of the testing of the entire population.

In addition to recording data, inspection is a significant QC activity. The QC team examines the product or service to determine whether it meets the documented standards and requirements. Inspection activities can range from measurements, reviews, peer reviews, audits, or walk-throughs. They can take place at a certain checkpoint or on the final product or service result of the project.

Finding Causes of Quality Problems

You and your project team can use the measurement data the QC team collects to help solve systemic or recurring problems. In this way, QC feeds the continuous improvement process.

QC data can be used with the following tools and techniques to help analyze the root cause of a problem and then determine the appropriate solution to that problem:

- **Cause and effect diagram:** Illustrates how various factors might be linked to potential problems or effects. The effects commonly examined are machine, method, material, measurement, time, personnel, energy, and environment. The cause and effect diagram is also known as the *Ishikawa diagram* or *fishbone diagram*.

- **Histogram:** A vertical bar chart with the height of each bar representing the frequency of a particular occurrence. In this way, the histogram can illustrate the most common causes of a process problem.

- **Pareto chart:** A type of histogram, or vertical bar chart, which arranges the causes of the defects or errors in rank order. The Pareto chart is based on *Pareto's Law*, also known as the 80/20 principle, which maintains that 80 percent of the problems are due to 20 percent of the causes. Using a Pareto chart, you can focus on the causes of the greatest number of defects.

- **Process flowchart:** A graphical representation of a process showing activities, decision points, outputs, and sequence. A process flowchart can help you anticipate or troubleshoot quality problems in a process.

Summary

Quality management in a project ensures that the product, service, or other result meets the customer's quality standards, which are typically defined in the requirements document. The customer might ask that you adhere to a specific quality standard or you might create the quality standard definition based on the customer's unique requirements. Likewise, you might follow a quality methodology such as Six Sigma or Continuous Improvement or develop your own processes for meeting the quality standard.

The quality management plan defines your quality standards and how they will be implemented in your project. As part of this plan, you can determine the cost of quality or the cost-benefit analysis for meeting quality requirements. The plan includes details for quality assurance and quality control, ensuring that processes are in place for auditing, measuring, and validating the quality of the project's deliverables throughout the project life cycle.

Coach's Review

Use this section to assess what you've learned in this chapter and to apply it to a real-life project you're currently working on.

Test Your Knowledge

Test your knowledge of the material in this chapter by answering the following questions. See Appendix A for the answers.

1. Name two possible sources of quality specifications.
2. Define quality management.
3. What is the difference between quality assurance and quality control?
4. Name two widely used quality methodologies.
5. List three elements of a project's quality management plan.

Project Challenge

Practice the knowledge you've gained in this chapter with the following challenge. Use the project you're planning as you continue to work through the chapters in this book.

1. In your project workbook, review the project objectives, scope statement, and requirements document you've developed. Find any quality specifications and use those as the basis to create your quality management plan. If necessary, get more details from your project sponsor or customer.
2. If you are expected to adhere to a particular standard and quality methodology, specify the details as part of the quality management plan.
3. Create a cost of quality analysis and include it in your quality management plan.
4. Specify the QA and QC processes for the project.
5. Adjust the work breakdown structure, project schedule, budget, and other planning documents to accommodate the quality management plan.

CHAPTER 10

Setting Up a Communication Plan

You might wonder why you have to *plan* communication. After all, you've been communicating all your life. Unfortunately, communication is the source of many problems and projects are no exception. Are you overwhelmed with emails — and frustrated when you receive emails that have nothing to do with you? Have plans gone awry because someone didn't listen to a voicemail message you left? Or do you sit in a meeting and wish that the person talking would get to the point?

There's always room to improve communication, whether you want to get your point across more effectively or truly listen to what others are saying. This chapter discusses techniques for communicating better, whether you're talking or listening, meeting in person, or communicating via email or some other means.

As a project manager, you spend most of your time communicating with others. You might communicate with the customer, management team, and other stakeholders to gain their concurrence on project objectives. You communicate assignments to team members and receive reports on work status from them in return. Perhaps the sponsor or another stakeholder tells you about an issue that needs to be resolved. And you update everyone involved about the project status — except that the status you provide to team members is a lot different than the status you deliver to the management team.

Communication becomes an especially big job when dozens or even hundreds of people are involved with a large project. If the project team is geographically dispersed around the globe, you can't ask everyone to join you in the conference room or set up a conference call at the last minute.

The success of a project relies on the right people getting the right information at the right time and in an effective way. To do that, you need to plan communication on your project. This chapter describes the components of a communication plan. You'll learn about the audiences that require project information, the information they need to know, and when they need to receive it. This chapter also discusses different methods for communicating and when to use each method.

CROSS-REFERENCE The information in this chapter relates to the PMP Exam's Domain II: Planning the Project, Task 6, "Develop a communication plan based on the project organization structure and external stakeholder requirements, in order to manage the flow of project information."

THE IMPORTANCE OF PROJECT COMMUNICATION

Good communication is crucial to project success, whether you're communicating the goal and objectives of the project so the team understands the purpose of their work or you're recording the results of the project you just completed for the benefit of future teams working on future projects.

Your job as project manager is actually easier when communication works well. Management has the information it needs to make good decisions. Your team members know what they're supposed to do. If there is any confusion, they ask questions so work isn't delayed. In addition, team members accomplish more when they have the information they need or can find it quickly. At the same time, good communication can help reduce errors.

Guidelines for Good Communication

You've probably had more than one conversation in which you thought you made your point crystal clear only to discover that the other person did not understand what you meant. For example, you explain an assignment to one of your team members. But the work he delivers isn't what you asked for. Why do people have so much trouble understanding one another? As long as you're speaking the same language, the problem could be that you aren't communicating effectively.

What Is Communication?

The most important aspect of communication is that it travels in both directions. It isn't enough that you send a message. The recipient of your message has to receive it *and* understand it. Here is a breakdown of the steps in a successful communication process:

1. **Transmit the message.** You transmit information to a recipient whether you send an email, call someone on the telephone, speak to them in person, or even frown without saying a word.

2. **Receive the message.** However, just because you send a message, the recipient doesn't necessarily receive it. Have you ever deleted a voicemail without listening to the whole message? Recipients might do the same thing and delete a voicemail or email without listening to or reading the entire message. Or they might do something else while they listen or read, in which case the message gets lost in the distraction. In addition, people might psychologically block out information they don't want to hear. Although you can't guarantee that your recipients will receive your message, you can design your messages to increase your chance of success.

3. **Understand the message.** Even if the message is received, the recipient might not understand it. With so many meanings for certain words, it's a wonder that we understand any messages at all. Understanding requires a variety of skills. The recipient of a message might have to process context, body language, sarcasm, irony, unspoken details, vaguely worded or convoluted messages, and more. In addition, some concepts, like quantum physics, earned value, or how a teenager's psyche works, take some brainpower to digest. You can improve the probability of understanding by encouraging a two-way conversation. Make a point of listening (or help the recipients do the same) and ask questions to clarify information that isn't clear. The section "The Importance of Listening" later in this chapter provides some guidelines for listening effectively.

4. **Reach agreement.** In many situations, you communicate in order to obtain a result. For example, you might ask the management team for additional funds or a resource manager for a specific resource. When you're trying to obtain agreement, you must help the recipient see your perspective. You might have to move your communication up to a higher level to negotiate with your audience.

5. **Take action.** Reaching agreement isn't necessarily the last step in successful communication. If you communicate because you need something to happen — funds released to your project or a resource assigned to your team, for example — the communication isn't successful until the action has been completed or everyone agrees on an alternative solution. You must also communicate in such a way that the responsible parties know that they're responsible, understand what they're supposed to do, and follow through.

How to Get Your Message Across

Communication is a two-way street. However, the person sending a message is responsible for making sure it gets communicated successfully. Here are some techniques you can use to help a message get through:

- **Understand your audience.** One key to good communication is understanding what your audience cares about. Once you know that, you can tell your audience why the message you're sending is important and also motivate them to take action, if that's your goal. Suppose you plan to ask your team members to put in extra effort to get an important task back on track. The team members care about doing a good job. They don't want to get sucked into a drawn-out struggle with long hours. In your message, explain how your request will help them deliver what the project needs and also describe your plan for completing the work without superhuman effort.

- **Get to the point.** Newspaper reporters make sure to put the most important information in the first few sentences of an article. Your messages will be more successful if you follow that model because you can't assume that people will read or listen to your entire message. Include the key points at the beginning of the message, including action that you want the recipient to take. Take the time to make your message brief while still including all the pertinent information. (Keep in mind that it takes more time to prepare a short informative message than it does a long one.)

- **Be clear and accurate.** Spend time making sure your message is both clear and accurate. Double-check that you are clearly communicating your information. For example, don't say "I need this by the end of the day." You might mean by 5 p.m., but your team member thinks she has until midnight. For significant messages, consider asking others to review your message. They might point out areas that are confusing or can be interpreted in different ways. Check your facts to ensure that the information is accurate.

- **Be engaging and persuasive.** Present your message to keep your audience's attention. If you don't, your information falls on deaf ears. A long presentation of dry statistics is certain to make all but the diehard mathematicians tune out. Instead, summarize the significance of the numbers and follow up with the detail for people who need to study the information more closely. For example, say something like, "The tasks on the critical path are on schedule because we have reassigned key resources to the critical path. We are monitoring noncritical tasks as well and will take action if they threaten the project finish date."

■ **Confirm the transmission.** Make sure that your message is received and understood. If you don't receive a response to a request, follow up with another transmission, preferably using a different communication channel. For example, if you sent an email, follow up with a phone call. After you know the message was received, ask questions or paraphrase someone else's message to make sure that both sides understand the information.

THE CANDID COACH: BALANCING POSITIVE AND NEGATIVE

Highlighting project and individual successes is a great way to motivate team members and assuage any concerns your audiences might have. However, putting a positive spin on every message can backfire, as team members and management alike begin to wonder if you are telling the whole story. Going too far in the other direction has its pitfalls. No one wants to listen to whining or a litany of problems with no sign of solutions. Like good journalism, a balanced perspective is the best approach.

When you need to communicate less than positive information to individuals, such as team members who have made mistakes, be direct yet diplomatic. Explain what you need them to do to improve. For example, "This software module came back from testing with a lot of bugs. I need you to test your code more before you turn it over to the integration and testing teams." If other team members start to play the blaming game, help them focus on the issue rather than the person.

Delivering bad news to a management team doesn't make it to anyone's top-ten list of favorite experiences. For that reason, many project managers try to put the information they present to management in a positive light. "Well, yes, there was an explosion in the lab and the building has collapsed . . . but everyone got out safely, only one car was crushed by debris, and our insurance will cover all the damage!"

If a project runs into significant problems, inform the customer, sponsor, and any management stakeholders who may be affected. You can ease the tension by explaining what you plan to do to resolve the situation and ask the stakeholders for assistance if you need it. Management might not be happy to receive bad news, but they would rather hear about it early enough to do something than get the news when there's no time to recover.

In addition, provide your management stakeholders with the truth — the whole truth. Perhaps a problem has come up, but you think you can handle it on your own. Tell the management team about the problem and what you're planning to do. If your plan for resolution doesn't pan out, you can escalate the issue to management. Because they've already heard about the problem, they are less likely to overreact to surprise bad news.

The Importance of Listening

Communication is a two-way street, so listening is just as important as sending the right message. Your ears might hear that someone is speaking, but that doesn't guarantee that the words reach your brain. Here are a few techniques for being a better listener:

- **Keep an open mind.** If you have already made up your mind about a topic, a discussion about it simply wastes the time of everyone participating. Instead, listen to what others have to say before you form an opinion or make a decision.

- **Focus your full attention on the speaker.** As a project manager, you have to juggle several tasks at once. When you listen, you must drop the multitasking and focus on the person or people speaking. A quiet location without distractions can help. Don't forget to switch your mobile phone to the silent mode.

TIP If you're talking to someone and she turns her attention to something else, try stating that you're going to get back to your work and suggest rescheduling the meeting or conversation to a better time. If the person returns her attention to you, finish the interaction. If she doesn't, you can resume the communication later.

- **"Listen" to body language and facial expressions.** The majority of information is communicated nonverbally through facial expressions and body language. In addition to listening to what someone says, pay attention to how they say it and whether body language sends conflicting signals.

TIP Because so much of communication comes through nonverbal channels, you must pay extra attention to telephone calls and email messages. When you can't see the other person or people, be sure to ask questions to make sure you understand the message.

- **Paraphrase the message.** To make sure that you listened successfully and understand the message, recast what the other person said in your own words and ask for confirmation that you understood what he or she was trying to say.

The Components of a Communication Plan

To make sure that communication works well on a project, you need to set up a structure for it. But communicating is a complex endeavor, so a communication plan must take into account your work environment, your organization's culture, and the standard and expectations that people have. There is also a technical aspect to communication: the technology and tools you use to interact with others.

A communication plan includes several components, which you can summarize in a table as shown in Figure 10-1. Each of these components is covered in detail in later sections:

- **Audiences:** Different groups involved with a project, such as the sponsor, stakeholders, and team members, need different information, often delivered in different ways. A communication plan identifies each audience, although you can call each audience by the name that makes the most sense to you.

- **Content:** Describe the information that each audience needs, such as high-level status and significant issues that you present to stakeholders audience, or details about accomplishments and progress that your team members send to you, the project manager.

- **Method or channel:** Today, you can choose from numerous methods and channels for communicating, including in-person meetings, videoconferencing, telephone, email, and written documents. Each approach has its pros and cons, so it's important to match the method to the message.

- **Schedule:** Some communication is ad hoc, such as questions that arise or sending a notification about a serious problem that just occurred. However, much of the communication on a project occurs on a regular schedule. For example, you might request status from your team members every Friday afternoon, whereas you meet with stakeholders to review progress every other week at 9 a.m. Monday morning.

- **Responsible party:** As project manager, you are responsible for managing communication. Fortunately, you aren't directly responsible for every type of communication that occurs. Part of the communication plan is specifying who is responsible for sending communication to your audiences. For example, if you designate team members to monitor risks or track change requests, those individuals are responsible for communicating information about those aspects of the project to you and possibly to the management team.

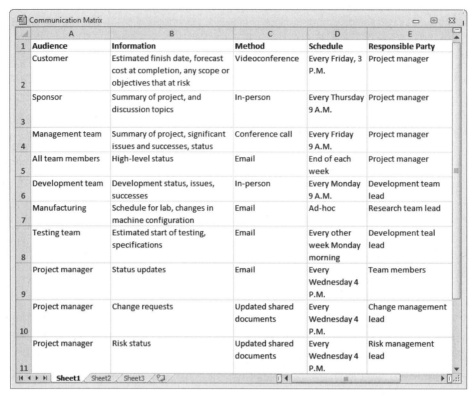

	A	B	C	D	E
1	**Audience**	**Information**	**Method**	**Schedule**	**Responsible Party**
2	Customer	Estimated finish date, forecast cost at completion, any scope or objectives that at risk	Videoconference	Every Friday, 3 P.M.	Project manager
3	Sponsor	Summary of project, and discussion topics	In-person	Every Thursday 9 A.M.	Project manager
4	Management team	Summary of project, significant issues and successes, status	Conference call	Every Friday 9 A.M.	Project manager
5	All team members	High-level status	Email	End of each week	Project manager
6	Development team	Development status, issues, successes	In-person	Every Monday 9 A.M.	Development team lead
7	Manufacturing	Schedule for lab, changes in machine configuration	Email	Ad-hoc	Research team lead
8	Testing team	Estimated start of testing, specifications	Email	Every other week Monday morning	Development teal lead
9	Project manager	Status updates	Email	Every Wednesday 4 P.M.	Team members
10	Project manager	Change requests	Updated shared documents	Every Wednesday 4 P.M.	Change management lead
11	Project manager	Risk status	Updated shared documents	Every Wednesday 4 P.M.	Risk management lead

Figure 10-1: A communication matrix summarizes the communication plan for a project.

Who Are the Audiences?

A significant part of managing a project is making sure that people involved with the project get the information they need. The audiences for information span the project food chain from the customer and sponsor to the management team and key stakeholders to team members assigned to perform work. Information about your project is important to people outside the project organization, such as vendors you hire or project managers in charge of projects that share your resources. This section describes the typical audiences for project information that you include in your communication plan.

CROSS-REFERENCE Each audience with which you communicate represents some subset of your project stakeholders, but, in the end, you communicate with all your stakeholders in some way. The section "Identifying the Project Stakeholders" in Chapter 3 describes various groups and individuals who represent stakeholders for you project. As you identify these stakeholders, you can ask them to suggest others who need information about your project.

The Project Sponsor

Similar to sponsors for events, project sponsors are individuals or groups who provide the resources that make projects possible. For that reason, a project sponsor is deeply involved with the project, more so than any other stakeholder. (If the sponsor isn't involved, you, as project manager, face an uphill struggle.) A good relationship with the project sponsor can make your job much easier and effective communication gets that relationship off to a good start.

Because project sponsors foot the bill, your best bet is to give them what they want. Start by asking what information they want, when they want it, and the method that's most convenient for them. In addition, as the project proceeds, don't be shy about communicating information that's important to the sponsor — for example, an issue that might negatively affect the project if it isn't resolved quickly.

Management Stakeholders

Management stakeholders might be the top-level management of departments involved in a project, such as software development, manufacturing, and technical support. A leadership team, functional managers who provide resources to your project, and the members of your change review board are other examples of management stakeholders.

As you will learn in the section "Information for Management Stakeholders" later in this chapter, your management audiences generally want summary-level information. They don't care to know about the squabble that broke out between the developers and the testers. However, if you ask for their help with a significant issue or request funds from the management reserve, they are bound to ask for more detail.

Team Members

The members of your project team work on project assignments every day. Communication with your team is frequent and regularly goes both ways. You need to tell team members what's going on and what they are supposed to work on. But they also tell you about the progress they're making, issues, problems, successes, and other details.

External Audiences

In addition to your project team and the stakeholders directly involved in your project, external audiences may need information, too. For example, third-party vendors and suppliers need to know when you need their deliverables or whether there has been a delay that affects their portion of the project. Project managers for other projects in your organization might need to know the status of your project if the projects share resources.

External audiences don't get as much information as your internal audiences. For example, if your project must report to a regulatory agency, you deliver the information the agency requests in the specified format and on the agency's schedule.

You might work with supporting groups that pitch in every so often. For example, the legal department steps in when you need contracts prepared or help with legal issues.

TIP When in doubt, send information to a broader audience. Then, provide individuals with the ability to opt out of receiving specific categories of communication. If you allow people to opt out of receiving communication, make sure they understand that they also opt out of participating in making decisions about the information in those messages.

What Do You Communicate?

For the audiences you've identified, the next step to planning communication is determining what your audiences *need* to know. For example, the team members on your project might not ask about the problem statement or project objectives, but that information can help them make the right decisions in their day-to-day work on the project. You can also find out what audiences *want* to know. If you have the authority to do so, providing that information can enhance your relationships with others.

What Information Do Audiences Need?

Different audiences need different information. Management doesn't want detail, unless it has to step in to make decisions or resolve issues. With the team members who perform project tasks, detailed information is sent in both directions.

A good approach for determining the information to provide is to ask your audiences what information they want to receive. From there, you can include additional information that you know is important to those audiences, even if they didn't ask for it.

Information for Management Stakeholders

The project customer, sponsor, and other management-level stakeholders need information throughout the life of a project from the initial goals, objectives, and constraints to project status and performance once it's underway.

Management stakeholders review high-level summaries, unless a decision or problem requires their attention. Then, they won't be bashful about asking for the details they want.

The following list provides some examples of information that management stakeholders provide and what they usually want to receive:

- **Project definition and plan:** The project sponsor and other management stakeholders play a large part in the project definition. They provide input on the problem statement, project goal, and objectives. They provide feedback on the possible strategies and other components of the project definition and plan. Eventually, they review documents you prepare (a project definition and then a project plan) so they can decide whether to approve the project to proceed.

- **Status:** Management stakeholders want to know about high-level accomplishments, such as major milestones that are complete. See "Status Reporting" for guidelines on information to include in status reports.

- **Performance:** Performance, such as whether the project will deliver its objectives on time and within budget, is one of the measures of project success that you can see while the project is in progress. Management stakeholders want the current values for whatever metrics you use to measure performance, whether it's the return on investment or number of defects outstanding. If a project is recovering from problems, they probably want to see performance trends, such as whether budget overruns are decreasing as the project proceeds.

- **Risks and issues:** As you learn in the section "Setting Up Contingency Funds" in Chapter 12, part of risk management is setting aside reserves of money and time to handle some of the risks that come to fruition on a project. Management stakeholders want to hear about the status of the project risks you track, whether any might turn into real issues, and how risk responses that you've implemented are performing. If significant issues threaten the project from achieving its objectives, you can be sure that management wants to know.

- **Change requests:** The change review board usually includes management stakeholders. The change review board needs information about change requests that have been submitted and/or evaluated. Chapter 11, "Setting Up a Change Management Plan," describes in detail the role of the change review board and the information that flows through the process.

Functional Managers

If you obtain resources in-house, you communicate with the functional managers who manage those resources. Here is the information functional managers typically need:

- **Resource requirements:** During planning, you distribute work packages with information about the skills the work requires and constraints such as cost. Once the schedule is built, you let functional managers know when you need members of their staff.

- **Assignment status:** Once project work is in progress, functional managers need to know how their people are performing. They also need to know when the people assigned to your project will finish their assignments and be available for other work.

Team Members

When team members join your project, the first thing they need to know is how you plan to run the project. (As you learn in Chapter 13, a kickoff meeting is a great opportunity for publicizing the project processes.) Team members also need to know what work they are supposed to do and how it fits into the overall project. That way, you empower them to make decisions about their work that support the project goal and objectives.

As work progresses, you need to communicate assignments to team members along with status about work that's been completed. In turn, team members report their progress to you, as you learn in the next section, "Status Reporting."

Status Reporting

Face it. A lot of information about progress and status flies around during a project's lifetime. Team members send status reports to you, the project manager. You summarize that information, gather additional project info, and send status reports back to the team members, project sponsor, stakeholders, and perhaps external audiences.

Status reports come in different forms and contain different information depending on the audience. Because of the volume of status reporting, it's important to automate this type of communication as much as possible. Use all the technology at your disposal to make it easy for team members to submit their status. Then, as you learn in the section "What's the Best Communication Method?" later in this chapter, you need to send status reports in a way that makes it easy for audiences to read and digest the information.

Status from and to Team Members

Status from your team members is the beginning of the food chain for status reporting. The people working on project tasks provide the progress they've made on assignments, estimates of the work to come, and other relevant tidbits, such as issues and lessons learned.

To get a complete picture of progress, you need actual dates and actual hours completed for the tasks team members are working on. For tasks that aren't complete, you also need your team members' forecasts for the hours remaining and the completion date. If your organization uses a project management application, you might find a built-in time reporting form that you can use. In that situation, team members fill out the form and the data they submit is automatically incorporated into your project database. If that isn't an option, another approach is to set up a spreadsheet for team members to fill in, as shown in Figure 10-2.

144244 F1002.xlsx

	A	B	C	D	E	F	G	H	I	J
1	Team Member:	Julia	Time Period:	5/5/12 - 5/11/12						
2			Scheduled Start	Scheduled Hours	Scheduled Finish	Actual Start	Hours Prior to This Period	Hours This Period	Est. Remaining Hours	Est. Finish Date
3	Assigned Tasks:	Task 1	5/2	40	5/8	5/4	8	24	8	5/15
4		Task 2	5/8	8	5/11	5/2	0	8	0	
5		Task 3	5/10	40	5/18	5/10	0	8	24	5/18
6										
7										
8										
9										

Sheet1   Sheet2   Sheet3

Figure 10-2: An example of a worksheet for reporting task progress.

TIP Simplifying progress reporting is essential. However, the level of stream-lining you can provide depends on the tools that are available. For example, if you use a spreadsheet template and know your way around program macros, you might be able to produce customized spreadsheets for each team member with the tasks they have assigned and existing values from your project management program. Then, you can import the data you receive into your project file.

The box "Reality Check: Collecting Project Time" in Chapter 17 discusses the challenges of collecting project time using your organization's time tracking system.

In addition to task progress, you also need to know more about how things are going. If issues or obstacles are slowing work down, you need to know about them so you can help your team if necessary. If someone resolved an issue successfully, that information might help others in the future. Gather lessons learned from team members. That way, everyone on the team can take advantage of effective techniques or stay away from approaches that don't work.

Depending on the size of your project, you might use different communication channels for obtaining status from your team members. For a small project, a face-to-face meeting might be the quickest and most effective way to obtain and distribute status among team members. When a project team is made up of hundreds of people, you might plan for different channels at different levels of the reporting structure. For example, team leads might meet with their team members face to face and then send you a team status report. You, in turn, might meet with the team leads to discuss some of the items on the reports.

CROSS-REFERENCE Sometimes, lessons learned are difficult to obtain. Team members might be uncomfortable talking about their failures as well as their successes. The section "Gathering Lessons Learned" in Chapter 22 provides tips for gathering lessons learned.

Information doesn't flow solely from team members to you. They need to know what's going on with the project, albeit at a different level of detail than the management team does. After you collate the status data that team members submit, you distribute project status reports to them. These reports include more detailed information than the status reports you prepare for management. Depending on the size of your project team, you might prepare a single status report for team members or you might prepare a status report for team leads who then communicate information to the members in their groups.

Here is the information you might distribute to team members:

- **Decisions:** Communicate decisions (or changes) that have been made that affect the project. For example, if the management team has decided to eliminate items from the project scope, you need to pass that information on to team members so they don't work on those assignments.

- **Kudos:** Share positive feedback with your team members.

- **Issues:** Distribute information about issues that might affect team members, including solutions that have been proposed and solutions that resolved issues. For example, one team member might encounter an obstacle. Another team member sees the issue in the status report and sends you the solution he used to resolve the problem.

- **Lessons learned:** Everyone on the project team can benefit from lessons that other team members have learned. The section "Documenting Lessons Learned" in Chapter 22 describes methods for archiving lessons learned so they can be easily retrieved and reused in the future.

- **Assignment status:** Team members already know where their assignments stand. However, they also need to know about the status for related tasks and how their assignments fit in. For example, it can be very motivating to see how a delayed task affects the work of other team members and the progress for the entire project.

HOLDING STATUS MEETINGS WITH TEAM MEMBERS

Status meetings can take up a lot of team time — time that you would probably rather have your team members spend on assignments. However, status meetings are preferable to reports when your team members need to work together to resolve issues, make decisions, or coordinate the work that each person should do. In addition, status meetings can help team members establish relationships with one another, if individuals don't collaborate otherwise.

Use a status meeting to discuss smaller issues and brainstorm solutions. (For larger issues that require significant discussion or don't require the entire team, set up a separate meeting.) A status meeting can be a convenient time to share lessons learned so that every team member can benefit from what others have learned.

Status for Management

The project customer, sponsor, and other management stakeholders want to know the progress that's been made on your project and what to expect from it in the future. The status that you provide to management might determine whether your project receives kudos, extra scrutiny, or even continued funding. Like other information you communicate to management, status needs to be clear and succinct.

Here are status items that most management teams want to see:

- **Summary:** Start with a summary of the project. For example: "The project is on schedule and 5 percent over budget. Two identified risks have occurred and we are tracking the results of the risk responses, which seem to be working. Change requests have been minor." If you distribute a status report, managers can decide whether they want to read the entire report. For a status meeting, they can determine what questions they want to ask.

- **Review of cost and schedule:** Provide a slightly more detailed description of the project cost and schedule. Include the budgeted and actual costs and planned and actual dates. Explain significant variances, such as those greater than 10 percent.

- **Accomplishments:** For management audiences, include only major accomplishments and project activities. Typically, this list should include no more than six items.

- **Significant risks and issues:** Include only the risks and issues that require management decisions or actions. Describe the efforts and results of the risk management plan: risks that became issues, the progress on responses, and the results of risk management. Ask for any management assistance that you need. Identify issues that have been resolved.

- **Lessons learned:** Share significant lessons learned that management can use to make better decisions in the future.

What's the Best Communication Method?

A communication plan also identifies the communication methods or channels you plan to use. The best channel is the one that accomplishes the goal of communication with the least amount of effort. Each method has its advantages and disadvantages, so it's important to match your messages with the right communication method. For example, face-to-face communication works well when you need to discuss issues with others or you want to receive information people are sending through body language. This section describes different methods of communication and the pros and cons of each.

In-Person Meetings

Meeting face to face is usually the most effective way to communicate. Meetings are interactive. One person presents information and the others in the meeting can immediately provide feedback or ask questions if they don't understand.

The real power of a meeting is that the people present can see one another's reactions, both in body language and facial expressions. Because meetings enable back-and-forth communication, they're ideal for discussions, collaborative decision making, and brainstorming. The downside to in-person meetings is that they aren't always possible; for instance, when your team is dispersed between different locations or even continents.

CROSS-REFERENCE To learn how to hold effective meetings, see the section "Running Effective Meetings" in Chapter 15.

Videoconferencing and Conference Calls

Videoconferencing and conference calls are an alternative when you need an interactive discussion but people aren't in the same location. Although they provide interaction between participants, they aren't as effective as face-to-face meetings.

Technology has reduced the cost of videoconferencing so it is often a viable alternative. For example, you can use software products or web-based services, such as GoToMeeting, Adobe Connect, WebEx, or Microsoft Office 365. These services enable you to see one another or share presentations online. Keep in mind that videoconferencing isn't as smooth or seamless as meeting face to face. Cameras don't always capture the entire scene. People move out of view or don't act naturally because they are on camera.

Teleconferencing does not provide the visual component that face-to-face meetings and videoconferencing do. However, with conference calls, participants can hear the intonations in speakers' voices. Conference calls enable interactive discussions up to a point. Similar to in-person meetings, discussion works only if a limited number of people speak or you use rules to facilitate when individual participants can speak.

NOTE In-person meetings, videoconferencing, and conference calls can also provide one-way communication when it's important for the audience to see or hear the person speaking, for example, if the project sponsor delivers a motivational message to the entire team.

Email

Email has grown to be one of the most popular methods of communicating. You can send messages at any time of the day or night. Your recipients can read the messages when they're awake and have time. In fact, email at least partially overcomes time zone challenges for global teams. In addition, many people would rather communicate via email than by telephone or in person.

However, email has several disadvantages. The volume of email that people receive is almost always overwhelming. And email transmission can fail in a variety of ways. Rather than dashing off emails without thinking, you need to pay as much attention to email communication as you do other methods. Here are some guidelines for using email effectively:

- **Use meaningful subject lines.** How do recipients determine which emails require their immediate attention, which ones can wait, and even whether an email is something they need to look at? Subject lines are the first thing recipients see. By putting the meat of your message there, you can help your team members get through their Inboxes more efficiently. In fact, some email messages can stop right at the subject line, for example, "Provide feedback on this change request by 2PM Wednesday the 17th."

   In addition, if the topic changes in the middle of an email thread, change the subject line. If you don't, messages are difficult to find later on because you must read the body of the messages instead of just the subject.

TIP For emails that include information only and don't require action, include an identifier in the subject line, such as "Info only:" That way, recipients can filter these emails into a different folder to read at their convenience.

- **Start with the most important information.** Many recipients manage the flood of email by reading the first few lines of a message to decide whether they need to continue. If you begin email messages with wandering explanations rather than the point of the communication, your readers might not reach the significant information that you sent. Draft email messages the way newspaper reporters write articles. Stuff all the crucial information in the first few sentences and fill in the detail later.

- **Make your point quickly and clearly.** This approach applies to all forms of communication, but it's especially important with email. Making your point quickly is similar to starting with the most important information, except that it applies to the entire message. Many team members think of email as more informal than other types of written communication so they write without thinking. The result is often a long, disorganized, and unclear message, which exacerbates the problem of too much email because these messages take so long to read and digest. In addition, a confusing message launches a string of emails with questions, answers, more questions, more answers, and so on. These exchanges become torture if recipients reply to everyone in the "To" list.

- **Avoid humor.** Unless you know your recipients very well, keep humor out of your messages. Readers can't see your body language or facial expressions and can't hear the intonation of your voice. Without those cues, they might misconstrue your humor as something less pleasant.

- **Don't assume your email reached its destination.** Email gets caught in spam filters and bounces off unresponsive servers, or your recipients might delete them by mistake. If you don't receive a response by the time you requested, follow up with another message. You can try another email message, but it might fall into the same trap as the first one, so consider a phone call or a face-to-face visit, if that's feasible.

- **Stick to a schedule for responding to email:** Let your team members know your time frame for responding to emails so they know when they can expect a reply. If you won't be able to respond in that time frame, due to travel or other exceptions, notify your team members of that, too.

Telephone

If the person you're calling actually answers the phone, you can have a two-way conversation, which means you can exchange ideas, discuss issues, and get feedback. You also obtain additional information through the other person's tone of voice.

However, telephone calls are no longer the sure-fire interactive communication channel that they used to be. With so many calls going straight to voicemail, your telephone calls might be a one-way channel. In that situation, follow the same guidelines for the voicemail messages you leave as you do for emails. Keep in mind that some voicemail systems limit the length of messages. In addition, people are less patient listening to voicemail messages than when scanning an email message, so be sure to make your point right away and keep the message short.

Written Documentation

Documents, whether printed or stored in electronic format, are the best communication channel for large amounts of information or complex information that requires time to review and study. Documents are also an effective format when you work and communicate with team members in other locations.

One way to deliver written information is by *pushing* it to your audiences, that is, emailing it or delivering a hardcopy to the recipients. If the audience is very large, you can cut down on postage costs and unclog your email system by using a *pull* method, in which you store documents in a shared location. The team members who need or are interested in the information can access the documents when they need them.

NOTE If you distribute documents electronically, be sure to use software formats that everyone in your audience can open. For example, some team members might use older versions of programs or might not have project management software to open your project schedule. Consider saving documents intended for a wide audience in a commonly used format such as portable document format (.pdf).

Who's Responsible?

As you identify different types of communication in the project communication plan, you also document who is responsible for each type. For example, members of small teams might send status to their team leads or attend status meetings; the team leads then send status to the project manager; the project manager holds status meetings with the management team and perhaps a separate meeting with the project sponsor. In addition, you might hold meetings to discuss issues or lessons learned.

Frequency and Timing

How often communication occurs and when information arrives are both important to the success of communication. For that reason, the communication plan also spells out the frequency and timing of project communication.

The frequency depends on factors such as the length of the project, the typical duration of project tasks, or whether the project is in trouble. For example, status reports scheduled every two weeks won't work well on a project that's only a month long. On the other hand, daily meetings would chew through excessive amounts of team members' time if the project is scheduled for four years and tasks run for weeks at a time.

At the same time, the project customer or sponsor might ask for more frequent updates if the project is in trouble. They want to see whether your plans to get the project back on track are paying off.

When people receive information does matter. Perhaps you've received an invitation to an event so far in advance that you forgot about it by the time it occurred. Or you received coupons from the store the day after the sale ended. Information needs to arrive when your audiences need it.

With technology that's available, you can easily set up reminders to send information, whether it's one-time communication or a status report that goes out regularly. You can even set up distribution lists to simplify the distribution of information to the right people.

Summary

Projects are performed by groups of people working together, so, naturally, communication is an important part of project success. However, the communication that occurs isn't always as effective as it could be. The breakdown can occur in several places. You can improve your communication with others by making sure that the messages you send reach their destination and that the audiences you communicate with understand what you're saying. Follow-through is especially important when you want people to take action.

When a project team is large, you need to plan communication so information gets to the right people when they need it. The communication plan maps out the communication that will occur on your project: who needs information, what information they need, how the information is transmitted, who sends it, and how often.

Coach's Review

Use this section to assess what you've learned in this chapter and to apply it to a real-life project you're currently working on.

Test Your Knowledge

Test your knowledge of the material in this chapter by answering the following questions. See Appendix A for the answers.

1. What three things are a minimum for successful communication?
2. How can you determine whether you understand what someone else is saying?
3. What aspects of communication does the communication plan address?
4. Why are meetings the best communication method for topics that require interaction?

Project Challenge

Set up a worksheet similar to the one in Figure 10-1. With a project that you're working on or one you've worked on in the past in mind, identify the different types of communication that occur. For each type, fill in all the fields based on how that communication was accomplished.

Now that the matrix is filled in, review the communication plan and identify any changes you would make to the audiences, information, methods, sender, and schedule. Describe why and how each of those changes would improve project communication.

Finally, based on the technology that's available in your organization, list several features you can use to simplify communication on your project.

Setting Up a Change Management Plan

In the good old days, you could race up to your airplane gate at the last minute, your suitcase weighted with clothes and personal products like shampoo and nail files. Over time, airport security added rules to keep us safe: what you can bring on board, the quantity and how it's packaged, and how long before the flight you can check your bag. Now, you spend hours longer than you used to and spend more on luggage fees. And what was once a simple, straightforward goal is now a complicated burden.

Change requests for a project are a lot like that. As the requests come in, they seem to make sense and seem doable. But then, at some point, you find your schedule longer, your costs higher, and your objectives almost impossible to achieve.

However, change is a fact of life. You can't say no to every change that's requested. Someone forgot a requirement that's important to your project. Or a team member comes up with a new design that makes the final product easier to use. If changes make sense, you want them to become part of your project. At the same time, you don't want the project overwhelmed with changes that aren't of value.

You don't know everything you need to know at the beginning of a project. A change management process accommodates that reality. It helps you include the changes you want and block the ones that don't make sense. It provides a way for people to submit change requests. Team members evaluate the requests and a change review board decides which ones to add to your project. The change requests become additional work for the project that you track as you would the tasks in your original plan.

This chapter begins with a discussion of when you do manage changes and when you don't. It identifies the people who are likely to belong to the change review board. And it describes the steps in a simple change management process.

CROSS-REFERENCE The information in this chapter relates to the PMP Exam's Domain II: Planning the Project, Task 9, "Develop a change management plan by defining how changes will be handled in order to track and manage changes."

When to Manage Changes

Change isn't necessarily bad. There are times when you want changes, such as when you're initially identifying requirements or coming up with alternative designs. But at some point, that free-flowing brainstorming has to slow down or you'll never see the end of your project. Managing changes becomes an important part of project success. Change management isn't a project lockdown against changes. The idea is to assess the changes that are asked for and make conscious decisions about whether to incorporate them into your project.

When You Don't Manage Changes

Change management isn't always required or even possible. Sometimes, the best results come from the free exchange of ideas. At the same time, you can manage change only if you can identify what changes are. Here are two situations in which you don't manage changes:

- **You are exploring alternatives.** Early on in a project, you identify alternative strategies to help find the best solution. When it comes to design, the results are often better when people are free to explore alternatives. Brainstorming sessions help identify solutions to issues or problems and help promote creativity and innovation. When people are in the groove, you don't want anything to get in the way of this creativity. If your project requires this type of work, give people time to explore. However, once designs, solutions, or results from other brainstorming sessions are signed off on by stakeholders, it's time to move them under change management.

- **You don't have a baseline to compare to.** When you're working on a first draft of your project plan or another type of deliverable, you don't track and manage every change you make. All your additions, modifications, and deletions are part of your creative process.

In fact, you don't manage changes until you have a baseline document, that is, a document or deliverable that stakeholders have approved, such as requirements, specifications, or your project plan.

For example, stakeholders might review your draft project plan and ask you to shorten the schedule. You go back and rework your plan and then submit it to them again. Although you might use a program's Track Changes feature to show the edits in the new version, you don't have to follow the steps in your change management process because the plan isn't yet approved.

TIP Suppose your project is informal and you don't have an official set of objectives or requirements to work toward. You don't have baseline documents to compare to, so you don't have to follow a change management process. This laissez-faire approach might work on a small project with a close-knit team. However, if you find that you're spending lots of time putting out fires or soothing the customer about delayed dates, it's time to introduce some type of change management.

When You Do Manage Changes

Once stakeholders approve documents or deliverables, they go under the control of your change management process. Those approved items are called your baseline documents and you control changes made to them. That way, you make conscious decisions about which changes you make and track the effect the changes have on your project. For example, if you baseline the requirements for your project, you can decide whether to add new requirements. If you add them, you do so knowing the effect they will have on your plan. And you also track them so you're aware of the end results. Without a baseline, your project could take longer or cost more and you're left to wonder why.

NOTE The good news is that people often take change management more seriously as the end of the project approaches. That's because changes made near the end are riskier. For example, a change can affect work that's already complete, triggering an avalanche of other changes. Or a change can take more time or money than estimated and there are fewer options for correcting the issue when you're closer to the project end.

Who Sits on a Change Review Board

Change requests can originate from anyone from the project customer to someone working on a project task. On the other hand, the change review board is the primary group that decides whether or not change requests become a part of your project. A change review board is typically made up of key project stakeholders, including:

- **The project customer:** Although the project customer often asks for all sorts of changes, the customer's representatives on the review board have the largest influence on whether changes are approved. The customer is in control of the project's goal, objectives, scope, and budget, all of which can be affected by changes that are requested.

- **The executive team:** Your management team has a lot of say about changes that affect your organization, such as the addition of more resources or contingency funds.

- **Representatives from groups involved in the project:** Groups involved in your project are particularly helpful for determining whether change requests are risky or affect other aspects of your project.

- **Team leads:** Team leads use their in-depth knowledge of project work and resources to determine the impact of change requests.

- **The project manager:** It's no surprise that the person who probably knows the most about the project is a member of the group that makes decisions about change requests. As project manager, you help with decisions by providing the board with opinions and an insider's insight.

The Anatomy of a Change Management Process

Change management doesn't have to be a complex, convoluted process. In fact, the ideal approach controls changes without tying them up in red tape. Basically, change management boils down to six steps, which are described in detail in the following sections:

1. Define the baseline documents
2. Document change requests
3. Evaluate change requests
4. Make decisions about change requests
5. Update your baseline documents
6. Monitor change requests

TIP Depending on the size and complexity of your project, your change management process could include fewer or additional steps. For example, if change requests require a great deal of time just to evaluate them, you might submit them to the change review board to approve the evaluation step.

Defining the Baseline Documents

The first thing you need to manage change is the baseline documents you're going to control. Baseline documents are items that stakeholders approve, so they may be documents, such as requirements or specifications, spreadsheets, or your project schedule. For example, you work on your project plan without change management until the stakeholders sign off on it (described in the section "Obtaining Approval" in Chapter 13). After that, every component of your project plan — scope, requirements, deliverables, schedule, procedures, and so on — goes under change management. Similarly, when the customer and other stakeholders approve a design later in the project, that design becomes a baseline document.

In some cases, you designate a specific version of a document as your baseline. For example, suppose the stakeholders asked for several rounds of changes before they approved your project plan. You kept copies of each revision just in case the stakeholders decided to go back to an earlier version. When they approve version 3 of the plan, that's the one that becomes your baseline.

WARNING It's important that everyone understands the change management process and how it helps. If they don't, changes could go unmanaged and under the radar. People might have the best of intentions. For example, a customer with a great idea talks to a well-meaning project team lead, who agrees to a small change. Everything looks great initially, but over time, these requests grow into weeds that drain resources from your project.

Documenting a Change Request

After you put items under change management, you begin the ongoing task of processing change requests that come in. The first step when someone submits a new change request is to make sure that the request has all the information you need and that what's being requested is clear.

Using a Change Request Form

A standard change request form, like the example shown in Figure 11-1, is a great way to get a change request off on the right foot. People submitting change requests have a better idea of the information they have to provide. People assigned to analyze change requests understand the request without having to ask a lot of questions. And the change review board gets the information it needs to make a decision.

Change Request

Project:
Project manager:
Submitted by:
Date submitted:

Submitter fills in:
Business justification:

Connection to project goal and objectives:

Description of change, design, and deliverables:

Project manager fills in:
Change request number:
Evaluation:
Estimate:

Hours	Cost	Duration	Effect on project

Recommendation and analysis:

Approved	Denied

Signature: _____   Date: _____

Print name: _____

Figure 11-1: A sample change request form

A change request doesn't have to be a long document. One or two pages are enough. The information you need from the requester includes:

- **The business justification:** This is the reason the change is needed. For example, the training course doesn't cover two topics on the corresponding certification exam, which will significantly affect students' satisfaction with the course and, therefore, the course's ongoing sales.

- **The relationship of the change to the project goal and objectives:** This relationship helps you prioritize the change. If you end up with more changes than you can handle, changes that relate to more significant objectives can get a higher priority. If the training course is intended to be a preparation for taking the certification exam, the change is connected directly to the project goal.

- **A description of the change request and the deliverables:** The requester describes the change and the results. The description provides detail that helps with analysis. For example, the change request identifies the missing topics and the corresponding certification exam objectives.

- **A description of the effect on project risk:** The requester can describe the effect that the change request has on risks in your project. Changes might increase or decrease risk.

If the change request isn't clear, you, the project manager, or someone you delegate clarifies and summarizes the change request, so everyone else in the change management chain can do their jobs.

CROSS-REFERENCE This sample change request form is available in the companion files for this book. You can download it at `www.wiley.com/go/ ProjMgmtCoach.`

TIP One way to manage lots of changes is to stockpile them until you have enough to bundle into a work package. For example, you can assemble change requests associated with the same portion of your project into a new work package and assign it to one of your team members. This approach makes it easier to estimate the effort and cost. And the assigned team member will be more productive working on a chunk of work instead of switching between assigned tasks and teensy change requests.

Tracking a Change Request

Most projects end up with dozens, perhaps hundreds or thousands, of change requests, so you have to organize them to track them all. When someone submits a change request, you add it to the log. As you learn in subsequent sections, you also update the log as requests weave their way through your change management process.

You can use different technologies to build a change request log, such as the spreadsheet shown in Figure 11-2 or an electronic issue-tracking system. If you use a spreadsheet, fill in key change request information, such as estimates of effort and cost, the person responsible for the request, and its current status. The advantage of an electronic issue-tracking system is that it pulls information from your change request forms into a change request report.

CROSS-REFERENCE This sample change request log is available in the companion files for this book. You can download it at `www.wiley.com/go/ ProjMgmtCoach.`

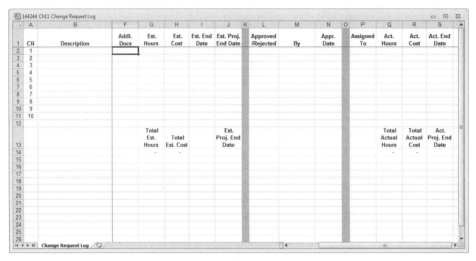

Figure 11-2: Using a spreadsheet for change request log

ACCEPTING CHANGES WHILE PREVENTING PROJECT DELAYS

If your project is like most, many small change requests come in throughout the life of the project. Requesters assume their small changes can easily be incorporated into the plan. The reality is that all those changes add up to significant increases in time or cost. Here's a two-phased approach that helps prevent schedule delays by introducing a more restrictive change management plan when you get close to your project's finish date.

Suppose your project must stick to a 12-month schedule. You can use your normal change management process for the first 11 months — assuming you haven't veered away from your timeline and are on schedule. Then, the 11-month mark triggers a more rigorous approach to managing new changes. Any new change that you add to the project means another change your team hasn't worked on yet has to come off the list. Your team evaluates each new change individually and also reevaluates every change already in the queue to determine which changes come or go.

The advantage of this method is that it doesn't freeze your project to changes, so important changes can still be made. However, it decelerates the pace of change, which helps you stick to your finish date.

Evaluating a Change Request

The person who submits a change request may not know the work that the change entails behind the scenes. So the next step is to analyze the request and estimate what it will take to perform. Assign someone who's familiar with the corresponding part of the project, such as a business analyst for a requirement change or a programmer for a new program feature.

The person who evaluates a change request answers the following questions:

- **Is the change needed?** Not all changes are necessary. For example, someone might submit a change request because he misinterpreted the requirements or didn't realize that the feature requested is available in another area of the application. If the change isn't needed, the evaluator fills in the reason why.

- **Is the description or design of the proposed change correct?** As you learned in Chapter 3, people like to suggest solutions instead of identifying the problem. If a change request proposes a solution that won't work or a design that isn't appropriate, the evaluator describes the correct approach for the change or recommends an alternative.

- **What's the estimated effort and cost?** You need an estimate of the time and cost to perform the work. Another common evaluation item is the impact on resources that are in great demand. With this information, the review board can decide whether the change request is worthwhile.

- **How does the change affect the project?** The change review board also needs to know the impact on the project, such as delays to the finish date or increases to the project cost.

- **Are there any risks?** Ideally, you want to know whether the change request introduces any risks to your project. In addition, you need to evaluate whether the request increases or decreases the risks already identified. For example, change requests could have side effects on other parts of the project, which might introduce unexpected delays or cost increases. On the other hand, a change request could simplify a machine's design, which reduces the risk of problems manufacturing the equipment.

When the evaluation is complete, you update the change request log with the new status and high-level information. If the evaluation is in a separate document, keep it with the original change request form.

Making Decisions About Change Requests

The change review board doesn't sit around waiting for change requests to come in. Typically, the review board meets regularly, such as weekly or every other week. During that meeting, the review board considers the new crop of change requests. One of three things can happen with each request:

- **The change request is approved.** In this case, the change request becomes a new work package in your project, as described in the next section. You update your change request log with the approval and notify the team assigned to perform the work.

- **The change request is denied.** You notify the requester of the decision (and the reason for it) and update the change log to reflect the request's status.

- **The board asks for more information.** The board might ask the requester or the evaluator questions. It also could ask the requester to rework the request.

EXCEPTIONS TO THE CHANGE MANAGEMENT PROCESS

Change management is a balance between controlling changes and keeping your project bubbling along. You don't want your change management process to get bogged down. For that reason, you might include some exceptions to the full-blown change management process. Here are a few special cases to consider:

- **Incomplete or inappropriate change requests:** If a change request doesn't have the information you need, ask the requester to rework the request before you add it to your change request list. Or a change request could be so odd that you simply notify the requester that it's denied without going any further.

- **Changes with a small impact:** If a change request doesn't affect the schedule or budget, you can work with the appropriate team to create a plan for the change without involving the change review board. Another alternative is to specify people who can approve change requests based on thresholds for schedule and cost impact. If a change request is below the threshold, that person can make the decision instead of the change review board. You still track the change in the change request log.

- **Changes with broad impact:** The change review board for a project has limits to its authority. If a change affects the business case for the project or significantly affects other projects in your organization, you need to take the request higher in the food chain. For example, the customer and project sponsor must approve changes that affect the business case. Your executive team must approve changes that affect other projects.

- **Emergencies:** If a change has to be done quickly, for example, to correct an issue that is sitting between you and project acceptance, you can use an emergency change process to expedite the process. One option is to convene an emergency meeting of the change review board. Or you might ask the customer and management team to step in to approve the work.

Updating the Baseline Documents

When a change request is approved, you must update your baseline documents to reflect the work. The documents you update and the modifications you make depend on the change request. For example, if the request is for a new requirement, you add the requirement to your requirements list. You also add new tasks to the work breakdown structure (WBS) and update the schedule with tasks and assignments.

> **TIP** When you update baseline documents, it's a good idea to identify the change request that generated the updates. That way, it's easy to see the source of every revision to a document. For example, you might include the change request number in the new tasks in your schedule, color code change request tasks in a Gantt chart, or add the change request number in parentheses when you edit a document.

Monitoring Change Requests

After you add an approved change request to your project, you or people you delegate monitor and control the work as you would any other tasks. When the change is complete, you make a final update to your change request log to show the actual results of the change in hours, cost, and change to the project finish date.

Summary

Change is inevitable, so you can't refuse to change your project. Instead, the goal is to assess changes that are requested and approve the ones that make sense. Change management doesn't have to be complicated. You can tailor the process to fit the size and complexity of your project.

Coach's Review

Use this section to assess what you've learned in this chapter and to apply it to a real-life project you're currently working on.

Test Your Knowledge

Test your knowledge of the material in this chapter by answering the following questions. See Appendix A for the answers.

1. What is the goal of a change management process?

2. What do you need in order to manage changes?

3. What information does an evaluator provide?

4. Identify at least three ways to keep change management from becoming bureaucratic.

Project Challenge

Consider your work environment and the projects you work on. Design a change management plan that fits with your environment and culture. Identify any special cases that your change management plan should handle and design procedures for them. Then, document your plan so you can use it as a template for your next project.

CHAPTER 12

Managing Risk

Planning a project is a bold attempt to predict the future. Anyone who has indulged in a bit of gambling or invested in the stock market can tell you that attempts to tell the future are fraught with uncertainty. And that uncertainty equals risk.

A project *risk* is an uncertain event or condition in the future, which, if it occurs, will affect the project in some way. While that effect can be positive, in risk management, often the focus is on the negative effects — the threats — that can debilitate, derail, or even destroy the project.

Whether negative or positive, some risks are more likely than others, and some risks would have a greater impact than others. So as the project manager, it serves you well to pay attention. You want to identify which risks or threats exist in your project, assess their probability and impact, determine which ones are worth your attention, plan responses for those risks, and track and monitor them so you are not blindsided if any of them become reality.

Having such a risk management plan in place for your project helps keep your project on track. If you and your team are aware of and prepared for risks, you're less likely to panic and overspend time, money, or effort recovering if a risk comes to fruition. Knowing what you'll do if certain things go wrong actually reduces the anxiety and angst when a risk becomes reality.

This chapter covers the risk management life cycle and the development of the risk management plan in support of your project.

CROSS-REFERENCE The information in this chapter relates to the PMP Exam's Domain II: Planning the Project, Task 10, "Plan risk management by developing a risk management plan, and identifying, analyzing, and prioritizing project risks in the risk register and defining risk response strategies, in order to manage uncertainty throughout the project life cycle."

Identifying Risks to a Project

The first step toward developing your risk management plan is to identify risks. The best method is to call your team together for the sole purpose of identifying risks.

METHODS FOR IDENTIFYING RISKS

While group brainstorming is a great method for identifying risks, you might find other techniques helpful as well:

- Review your work breakdown structure with an eye toward risks. Business-critical functions as well as work that is new to the organization tend to increase risk.

- Review lessons learned from similar past projects.

- Interview experts.

- Complete a cause-and-effect diagram to identify risks and their causes. In such a diagram, also known as the *fishbone* or *Ishikawa diagram*, you consider categories such as time, machinery, methods, material, energy, measurements, personnel, and environment to identify risks and their causes.

- Examine a system or process flowchart for risks.

- Do a *SWOT analysis* to examine strengths, weaknesses, opportunities, and threats to the project.

For a large project, decide how you want to break down the identification of risk. You can work your way through major components of the project, such as phases or subsystems. Or you can think in terms of risk categories. Commonly recognized risk categories include:

- Technical
- External
- Organizational
- Project management

See Table 12-1 for examples of risks in these categories.

Table 12-1: Risk Categories and Examples

RISK CATEGORY	RISK SUBCATEGORY	RISK EXAMPLE
Technical	Requirements	Vague requirements can cause scope creep.
	Technology	The product depends on new technology that's not fully tested, which can increase R&D time.
	Complexity and interfaces	Design might take longer to determine how the technology will interact.
	Performance and reliability	The product speed and reliability are unknown and might not satisfy requirements.
External	Subcontractors and suppliers	Delays in shipments might delay the schedule.
	Regulatory	Legal requirements could change, increasing project scope and cost.
	Market	An unknown competitor could get its version to market first, which would impact the return on investment.
	Customer	The customer could change the project direction.
	Weather	Construction will continue into hurricane season, which could mean delays.
Organizational	Project dependencies	A critical task depends on a deliverable from another project, which has been delayed several times already.
	Resources	Another high-profile project could take resources this project depends on.
	Funding	The project budget could be cut as a result of a drop in sales.
	Prioritization	Management is more focused on new development than on projects like this, which could affect the ability to get resources and funding.

Continued

Table 12-1 *(continued)*

RISK CATEGORY	RISK SUBCATEGORY	RISK EXAMPLE
Project management	Estimating	The estimates of work and cost might be sketchy and inaccurate.
	Planning	There's a steep learning curve on the new project planning software.
	Controlling	The method for collecting progress data might change, causing inconsistent schedule and cost tracking.
	Communication	A new tracking system could require redesigning all the project's reports and communication plans.

You can also think in terms of the project triangle and the major drivers of your project, that is, what possible event or condition could affect one or more of the following:

- Scope
- Schedule
- Budget
- Resources
- Quality

While you can look at these drivers independently for risks, you can create a matrix that intersects the risk categories (technical, external, organizational, and project management) with the project drivers. In other words, you can identify technical risks against scope, schedule, budget, resources, and quality.

The nature of your project can suggest other categories that you'll want to examine as a group for risks. Also remember to consider positive risks in each of the categories you choose to examine.

Collect the risks into the risk register or log. This can be a simple list of risk statements for now, as shown in Figure 12-1. Be sure the statement indicates the effect the risk would have on your project, if it's not already obvious. And if the condition described is already a reality, treat it as an issue rather than a risk.

WHEN RISKS ARE OPPORTUNITIES

A risk is an uncertainty, and that uncertainty is not necessarily a bad thing. A prudent project manager would not bet on getting lucky about various possibilities.

However, you can plan for what you would do if specific opportunities were to come your way. The following are examples of positive risks — occurrences that are not certainties but would be great advantages if they did happen:

- The new technology could integrate more easily than expected.

- A key resource might not be as expensive as budgeted.

- Materials could be delivered in half the time scheduled.

- A light hurricane season could result in less downtime than planned.

- The regulations under review could not change after all.

- A key competitor could drop out of the market.

As with negative risks, you can identify positive risks, rate their probability and impact, and plan for responses. This way, if any of your positive risks come true and shine a light on your project, you'll be prepared to take full advantage of the new opportunity.

Risk Log			
Risk ID	Risk Statement	Probability	Impact
1	Vague requirements can cause scope creep.		
2	The product depends on new technology that's not fully tested, which can increase R&D time.		
3	Design might take longer to determine how the technology will interact.		
4	The new technology could integrate more easily than expected.		
5	The product speed and reliability are unknown and might not satisfy requirements.		
6	Delays in shipments might delay the schedule.		
7	Materials could be delivered in half the time scheduled.		
8	Legal requirements could change, increasing project scope and cost.		
9	The regulations under review could not change after all.		

Figure 12-1: Risk log

As you go on to evaluate the risks and develop your risk management plan, this log will serve as a tool to help you prioritize the risks you'll choose to manage and also help record the chosen risk response.

> **CROSS-REFERENCE** A sample risk log is available in the companion files for this book. You can download it at www.wiley.com/go/ProjMgmtCoach.

Analyzing the Risks

It would be impossible for any team to track and manage each and every risk you can think of. So to scale the risk management effort to a reasonable level, you assess the risks you've identified according to probability and impact. The outcome of this assessment is that you'll have a prioritized list of risks on which to focus.

The questions you're asking of each risk are simple. How likely is this risk to come true? And if this risk comes true, how bad (or how good) will it be? Although the questions are simple, the answers sometimes are not because they can be quite subjective. But with your team members and experts working together, you can come to consensus that will help you prioritize the risks.

So after brainstorming and identifying risks with the team, it's time to go through that list and do the necessary analysis together. As you examine each risk, have the team assess its probability and its impact according to the measurement you've decided to use. That assessment leads to a risk priority score, which helps you decide which risks get the most attention in your risk management plan.

> **TIP** As you and your team assess the probability of risks you've identified, you might discover that some of the risks are actually a current condition already realized. In this case, they're not risks; they're existing issues that you need to resolve. For more information about issues, see "Tracking Issues" later in this chapter.

The following sections outline some simple options for rating risk probability and impact.

Rating Risks as Low, Medium, or High

For each risk, specify whether the probability is low, medium, or high. Then specify whether the impact is low, medium, or high. Plot those two ratings on a 3×3 matrix as shown in Figure 12-2.

The matrix shows a 3×3 grid with IMPACT on the vertical axis (High, Medium, Low from top to bottom) and PROBABILITY on the horizontal axis (Low, Medium, High from left to right):

	Low	Medium	High
High	Consider	Plan Response	Plan Response
Medium	Disregard but Monitor	Consider	Plan Response
Low	Disregard but Monitor	Disregard but Monitor	Consider

Figure 12-2: Low-Medium-High risk matrix

Risks with high probability and high impact fall into the "plan response" category because they're too dangerous to ignore. Your project must be prepared to deal with these risks should they occur. Those with low probability and low impact fall into the "disregard but monitor" category. They aren't likely to occur and they don't do much damage if they do. You don't have to plan for them, but you still monitor them. Those risks with a middle score fall into the "consider" category.

If you need more than just three priority levels for probability and impact, consider a 5 × 5 matrix with labels such as Low, Medium Low, Medium, Medium High, and High.

Rating Risks Numerically

If you prefer to use numbers, or if you intend to use a spreadsheet to calculate risk priorities, you can substitute numerical values for the Low, Medium, and High ratings. For each risk, answer the probability question with a numerical rating. The number can be on a scale of 1–3 or 1–5, with 5 being the highest likelihood.

Answer the impact question with another numerical rating, such as 1–3 or 1–5 again. Then multiply the two ratings to get the risk's priority score. It's simplest if you use the same scale as for probability.

So if you're scoring on a scale of 1–5 for both probability and impact, the highest score would be 25 while the lowest would be 1. Any score of 13 or more would fall into the "Plan Response" category.

Another variation is to answer the probability question with a percentage. The higher the percentage, the higher the likelihood. Then express the percentage as a decimal and multiply it by the impact rating of 1–3 or 1–5 to get the risk's priority score.

NOTE If your team assigns a risk of 100 percent likelihood, it really isn't a risk. It's an issue that you will have to address. See "When a Risk Becomes Reality" later in this chapter for more information.

Recording the Risk Ratings and Scores

Record each risk's priority score on the risk log, as shown in Figure 12-3. Having the scores all together is instrumental as you move to the next step of prioritizing the risks.

Risk ID	Risk Statement	Probability	Impact	Priority Score
1	Vague requirements can cause scope creep.	HIGH	MEDIUM	CONSIDER
2	The product depends on new technology that's not fully tested, which can increase R&D time.	HIGH	HIGH	PLAN RESPONSE
3	Design might take longer to determine how the technology will interact.	MEDIUM	HIGH	PLAN RESPONSE
4	The new technology could integrate more easily than expected.	LOW	MEDIUM	MONITOR
5	The product speed and reliability are unknown and might not satisfy requirements.	MEDIUM	MEDIUM	CONSIDER
6	Delays in shipments might delay the schedule.	MEDIUM	MEDIUM	CONSIDER
7	Materials could be delivered in half the time scheduled.	LOW	HIGH	CONSIDER
8	Legal requirements could change, increasing project scope and cost.	LOW	MEDIUM	MONITOR
9	The regulations under review could not change after all.	MEDIUM	LOW	MONITOR
10	An unknown competitor could get their version to market first, which would impact our return on investment.	MEDIUM	HIGH	PLAN RESPONSE

Figure 12-3: Risk log with ratings and scores

The ratings and priority in the risk log are essential for monitoring and tracking risks throughout the project life cycle. Conditions can change such that risks with a low score early on end up having a higher score later, and vice versa.

Choosing the Risks to Manage

With the risks identified, rated, and scored, you can decide which risks are worth the time and cost to plan and manage. Risks with a high probability and high impact must not be ignored. You must be well prepared for them, or they will have you for lunch. On the other hand, risks that aren't as likely to happen or that would have little impact on your project are not worth the effort.

The easiest way to select the risks you should manage is to arrange the risks by their priority score, as shown in Figure 12-4.

Risk ID	Risk Statement	Probability	Impact	Priority Score
2	The product depends on new technology that's not fully tested, which can increase R&D time.	HIGH	HIGH	PLAN RESPONSE
3	Design might take longer to determine how the technology will interact.	MEDIUM	HIGH	PLAN RESPONSE
10	An unknown competitor could get their version to market first, which would impact our return on investment.	MEDIUM	HIGH	PLAN RESPONSE
13	Construction will continue into hurricane season, which could mean delays.	HIGH	HIGH	PLAN RESPONSE
15	A critical task depends on a deliverable from another project, which has been delayed several times already.	HIGH	HIGH	PLAN RESPONSE
16	Another high-profile project could take resources our project depends on.	HIGH	HIGH	PLAN RESPONSE
1	Vague requirements can cause scope creep.	HIGH	MEDIUM	CONSIDER
5	The product speed and reliability are unknown and might not satisfy requirements.	MEDIUM	MEDIUM	CONSIDER
14	A light hurricane season could result in less downtime than planned.	LOW	HIGH	CONSIDER
22	A new tracking system could require redesigning all the project's reports and communication plans.	MEDIUM	MEDIUM	CONSIDER
4	The new technology could integrate more easily than expected.	LOW	MEDIUM	MONITOR
8	Legal requirements could change, increasing project scope and cost.	LOW	MEDIUM	MONITOR
9	The regulations under review could not change after all.	MEDIUM	LOW	MONITOR

Figure 12-4: Risk log sorted by priority

The risks that are grouped as "Plan Response" or have the highest priority score have the highest *risk value*, indicating the cost of the consequence should a risk become reality. The risks with the higher risk value scores are likely to cost the project more money. Such costs can be more precisely quantified and used to negotiate the project contingency fund. Keep in mind that you will analyze the cost of the realized risk against the cost of the response when determining which response is appropriate.

CROSS-REFERENCE Read more about the costs of risks in "Setting Up Contingency Funds" later in this chapter.

Planning Risk Responses

Now that you've selected the highest priority risks (whether negative or positive), you can plan your responses to them. Assemble your identified risks, the risk analysis tool, the risk log, and any detailed risk information, including the risk responses and risk detail sheets.

TIP Although you've judiciously selected a subset of the highest priority risks for detailed risk planning, it doesn't mean the lower-priority risks are forgotten. They remain a part of your risk management plan, still visible on your risk radar. You or assigned team members will keep a watchful eye on them as the project moves along. If conditions transform a lower-priority risk into a higher-priority one, you'll develop a risk response plan for it at that time.

Planning Responses to Negative Risks

Analyze each of your high-priority negative risks, and determine the best response. The following are response strategies for negative risks:

- **Mitigate the probability or impact of the risk.** Lessening the risk's likelihood, the impact, or both can be a good strategy if doing so is cost-effective. Mitigation efforts are often more effective earlier in the project life cycle and cost less than recovering from damages later on. For example, if you're planning an outdoor event and bad weather is a risk, you can mitigate the impact by renting party tents.

- **Plan a contingency for the risk occurrence.** Contingency planning is a form of accepting the risk and being willing to use an amount of contingency time, money, or resources to deal with the risk if it occurs. More monitoring of this risk is required and contingency trigger points should be developed.

- **Transfer the risk to another party.** Shifting some or all of the risk to a third party doesn't eliminate the risk, but it outsources it to a third party who takes on the risk for a price. Examples include contracts for insurance or warranties. If the cost of the transfer is less than the risk value, it can be well worth it.

- **Avoid the risk.** A project requirement, objective, or task might not be worth the risk it's causing. In such a case, you might avoid the risk by choosing another approach to that portion of the project. For example, if one risk is that a key resource won't be available, you can avoid the risk by determining how to assign the work to other qualified resources.

- **Accept the risk.** Even a high-priority risk might just need to be accepted if it happens. This is especially true if the cost of any other response (mitigation, contingency planning, transfer, or avoidance) would be greater than the expected loss. No action is required except to have the project team deal with the risk as it occurs and document the issue accordingly.

Note that all responses except for acceptance require preparation before the risk is realized. Two responses take place after a risk comes into being: activating the contingency plan or accepting the risk.

IDENTIFY CONTINGENCY TRIGGER POINTS

If the response to any of your negative or positive risks is the development of a contingency plan, you need to specify the trigger points. These trigger points indicate when you and your team should spring into action and implement the contingency plan.

Add these trigger points to your risk log or other risk tracking mechanism.

With each risk response identified, you can estimate the impact of taking that response. Will project scope change with tasks added? How much time will this add to the project finish date? How many more resources, and what kinds of resources, will be needed? How much would this risk response cost?

In your risk log or other risk tracking mechanism, record the risk response plan for each high-priority risk as shown in Figure 12-5. Also note the time, cost, and other needs for the risk response.

Risk ID	Risk Statement	Probability	Impact	Priority Score	Response
2	The product depends on new technology that's not fully tested, which can increase R&D time.	HIGH	HIGH	PLAN RESPONSE	Plan contingency.
3	Design might take longer to determine how the technology will interact.	MEDIUM	HIGH	PLAN RESPONSE	Plan contingency.
10	An unknown competitor could get their version to market first, which would impact our return on investment.	MEDIUM	HIGH	PLAN RESPONSE	Plan contingency.
13	Construction will continue into hurricane season, which could mean delays.	HIGH	HIGH	PLAN RESPONSE	Transfer risk (insurance).
15	A critical task depends on a deliverable from another project, which has been delayed several times already.	HIGH	HIGH	PLAN RESPONSE	Mitigate the probability.
16	Another high-profile project could take resources our project depends on.	HIGH	HIGH	PLAN RESPONSE	Plan contingency.
17	Our project budget could be cut due to a drop in sales.	MEDIUM	HIGH	PLAN RESPONSE	Accept the risk.
18	Management is more focused on new development than on projects like ours, which could affect ability to get resources.	MEDIUM	HIGH	PLAN RESPONSE	Accept the risk.
19	The estimates of work and cost might be sketchy and inaccurate.	MEDIUM	HIGH	PLAN RESPONSE	Mitigate the probability.
20	We have a steep learning curve on our project planning software.	HIGH	MEDIUM	PLAN RESPONSE	Mitigate the probability.
21	Our method for collecting progress data might change, causing inconsistent schedule and cost tracking.	HIGH	MEDIUM	PLAN RESPONSE	Mitigate the impact.
1	Vague requirements can cause scope creep.	HIGH	MEDIUM	CONSIDER	Mitigate the possibility.

Figure 12-5: Risk log including response plan

CONSIDER RATING THE RESIDUAL RISK

Some organizations add a High, Medium, or Low rating value after the risk response has been identified. That is, given the risk response, what is the adjusted probability and impact? With this new priority rating, you have a determination of *residual risk*, that is, the risk that's left after you've identified the planned response.

For example, suppose your project has a high-priority risk that indicates the project might experience schedule and budget overruns because of suspect work and cost estimates. You decide to mitigate the risk by revisiting and adjusting the estimates according to historical data. Looking at residual risk, you determine that the high-priority risk is now a medium priority.

By now, you and your team have worked out significant details about the high-priority risk responses. In most cases, you add this detailed information to a risk detail sheet (see Figure 12-6) that can be linked or referenced from your risk log.

Risk Detail Sheet

Risk ID #	Risk Statement	
Owner	Risk Description	
Probability Rating:	X Impact Rating: = Priority Score:	

Response Strategy (mark one)

Mitigate   Plan   Transfer   Avoid   Accept
                Contingency

Response Description (include trigger if applicable)

Action Plan

Relevant Dates

Scope Impact	Schedule Impact	Cost Impact	Resource Impact	Quality Impact

Status (mark one)   Inactive   Active   Resolved   Closed

Figure 12-6: Risk detail sheet

CROSS-REFERENCE A sample risk detail sheet is available in the companion files for this book. You can download it at www.wiley.com/go/ ProjMgmtCoach.

Quantifying the impact of the risk response for high-priority risks is a concrete way to determine the amount of schedule buffer and contingency funds needed in case any the risks come to pass.

Planning Responses to Positive Risks

Analyze each of your high-priority positive risks, or opportunities, and choose the appropriate actions. The following are response strategies for positive risks:

- **Enhance the probability or impact of the opportunity.** Identify the elements that are driving this opportunity and do what you can to increase the likelihood of the opportunity, its positive effects on the project, or both.

- **Plan a contingency for the opportunity occurrence.** In some cases, a positive risk saves a project time, money, or resources. In other cases, it might need some contingency time, money, or resources, possibly to change or expand scope, but the benefits outweigh the costs. Contingency trigger points should be developed and the likelihood of the opportunity should be closely monitored.

- **Share the opportunity with another.** A strategic partnership or joint venture with a third party in an advantageous position can increase the likelihood and ensure that the opportunity bears fruit, and that the benefits are shared.

- **Exploit the opportunity to ensure it happens.** You can create conditions to turn the uncertainty of the opportunity into a reality. You might add a requirement, objective, or task to the project, or assign the best resources to certain tasks. For example, if the opportunity is that your product's feature set might be better than the competition's, you add two more key features to make sure that's the case.

- **Accept the opportunity.** A more passive approach than the others, acceptance takes advantage of the opportunity if the situation arises, but the team does not go out of its way to actively pursue it.

With the response to each possible opportunity identified, estimate the impact on the project of implementing that response. Consider scope change, schedule adjustment, addition or reduction of resources, and added or reduced cost. Many realized opportunities will benefit the project in terms of schedule, cost, or quality. Other realized opportunities will cost a bit, but their benefits will ultimately outweigh the cost.

In your risk log or other risk tracking mechanism, record the risk response plan for each high-priority opportunity. Also note any positive or negative impacts on the project for taking advantage of the realized opportunity.

Compiling the Risk Management Plan

By the time you and your team have identified and analyzed risks to your project, selected the high-priority risks and opportunities you're going to manage, and developed risk response strategies for each one, you've already created your risk management plan. Now it's just a matter of compiling the information and making it available to the team members and other stakeholders who need it.

The key elements of the risk management plan are as follows:

- **Risk categories:** The categories that are examined for risk identification, possibly the risk breakdown structure.

- **Identified risks:** The list of all risks identified through the risk identification process, even those that have been determined to be low priority.

- **Risk analysis tool:** The matrix used to assess risk probability and impact.

- **Risk log:** The register, which includes the risk ID, statement, probability, impact, priority score, response, cost, and other information. This log includes all identified risks, even though you initially plan responses only for the higher-priority ones.

- **Risk detail sheet:** Detailed information about each of the high-priority risks, including response description, owner, action plan, trigger, applicable dates, scope and schedule impact, risk cost, and status.

- **Risk monitoring plan:** The process being used to monitor and track risks throughout the project life cycle.

More complex projects might need an elaborate risk management plan that describes risk management methodology, the roles and responsibilities of a dedicated risk management team, the risk budget and schedule, reporting formats, and risk tracking mechanisms and metrics.

The risk management plan becomes part of your project notebook and should be maintained in the same format — whether that's a binder, electronic files on a shared drive, or documents on a project intranet. The risk management plan is continually referenced by you, managing stakeholders, team members, and those who have risk tracking responsibilities. The risk management plan is also continually monitored and updated, especially as risks are tracked and change over the span of project planning and execution.

THE CANDID COACH: BETWEEN YOU AND ME, WE HAVE A RISK

Suppose one of your key stakeholders is a bit of a "hothead" whose antagonistic approach is a risk to the consensus you've gained for the project. You can't very well add that to the risk management plan you share with the team. But it's a risk you must manage like any other.

In a situation like this, you might set up an internal risk plan that only you and your project sponsor share.

Establishing Contingencies

With each high-priority risk associated with a specific response plan, it's easier to determine what would be needed if the risk is realized. Those contingent needs correspond to the project constraints of scope, time, money, resources, and quality.

For example, suppose a high-priority risk states that more R&D would be needed to evaluate a new technology being used in the development of a new product. If this risk is realized, scope might increase with new tasks added to accommodate that research and testing. Even if new tasks are not added, certainly time on existing tasks would be lengthened, and this would probably require more money and possibly more resources.

Or, imagine there's a risk stating that materials could ship slower than needed. If this risk is realized, it causes a project delay, which lengthens the schedule, especially if there's no slack time to compensate for the delay.

It's wise to build in an amount of contingent time and funding for the project to accommodate the fact that a number of high-priority risks (although probably not all of them) are likely to be realized. In some cases, you might also want a plan for contingent resources if you need more people to deal with a scope change caused by a realized risk. Of course, these resources would also use some of the contingent funding, and the scope change might need to be handled through your change management process.

PRIOR APPROVAL FOR IMPLEMENTING A CONTINGENCY PLAN

If your response to one or more high-priority risks is to create a contingency plan, and if that plan consists of a project scope change, you can notify the change review board of the contingency plan and get its input and approval ahead of time. If the risk does occur, you can inform the change review board if you have time, but you can also immediately implement the contingency plan without having to wait for approval in the case of an emergency.

For lower-priority risk contingencies or those for which implementation speed would not be essential, you might submit the change request at the time the risk becomes a reality. Use your judgment and the resources of your change review board sensibly.

For more information about the change review board and project scope changes, see Chapter 11, "Setting Up a Change Management Plan."

Building in a Schedule Buffer

Because of the uncertainty inherent in project schedules, especially early in the planning stages, building in a *schedule buffer* is a safety technique. The schedule buffer, also known as *contingency reserve*, *time reserve*, or *management reserve*, is a period of time typically added to the end of the project schedule. This buffer is like an emergency savings account of time used as needed to help keep the schedule from slipping past its contracted finish date. If a critical task slips by 2 days, for example, 2 days can be taken from the schedule buffer to compensate, thereby preventing the overall schedule from slipping by 2 days.

If a risk consequence requires the addition of tasks or time that affects the critical path, you can use time from the schedule buffer. The schedule buffer might be a percentage of the overall project time span, it might be a certain number of days or weeks, or it might be determined by a particular formula or analysis.

In some instances, the amount of the schedule buffer is at the discretion of the project manager. However, the project customer or sponsor might choose to control the use of the buffer.

Setting Up Contingency Funds

Like the schedule buffer, *contingency funds* are established as a safety measure or emergency savings account against risks in the project schedule. Contingency funds, also known as *contingency reserve*, *contingency allowance*, or *management reserve*, are an amount of money set aside for unknown occurrences in the project. If materials cost more than planned, if additional resources are needed to keep the project on track, or if a weather-caused delay adds time and cost to the project, the contingency funds might be used to keep the project within budget.

Contingency funds might be a percentage of the overall project budget or a fixed amount, or the amount might be determined by a particular formula or analysis. If the contingency funds are not an established percentage or fixed amount, you might need to negotiate the amount with the project customer or sponsor. A good place to start is to add the estimated costs of the high-priority risk responses and to take a percentage of that total. It's unlikely that all high-priority risks will become an actuality.

Project managers are typically given an authorization threshold for use of the contingency funds. Beyond that amount, approval from managing stakeholders would be needed. Often one side of the threshold is called the *project reserve*, and the other side is the *management reserve*.

Establish and publicize when and how the contingency funds will be used. You might parcel the contingency funds by phase or functional area. Make sure it's clear that contingency funds are to be used only to cover the costs of realized risks.

Tracking Risks

The risk management plan might change as you work through the project planning processes. While you're refining your work breakdown structure, estimating work and cost, planning resources to do the work, and building the schedule, you're also planning how you're going to manage quality, communications, and change in the project.

CROSS-REFERENCE The information in this section relates to the PMP Exam's Domain IV: Monitoring and Controlling the Project, Task 4, "Update the risk register and risk response plan by identifying any new risks, assessing old risks, and determining and implementing appropriate response strategies, in order to manage the impact of risks on the project."

Developing the different aspects of your project plan is likely to uncover new risks as well as shed more light on ones you've already identified. Be prepared to start tracking risks well before the ink is dry on the risk management plan and well before you move out of the planning processes and into the executing processes.

Overall risk tends to be higher earlier in the project life cycle when uncertainty is greater and the unknowns are more, well, unknown. As the project moves through its life cycle, some of that uncertainty, and therefore risk, is removed. But other types of uncertainty can crop up. Risk tends to fluctuate over the course of the project.

When tracking and monitoring risks, the assigned risk owners do the following:

- **Implement proactive negative risk responses:** Carry out the proactive response actions of mitigating the risk, planning the contingency, transferring the risk, or avoiding the risk. Think of these as emergency preparedness measures that are done before the risk has an inkling of raising its ugly head.

- **Implement proactive positive risk responses:** Execute the proactive response actions of enhancing the probability or impact, planning the contingency, sharing the opportunity, or exploiting the opportunity. Good preparation prepares the soil for such opportunities to take root.

- **Look for risks becoming reality:** Pay attention to the symptoms or indications that high-priority risks are coming true, and monitor them closely.

- **Look for events that trigger a contingency plan:** Stay aware of occurrences that trigger a risk contingency plan.

- **Look for possible new risks:** As project conditions change, be vigilant of new risks cropping up. As appropriate, add them to the risk log and identify their probability and impact. If they're assessed as high-priority risks, develop their risk response plans and assign owners.

- **Keep an eye on lower-priority risks:** Conditions can change the probability or impact of lower-priority risks to transform them into higher-priority risks. While lower-priority risks would generally not be assigned to anyone, as a team, you should all be on the lookout for changes as details are uncovered.

- **Regularly report on risk status:** Risk should be a regular agenda item at your project status meetings and in status reports. Risk should also be included in your reports to the managing stakeholders.

- **Update the risk log and risk detail sheet:** These should always reflect the current status of risks. Close or inactivate risks that are no longer relevant, perhaps because a phase or activity has been completed. Downgrade or upgrade the probability or impact of risks whose conditions have changed.

TRACKING RISKS AND ISSUES WITH SHAREPOINT

Your organization can use Microsoft SharePoint to help track risks. SharePoint has a risk tracking feature that enables you and your team to add, describe, score, and assign a risk. You can also describe the response plan and enter the current status. Risk owners can track and update information about their assigned risks.

SharePoint also has an issues tracking feature. You can add and assign issues, along with due dates, categories, notes, and resolutions. Issue owners can track and update information, and the entire team can review information about all issues.

When a Risk Becomes Reality

The more prepared you are for an emergency, the more calmly you can handle it if it happens. In the same way, having a well-developed and well-maintained risk management plan makes it easier for you and your project team to deal with an anticipated risk that becomes a reality.

For a negative risk, the response you chose during planning will now be implemented, whether it's to activate a contingency plan, accept the results, or some other response. If a positive risk or opportunity lands in your lap, you'll be primed to maximize the advantage it provides to your project.

When a risk is realized, it becomes an *issue*, and you can track it as such. In your risk log, record that the risk did indeed become a reality. Cross-reference the risk to its place in your issues system and continue the tracking there, including the chosen risk response and the result.

Continue to monitor the issue, report on it in status reports and meetings, and document the results of the response. If the response is not working as well as you had hoped, re-evaluate and adjust.

CROSS-REFERENCE The information in this section relates to the PMP Exam's Domain III: Executing the Project, Task 5, "Implement approved actions and follow the risk management plan and risk register, in order to minimize the impact of negative risk events on the project."

Tracking Issues

An *issue* is an event, condition, or problem that affects your project in some way, typically in terms of one or more of the project constraints — scope, time, money, resources, or quality. The following are examples of issues that can affect your project:

- The technology the new product is depending on doesn't meet speed requirements.
- The rainy season was longer than usual, causing two more weeks of delay.
- The materials cost 10 percent more than budgeted.
- Another high-profile project in the organization has committed certain resources this project was counting on.
- The quality assurance team is backlogged and won't be able to do the audits as scheduled.

CROSS-REFERENCE The information in this section relates to the PMP Exam's Domain IV: Monitoring and Controlling the Project, Task 5, "Assess corrective actions on the issue register and determine next steps for unresolved issues by using appropriate tools and techniques in order to minimize the impact on project schedule, cost, and resources."

Unlike risks, which are possible conditions in the future, issues are conditions that exist for your project. Risks and issues are related, however. Often when identifying risks with your project team, you will also uncover issues. And, whenever one of your risks is realized, you have a new issue on your hands.

Issues are also identified throughout the life of your project. Your team members can bring them up as they discuss obstacles in your project status meetings. Your stakeholders might come to you with a new problem that affects the project. So you see that a significant part of managing your project is identifying, tracking, and acting on project issues.

As an issue is identified, record it in some kind of issues tracking mechanism that works for you and your team. A spreadsheet is a great option, with the following fields related to each issue:

- Name
- Description
- Category (optional)
- Priority
- Owner
- Deadline for resolution
- Status

- Resolution
- Notes

Like assigned project tasks and assigned risks, you and your team should discuss issues at your project status meetings, especially the ones with the higher priorities or whose deadlines are approaching.

The issue remains an issue until you and your team decide on the action to take to deal with it. Often that decision leads to a change to the project plan. After that change is made, the issue is considered resolved and can be closed.

Summary

Because managing a project is rooted in so much uncertainty, especially in the earlier phases, risk management is essential to success. A project risk is an uncertain event — negative or positive — that could happen in the future and have an effect on the project's scope, schedule, cost, or quality.

As a project manager, you and your team can plan for risks and reduce the impact on the project that risks cause by developing and executing a risk management plan. In this process, you identify project risks, analyze the probability and impact of each identified risk, and prioritize risks for monitoring and tracking. For each prioritized risk, you and your team develop an appropriate response such as mitigation or contingency planning.

As the project is executed, your team tracks and monitors the higher-priority risks. Before risks come to pass, your team completes any needed mitigation, avoidance, or transference and develops contingency plans as appropriate. If any risks come to pass, your team converts the risk into an issue, implements the contingency plan or other risk response, and records the effort.

Realized risks and other events or problems that affect your project are issues that need action and decision. Like risks, you need to assign issues to team members who will track and resolve them.

Coach's Review

Use this section to assess what you've learned in this chapter and to apply it to a real-life project you're currently working on.

Test Your Knowledge

Test your knowledge of the material in this chapter by answering the following questions. See Appendix A for the answers.

1. What is project risk?
2. Name at least three methods for identifying risks in the project.
3. Name the four commonly recognized project risk categories.
4. What are some characteristics of a technical risk category? Name an example from your experience.
5. Name the two key factors for analyzing risks.
6. List the five response strategies for negative risks.
7. What does it mean to mitigate a risk?
8. What is an issue, and how do risks relate to issues?

Project Challenge

Practice the knowledge you've gained in this chapter with the following challenge. Use the project you're planning as you continue to work through the chapters in this book.

1. Develop a risk assessment tool that you will use to analyze identified risks. Also develop a risk log and risk detail sheet to use for recording and tracking project risks.
2. With your team or on your own, develop a risk management plan for your project. Identify project risks, analyze risks using your risk assessment tool, prioritize the risks, and develop appropriate risk responses.
3. Estimate the impact to your project if your high-priority risks were to become reality. Based on that, determine a fair amount for your schedule and cost buffers. Imagine how you would present the request to use one of the buffers to the project sponsor or customer.
4. Create an issues tracking tool. Add any current issues to it, along with owners and resolution deadlines.

Part

III

Executing a Project

Chapter 13: Kicking Off a Project
Chapter 14: Taming Processes, Problems, and Conflicts
Chapter 15: The Keys to Successful Meetings
Chapter 16: Transforming People Into a Team

Kicking Off a Project

The executing portion of the project life cycle starts with a few kickoff activities before your team members can dig into the work on their assignments. Getting stakeholders' approval (in writing) for your project plan segues from planning into executing.

The approved project plan means that you can set the baseline for your project. You save versions of all the approved plan documents so you can track any changes that are made going forward. If you haven't done so already, you set up the storage system for your project notebook, which is the repository for all project documentation and communication.

At the same time, you need your project team on board to start work. If team members come from within your organization, now is the time to communicate with their managers that the project is a go and when their folks should report for duty. However, if you need people and other resources from outside your organization, it's time to procure those resources.

In some very large projects, planning is so extensive that you have a kickoff meeting when planning starts. But after the plan is approved, you're ready for the kickoff of project tasks. You can assemble all the players — the stakeholders and your team — for a kickoff meeting, during which you review the project, outline the schedule, and explain the ground rules.

Preparing to Execute the Project

Before you hand out assignments to team members, you have a few additional project management tasks to perform. In fact, you have to complete a few steps before you can finalize the arrangements for some of the resources you plan to use. This section describes the flurry of activity that occurs at the beginning of project execution.

Obtaining Approval

Before you implement your project plan, you have to get the stakeholders (the project sponsor, customer, and others you've identified) to approve it. That approval is the final task in the planning process group and it triggers the start of the executing process group.

CROSS-REFERENCE   Obtaining approval for the project plan is Task 11, **"Present the project plan to the key stakeholders (if required), in order to obtain approval to execute the project," in the PMP Exam's Domain II: Planning the Project.**

As with other approvals, a face-to-face meeting with all the people who must sign off on the plan is ideal. That way, you have an opportunity to present the project plan and ensure that the stakeholders know what they're signing. This meeting is a great time to review the following aspects of the project plan (which you learned about in Chapter 3, "Getting a Project off the Ground," and Chapter 4, "What Goes into a Project Plan"):

- Objectives
- Requirements
- Success criteria
- Scope
- Deliverables
- Risks, assumptions, and constraints
- Schedule
- Budget
- Project management processes (quality, communication, change, and risk management)

If an in-person approval isn't feasible, you can set up a conference call or send the plan to the appropriate stakeholders. With either of these approaches, ask the stakeholders to sign the signature pages and send them to you to add to the project notebook. Regardless which method you use, be sure to review or highlight portions of the plan that required compromises or tweaks to satisfy all the parties.

WHAT IF THE PLAN ISN'T DONE?

Sometimes, you have to start work before the project plan is approved or even complete. If you're in such a situation, you can start managing the project based on the plan as it stands. The absence of an approved plan puts the project at risk, so you must work hard to propel the plan to completion and approval.

On the other hand, iterative projects don't start with a fully detailed plan. As described in the section "Iterative and Agile Project Management" in Chapter 2, project plans lay out an overall direction for the project. Then, you develop more detailed plans for each iteration.

If you can't get approval for the entire plan, ask for approval for part of the project plan so you can at least set a baseline for that part. Then, you can use a rolling wave approach to obtain approval for the remaining parts. With rolling wave planning, you prepare a detailed plan for a few weeks of work, for example, four weeks. At the end of each week, you add another week's worth of detail to the plan.

Saving Project Baselines

As soon as work begins on project tasks, you begin tracking progress and comparing the actual results to your plan. But before you can make those comparisons, you need to save a copy of your approved project plan, which is the baseline against which you compare progress and identify changes.

One part of the project baseline is numeric. You save the start and finish dates for tasks in your schedule, duration and effort for tasks, and costs. That way, as the project progresses, you can compare your actual values to planned values to determine whether the project is on track.

CROSS-REFERENCE Chapter 18, "Evaluating Progress and Performance," describes methods for comparing actual results to your plan.

Your project baseline also includes all your approved plan documents, such as the project scope, requirements, success criteria, change management plan, risk management plan, and so on. When the stakeholders approve your plan, you also save the approved versions of all the documents in the plan so you can keep track of changes made to them during project execution. For example, if the project ends up taking too long or costing too much, the key stakeholders may decide to remove items from the scope. Or someone might identify requirements that weren't included in the original plan. When the project is complete and you prepare your project closeout report, you identify significant changes such as these.

CROSS-REFERENCE You learn about final project reports in the section "Documenting the Project: The Project Closeout Report" in Chapter 20.

Updating the Project Notebook

By the time you complete your draft project plan, you'll have a plethora of documentation: text documents, a project schedule, spreadsheets, communication, and so on. The paperwork just keeps coming as you launch into project execution. So, it's time to add all your project plan documentation to your project notebook or register.

CROSS-REFERENCE The section "Assembling the Project Notebook" in Chapter 3 describes several methods for storing project information — both electronically and on paper.

The filing system you use depends on the technology available within your organization and, to some extent, your project. At the very least, you'll want to make the following information easy to find and access:

- **Approved project plan:** The approved plan consists of a variety of documents and files: the work breakdown structure, project schedule, budget, resource plan, project management processes, and so on. The documents that make up your plan represent the baseline to which you compare your project's progress and performance.

- **Current versions of documents:** By keeping current and previous versions of your project documentation, you can track progress and flag changes made to documents and other files as the project progresses.

- **Change management:** Keep records of change requests and their status, as described in Chapter 11, "Setting Up a Change Management Plan," so you know which changes have been approved and incorporated into your project.

- **Risk management:** In addition to your original risk management plan, keep records of risks that have occurred, the responses you implemented, and the results.

- **Quality management:** Track your quality management tasks, the results, and actions you implement to improve quality if necessary.

▪ **Communication:** This could be the most prolific portion of your project notebook. Keep track of reports, meetings minutes, and all forms of correspondence.

Obtaining Resources

During planning, you started to flesh out your project team. As you learned in Chapter 7, "Planning Project Resources," you put together an inventory of the skill sets you need on the project, which you then use to develop a resource plan. If you're using in-house resources, you work with resource managers as you develop your schedule. For people and other resources you obtain from outside your organization, you follow a procurement process. Now that the project plan is approved, the funding for the project is in place and the dates that you need resources are official. It's time to bring resources on board.

NOTE Depending on the project, you might be able to start procurement work before the project execution stage. By doing so, you can mitigate risk and manage teams so resources are available when you need them. Although you wouldn't typically sign contracts prior to execution, you can perform many procurement tasks as plans start to take shape.

CROSS-REFERENCE The information in this section relates to Task 1, "Obtain and manage project resources including outsourced deliverables by following the procurement plan, in order to ensure successful project execution," in the PMP exam Domain III: Executing the Project.

Obtaining In-House Resources

Chances are you have been working with resource managers to line up people for your project before the plan was approved. Those managers know what other commitments have been made, so they can help you develop a realistic schedule that reflects the availability of resources. Whether or not your organization has a formal resource assignment process, your best bet for obtaining the best people is to develop relationships with potential team members and their line managers. As your project plan closed in on its final form, you started obtaining commitments for specific skills and levels of experience — and in some cases, specific people.

Now it's time to call in those commitments. You can notify the resource managers that the project is starting and give them the start dates for assignments. If some of your resources are still unnamed, contact the appropriate resource managers to work out who those people are. You perform similar steps to finalize commitments for other resources, whether you need office space, computers, or other types of equipment.

Procuring Resources from Vendors

Obtaining resources from outside your organization is a little more complicated because you must set up business relationships with other companies or individuals. A procurement process helps you find and select the vendors you work with, sign contracts with them, and manage the relationships until they're complete. This section provides an overview of what occurs during each part of a procurement process.

Many organizations have a procurement department, or in smaller companies, someone whose job it is to manage procurements. If that's the case, you provide the procurement department with your requirements and they take care of lining up vendors and managing contracts.

> **NOTE** As you'll see from the steps described in this section, a procurement process might take quite a bit of time. On the other hand, large companies often have standing contracts in place with vendor companies, which can make the procurement process relatively quick. If you're going to use outside resources, be sure to understand the procurement process in your organization and then add the appropriate procurement tasks and lead times to your project schedule, so you know when people will be available to start their assignments.

Soliciting Vendors

The first step in a procurement process is typically obtaining bids from several vendors so you can choose the one that best meets your needs. How you go about getting bids depends on whether you already have a list of vendors you work with or are starting from scratch.

You can start your candidate vendor list with vendors you've used in the past (and who did a good job). You can also ask for references from colleagues, scan ads in trade magazines, or attend trade shows.

If you're starting at the very beginning, you need to identify vendors who are suitable for the job. In this case, you put together a request for information (RFI), which is simply a request for more information about the services or products that vendors offer. Based on the responses you receive, you can decide which vendors you will ask for bids.

Then, to solicit bids, you typically send a request for proposal (RFP). An RFP describes what service or products you need along with other information that vendors need in order to put together a bid, such as the following:

- **An overview of the project:** Provide a brief description of the project so that vendors can put your requirements into context.

- **The services or resources you require:** Describe what you need. For example, you can provide your skills inventory for human resources or specifications for equipment or services.

- **Timeframe:** Specify when you need resources and how long you need them for.

- **Selection criteria:** Specify the criteria you will use to choose the vendor. For example, you might use criteria such as the lowest bid, the most experience performing the work you need done, proximity to your location, financial stability, or good references.

- **Deadlines:** Specify the deadline for responding to the RFP and how you prefer to receive responses. Also include when you will make your decision.

NOTE In most organizations, the legal department or an attorney reviews the RFP before it's distributed to vendors.

Regardless how carefully you prepare your RFP, vendors often have questions. You don't want to answer the same questions time and time again. Likewise, you want to make sure every vendor gets the same information so you can compare responses. A bidders' conference is a meeting where every vendor has the opportunity to ask questions and hear your answers to all the questions asked. Another approach is to publish your RFP online and include an online forum. That way, vendors can post their questions electronically and review your answers to everyone's questions.

Selecting Vendors

Once you get responses from vendors, it's your turn to assess those responses and choose the vendor or vendors you're going to work with. You can use different methods to evaluate responses. But the bottom line is that you use the criteria you put together and choose the vendor whose response does the best job of satisfying your criteria. For complex RFPs or long lists of vendors, you might run an initial round of evaluations to identify a short list of candidates. Then, you might ask those vendors to provide more information or give demonstrations.

Contracting

The next step is to sign contracts with the vendors you choose. Typically, a contract includes a statement of work, deliverables, terms and conditions, due dates, and price information.

A contract should also include your acceptance criteria and acceptance process, so both parties understand how you will verify that the contract is complete. Finally, describe the processes you want the vendor to follow, such as change management, status reporting, invoicing, and so on.

If your organization has a legal department, ask them to prepare a contract based on the RFP. If not, you can ask an attorney to prepare a contract. For simple agreements, you can use a standard contract with an attachment for the statement of work and other details.

If you aren't familiar with contracts, here are the most common arrangements:

- **Time and materials:** This type of contract pays for the hours worked and reimburses for expenses. In this situation, the vendor submits timesheets for time worked and receipts for expenses.

- **Cost plus:** This contract is like a time and materials contract except that it also includes rewards or penalties based on the vendor's performance.

TIP Time and materials and cost plus contracts are risky for the customer. If the vendor takes longer than estimated or incurs more expenses than estimated, you still have to pay. For that reason, these types of contracts usually include a "not-to-exceed clause" that specifies the maximum amount for which you're responsible. If the time or expenses look like they will exceed the limit, the vendor would notify you and negotiate to increase the maximum.

- **Fixed price:** This type of contract works well when requirements are well defined or the work is familiar. The vendor receives a fixed amount regardless of how long it takes to complete the work or the expenses incurred. Although the vendor accepts the bulk of the risk, a fixed price contract can be profitable if the vendor is able to complete the work quickly and cost-effectively.

NOTE A retainer is another form of contract that's helpful when you don't have details about the work you want a vendor to perform. Instead of providing a statement of work, you simply contract for a number of hours during a period at a given rate — for example, 40 hours a month at $100 per hour. You send the vendor assignments as you identify work. If the work requires more time, for instance, 50 hours during a month, you can opt to pay more that month or extend the assignment into the next month.

Next Steps

At long last, you're ready to launch the project work. A significant milestone shouldn't slide by unnoticed. Take this opportunity to get everyone together so you can introduce the players.

Holding a Kickoff Meeting

Now that your team is assembled, a kickoff meeting is an effective way to introduce everyone and orient the entire team to their new assignments. You can confirm what everyone already knows about the project and get them enthusiastically pulling in the same direction by reviewing how the project is going to work. Here are some common elements of a kickoff meeting:

- **Introductions:** Because many of the team members haven't met, the kickoff meeting is perfect for introductions. Start by introducing yourself (the project manager). Then, introduce the project sponsor, project customer, and other stakeholders. If the team is small enough, you can introduce every member of the team. Otherwise, at least introduce the key players.

- **Project purpose:** A great way to get people jazzed about the project is to have the project sponsor talk about the purpose of the project, what it's supposed to achieve, and why it's so important.

TIP If you can, arrange for the project sponsor to record a short video so your team can see and hear the sponsor directly. This approach can be more motivating than having the project manager or someone else speak on the sponsor's behalf.

- **The project plan:** Step through the project plan with the entire team. Depending on the size of the team, this might be the first time some team members see the plan. This review helps everyone see how all the pieces fit together.

- **Ground rules:** Similar to the rules the referee rattles off at the beginning of a boxing match, project ground rules let people know what you expect from them and what you won't tolerate. For example, some of your ground rules might be that you ask people to suggest solutions to the issues or problems they identify, treat their team members with respect, or communicate bad news early enough that you can do something about it.

- **Review processes:** In addition to ground rules, you can also review your change management, risk management, communication, and quality management plans and processes, as well as any other processes you've put in place. That way, team members can be more productive because they know how to get the administrative aspects of their assignments done.

Implementing Your Plans

During planning, you put together plans for managing changes, risks, and the quality of results. At this point, you're ready to implement those plans:

- **Change management:** The process for requesting changes is in place. You don't have to do anything more until change requests start coming in.

- **Risk management:** You appoint people to track the risks you've decided to monitor. Then, they look for signs that risks are turning into reality.

- **Quality management:** Once work is underway, you and your team begin performing the processes in this plan to measure the quality of results, analyze the measurements, and take corrective action, if necessary.

- **Communication:** When execution begins, you also implement your communication plan: obtaining status and other information from your team, holding meetings, and disseminating information to project audiences.

CROSS-REFERENCE In the PMP Exam's Domain III: Executing the Project, Tasks 3, 4, and 5 correspond to implementing the change, risk, and quality management plans.

Summary

To move from planning to executing, you must first get the key stakeholders to approve your project plan. Once that hurdle is behind you, you can set the baselines for your project and set up the storage repository for the project documents you've produced so far and the ones yet to come. You finish acquiring the resources you need, whether they come from other departments or must be procured from other companies. Finally, you hold a kickoff meeting to introduce the team and explain how the project is going to run.

Coach's Review

Use this section to assess what you've learned in this chapter and to apply it to a real-life project you're currently working on.

Test Your Knowledge

Test your knowledge of the material in this chapter by answering the following questions. See Appendix A for the answers.

1. Why must you obtain approval for your project plan before beginning the executing process?

2. Why do you set a baseline for your project before beginning work?

3. What are the main steps in a procurement process?

4. Name three things you can accomplish with a kickoff meeting.

Project Challenge

Select a project you're working on and write up the steps you would perform to launch the project:

- Describe how you would obtain approval from stakeholders given the project environment and technology that's available.

- Design a repository for your project documentation based on the technology that's available.

- Identify the information you would baseline for the project.

- Describe the procurement process you would use for the resources you require.

- Prepare an agenda for the project kickoff meeting and describe how you would hold the meeting (in person, conference call, and so on).

CHAPTER 14

Taming Processes, Problems, and Conflicts

A project is like a journey. You start out in one place with the intention of getting somewhere else. But, unlike some treks, you don't want your project to be an adventure with twists and turns, surprises, backtracking from dead ends, and hair-raising exploits. It should be more like a trouble-free business trip — an efficient, cost-effective jaunt from point A to point B. Project ground rules are akin to a travel itinerary for your trip. You know whether to look for a driver or airport shuttle to pick you up, or hoof it to the nearest subway station. Ground rules help make a project run more smoothly and pleasantly for everyone.

Whether your project has a few people assigned or thousands, you want them all pulling in the same direction. The processes you put in place help people do just that. Processes are guidelines for how to get things done on your project so your team doesn't have to waste time figuring out what to do next. At the same time, those processes should be flexible enough to cover a variety of circumstances as well as allow for better ways to produce results. This chapter begins with a discussion of the characteristics of effective processes — and what you can do if you're stuck with some that are less than ideal.

As you learned in Chapter 1, a project is about solving a problem. Once your project starts, you realize that you end up solving lots of small problems and making lots of decisions every day. In this chapter, you learn some guidelines for improving your problem-solving and decision-making skills. Unfortunately, another important project skill for a project manager is resolving conflicts, whether stakeholders have conflicting objectives or have different ideas about how to achieve the goal. As a project manager, you can work on improving your conflict resolution skills over your entire career. This chapter provides a few effective techniques for conflict resolution and recommends a few resources if you want to learn more.

CROSS-REFERENCE This chapter covers many of the topics listed in the PMP Exam's list of Cross-Cutting Knowledge and Skills (which apply to all of the exam's domains), including conflict resolution, decision making, negotiating, prioritization, and problem solving.

Defining Project Processes

Most people would prefer to get things done right the first time, effectively and efficiently. And everyone wants to get through their work days with the least amount of annoyance possible. Effective project processes can go a long way toward helping your project get done when and in the way it should.

Processes are perfect for activities that people perform on a regular basis. A good process can provide guidelines for performing the work quickly and easily, and it can help people remember all the steps. In effect, a process helps automate tasks that are repeated during a project so people don't have to spend time and energy rethinking how to do things. For example, as you learned in Chapter 11, "Setting Up a Change Management Plan," a process for submitting and evaluating change requests helps you obtain the information you need to make better decisions about which changes to include in your project. In addition to project management processes such as managing change, managing risk, and reporting time and status, you can use processes to document the work content of the project, such as producing software builds or testing.

What Makes a Good Process?

The bottom line: Good processes help make your project successful. If they don't, get rid of them. When you're designing processes (or tailoring existing ones), ask whether they:

- **Help get work done:** Good processes don't get in the way. They actually help people get their work done more efficiently and effectively. If someone uncovers a particularly effective way to build a widget, you can document that process so everyone can build widgets with equal alacrity. Or consider your process for submitting a change request. With a procedure and a standard change request form, requestors know what information they need to provide and who to submit the request to.

- **Prevent problems:** No one wants to deal with the same problem over and over. Many processes are born to prevent problems from occurring or reoccurring. For example, the IT people notify your team of planned server maintenance so crucial software builds aren't interrupted. The trick is to avoid developing a process that is more onerous than the problem it was designed to solve.

- **Help deliver quality:** Improving quality is the flip side of preventing problems. You can develop procedures and processes to increase the accuracy of results or the quality of deliverables. For example, when people know what information is needed for a change request, you won't waste time sending questions and answers back and forth.

- **Provide needed information:** A lot of communication occurs in a project environment and it can be tough to keep track of who needs to know what and when. For that reason, many processes revolve around getting the right information to the right audiences, as you learn in Chapter 10, "Setting Up a Communication Plan." You might have processes for generating reports and distributing them to the project sponsor, stakeholders, team members, and other interested parties. But you probably also have processes for your team members to report their time and status.

TIP The best processes will dovetail with the characteristics of your project and those of your team. For example, if you have closely knit teams that work together like clockwork, you might opt for basic checklists or leave it up to them to work out their own processes. If your teams design their own processes, it's a good idea, as project manager, to understand how they work so you know how to get the info you need.

Making Processes a Success

The processes you design won't deliver their intended benefits if no one on your team uses them. If you design good processes, chances are your team will feel comfortable that the project is in good hands, give its nod of approval, and use your processes. However, you can take a few additional steps to make sure your processes are a hit.

Once you have a process mapped out, whether it's to prevent a problem or speed things along, perform a small-scale test to work out the kinks. Pick an area within your project that's small, low-risk, and, if possible, out of the mainstream. Set the test up as you would any other. Identify the results you expect and define success criteria. Then, ask the people in the pilot to use the process. Measure the results and get feedback from the testers. If the results weren't what you expected, correct the process as necessary and run the test again. Bob McGannon, this book's technical reviewer, shared a friend's take on getting things right: "You don't have to be perfect to start, but you have to start to be perfect."

When a process is finally ready for prime time, people need to know about it. Publicize the new process to the audiences that will use it. Make information about the process easy to find, for instance, by posting instructions or forms on your company intranet. Use technology to simplify following the process or ensure that a process is performed correctly, similar to the work flows that are automated using online collaboration tools. Just as important, make it clear that people must follow the process. Don't allow work to move forward unless the process has been followed — unless you agree ahead of time to make an exception.

BUILDING A PROJECT CULTURE

The culture of your organization influences your project. After all, the project came about to achieve goals within your organization. In addition, your work environment is molded by the organization's values. For example, things will work one way when teamwork, accuracy, and traditions are the goals. The environment will be different if innovation, creativity, and individuality are prized.

Over time, the flavors of the project goal and objectives, the team, and how people work meld together as they do in a tasty soup. From that, a project starts to develop a culture of its own. But you don't have to leave that to chance. As project manager, you can use ground rules to shape and nurture the culture within your domain.

To build a project culture, you need to know the values you want to encourage. Think about what you consider important in your life and your work. In some cases, you might think about what you'd like to see different about your work environment.

With a set of values defined, you can publicize them within your project. Values can be built into your project mission statement at the beginning of the project. You can also communicate them when you hold a kick-off meeting with the stakeholders and your project team. In addition, you can design your project processes to promote the values you've targeted. Most important, you demonstrate those values with everything you do as project manager: how you act, how you communicate, how you handle problems, and how you treat people, which are sometimes detailed in a team charter.

Defeating Poor Processes

Processes get a bad rap, due primarily to the multitude of poor processes float-ing around the business world. Bad processes are like barnacles on the keel of a boat: They slow people down and increase their levels of frustration and annoyance — without providing the benefits that repeatable processes should.

Some of these recalcitrant processes started that way. They may have been developed without a good understanding of why they were needed or the prob-lem they were supposed to solve. On the other hand, some processes worked just fine when they were first set up. The problem could be that they're ill-suited to your current situation, but no one bothered to change them with the times.

Then again, some processes are ridiculously complex or grow that way over time. (Tax returns are a classic example.) Changing these processes can be a los-ing battle because the underlying work is so complex. However, sometimes the processes themselves can be burdened with double- and triple-checking results.

Bad processes may come to light when your team rankles about perform-ing them. If team members blame specific processes for preventing them from completing their assignments on time, you should investigate to see if the accusations are true. Measuring and analyzing the time people spend perform-ing a process can help determine whether it's effective. If people make a lot of mistakes performing the process, streamlining or automation might be in order.

Regardless of the reasons, you have a few choices if you've inherited a bad process or two:

- **Come up with a better process.** If there's a good reason for the process, such as managing changes or risks, design a new and improved one. The first step is to make sure you understand what problems the process is meant to solve or which results it's meant to ensure. When you take this approach, you might have to convince the management team to give your new process a chance. If the existing process is built into your business systems, there is some additional work to modify the current automation.

- **Deal with the process so your team doesn't have to.** For processes that aren't going anywhere, another option is to perform the process yourself so your team doesn't have to. Filling out requisitions for equipment is a good example of this type of process. You spend a little bit of your time satisfying the process masters and your team gets to work without inter-ruption. One side benefit to this approach is that you may earn brownie points from your team members.

- **Deliver successfully without the process.** Finally, you might consider doing your work without following the process as long as you are confident that you can deliver the required results without it. If no one asks why you didn't use the process, you're home free. And if you are questioned, you can show that the results were just fine without it, ask forgiveness, and suggest a different approach. Keep in mind that this tack can be risky in an organization that swears by its processes no matter what or within a regulatory environment.

Guidelines for Effectiveness

Every day, you perform many of the same activities and use certain skills whether you're managing a project, a team, or just yourself. You have to make decisions, solve problems, and make things happen. And every so often, you have to settle conflicts. As a project manager, you can boost your project's success by honing these skills in yourself and your team. This section provides some guidelines for increasing your effectiveness in these areas.

Making Decisions and Solving Problems

Making decisions and solving problems have a lot in common. In fact, most decisions are about how you're going to solve a problem, or preferably, preventing them from occurring in the first place. That means that you can become more effective in two essential skills using the same techniques. How's that for efficiency?

Focus on What's Important

You usually have too much to do and not enough time to do it. Although you would like to consider every decision carefully and analyze every problem with a gimlet eye, you won't be able to. Formal decision processes and problem solving take time and require data, both of which could be in short supply.

A significant technique for improving both your decision-making and problem-solving skills is to focus on what's important. You can perform a quick cut to classify each decision and problem that comes your way, so you can handle them appropriately.

Decisions and problems can be classified by their importance and urgency. Figure 14-1 shows some examples of each category. The secret to being effective is to ignore what isn't important, regardless of how urgent it seems to be. If a decision or problem lands in your lap, ask yourself if it is important. If it isn't, just let it go. If a decision isn't important for you, ask the person who requested the decision or identified the problem to recommend a way to address it. By delegating, you coach team members to handle issues more effectively.

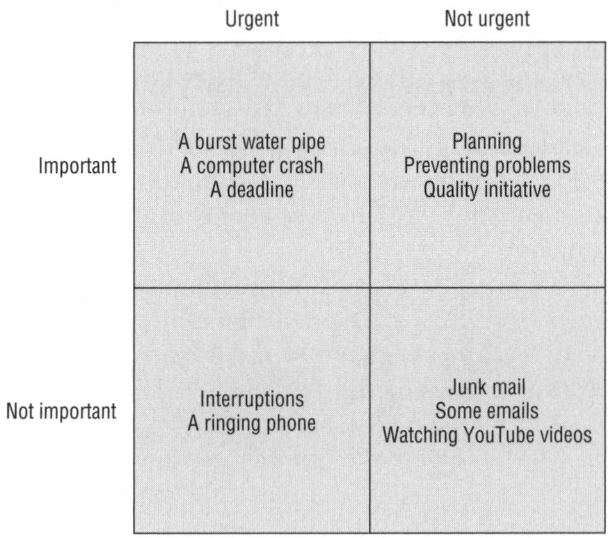

	Urgent	Not urgent
Important	A burst water pipe A computer crash A deadline	Planning Preventing problems Quality initiative
Not important	Interruptions A ringing phone	Junk mail Some emails Watching YouTube videos

Figure 14-1: Decisions and problems can be classified by their importance and urgency.

TIP Urgency can make things seem more important than they are. Someone races into your office, drops a folder on your desk, and says "This has to be done in an hour!" It's easy to fall into the trap of "doing" whatever it is immediately without determining whether or not it's important. With most urgent requests, you have time to ask a few questions to find out if the task is truly important and why it's so urgent.

The decisions or problems that are left are important, but some are simple enough that you can handle them quickly using your intuition and experience. If the decision or problem is an easy one, take care of it immediately. For example, if a few simple criteria are satisfied, any alternative might do. By closing out the straightforward ones, you free up your head to focus on the decisions and problems that remain. The rest of this section describes an overall approach to solving problems and making decisions. Because many problem-solving methodologies are grounded in quality processes, you can learn about additional problem-solving techniques, such as Ishikawa fishbone diagrams and root cause analysis, in Chapter 9, "Planning for Quality."

TIP Some very important activities aren't urgent, so they might get lost in the shuffle of more pressing endeavors. Planning, prevention, and gathering lessons learned are examples of activities that might get ignored even though they can dramatically improve your results. Be sure to map out some space in your calendar to attend to important, but not urgent, work.

Define the Problem

Whether you're hunkering down to solve a problem or getting ready to make a decision , the heart of the matter is the problem — just like a project boils down to a problem to solve, as you learned in the section "Discovering the Problem or Opportunity" in Chapter 3. Before you go any further, make sure you understand what the problem is. That's the best way to improve the quality of the decisions you make and the actions you take.

You also learned in Chapter 3 that people struggle to identify problems because they tend to focus on symptoms. To determine the problem, talk to other people to gather different perspectives and information. Ask questions to get to the bottom of the issue. Ask why people think there's a problem. Ask others what is happening that shouldn't be, or what isn't happening that should. Ask for details: why, when, where, how, who is involved (not who is to blame). Find out what the potential causes are.

TIP With complex problems, break them down into more manageable pieces. Decomposition works on problems just as it does for breaking down work in a work breakdown structure. Then you can tackle each part of the problem separately. See Chapter 9, "Planning for Quality," to learn techniques that help dissect problems into smaller chunks.

Prioritize

Decisions and problems aren't created equally. Some have more significance. Their effects last longer or affect more of your project. You evaluate the impact of the decisions and problems you have to deal with and work on the ones with the greatest effect on your project. How long a decision will affect your project is another consideration. A decision with far-reaching and long-lasting effects is one to consider carefully.

TIP Find out how long you have to make a decision or solve a problem. If you don't take action within that time, someone else might do it for you. Not making a decision can be bad for your project and your reputation – possibly worse than making the wrong decision.

Consider Your Options

When you're addressing decisions and problems that are complex, crucial, or both, you need to evaluate your options, just as you do with project strategy, as described in "Deciding on the Project Strategy" in Chapter 3. Considering alternatives helps you work through decisions that have several variables or a variety of consequences, or that are unfamiliar to you.

Even with big decisions, don't ignore the option of doing nothing. Purposely taking no action is an action in a way, and it might be an acceptable alternative. For example, suppose you're in charge of a project for attending a trade show and you have materials from previous events. If your company's products haven't changed, you might decide to go with the materials you already have.

Listing pros and cons is a tried and true method of evaluating options. For each one, document the advantages and disadvantages. Then, you can weigh the suitability of each option. Ask questions such as "Which option is the most realistic given the constraints on resources, time, cost, and other factors?" "Which option solves the problem for the long term?" and "What are the risks associated with this option?" Sometimes, none of the options are satisfactory, but they're all you have. If that's the case, start by eliminating the worst ones. When you're left with one, you have the best option you're going to get, even if it's broccoli over Brussels sprouts.

Ask for Help

Although you might make some decisions and solve some problems on your own, don't be afraid to ask for help if you need it. Brainstorming with others can identify options you might not have thought of. Other people might spot flaws in your reasoning. In addition, working with others can help you to be more dispassionate about your decisions.

TIP You can improve your decision making and problem solving by evaluating how you did on the decisions that are complete, similar to the lessons learned during a project. Were the results what you expected? Were there ramifications that you didn't expect? Did you involve the right people? Could you have improved your results by doing things differently ?

Making Things Happen

Project managers spend a lot of time making things happen, so this is another skill that you hone every day. When you're trying to get something to happen, the critical step is to clarify what that something is. In effect, each thing you want to happen is like a project in miniature, so knowing the goal is important for achieving success. Be very clear about what you need (whether it's resources, time, money, an answer, a decision, authority, and so on) so you can clearly communicate that need to the team member responsible for delivering.

The other key is to figure out who can give you what you need. In some situations, you may need assistance from others in your quest. For example, if the person in power is several levels up the chain of command, find out to whom that person listens and ask this advisor to help you. You can run your request by this advisor to see what he or she thinks and learn ways to tweak the request to improve its chance of approval by the person higher up. When you ask someone, whether an executive, stakeholder, or team member, to do something, make sure that your request is clear and specific, much like you do when you prepare a project proposal (see the section "Defining a Project" in Chapter 3).

HOW TO GET RESULTS

You might wonder how you can propel people to action without carrots, sticks, or influence. Here are a few techniques to try, regardless of your audience:

- Take some time to understand what your audience cares about and then frame your request in terms of the benefits they'll receive by helping you. For example, if you need help from the operations team, explain how your request can help them streamline their day-to-day work.

- If you need the help of another person to make one of your ideas become reality, help that person come up with your idea on his or her own. This approach takes practice and a deft touch. You ask the person key questions and guide them toward the answer you want.

- If you need something from a person who is renowned for being unresponsive, make your request and set a deadline for delivery. As a last resort, to motivate the person to respond, tell him or her what you plan to do if they don't provide a response to your request by that time. You can stack the deck in your favor by choosing the alternative that you feel is best. For people who mimic immovable objects, you might resort to choosing the alternative the person would find most distasteful. For example, if one of your stakeholders wants to publicize his role in the project, you might remind him that you won't be able to include his name on the list of contributors if he doesn't provide information that you need.

How to Resolve Conflicts

Different perspectives are great for truly understanding something and for solving problems. Each person might see something or come up with an idea that no one else would. Differences of opinion and disagreements are good ways to evaluate the merit of an idea, approach, or plan. You hear someone else's side and you have to defend your own reasoning. On the other hand, conflicts can be devastating if they aren't resolved or resolved well. As a project manager, you will have to resolve your share of conflicts, whether they are conflicts you have with someone else or conflicts between people involved with your project. Your team will be more effective if the team members can resolve their own conflicts — and you can help them learn to do that.

Like project management itself, conflict resolution isn't something you master in a day, or ever. But you can improve your skills with a few techniques and some practice:

- **Look for something positive to start with.** Rooting for the same sports team isn't enough. Conflict heightens people's emotions. Part of finding a solution to a conflict is to eliminate or at least reduce the emotions that people feel. One way to do that is to find something that the parties agree on and go from there. Say that two groups are arguing over who gets a key resource. The point they agree on is that both groups value that resource highly. For this situation, you can start the discussion with what makes this key resource so valuable.

- **Understand what the other side cares about.** People often disagree heatedly on details, even though they're interested in the same things at a higher level. You can smooth the way to a successful resolution by taking the time to understand what the other side considers important. You may discover that the other side places a high value on something that isn't that important to you. One side might want that specific resource because she's worked with the group before. The other side might not care which resource it gets, as long as the person is competent and fits the budget.

- **Pick your battles.** Every side in a conflict has items they must have and others that they're willing to compromise on. Before you begin the discussion, determine your must-haves and negotiable points. Then, once the interaction begins, you can negotiate with your less important points in order to maintain your stance on your must-haves. For instance, one group in the resource discussion from the previous bullet point might be comfortable hiring a contractor but balks at the price. One solution is to divide the cost of the resource between the groups.

CROSS-REFERENCE Although the business shelves at bookstores are rife with books about negotiating and handling conflict, two truly stand out. In the *7 Habits of Highly Effective People* (Covey, Free Press, 1989), Habit # 4 is "Think Win-Win." Conflicts frequently arise when people view life as one side winning and the other losing. Think win-win is an approach that looks for solutions that benefit both sides. *Getting to Yes: Negotiating Agreement Without Giving In* (Fisher, Penguin Books, 1991) is a classic book about how to turn a competitive negotiation into a collaborative one.

Summary

Good processes help your project become a success. People work more effectively and sidestep problems that tripped others up in the past. The key is to develop processes that help rather than hinder results. Processes need to fit your project and your environment.

Problem solving, decision making, and conflict resolution are all skills that help you get things done in your projects. In addition to becoming more effective yourself, you can help your team improve in these areas.

Coach's Review

Use this section to assess what you've learned in this chapter and to apply it to a real-life project you're currently working on.

Test Your Knowledge

Test your knowledge of the material in this chapter by answering the following questions. See Appendix A for the answers.

1. What steps can you take so that your team uses a process?
2. What is the most important thing you can do to solve problems and make decisions more effectively?
3. Describe three steps for making decisions.

Project Challenge

Consider your work environment and the projects you work on. Choose a project process, such as risk management, and design a process that fits your environment and culture.

CHAPTER 15

The Keys to Successful Meetings

Suppose you go to great lengths to enlist a valuable resource as a project team member, only to hear her say, "I'll be delighted to work with you on this project, but don't make me come to any meetings." It's understandable. Sometimes meetings are merely interruptions to work on project tasks. When meetings are dominated by people posturing, pontificating, and politicking rather than achieving the business at hand, they're not only a waste of time, but downright annoying.

However, good meetings move your project forward. With the right people collaborating, a good meeting can be the most effective way for the project team to generate creative ideas, collect facts, develop a deliverable, troubleshoot a problem, and make a decision.

This chapter provides a dose of common sense and best practices about conducting meetings for your project. You learn tips and techniques about setting up and running effective meetings, conducting different types of meetings, and following up afterwards.

CROSS-REFERENCE The information in this chapter relates to the PMP Exam's Domain II: Planning the Project, Task 6, "Develop a communication plan based on the project organization structure and external stakeholder requirements, in order to manage the flow of project information."

Running Effective Meetings

It's been said that the test of a true leader is whether people come when that individual calls a meeting. Even when meetings are mandatory, people find a way to avoid meetings they consider useless. They'll have a conflict, forget, or get sick. The kicker is when you start to hear people say they can't come to your weekly status meeting because they're "too busy" or "have to get some work done." This is when you might want to evaluate the effectiveness of your meetings.

This section includes tips, techniques, and best practices for all your meetings. You can be sure that people will come and participate in your meetings if you develop a pattern and reputation for respecting everyone's time, making every minute count, and accomplishing important work at every meeting.

CROSS-REFERENCE Learn techniques about specific types of meetings such as brainstorming sessions and status meetings in the section "Types of Project Meetings" later in this chapter.

Planning a Meeting

Before setting up a meeting, be sure that it's the best mechanism for accomplishing your objective. The most compelling reason to have a meeting is that you need several minds present in the room at the same time in order to most efficiently achieve your goal.

Once you've decided that a meeting is the thing to do, determine who needs to be there. Be sure that only the people who are essential to the meeting are invited. In some cases, everyone on the project team is essential, but most of the time only a small subset of people, such as those working on a particular activity, need to be there. Don't worry about hurting someone's feelings by not inviting them to a given meeting; they'll probably be grateful. If it's a gray area, you can send optional attendees a courtesy copy of the meeting invitation.

Decide on the meeting duration, which is often dictated by the nature of the meeting. Some meetings, such as status meetings and management meetings, tend to be more effective with shorter durations — a sense of urgency makes everyone get down to business more quickly. On the other hand, you might need a longer period of time for a brainstorming session or work breakdown structure planning meeting to foster creative and process-oriented thinking.

THE SCRUM HUDDLE AND THE 22-MINUTE MEETING

Scrum huddles and the "22-minute meeting" philosophy offer precedents for the effectiveness of really short meetings and their ability to get a lot done and get everyone back to working on their tasks immediately.

A fixture of agile project management is the *daily Scrum*, also known as the daily standup, the Scrum huddle, or morning roll call. It's a quick daily check-in, in which the team members stand in a circle, and one at a time, everyone reports on the tasks they worked on yesterday, the tasks they're working on today, and any risks or obstacles that stand in the way of today's plan. The daily Scrum doesn't take more than 15 minutes.

The "22-minute meeting" asserts that many meetings can be handled in about 22 minutes. The meeting has a goal-based agenda, required reading is done in advance, the meeting starts on time, participants stand rather than sit, laptops and mobile phones are not allowed, the facilitator keeps the meeting focused on the goal, and meeting notes are sent immediately.

Settle on a date and time that's most convenient for the essential attendees. This is often a challenge, but it's much easier if you have shared appointment calendars on your network.

Book a meeting room that's conducive to the work being done. For example, if you're conducting a brainstorming session or developing the work breakdown structure, reserve a room with at least one white board and perhaps a computer projector. If you're conducting a quick check-in status meeting, you might consider an open common area large enough for all attendees to stand for about 10 or 15 minutes. If you're facilitating a strategic planning session or risk identification and assessment session that will require more concentration and focus over several hours, consider an offsite location.

Setting the Agenda

Have an agenda for all meetings. The agenda sets the context and framework for the meeting and conveys the purpose and significance of the meeting to participants.

This is true even for weekly status meetings. You might use the same agenda every week and just change the date. The agenda ensures that you cover all your items without getting sidetracked. Participants can use it for notes and action items.

A good agenda includes the following items:

- Meeting name and date
- Meeting goal, expected outcome, and overall time limit

- Topic names, time limits, and person leading the topic discussion
- Expected outcome of the topic discussion, such as decision or action

Next to each topic discussion, include space for notes, action items, and due dates (see Figure 15-1).

Mobile Web Eyeglasses
Development Project

Meeting Agenda

Project Goal
Research and develop the new mobile Web eyeglasses product.

Meeting Name:

Meeting Date and Time:

Meeting Goal or Outcome:

Topic	Responsible	Time Limit	Decision, Action Item, Due Date, Owner, Notes

Figure 15-1: Meeting agenda

CROSS-REFERENCE **A sample of a meeting agenda is available in the companion files for this book. You can download it at `www.wiley.com/go/ProjMgmtCoach`.**

You might also consider including the project goal on every agenda. It's an easy way to keep the project goal constantly at the forefront for all team members.

Inviting Participants

Your meeting invitation is the first signal to the participants that your meeting will indeed be worth their time. The following are tips for making the meeting invitation compelling and indicative of your facilitation style:

- In the subject, state that this is a meeting invitation and state the meeting topic.
- In the first one or two lines of the email message, indicate the date, time, place, purpose, and length of the meeting. You want to make it easy for

attendees to quickly digest the basics of the meeting, and you don't want the invitation to look like too much work to read through.

- Include the agenda or any background information below those first couple lines or as an attachment to the email.

- As with most emails, keep your sentences and paragraphs — in fact the entire email — short and scannable. Use bulleted or numbered lists where possible. If you can't avoid a longer email, use subheadings.

- Make sure that everyone who receives the meeting invitation can see everyone else who's invited.

TIP If available, use the meeting invitation feature of your email program's calendar. Participants can accept your meeting invitation and have it added to their online calendar. They can also decline or mark it as tentative.

Preparing for the Meeting

As a project manager, you already know that planning and preparation are keys to success. Of course, the same is true for your project meetings. Give yourself ample time to prepare.

For the status update meeting, for example, you might just need an agenda. For a project plan approval meeting, you probably need a slide presentation. For working meetings whose result is brainstormed ideas, the work breakdown structure, or risk identification and assessment, you might need forms or other materials to facilitate the process.

Also consider whether you need assistance. In many cases, as the project manager, you serve as the leader, meeting facilitator, and scribe. Sometimes you might ask others to play one or more of these roles to make the process go more smoothly.

REALITY CHECK: ACCOUNT FOR MEETING TIME IN YOUR SCHEDULE

In the tool you use to schedule your team members' tasks, never use eight hours as a full project work day. On average, because of meetings, training, and other activities that consume time, you can realistically assume no more than five or six hours per day of real working time dedicated to a project.

When the meetings have to do with the project, you can add them to the project schedule. This is especially true for major meetings that will take a day or more of preparation and perhaps significant team member time for participation as well.

However, for weekly half-hour meetings, you might not want to deal with the minutiae required to add them to your schedule, unless customer billing requirements dictate that you do. If you can, just leave these meetings to available administrative time.

In addition to your own planning and preparation, some types of meetings need the participants to prepare as well. In your meeting invitation, let participants know what's expected of them. Should they bring their latest status report and current task list? Should they prepare thoughts about risks and issues in their areas of responsibility? Will they be asked to report on a particular deliverable? Or do they just need to bring their brain and their brilliance?

Starting on Time

Timeliness is essential. When you start the meeting on time, you are training the participants that this is one meeting where it doesn't pay to be late.

Don't wait for latecomers, and don't catch them up when they arrive. (Don't even waste time making a sarcastic comment when they do arrive.) If you are depending on a particular person to achieve the results of the meeting, call them from the conference room, and try to work on other agenda items until they arrive.

Setting Expectations

At the start of the meeting, emphasize the goal and the outcome you expect to achieve. Do this even though you probably already stated it on the agenda and the meeting invitation. Because people deal with different issues, all clamoring for their brain's attention, restating the meeting goal helps focus everyone on your common purpose.

Briefly review the main points of the agenda. State the length of the meeting as well as the amount of time allotted to each agenda item to finish on time.

If the meeting has a special framework that you're facilitating, review that and any ground rules. If others are helping you with the facilitating or note-taking in the meeting, get them started. Set the stage for how the meeting will be conducted so participants can settle in and start the work.

TELEPHONE, WEB, AND VIDEO CONFERENCING

The level of sophistication available with Web and video conferencing has made it easy for project teams distributed around the world to collaborate around a virtual meeting table.

As the meeting facilitator, be aware of possible distractions. Sometimes the tendency is for the live participants to speak primarily to the speaker phone or video to the exclusion of participants across the table. Other times, the remote participants are ignored.

Whatever the virtual conferencing situation, facilitate the meeting to ensure that everyone is included and fully participating. The phone, Web, or video conferencing should enhance the collaboration process and allow more of the right people to participate.

Facilitating the Meeting

As the project manager, you are constantly called upon to facilitate various aspects of the project. Remember that facilitate means "to make easier." When you're facilitating a meeting, you're making it easy for everyone to fully participate and achieve the meeting objective.

Here are some tips for effectively facilitating a meeting:

- **Maintain the time limits:** Holding to the time limits you specified for each agenda item helps reduce socializing and unfocused discussion. People will get straight to the point if they know there's only five minutes or less to discuss a topic or convey information. If certain people take too much of the floor, consider using a timer for each agenda item, and possibly even a timer for each speaker if things are getting out of hand.

- **Have one speaker at a time:** Also have just one meeting at a time. Eliminate interruptions and side meetings with tactful facilitation and perhaps the use of a token such as a talking stick, a card, or whatever. Whoever has the token has the floor.

- **Stay focused:** Keep to the agenda items as well as the meeting's goal and outcome. Record the other important topics that are bound to come up in a "parking lot" or "issues bin" for future discussion. Staying focused on the meeting's outcome will ensure that your meetings will never be accused of "just talk and no action."

- **Allow everyone to contribute:** Make sure that everyone who needs to present or discuss has the opportunity to do so. If more dominant voices tend to overpower the quieter voices, where appropriate, have a round-robin discussion in which everyone has the opportunity to share their information or opinion.

TROUBLESHOOTING TROUBLED MEETINGS

Many problems with meetings can be solved with the simple solutions described in this section. But you might have bigger problems such as ongoing conflict among participants, people refusing to discuss difficult issues, or poor meeting attendance.

If you're not sure how to fix a problem meeting, ask someone else for his or her candid opinion. This can be a team member, a peer, a managing stakeholder, or someone unconnected with the project. As long as this person can offer you helpful and candid feedback, you might be able to see your blind spots about the meeting or figure out solutions to make the meetings work better.

Ending on Time

Be as scrupulous about ending on time as you were about starting on time. If another session is needed to finish the work you started, schedule it. As always, this is about respecting people's time and their roles on the project.

End the meeting on a positive note. Recap how you all achieved the meeting's goal and intended outcome. If you didn't achieve the meeting's goal, address what you'll do differently next time. Let participants know when they can expect to receive the meeting summary. Briefly review the action items and next steps. This will give you and the meeting participants a satisfying sense of accomplishment.

Types of Project Meetings

Although all types of meetings benefit from the best practices for effective meetings described in the previous section, different types of project meetings have additional requirements. This section examines how you can make the most of common types of project meetings.

CROSS-REFERENCE The information in this section relates to the PMP Exam's Domain II: Planning the Project, Task 1, "Assess detailed project requirements, constraints, and assumptions with stakeholders based on the project charter, lessons learned from previous projects, and the use of requirement-gathering techniques (e.g., planning sessions, brainstorming, focus groups), in order to establish the project deliverables."

Kickoff Meetings

In the kickoff meeting, you introduce and orient your team to the project and their new assignments. Hold the kickoff meeting very soon after the project plan has been approved and the team assembled — in effect, at the point when the project executing processes are starting.

During the kickoff meeting, your team members not only meet each other, but they also meet the managing stakeholders, especially the project sponsor or customer. It's ideal to have the sponsor or customer present at the kickoff meeting; if that's not possible, at least have him or her there by videoconference or a message that you relay.

Review the project goal and objectives so everyone starts out on the same page. Walk through the project plan so that each person understands the context of his or her role within the big picture of the project.

Explain the project's processes and procedures so that expectations are clear from the start. This includes everything from reporting status and handling issues to managing change and resolving problems.

CROSS-REFERENCE For more information about this initial orientation to the project, see the section "Holding a Kickoff Meeting" in Chapter 13.

Project Status Meetings

The project status meeting is a standing meeting with your team members to discuss ongoing project progress, namely, what tasks have just been completed, what tasks are currently being worked on, and any issues or obstacles with those tasks.

As the project manager, you determine when to start the status meetings and how often to have them. Status meetings are often held weekly, but sometimes, particularly in agile projects, there's a daily status meeting. You might decide to have more or less frequent meetings throughout the project lifecycle, and the frequency tends to be dictated by the needs of the project and the team.

The focus of the project status meeting is ongoing forward movement and information about dependencies between one another's tasks. Typically each team member reports on his or her accomplishments for the past week (or day) and his plans for the next week. Most project managers like team members to report on any obstacles or red flags that are impeding progress. This is also an excellent forum for reporting on risks, problems solved, and lessons learned. See Figure 15-2 for a sample project status meeting agenda.

Mobile Web Eyeglasses Development Project	**Meeting Agenda**	
Project Goal *Research and develop the new mobile Web eyeglasses product.*	**Weekly Status Meeting** November 14, 2014, 1-1:30 pm	
Meeting Goal: Weekly check-in from each team member about accomplishments, goals, and obstacles.		
Topic	**Time Limit**	**Notes**
Weekly check-in, round robin Tasks accomplished since last week Tasks in progress Tasks being completed in the next week Obstacles to completing tasks	1-2 min each 15 min total	
Other risks or issues	5 min	
Problems solved	5 min	
Lessons learned	5 min	

Figure 15-2: Project status meeting agenda

CROSS-REFERENCE A sample of a project status meeting agenda is available in the companion files for this book. You can download it at `www.wiley.com/go/ProjMgmtCoach`.

Because it is held more frequently, the project status meeting can be as short as the 15-minute daily check-in, but generally no longer than an hour for a weekly or monthly meeting. Note that details such as percent complete or the number of hours spent are typically handled in status reports and not in the status meeting.

NOTE In the daily Scrum meetings for agile project management, documented meeting agendas tend not to be used. However, Scrum meetings do follow a structured process, and some documentation might be part of the meeting discussion.

CROSS-REFERENCE For more information about project status meetings, see the section "Obtaining Time and Status" in Chapter 17.

Management Meetings

A management meeting is one you conduct with executive stakeholders, including the project sponsor or customer.

CROSS-REFERENCE The information in this section relates to the PMP Exam's Domain II: Planning the Project, Task 11, "Present the project plan to the key stakeholders (if required), in order to obtain approval to execute the project." It also relates to Domain IV: Monitoring and Controlling the Project, Task 6, "Communicate project status to stakeholders for their feedback, in order to ensure the project aligns with business needs."

You might conduct a management meeting to:

- Gain approval for a project proposal to move ahead with project planning.
- Obtain signoff and budget for a project plan to acquire your resources and start executing the project.
- Report on project cost and schedule performance upon completion of major deliverables or other milestones throughout the project.
- Review status of and responses to issues and risks.
- Obtain acceptance and sign-off on a completed project.
- Conduct a lessons learned session with managing stakeholders.
- Select the right mix of projects for the organization's project portfolio in support of the organization's strategic goals.

The key stakeholders involved in a given management meeting are determined by the purpose of the meeting and the functional areas and organizations involved. The following are tips for conducting an effective management meeting:

- Prepare a more formal and polished presentation. A slide presentation with a brief accompanying handout is ideal. Create the slides with graphically oriented, easy-to-digest information. Avoid project-insider jargon, although it's usually fine to use industry or organizational buzzwords.

- Present high-level summary information suitable to the management audience. In general, you'll do well to keep the material short, concise, and to the point. However, get to know the members of your management team so you can meet their preferences and expectations.

- Focus on strategic goals being met and benefits realized, while also pointing out the costs to the organization in terms of money, resources, time, and effort.

- Although your presentation focuses on summary information, be prepared for challenges about specific details. You might get tough questions about costs, schedule, why things are being done a particular way, and how aspects of a project integrate with other groups or efforts in the organization.

- Send advance material, such as a project proposal or acceptance report, two or three days before the meeting. Understand and work in conjunction with the organization's culture and expectations.

- Keep the meeting short, but be flexible in case the executives want to take it further. For example, schedule the meeting for a half-hour, but book the conference room for an hour.

CROSS-REFERENCE For more information about communicating with management, see Chapter 10, "Setting Up a Communication Plan," as well as "Obtaining Approval" in Chapter 13.

Brainstorming Meetings

Every project is full of creative work, often because the endeavor has never been done before, or at least not in this way. A new opportunity — perhaps a newly released technology — has arisen, and an organization needs to imagine ways it might take advantage of the innovation. Perhaps a problem has been identified, and you and your group want to think openly and creatively about all possible solutions before determining a course of action.

An excellent technique for fostering collaborative creativity is a brainstorming meeting in which all participants generate as many ideas as possible. Although there are many variations, essentially you conduct a brainstorming meeting as follows:

1. Gather the participants in a meeting place with white boards or flip charts and easels. Provide the participants with sticky notes, notepads, and pens.

2. State the subject of the brainstorming exercise. Review the rules of brainstorming. Also have the brainstorming subject and rules posted on one of the walls.

3. Have everyone contribute with their ideas. You can have everyone walk around the room and write their ideas. Have them write them on the sticky notes if you expect to move the ideas around. Otherwise, have them write directly on the white boards or flip chart paper. You can have people shout their ideas out, either in a free-for-all or in a round-robin fashion while a scribe scribbles them on the wall.

4. As people contribute their ideas, there is no evaluation, criticism, or judgment. Even the most outlandish ideas can help generate other plausible ideas.

The following are typical brainstorming rules:

- Refrain from any judgment or analysis of ideas.
- Show respect for every participant and their ideas.
- Encourage outlandish and exaggerated ideas.
- Build on ideas that others suggest.
- Encourage a quantity of ideas, not quality.

When all ideas are exhausted, you can either gather the ideas for later analysis, or you can take a break and then come back and start the analysis with the same group. One way to analyze is to arrange the ideas into three categories: excellent, interesting, and "a stretch." Another method is to have participants "vote" for the ideas they feel are the best, either with tick marks or sticky notes. You can discuss the ideas further to narrow them down as needed.

Planning Meetings

At various points in the project, you need to gather team members and other experts to collaborate and develop a specific planning document. Examples include the requirements document, solution design, the work breakdown structure, risk identification and assessment, and lessons learned. In such a meeting, you're collecting information related to a particular aspect of the project, and the outcome of the meeting is a document or other result that becomes part of the project plan.

A planning meeting has certain elements in common with a brainstorming session. The difference is that you're not generating new, creative ideas. Instead, you're collecting facts within a specific structure from experts on the topic.

Conduct a planning meeting in a fashion similar to the following:

1. Gather the participants in a meeting place with white boards or flip charts and easels. Provide the participants with sticky notes, notepads, and pens.

2. If necessary, list categories for different aspects of the project or planning activity on different white boards or flip charts.

3. State the subject of the planning activity — for example, risk identification.

4. Have everyone contribute information on the topic. As with the brainstorming, you can have everyone mill about the room and write their ideas on the sticky notes or directly on the white boards or flip chart sheets. Or, you can have a designated scribe record the information. You might consider having the scribe record the information on a computer with a projected screen.

5. Continue with the structuring or analysis of the information as appropriate until you're finished. The outcome of your meeting will be the completed information, which you can then format, submit for review, and add to the project plan.

CROSS-REFERENCE For information about developing the requirements document, see the section "Gathering Requirements" in Chapter 3. For information about conducting a work breakdown structure development meeting, see the section "Identifying Work" in Chapter 5. For more information about conducting a project risk session, see the section "Identifying Risks to a Project" in Chapter 12. For information about conducting a lessons-learned meeting, see the section "Gathering Lessons Learned" in Chapter 22.

Following Up after Meetings

After meetings are over, close the loop by following up as needed. Follow-up articulates the work that actually took place in the meeting: Decisions are remembered (correctly) and action items actually get completed. In addition, the project plan is updated as appropriate.

Good follow-up often marks the notable difference between an average project manager and a superior one. A superior project manager is able to synthesize and translate discussions into tasks and then follow up on those tasks to make sure they're done.

Documenting Decisions and Action Items

After most meetings, prepare a meeting summary and send it as soon as possible. You can do it as project manager, or you can ask a team member to do it.

The meeting summary doesn't necessarily need to be formal meeting minutes. In fact, it can be as simple as a brief email message. Whatever form it takes, record the following outcomes:

- Decisions, sometimes with next steps
- Action items, with owner and deadline

If the meeting brought to light any key information such as issues, risks, problems, solutions, or lessons learned, record those in the meeting summary as well.

Make sure that all meeting participants receive the meeting summary. Add the meeting summary to the project notebook. The summary can help jog your memory about the decisions and action items. These summaries will also eventually become a part of the project archives.

If it was a brainstorming meeting, compile the ideas and send them to the participants along with a thank-you for their participation and creativity. Let them know what will happen with the ideas, and keep them informed as the process moves forward.

If it was a planning meeting, compile the resulting product, such as the WBS or risk analysis document, and send it to the participants. Thank them for their time and expertise.

Adjusting the Project Plan

The outcome of a planning meeting typically becomes an integral part of the project plan — for example, the requirements document or lessons learned report. If information or activity from the meeting affected the project plan, then you need to update the proper section of the plan. This could be a change to the project schedule, the budget, issues tracking, risk management plan, or lessons learned knowledge base.

Information or activity from the meeting can lead to bigger changes. For example, if a new obstacle might require a scope change, you'll probably need to submit a request to the change review board. If the change is adopted, you'll need to update the work breakdown structure, the project schedule, and possibly the budget.

Summary

Meetings are a great project management tool for moving your project forward. However, maximizing the productivity of meetings can sometimes be a challenge.

It's important for you to decide when a meeting is the best mechanism for the issue at hand. You also need to discern the right people to be invited and the appropriate length of time. Even composing the meeting invitation must be done with care.

Your team members and other meeting participants will give their time and attention to your meetings if you develop a reputation for running efficient meetings that accomplish important work for moving the project forward. Ensuring an efficient meeting involves good preparation, starting and ending on time, following an agenda, setting expectations and ground rules, and facilitating the meeting skillfully. This is true for all types of meetings, whether it's the project kickoff, a weekly status check-in, a brainstorming session, a management sign-off presentation, or a lessons learned meeting.

Coach's Review

Use this section to assess what you've learned in this chapter and to apply it to a real-life project you're currently working on.

Test Your Knowledge

Test your knowledge of the material in this chapter by answering the following questions. See Appendix A for the answers.

1. Name four key techniques for effective meetings.

2. How does good facilitation contribute to an effective meeting?

3. Name one thing you can do if a participant consistently takes too much time in meetings.

4. What type of meeting might you hold if you need to design a solution to a problem? How would you conduct such a meeting?

5. In a brainstorming session, what are the advantages of refraining from judgment and encouraging quantity over quality of ideas?

6. What must be documented after each meeting?

Project Challenge

Practice the knowledge you've gained in this chapter with the following challenge. Use the project you're currently planning as you're working through the chapters in this book.

1. As part of your communication plan, you've determined that you'll have periodic status review meetings with your project team. Based on the culture and preferences of your organization, prepare the ground rules for these meetings.

2. Think of a problem or opportunity faced by your project or organization. Following the effective meeting practices, invite a group to participate in a brainstorming session about the problem or opportunity. Prepare the room, set the ground rules, and conduct the brainstorming session.

Transforming People Into a Team

The people assigned to your project work together only temporarily but you need them to pull together as a team if you want to get their best. Although the trek to teamdom might not be pretty, you can help your team members make the journey.

Another challenge is that the people who work on your project report to other managers. You have to learn how to motivate people without direct control over their careers and salaries.

This chapter introduces several techniques for managing people — techniques that work whether folks are team members or direct reports. Everyone is different, so this chapter is only the beginning. You have to figure out which approaches work best with your personality as well as the resources assigned to your projects.

CROSS-REFERENCE This chapter relates to Task 6, "Maximize team performance through leading, mentoring, training, and motivating team members," in the PMP Exam's Domain III.

Developing a Team

You can throw people together on a project, but that doesn't mean they're a team. People learn to work together over time and the process can be disconcerting both for the team members and people like you watching from the sidelines.

To add to the challenges, teams need different types of support as they grow. For that reason, it's helpful for you to understand the phases that teams go through and how you can help at each stage of the game. For example, a newly formed team requires detailed instructions and lots of guidance. Once a team matures, you can provide the team with a goal and some brief guidance and let team members handle the rest.

Turning Individuals into a Team

Bruce Tuckman developed the "Forming, Storming, Norming, and Performing" model to describe the stages that teams go through on their way to high performance. The following list describes the four phases and the best way to lead teams at each phase:

1. **Forming:** In the beginning, the people within your team are still sorting things out. They aren't sure about their roles and who's responsible for what. They aren't clear about their goals as a team. The bottom line is forming teams need guidance and they will look to you for that.

   To help a young team grow, give it clear directions. Define the team's goal, explain why that goal is important, and spell out what you expect from the team. Take time to answer questions from team members or the team as a whole.

TIP Don't be surprised if a forming team starts to challenge your authority. For example, the team might choose to tackle a problem in its own way instead of taking your advice. Just like a youngster, a young team resists authority as it matures.

2. **Storming:** Power struggles and disagreements are to be expected as team members sort out their relationships with one another. People pick sides within the group, which means that the team has trouble making decisions. To make matters worse, the team will increase its challenge to your authority. Although the seas look stormy, the team members are talking, and eventually the discussion will help them work out their issues.

   As project manager, you have to help the team make decisions or work out a satisfactory compromise. In addition, you have to watch for storms that aren't going away or relate to non-project issues. If those occur, you must step in and refocus the team on its objectives.

3. **Norming:** Once a team has weathered the storm, it's really a team. At this point, a team can make decisions effectively and, at the same time, know when to let individuals or subsets of the team handle smaller issues. The

team will fine-tune how it interacts and the team members will truly bond. They may begin socializing with one another.

As project manager, you can let the team take more control. In fact, you might not need to do anything unless the team asks. You can keep an eye on the team just in case it goes off track, and then, you can diplomatically bring the team back on course.

4. **Performing:** The members of a performing team will still disagree from time to time, but the team resolves its own issues. A performing team leads itself. The team will even develop its own processes to increase its performance.

    As project manager, you can hand off tasks or subprojects to the team and let the team figure out the best way to deliver.

NOTE Performing teams are usually small groups of people, so don't expect that level of performance from your entire project team. However, you can sow the seeds of high performance by giving teams something to strive for. Give mature teams challenging, but achievable goals. They will figure out how to increase their performance to tackle the challenge.

TIP Regardless of a team's stage, be there for team members if they ask for your assistance. Even performing teams need help from time to time. And if a team at that level asks for something, it's probably important.

Building Relationships with Your People

Leadership and relationships are an important aspect of your job. In addition to keeping the project pointed in the right direction, you also have to be able to work effectively with people who are essentially on loan to your project.

The nature of projects can make developing good working relationships challenging but also essential:

- **Temporary assignments:** Sometimes, working on projects can feel a lot like the premise of the movie *Fifty First Dates*. You work with lots of people you've never worked with before. You have to get to know them and they have to get to know you and the other members of the team.

- **Assignments on multiple projects:** In addition, people on your team might be working on more than one project at a time. When people work on several projects simultaneously, they need to know more than the work they're supposed to do. Ideally, they also need to know the priority of each assignment, so that the most critical work is done first. As project manager, the best approach is to assess the work under your control, prioritize it, and present your prioritization to management. If necessary, you can adjust your priorities based on the executives' input.

Keep in mind that most team members either set their own priorities or have them set by their functional managers. Members of teams that reach Tuckman's performing stage know what's important and take responsibility for getting it done.

■ **Reporting to more than one manager:** People who work on projects usually report to a regular line manager as well as a project manager or team lead. Even if you work with line managers, your team members may feel like their loyalties are stretched in several directions.

Each person on your team is different and you have to get to know all team members if you want to build good working relationships with them. The following guidelines help you develop effective working relationships with almost everyone:

■ **Clarify roles, responsibility, and authority.** Because most projects today are complex, the work requires a lot of interaction between team members. For teams to function effectively, everyone needs to be able to depend on their teammates. They need to know what each person, including you, the project manager, is supposed to do; who is responsible for each part of the work; and who has the authority to make different decisions. This up-front knowledge, combined with the actual experience of working with others, builds the trust that makes everything run more smoothly.

SETTING AN EXAMPLE FOR YOUR TEAM

Relationships are built on trust, so it's important for team members to trust one another and to trust you, the project manager. Let your team members know that you value integrity and dependability. Be a good role model for your team by taking the high road and telling the truth even when faced with difficult situations.

Another way to bond with your team is to be open about your strengths and weaknesses as a project manager. For example, you can start by explaining how many different things a project manager is supposed to do and how many skills the job requires. That can be your lead into admitting that you aren't good at everything. You can share with your team your self-evaluation: what you think you're good at, what you don't do that well, and what you don't like doing. At that point, you can ask your team to help you fill in the gaps.

In addition to boosting your team's confidence ("Hey, the PM needs our help!"), you also show by example that imperfection is okay and that it's safe for team members to be open with each other about their strengths, weaknesses, likes, and dislikes. You send a message that pitching in and helping one another enables the team to capitalize on each team member's strengths and builds a team that's more than the sum of its parts.

TIP When times get tough, roles and responsibilities are even more critical. Under pressure, people might become fearful and blame others for what goes wrong. That's your opportunity to lead your team. Reiterate everyone's roles and responsibilities. Emphasize what is expected from each person. Reinforce that team members are depending on each other. Express your confidence in the team. Talk with people individually to make sure they're comfortable or to reduce their anxiety.

■ **Set specific, challenging, yet attainable goals.** Regardless of whether you're defining the overall goal of a project or a single work package, specific goals give people something to aim for. But don't make the mistake of giving people goals that are too easy. In addition to boring your team members, they might assume that you don't have faith in them. Over time, they lose interest and motivation, which leads to less productivity and lower-quality results. In contrast, individuals and teams grow by overcoming challenges. You can start off easy to gauge team members' abilities. As they prove themselves, you can set the bar higher. And there's nothing wrong with asking your folks what you can do to help them do even better.

■ **Provide assistance and remove obstacles.** Team members want to know that you're in their corner. On the one hand, you can earn their loyalty by making sure they have what they need to do their jobs, such as enough time and the right equipment. On the other hand, removing obstacles might earn their devotion. Ask team members if anything is getting in the way and take action to try to remove those obstacles. If you succeed, your people will be productive and grateful to you. Even if you can't eliminate some obstacles, you earn points by showing that you care.

TELL TEAM MEMBERS HOW THEY'RE DOING

Most people like to know that they're important and doing a good job. You can build people's confidence and your relationship with them by telling them why their work is important. When a team member does something right, jump in with positive reinforcement. Treating people with respect is another unspoken way to convey how you perceive them.

If something goes wrong, refrain from blame and other negative reinforcement. Instead, explain what the problem is and how this team member might avoid the problem in the future. Describe what you want people to do going forward. Although the redirection might still sting a little, your team members will appreciate the chance to get back on the right track.

▪ **Have some fun.** Play is just as important as work. Introduce some fun and games into your project environment, whether you hand out a humorous plaque each week or invite easy-going competitions. You can get the most laid-back teams to participate by offering prizes that require managers to make fun of themselves. Hold offsite events or spring an impromptu morale-booster on the team, like a team trip to the movies or bringing in a pizza lunch.

Increasing Your Influence

When it comes to influence, project managers have a challenging dilemma. They reflect the authority bestowed upon them by the project sponsor. However, the effectiveness of this authority is not a given. As a project manager, you can increase your power and influence in an organization by continually increasing your leadership skills, your relationships within the organization, and your expertise.

▪ **Leadership**: Project team members often do not directly report to their project managers, so methods of motivation beyond the carrot and the stick are necessary. Your team members will be confident that the project and their work is in competent hands when you communicate clearly with your team members, show that you value and recognize their contributions, seek their feedback, make sound decisions, and demonstrate your expertise. You'll command respect from your team members that you need to lead them through project execution to a successful finish.

▪ **Relationships:** Project managers must constantly negotiate with and persuade those in support departments to provide what's needed. The ability to foster good working relationships, not only with your team members and managing stakeholders, but also with people in support departments and vendor companies will help you get what you need for the project. Remember that give-and-take is essential in good working relationships. Be willing to help others, and then you are more likely to receive help when you need it. Following through on your commitments goes a long way building trusting relationships.

▪ **Expertise**: Project managers have experience in project management principles as well as the technical subject matter of the projects themselves. You've been through the project management school of hard knocks, and you know by heart the recipes for project success as well as disaster. You need to be able to share your know-how when key project decisions are being made. If you have your own project or idea you're trying to sell, or if there's a project being foisted on you that needs to be "unsold," using the influence you've garnered through your expertise can ensure that your ideas get the best shot.

Evaluating People's Performance

While a project's performance has a lot to do with how individual team members have performed, the performance of team members is more difficult to evaluate than the project itself. Unlike schedule and cost variances, many of the things you look at with people are hard to quantify.

CROSS-REFERENCE Chapter 18, "Evaluating Progress and Performance," describes methods for evaluating a project's performance.

Finding Out What's Going On

When you want to see how people are doing, you can start by looking at their assignments. Do they deliver their assignments on time? Is the effort they expend on track with the estimated hours and do they complete the work in the estimated duration? Were the results in line with what you expected?

Even if those answers are positive, there's more to performance. To get a better picture of how team members are doing, the personal touch is the way to go. Talk to your team members — whether in person, on the phone, or via email, if absolutely necessary.

Ask open-ended questions to find out how they think work is going and whether they have any issues. Here are several examples:

- Tell me what's going on with your assignments.
- Have you run across any issues? Tell me about them.
- What can I do to help?
- What can I do to make things run more smoothly?
- What are you most happy about with this project?
- If you had one wish, what would you like to see happen on this project? Okay, if you had a hundred wishes. . . .

CROSS-REFERENCE For more tips about effective communication, see the section "Guidelines for Good Communication" in Chapter 10. The section "Guidelines for Effectiveness" in Chapter 14 discusses techniques for solving problems and resolving conflicts. Chapter 15, "The Keys to Successful Meetings," discusses how to run meetings and get people to participate. Chapter 22, "Don't Forget Lessons Learned," includes tips for gathering information, including situations in which team members might be uncomfortable sharing.

Although some people aren't shy about talking about problems, others clam up when there's trouble. If things get too quiet around the office, ask more questions and listen carefully to the responses. Read people's body language.

Of course, you will get a lot of info about how things are going at your status meetings and lessons learned meetings. But you can also observe the interactions between team members to see how people are getting along. Lack of participation and strained conversations are signs of problems. Ask the attendees what's going on and what you can do to help. On the other hand, if your people are in good moods and teasing each other in good fun, you'll probably find that work is going well.

> **TIP** If communication is strained, the problem might be you. Consider bringing in someone you trust to get an objective reading on whether you're inhibiting the interaction. If you can, find out what other people see as your shortcomings. Then, if you make meaningful changes in your behavior, you can win the team over.

Working with Line Managers

Line managers will need information from you to complete evaluations of the people who report to them. But you can also get useful information about your team members from their line managers.

When you request resources, you typically ask for people with a specific set of skills. In some instances, you might ask for specific individuals — for example, if you know that a group with the skills you need has worked together in the past. However, when the folks assigned to your project are unfamiliar, you can ask their managers what they're like.

Later on, you return the favor. Line managers need input from project managers and other groups to complete someone's performance evaluation. You might receive a phone call from the manager or a questionnaire to fill out about how the person performed while working for you. You can enhance your working relationships with line managers by providing information without being asked. For example, make it a habit to provide line managers with one- or two-paragraph assessments for each team member you work with when they finish their project duties. The next time you need one of their resources, you'll probably have an easier time arranging the assignment.

> **TIP** Don't let a less-than-positive analysis of someone put you off. There's nothing that guarantees that a line manager gets along with every direct report. Give your new team member a chance, but keep a close eye on his or her work until you feel comfortable with the team member. If the assignment doesn't work out, see the next section to learn some steps you can take.

Handling People Problems

Sometimes, people simply don't work out. Whether it's a problem with the wrong or inadequate skills or personality clashes, dealing with the situation quickly is key. Otherwise, the performance of your entire team can suffer.

When someone's behavior causes problems, a tactful discussion often does the trick. In many instances, people don't realize the effect they have on other people. Try explaining the situation and helping the person see things from other people's perspectives.

If someone's performance doesn't meet your expectations, the issue could stem from several sources. Consider the following possibilities:

- Make sure team members understand their assignments and what you expect.

- Confirm that team members have the skills needed to perform the work satisfactorily.

- If team members don't have the right skills, discuss options with the line manager. For example, you might be able to find another assignment for the team member while bringing a new person onto your project. (In addition, you should go back to your work packages and resource requests to make sure you were clear about what you needed.)

NOTE If you decide to use people who don't have the level of skill you require, evaluate the effect that will have on your project. Depending on the magnitude of the changes, you might need to communicate them to the stakeholders.

- If someone has a negative attitude or isn't willing to perform to your expectations, your team and project will suffer. In a situation like this, work with the line manager and the human resources department to determine the best course.

Summary

Building and managing teams can be a lifelong vocation. Teams go through stages and mature in the same way children do. The methods you use for interacting with them change every step of the way. You also have to develop relationships with individual team members. Because you work with people temporarily and share them with other projects as well as with their department managers, building effective relationships takes a concerted effort. But following a few simple guidelines can do wonders.

Evaluating people's performance is more qualitative than quantitative. The same personal interactions you use to develop relationships can do double duty to help you see how people are doing.

Coach's Review

Use this section to assess what you've learned in this chapter and to apply it to a real-life project you're currently working on.

Test Your Knowledge

Test your knowledge of the material in this chapter by answering the following questions. See Appendix A for the answers.

1. What four stages does a team go through during its development?
2. When is it most likely that you'll need to help a team?
3. Name three ways to build relationships with team members.
4. How does evaluation of people performance vary from evaluation of project performance?

Project Challenge

Suppose that your team has been working on its assignments for a month. You notice that work is beginning to fall behind schedule and status meetings have gotten very quiet. People aren't talking much or sharing information. What would you do to find out what's going on? Prepare a list of questions you can use to coax team members into talking.

Part

IV

Monitoring and Controlling

Chapter 17: Gathering Progress Information
Chapter 18: Evaluating Progress and Performance
Chapter 19: Getting a Plan Back on Track

Gathering Progress Information

Before you can see how your project is doing and whether you need to take action to keep it on course, you need to know where things stand. That's why monitoring and controlling your project begins with collecting data about your project's progress from your team members.

Some aspects of gathering project data are consistent from project to project, while other facets vary depending on the project. The data you need typically includes how many hours were worked, when work was performed, how much cost was incurred, and so on. However, you might ask for more or less detail based on the size of your team or choose a frequency for updates to suit the project.

Because a project is a microcosm within a host organization, you often have to figure out how to get the project-related data you need while also working with the time and cost reporting for the overall organization. In this chapter, you learn some approaches for gathering project data without overtaxing team members with status reporting.

CROSS-REFERENCE The information in this chapter relates to the PMP Exam's Domain IV: Monitoring and Controlling the Project, Task 1, "Measure project performance using appropriate tools and techniques, in order to identify and quantify any variances, perform approved corrective actions, and communicate with relevant stakeholders."

Choosing the Data to Collect

The project finish date and the final price tag are almost always important factors for the success of a project. For that reason, the project customer, sponsor, and key stakeholders usually are keen to know how a project is doing schedule-wise and cost-wise; that is, they want to see quantitative results such as percentage of completed work, finish dates, and cost.

To give your audience (whether it is the project sponsor, customer, stakeholders, or team members) the information it wants, you have to collect the right data — both quantitative values and more qualitative information. For example, in addition to numbers such as dates, hours worked, cost for the hours worked, and ancillary costs, the reasons behind task performance can tell you a lot about what might happen in the future. In addition, other information such as quality results, issues, and risks plays an important part in determining the best actions to take if you need to get the project back on track.

Schedule and Cost Data

Most people involved in a project have an "Are we there yet?" mentality focusing on when the project will be done. However, there is more to a project than its finish date. While the project is under way, key stakeholders ask when individual tasks will be complete and how much money has been spent. Of course, your quest to deliver this information starts when tasks begin and follows with progress updates until all the tasks, and thus the project, are complete.

NOTE Most of the time, you use some type of project management software to track and manage your projects. When that is the case, you either collect the data directly into the program or you must transfer the data into your project file in some way. After that, you can evaluate how the project is doing, as described in Chapter 18, "Evaluating Progress and Performance."

It isn't enough to track which tasks are complete and when they started and finished. The number of hours that people work and when they work them combine to provide a true picture of progress.

TIP As you learned in the section "The Difference between Duration and Effort" in Chapter 6, estimating work hours provides a more accurate picture of a project schedule and cost than task duration alone. Then, when you execute the project, monitoring the hours worked provides a more complete depiction of progress. The comparison of your planned hours to actual hours helps you improve your estimates for resource requirements, schedule, and cost for future projects.

The following list describes the data you need for project status and how each piece of information contributes to the results:

- **Actual start:** Although your project plan includes a schedule with planned start and finish dates, you know that the schedule rarely sticks to the original plan. The first piece of data you need for each task is the actual date that assigned resources begin work. The actual start date is the point where progress on a task truly begins.

  For example, your schedule might show one task starting immediately after another task finishes. But, in reality, the second task might not start right away, perhaps because the assigned resources are still cleaning up different assignments.

- **Actual hours of work:** As you learned in Chapter 6, "Estimating Work and Cost," you need the number of hours people work on tasks and when they perform that work. The task duration (the number of work days between the start and finish dates) doesn't tell the whole story.

  Some people work part-time schedules. But even full-time workers end up spending some portion of each day on non-project work. In addition, team members might not work on task assignments every workday — for example, if they're home sick or get pulled off a task to work on something else. On the other hand, if you have several people working on the same task, you burn through more than a full-time quota of work hours each day.

- **Remaining hours:** You also need information about the work that remains to be done, including the current estimate of hours to complete the work and the estimated completion date. With actual hours worked, remaining hours, and estimated finish date, you can determine whether the task is on schedule and within budget.

  For example, suppose a task started on time and the assigned team member has worked 40 hours on the task during the first week, as you planned. So far, the numbers sounds good. However, if you estimated 50 hours for the task and the team member says she needs another 40 hours to finish the work, something is amiss. Perhaps you have a less-experienced resource than estimated or work that wasn't identified initially. As the project manager, you need to unearth the issue and determine what to do.

- **Cost:** The number of hours that people work determines the labor costs for your project. Whether you use employees or contractors, every hour that people work comes with a cost. For example, most companies calculate burdened hourly rates for employees, such as programmers, based on the average salary and cost of benefits for their positions.

You also have to collect data for other expenses that the project incurs, such as equipment rentals, materials used, travel, fixed-price contracts, and so on.

> **NOTE** If you hired a vendor on a fixed-price contract to deliver specific deliverables, you won't receive information about the hours worked by the vendor's employees or the actual costs the vendor incurred. You pay a fixed price to receive the contracted deliverables at a specific time.

Quality Data

As you learned in Chapter 9, "Planning for Quality," the quality management plan identifies the quality measures and processes you intend to use to determine whether the project is meeting its quality objectives. Once the project is underway, you launch those processes and begin gathering your quality data accordingly.

Quality data provides another perspective on progress. For example, if the testing team is finding a large number of software defects, the software development tasks might require more hours than estimated in the project plan. Depending on the issues, you might choose to bring in additional resources with expertise in resolving the problems.

In addition, the quality data you collect might identify problems for which the quality plan has a response. In that case, you implement the actions in your quality plan to achieve the quality objectives.

Issues and Risks

Issues and risks present yet another viewpoint of a project's true status. Obtaining information about the issues that are plaguing team members or risks that have occurred can help you understand the progress that's been made and what you have to do to improve it.

You need to know about issues and their effect on work so you can figure out how to eliminate them or, at least, reduce their impact. Issues can prevent team members from making as much headway on their assignments as you had planned. For example, tasks might be delayed because the necessary equipment hasn't shown up as scheduled. Team members might be interrupted with requests from other projects. Or administrative tasks are consuming a significant amount of time.

Negative risks that turn into reality are issues, as discussed in the previous paragraph. However, you also need to watch for risks that appear likely to occur. Chapter 12, "Managing Risk," describes the components of a risk management plan. When you begin monitoring and controlling the project, you also begin monitoring risks. If any of the risks that you track occur, you implement the risk response you planned.

TIP Remember, risks relate to uncertainty so they can have negative or positive consequences. Risks that have occurred might mean delays, but some risks might reduce hours or cost.

Determining the Level of Detail

The level of detail you request from team members depends on the size of the project and the maturity of the teams working on it. In addition, you need to decide who provides updates to you directly.

Although the amount of time that people work on assignments is essential to tracking project performance, you don't need to know what team members work on down to the minute. Most of the time, hours worked is enough. However, in some cases, you might need to track time in smaller increments — for example, if you are billing time to a customer who wants time reports rounded to 15-minute increments.

For small projects, you might request details from each team member — time worked, estimates for remaining work, quality, issues, risks, and so on. On the other hand, if your project has a cast of thousands, you don't have the time or attention span to digest detailed status updates from every team member. In that case, you need to rely on team leads to gather and summarize project information. The information you request depends on what you want to know and what you need to report to your superiors. You might ask for the high-level dates, hours, and costs for the tasks for which the team lead is responsible. In addition, you might request significant issues or successes. For example, your team leads can review the status updates that team members submit, help them resolve issues, and possibly determine how to get the team's work back on track. If the team needs help, then the team lead can ask you to weigh in with advice or to make a decision.

Obtaining Time and Status

Once you identify the data to collect, the next step is to determine the schedule on which team members will submit their updates. The ultimate test of your data collection process is actually obtaining updates from team members.

Choosing the Frequency

Collecting project data is a balancing act. You want enough data to determine your project's status and receive early warnings of problems on the horizon.

But you don't want your team members consuming time with status updates that they could be spending on completing project work. How much is enough and how much is too much?

Work package size is one way to choose the frequency of status updates. (The section "How Much Is Enough?" in Chapter 5 discusses how to determine the appropriate work package size for your project.) Setting the frequency to a time period equal to half the hours in a typical work package means you get one or two updates before a task completes. For example, suppose the majority of your project's work packages are 80 hours of work. Requesting status updates every week will provide one update while a task is in progress and a second update when it completes. For short projects, daily updates might be more appropriate.

In many projects, you don't have a choice about the frequency of updates. If the management team meets on a specific schedule and expects an update at every meeting, you're going to request updates a few days prior to those meetings.

ADJUSTING FREQUENCY OVER TIME

Have you noticed that projects get a lot more "exciting" as the finish date approaches? If the finish date is crucial, you have to pay more attention to progress as the deadline approaches, particularly when tasks are running behind schedule. For that reason, you might change the frequency of status updates as your project progresses. Perhaps you start out with updates every two weeks. But during the last few weeks or months, you might request updates every week. If the project is behind schedule as a hard deadline approaches, you might even switch to daily updates. Keep in mind that tracking time and reporting status takes time. If your project is running late, more frequent updates reduce the amount of time team members can spend on finishing their assignments. Updates don't have to occur exclusively in meetings. For example, team members might check in via email.

Sources of Data

The data you use to evaluate performance comes from several sources. In some cases, you receive data from team members in accordance with the plans you developed during project planning. Some data comes from your organization's business systems — as long as you provide them with the initial setup information they need.

NOTE Regardless of the source of data, make data collection as automatic as possible. If your organization uses an enterprise project management system, you can set up that system so team members can submit project time, quality results, issues, and risks according to a format you specify. The system

can also remind team members to submit their reports on a regular basis. Otherwise, you can set up a template for status and reminders about when reports are due to help your team members provide the information you need.

The following are some of the sources you might use to obtain project data:

- **Task status forms:** You need hours and estimates for the remaining work to update your schedule. For all but the tiniest of projects, you want tools in place that streamline that data entry for your team members. For example, you might set up a system that sends task update requests to the team members. The form includes the names of the tasks currently scheduled. If the task is in progress, the form might include the actual start date, the hours worked so far, and the estimated hours remaining and the estimated finish date, as shown in the sample in Figure 17-1. Team members then fill in the hours worked during the reporting period and update the remaining hours and finish date, if necessary.

144244 F1701.xlsx

	A	B	C	D	E	F	G
1	Status for:	<Resource name>					
2	Tasks	Actual start date	Hours worked	Estimated remaining hours	Estimated completion date	Issues	Other comments
3	Assigned task 1						
4	Assigned task 2						
5	Assigned task 3						
6							
7							
8							
9							
10							

Sheet1 Sheet2 Sheet3

Figure 17-1: A template for task status helps team members provide the information you need.

TIP Some people deliver the information you request on time and without drama. But others might balk at the time it takes or try to skate past without reporting in. You can try explaining the importance of reporting time and status. But in many cases, incentives motivate people to do what you want. For example, offer a cupcake bribe to the first person who submits his or her timesheet each week.

If your organization doesn't include project performance in employees' goals and compensation measures, ask management to consider adding it.

- **Narrative status reports:** Your communication plan (described in Chapter 10, "Setting Up a Communication Plan") for the project spells out what information people communicate and when. This communication includes status reports, which usually include information about tasks, risks, issues, and quality results. You can set up a template for status reports to make it easy for your team members to include the information you require. (See the section "Status Reporting" in Chapter 10 for an example of a status report.)

▪ **Organization accounting system:** At the beginning of a project, you request accounting charge codes for your project so you can track your project's expenditures. Once work is underway, you can assign costs associated with the project to those charge codes. And when people fill out their organizational timesheet, their time gets allocated to the project. Reports from the accounting system provide data about project costs, including labor, materials, and so on.

REALITY CHECK: COLLECTING PROJECT TIME

You might think you can keep things simple by relying on your organization's time tracking system to collect time data for your project. In reality, that system most likely isn't set up to track work hours to the level of detail that you need. For example, it might track the time people work on broad categories of work as well as by customer or by project. But time tracking systems typically don't include entries for the individual tasks within a project. In addition, contracts and accounting codes can affect how time is recorded. For example, if a customer's contract places limits on the hours for different portions of a project, management might ask you to record hours worked on one part of the project to the accounting code for another part. As a result, you often need to set up a separate time tracking system to obtain data for project tasks.

If you choose to use a separate system, automate data entry and collection as much as possible. For example, if your organization doesn't use enterprise project management software with built-in time tracking features, consider purchasing a software program for task-oriented time tracking. If possible, assign accounting codes to the tasks that you track so you can export your project time and import it into your organization's time tracking system.

Summary

To evaluate project performance, you need progress data for your project, such as hours worked, start and finish dates, and how much of the work is complete. Additional information, such as issues, risks, and quality results, can help you determine whether tasks are really as far along as the numbers indicate.

Because you want your team members devoting most of their time to completing project work, you don't want to saddle them with onerous reporting.

For that reason, you want to set up an appropriate status update frequency. The ideal frequency helps you spot problems early on while also delivering updates to management when they need it.

Much of the data comes from project status reports you define in your communication plan. However, time worked can present some challenges, particularly because organizationally imposed time tracking typically doesn't capture the details you need about hours worked on your project tasks. For that reason, you'll want to set up a process specifically for collecting project time.

Coach's Review

Use this section to assess what you've learned in this chapter and to apply it to a real-life project you're currently working on.

Test Your Knowledge

Test your knowledge of the material in this chapter by answering the following questions. See Appendix A for the answers.

1. What data should you collect to get an accurate picture or project status?

2. How often should you collect data about project status?

3. Identify four sources for project data.

Project Challenge

Considering the accounting system in your organization and a project you're working on, design a method for tracking project time that will provide you with the data you need to evaluate project performance and make it easy for team members to fill in their regular timesheets.

- If you work with enterprise project management software, set up timesheets to record project-oriented detail while also summarizing time worked by accounting codes.

- If you don't have automated tools, develop a spreadsheet that records time worked on tasks and also summarizes time according to accounting codes.

Evaluating Progress and Performance

During project execution, team members work on their assignments and send you information about their progress. The status information you receive includes the progress data for individual assignments or tasks (as described in Chapter 17, "Gathering Progress Information"). To evaluate the health of your project, you need to examine progress data from different perspectives.

So where do you start with this examination? You're likely to get questions such as "Is the project on schedule?" and "Is the project within budget?" so it makes sense to start by comparing your progress to your original plan. If tasks run according to plan, you don't have to take action. However, if tasks don't mirror your baseline dates, hours, and costs, you'll see *variances*, that is, differences, between your actual schedule and cost data and what you had planned. You can investigate the causes of these variances by digging deeper into the status reports or talking to team members. For example, obstacles could be preventing your team members from completing their work or issues might be reducing their productivity.

Variances alone don't provide the complete picture of your project's health. For example, suppose the hours worked are less than what you had planned. That variance doesn't necessarily mean that your team members are completing work in less time than the baseline estimate. In fact, the most likely answer is that their assignments are behind schedule because the team members have worked fewer hours than you had planned. In this chapter, you learn how to use earned value analysis to determine whether your project is on time and within budget.

Although some project managers aren't responsible for analyzing the financial details of their projects, it's a good idea to understand how management evaluates financial performance. The fate of many projects hinges on whether they deliver specific financial benefits, such as earning back the cost of the project within a given payback period or providing the annual return on investment that management requires. This chapter describes several financial measures often used to evaluate project success.

CROSS-REFERENCE The information in this section corresponds to the PMP Exam's Domain IV: Monitoring and Controlling the Project, Task 1, "Measure project performance using appropriate tools and techniques, in order to identify and quantify any variances, perform approved corrective actions, and communicate with relevant stakeholders."

Evaluating Progress and Variance

The best way to digest the task of evaluating performance is one bite at a time. Start by looking at progress from a high level, such as whether milestones are complete and when they were completed. You can also compare actual values, such as start and finish dates, hours worked, and cost incurred, to your baseline values to determine the variances from your plan. This section describes these basic measures of progress and performance and explains several ways to present the information to make it easy to analyze.

Reviewing Milestones

Milestones play several roles in a project schedule, as you learned in the section "Indicating Milestones" in Chapter 8. Whether milestones represent decisions, approvals of project documents, events such as a delivery of materials, or indicators that related collections of work are complete, they can act as yes/no flags for project progress.

Because milestones have no duration, they remain incomplete as long as the tasks leading up to them are incomplete. As soon as all that work is done, the corresponding milestone is done, too. For that reason, completed milestones and their completion dates provide a high-level view of your project's performance from a schedule perspective. For example, you might include the completed milestones in your status report to management.

Even before a milestone is complete, you can use its forecasted completion date to check on the prognosis for delivery. The trend in the milestone's forecasted completion date can provide early warning that the work leading up to the milestone is in trouble. Figure 18-1 shows the forecasted completion date of a project milestone over time. Beginning in the fourth month, the forecasted date begins to slip later each month, an indication that the work for that milestone is in some kind of trouble. There are still five months remaining in the schedule, so the project manager can take action to correct the slippage.

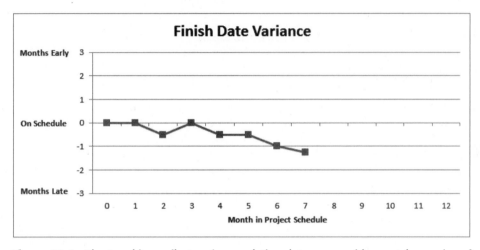

Figure 18-1: The trend in a milestone's completion date can provide an early warning of schedule problems.

Evaluating Variances

When you save a baseline of your project plan, you save the approved values for your project schedule and budget: start and finish dates, work hours, task durations, and costs. Once your team members start working on their assignments, you can compare what actually happened on the project to your baseline. The difference between an actual and baseline value is called a *variance*.

A positive variance means that the project or individual task is, as of the status date, ahead of schedule or that the actual cost is less than the baseline cost, because both of those situations are considered to be positive results. On the other hand, a negative variance indicates, at first glance, that the project or task is behind schedule or that the actual cost is greater than the baseline cost. Of course, if the variance is zero, your actual and baseline values are equal, which means the actual performance matches your plan.

Variances for task dates are often the first ones you look at. The date variances tell you whether a task or the entire project is ahead of or behind schedule. In Figure 18-2, the lower bar for each task indicates the baseline dates. The solid upper bar for each task shows the actual start date and the progress so far. The lighter upper bars indicate the remaining work and the forecasted finish dates. The difference between where the upper and lower bars end represents the finish date variance. For example, Task 1 is forecast to finish before the baseline finish date. However, Task 2, Task 3, Task 5, and Task 6 are all due to finish later than their baseline finish dates.

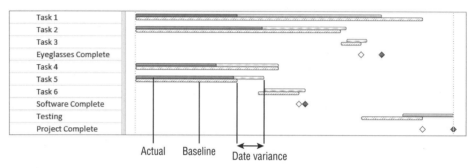

Figure 18-2: Variance between the baseline finish date and the forecasted finish date.

Cost variances indicate whether the project has spent more than or less than you had planned up to this point in the project. However, on their own, they can be misleading. Is a positive cost variance good or bad? It depends on the reason behind it. Unfortunately, the most common source of positive cost variances is that the team members haven't worked as many hours as you planned, so the labor costs are less than you estimated. However, a positive cost variance could have come about because your team members found an elegant shortcut for completing their work. Similarly, a negative cost variance isn't always a bad thing. For example, a negative cost variance might come from team members working more hours than you planned. If they also completed more work, the finish dates might be ahead of schedule.

CROSS-REFERENCE The next section, "Earned Value Analysis," explains how to look at both schedule and cost results to obtain a more accurate picture of progress than you get from schedule variance or cost variance alone.

To uncover the source of schedule and cost variances, look at the work hours that have been completed and the estimated hours remaining. If team members haven't worked as many hours as you had planned up to the current date, the finish date will be delayed. However, the team members might have worked the planned hours but didn't accomplish as much as was expected.

REPORTING STATUS WITH A STOPLIGHT REPORT

Determining how tasks are doing can be a challenge if you produce a report with nothing but rows and columns of variance values. A stoplight report provides a visual indication of whether tasks are ahead of, behind, or right on schedule. With a stoplight report, you replace variance values with green, yellow, or red "stoplight" icons. For example, if a task is ahead of or on schedule, the light is green. For a task that is slightly behind schedule, you display a yellow light. A red light indicates that the task is significantly behind schedule. That way, you or the management team can quickly locate the tasks most in need of help. Then, you can dig into the task's values to learn more.

You can choose your criteria for categorizing tasks as slightly behind or significantly behind schedule. For example, if you calculate variances as a percentage of task duration, you might consider any variance up to 5 percent slightly behind schedule. Variances greater than 5 percent would then be significantly behind schedule. In addition, you add another stoplight flag to indicate whether performance is improving or degrading, depending on whether the variance is decreasing or increasing as time passes. That way, management can easily see whether the variance is being handled effectively.

Earned Value Analysis

Getting a true picture of project performance is a challenge. Suppose the planned cost at the three-month mark of your project was $50,000. Three months have passed and you've spent only $40,000. It sounds like the project is $10,000 under budget. But, is that a good thing? What if the $50,000 was budgeted for 500 hours of team members' time and they have worked only 400 hours in the first 3 months of the project? The cost is below your planned amount because the project is behind schedule. Earned value analysis looks at both cost and how much work has been completed to determine the real status of a project's budget and schedule at a point in time.

Understanding Earned Value Measures

The heart of earned value analysis is, not surprisingly, the earned value of the project. *Earned value* is the value (in dollars) that the project has, in effect, earned because of the work that is complete. But earned value analysis actually uses three measures to deliver the complete assessment of your project's health.

Planned Value

The *planned value* (PV) of a project is the baseline cost you estimated up to the status date you're using. The baseline cost is how much you planned to spend on work that was scheduled to occur prior to the status date in your baseline project plan. For example, say your project plan includes work that is supposed to occur between April 1 and April 13 and costs $10,000. The planned value as of April 13 is $10,000.

Earned Value

As you learned at the beginning of this section, the earned value (EV) represents the value (in dollars) of the work completed up to the status date, which is the same as the baseline cost for the completed work. In other words, your project earns value as its work is completed. For example, if the baseline cost for the work that has been completed through April 13 is $6,000, the earned value is $6,000. Figure 18-3 illustrates earned value. The schedule slipped so that only $6,000 of work was performed up to the status date. If the work had started on time, all the work would have been complete and the earned value would be $10,000.

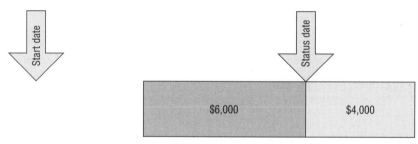

Figure 18-3: Earned value.

Actual Cost

The actual cost of work performed (AC) is how much has been spent for the work completed up to the status date. Suppose you spent $5,000 for the work completed through April 13, then $5,000 is the actual cost.

CHOOSING UNITS FOR EARNED VALUE ANALYSIS

In earned value analysis, planned value, earned value, and actual cost are usually converted to monetary values so you can compare the values to one another. To do that, you multiply work hours by labor rates to calculate labor costs.

   If you don't have access to labor rates and other project costs, you can still put earned value analysis to work. In this situation, you rely on work hours. Planned value becomes the baseline hours for the work that should have been completed up to the status date. Earned value becomes the baseline hours for the work that was completed. And actual cost turns into actual hours, which are the actual hours for the completed work.

Analyzing Performance with Earned Value

The key to earned value analysis is that planned value, earned value, and actual cost are all measured in dollars (or another currency). Because of that, you can calculate schedule and cost variance in the same units, dollars, for example.

- **Schedule variance:** This is earned value minus planned value. In other words, the schedule variance is the baseline cost of the completed work minus the baseline cost of the work that was supposed to be completed. If more work was completed than you planned, the earned value would be greater than the planned value, resulting in a positive schedule variance. Using the example in the previous section, schedule variance equals earned value ($6,000) minus planned value ($10,000), which is –$4,000. The negative schedule variance means that the project is behind schedule.

- **Cost variance:** This measure is earned value minus actual cost. In other words, the cost variance is the baseline cost of the completed work minus the actual cost of the completed work. If the earned value is greater than the actual cost, you spent less than you planned for the completed work: a positive cost variance. In the example in the previous section, cost variance equals earned value ($6,000) minus planned value ($5,000), which is $1,000. The positive cost variance means that the project is under budget for the completed work.

Evaluating Earned Value Measures in a Graph

A graph of planned value, earned value, and actual cost over time provides the complete picture of what's happening with both your project schedule and budget. Even better, an earned value graph depicts schedule and cost status visually, so you don't have to look at numbers at all. This section explains how to read earned value results in a graph.

Most of the time, the graph for planned value over time takes the shape of the letter "S," as shown in Figure 18-4, which is how these graphs became known as S-curves. The shape arises because work often starts slowly in a project, runs energetically through the middle of the project, and then tapers off at the end.

When you add the earned value line to the graph, the schedule variance appears as the gap between the planned value line and the earned value line. In the previous example, the earned value is below the planned value line, which means that the project is behind schedule.

Similarly, the gap between the earned value line and the actual cost line represents the cost variance. In this example, the actual cost is below the earned value line. So, although the project is behind schedule, the cost for the completed work is under budget. One explanation for this situation is that you are using less expensive resources, who are taking longer because they are less skilled than the resources you had planned for.

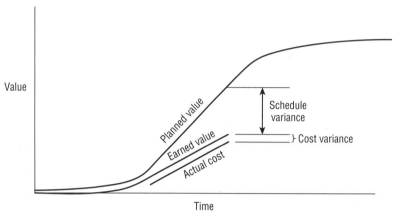

Figure 18-4: An earned value graph.

Using Additional Earned Value Indicators

As you can see in Figure 18-4, the schedule and cost variance show what has happened up to the status date. What if you want an idea of what might happen for the remainder of the project? You can use the three basic earned value analysis measures to forecast the future. This section describes additional measures and how to use them.

- **Schedule performance index (SPI):** This is a ratio of earned value to planned value, so it indicates how close the actual project schedule is to the baseline schedule. If earned value is greater than planned value, the project is ahead of schedule and SPI is greater than 1. Conversely, an SPI less than 1 indicates that the project is behind schedule. Continuing with the previous example, SPI is $6,000 divided by $10,000, or 0.6. If SPI equals 1, the schedule is on target.

- **Cost performance index (CPI):** This is a ratio of earned value to actual cost, which shows how close the planned cost for completed work is to the actual cost. A CPI greater than 1 means the project is under budget. A CPI less than 1 means the project is over budget. The CPI for the example is $6,000 divided by $5,000, or 1.2. If CPI equals 1, the actual cost is on track with the budget.

- **Estimate to complete (ETC):** You can estimate the cost to complete the project using CPI. To do that, first subtract the earned value from the baseline cost for the entire project, which is the baseline cost for the project's incomplete work. Then, divide that value by CPI. If the CPI is greater than 1 (the project is under budget), the estimate to complete will be lower than the baseline cost. For example, if the baseline cost for incomplete work is $100,000 and using the CPI of 1.2, the estimate to complete is $83,333.

Evaluating Financials

Most projects have to survive a gauntlet of financial hurdles before they obtain approval to proceed. Stakeholders look at the benefits the project might deliver and how much it's likely to cost. If the benefits and costs play well together, the project gains approval and proceeds from there. But that isn't the end of financial analysis. As work progresses, management makes sure that the project is still on track to deliver its promised benefits and that the cost is within the budget.

CROSS-REFERENCE To learn more about project selection criteria, see the section "Criteria For Selecting Projects" in Chapter 25.

As a project manager, you might not be responsible for running financial analyses on your projects. In some instances, you might not have access to the income and expense numbers you need to perform the calculations. However, it's helpful to understand the financial measures that management uses to evaluate projects. By doing so, you're better prepared to answer stakeholders' questions, manage their expectations, and make sound decisions for your projects.

Financial measures come in different forms, but they all provide insight into how effectively a project uses the money invested in it. This section describes a few of the most common financial measures.

Determining the Payback Period

The *payback period* is the length of time the project requires to earn back the money spent to perform the project. The payback period is the easiest financial measure to calculate, and it's easy for nonfinancial people to understand.

To determine the payback period, you need the cost and duration of the project. You also need to know how much the project is likely to earn or save per time period once its benefits kick in. Here's an example using the mobile Web eyeglasses project:

- The total project cost is estimated at $1.5 million.
- Initial sales are forecast at $10,000 per month for the first year.
- In subsequent years, sales are forecast to be $50,000 per month.
- Given the estimated income, sales will reach $1.5 million after 27.6 months.

As the project progresses, actual results can affect the payback period. For example, if the project schedule lengthens, the payback period increases by the amount of the delay. If the project cost increases, the project has to earn more income or save more money to pay back the cost. On the other hand, if the scope decreases such that the monetary benefits are reduced, the payback period will also increase.

NOTE   The payback period is a simple measure, but it has a few disadvantages. First, it ignores income after the payback period. If you use payback periods to compare potential projects, this measure penalizes projects that generate income later rather than sooner, even if the total income is greater than another project's revenue.

For some projects, income might not continue for the entire payback period. For example, what if another technology made the mobile Web eyeglasses obsolete after 24 months? The project wouldn't pay back the investment in the project.

The payback period doesn't take into account the time value of money. If a project continues for several years, the cost of money over time is a factor. One example of the cost of money is paying interest when you borrow money to fund a project. However, management usually requires a return on its investment, which is another form of the cost of money, as you learn in the next section.

Identifying the Net Present Value

Net present value (NPV) is a measure of the value that the project provides taking into account the money spent, the amount earned or saved, and the time value of money. Several factors can make the value of money vary over time:

- Inflation is one influence on the value of money. Over time, as product prices increase due to inflation, the purchasing power of your money decreases. In effect, each dollar is worth less because it purchases less.

- Borrowing money is another example of the time value of money. If you pay 5 percent interest on the money borrowed to fund a project, that cost of money adds to your project's price tag.

- The rate of return that management requires for investments is the time value of money factor that you encounter with projects. Your organization's management team probably has a specific annual rate of return they require on the money they invest in any kind of endeavor: a project, the purchase of a major piece of equipment, and so on. If management is going to fund a project, one of the project objectives is probably to deliver that rate of return (as a minimum) on the money invested.

NPV doesn't provide the actual rate of return that your project delivers. Instead, you use the required rate of return in the calculation and the result is a value for the project in today's dollars — the net present value. If NPV is greater than zero, the project exceeded the required rate of return. If NPV is less than zero, the rate of return fell short of the target.

When you calculate NPV, you specify the cash flows into the project and the cash flows out, as well as when they occur. (The "net" in "net present value" comes from the fact that you consider both income and expenses in the calculation.) For example, the cash flow data you provide might include an initial investment of cash, the money you spend each month while the project is underway, and then the money the project earns each month once it's complete, as illustrated in Figure 18-5.

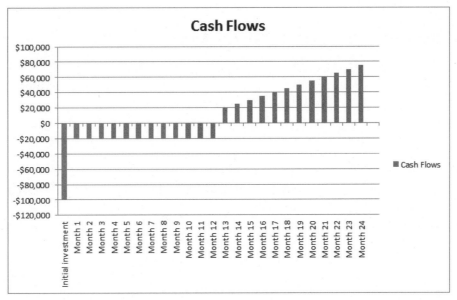

Figure 18-5: NPV uses cash flows to calculate a project's value, accounting for the time value of money.

The NPV calculation uses the required rate of return to convert the value of each cash flow into today's dollars. Then, it totals all the present values of the cash flows to obtain the net present value. For example, if the required rate of return is 10 percent annually, the value of a cash flow decreases a little (one-twelfth of 10 percent per month, in this example) for each month that the cash flow occurs in the future. For example, if you receive $20,000, 12 months from now, it's worth only $18,177 today, using a 10 percent rate of return.

> **NOTE** The further in the future a cash flow is, the greater the effect of the time value of money. For example, with a 10 percent rate of return, a $20,000 payment 24 months from now is worth $16,525. Critical chain project management schedules tasks to occur as late as possible. One advantage of doing so is that the net present values of project costs are reduced because they occur further in the future.

You don't need to learn and memorize the formula for NPV. A financial calculator or a spreadsheet function will calculate it for you. For example, Microsoft Excel includes the XNPV function. You specify the required rate of return, a series of cash flows in or out, and the dates on which those cash flows occur. The only thing you have to remember is that you enter money you spend with negative values, and enter income or money saved with positive values. NPV for the cash flows in Figure 18-5, using a 10 percent return, is $159,350, so the project exceeds the minimum return.

Calculating the Internal Rate of Return

The *internal rate of return* (IRR) represents the annual return that the project's cash flows deliver taking into account the time value of money. It's similar to the annual percentage yield (APY) that a bank savings account pays based on its annual percentage rate (APR). (The APY is different than the APR because of compounding during the year.) If the project's IRR is greater than the rate of return your organization requires, the project is good to go.

Although IRR shows the annual rate of return, the measure has one significant limitation. It works only if your project cash flows switch once from negative to positive. If cash flows switch back and forth multiple times, the calculation produces more than one mathematically correct answer. (The calculation for IRR actually requires you to calculate NPV using different rates of return. When the result is zero, the rate of return you used is the IRR.)

Summary

Once project work is underway, you begin to evaluate how your project is doing. One common comparison is the project's progress and task dates in relation to the original schedule. Another measure is how much money you've spent compared to the budget. The differences, or variances, between your plan and actual values provide an indication of the health of the project.

Earned value analysis is another popular approach that helps you determine whether your project is on time and within budget. This method compares how much the project has earned through completed work to the planned costs and actual costs. The comparison between earned value and the planned value provides insight into the project's schedule performance. The comparison between earned value and the actual costs is an indication of the project's budget performance.

Management evaluates financial performance in other ways. You can use measures such as the payback period, net present value, and internal rate of return to see whether a project is delivering the financial benefits it originally promised.

Coach's Review

Use this section to assess what you've learned in this chapter and to apply it to a real-life project you're currently working on.

Test Your Knowledge

Test your knowledge of the material in this chapter by answering the following questions. See Appendix A for the answers.

1. How do you determine schedule variance?

2. Explain one reason why a positive cost variance might not be a good thing for a project.

3. What is *earned value*?

4. If earned value is less than planned value, what do you know about the project?

5. If earned value is less than actual cost, what do you know about the project?

6. What are the pros and cons of using the payback period to evaluate project financial performance?

Project Challenge

Using a project you're working on or have worked on in the past, determine the data that is available to you. Then, assuming that you have saved a baseline for your project already, experiment with the following methods for evaluating performance:

1. If you have only schedule data, evaluate the project's schedule variance. Calculate the schedule variance for every milestone in the project. Using a milestone trend graph, plot the schedule variances for milestones that occur in each month of the project duration. Is there a trend in the variances,

such as milestones that occur later in the schedule being delivered further behind schedule? Examine the status of your project to try to explain any trends you see.

2. If you have schedule and cost data, calculate planned value, earned value, and actual cost for the project at the end of each week of the schedule. Plot the values in an earned value graph. Based on the relationship of the lines on the graph, determine whether the project is ahead of or behind schedule, and whether it is over- or under-budget.

Getting a Plan Back on Track

Your original project plan is a carefully crafted balance between your project's objectives and the amount of time, money, and resources available. Once the project gets going, reality hits: People aren't available when you need them, work takes longer than you expected, issues arise, or unmanaged changes wreak havoc on your schedule and budget. Next thing you know, your project begins to stray from the plan.

As project manager, your job is figure out what to do and how to do it. This chapter discusses a variety of methods for bringing projects back on track. Each one affects a project in different ways, so the best one to use depends on your project's objectives. For example, if your company's future depends on getting your product to market before the competition, you might be willing to spend more money, accept more risk, or pare down the scope to shorten the schedule.

If you have to resolve small issues, you might be able to modify your project plan without asking the customer, sponsor, or key stakeholders for their approval. However, most of the time, you do need them to approve the approach for getting the project back on track. In this case, you typically recommend multiple solutions and ask the stakeholders to choose.

If a project gets into serious trouble, you have to take action, and fast. The first step is to recognize that there's a problem. Then, you stabilize the project so you can take the time you need to evaluate the situation and make a plan for recovery. The processes you use to recover the project are the same ones you apply when you start a project from the beginning: initiating, planning, executing, monitoring and controlling, and closing.

Ways to Correct Course

When a project goes off track, you have to choose methods to bring it back into balance. For example, you might need to recover from schedule delays, but you can't spend more to do that. Perhaps management has asked you to cut costs without lengthening the schedule. Perhaps you've lost some of the resources assigned to your project and you're trying to figure out how to control the damage. This section describes several methods for adjusting different aspects of a project, including the advantages, limitations, and side effects of each one.

Fast-Tracking a Project Schedule

Fast-tracking shortens a project schedule by running tasks concurrently instead of one after the other. Overlapping tasks doesn't increase cost, because you're simply making adjustments to when work occurs. However, it works only if the tasks don't use the same resources. Fast-tracking does increase risk because you start tasks before their predecessors are complete.

Which Tasks Should You Fast-Track?

The critical path is the place to look for tasks to fast-track. That's because reductions in its length translate into an earlier project finish date.

CROSS-REFERENCE To learn more about the critical path, see the section "Understanding the Critical Path" in Chapter 8.

One way to minimize the risks you introduce is to fast-track the longest tasks on the critical path. You might be able to add a two-week overlap to a couple of multi-month tasks. If you overlap tasks that take only a few days each, you have to manage dozens of changes and risks to obtain the same two-week reduction. In addition, choose tasks that are early in the project schedule so you have additional time to make other project course corrections, if necessary.

NOTE Adjustments to a project schedule can change the tasks that make up the critical path. For example, if you fast-track two tasks on the critical path, their shorter duration might remove them from the critical path while making a different sequence of tasks critical. You might then want to turn your attention to the new critical path, if necessary.

Fast-Tracking Options

Fast-tracking comes in two variations. Shortening lag time isn't as risky as overlapping tasks, but some lag time isn't negotiable:

■ **Shortening lag time between tasks:** *Lag time* represents a delay between the end of one task and the beginning of the task that follows. (See the section "Scheduling with Lead and Lag Time" in Chapter 8 for a detailed explanation of the time between tasks.) For example, if it takes 2 weeks for materials you order to arrive, there is a 2-week lag between ordering materials and starting construction. Reducing lag time is the least troublesome method of shortening project duration. In most cases, the risk is low because you're merely shortening delays rather than overlapping tasks. For example, you might pay for expediting delivery to get your materials faster.

NOTE The length of lag time might be out of your control, such as the time it takes concrete to harden or glue to dry. For example, you can ask the management team to hold an interim meeting to approve a key change request. However, if the county government has a 4-week turnaround for building permits, you might not be able to speed that up.

■ **Overlapping tasks:** The most common fast-tracking method is to introduce a partial overlap between two tasks, also known as *lead time*. With this approach, you begin on the successor task after most of the work on the previous task is complete and the details are known. Some tasks are easy to overlap without introducing too much risk. For example, in a construction project, you can schedule electricians, plumbers, and other workers to work on the interiors of lower floors of a skyscraper, while the steel is fabricated for upper floors.

The more tasks affect one another, the more risk you take by scheduling them concurrently. Starting construction before the design is complete could result in major rework and delays, for example, if the foundation isn't sufficient to support the final building or it's the wrong shape or in the wrong location.

Crashing a Schedule

Spending more money to shorten a project schedule is known as crashing a project. This technique makes sense when the schedule is the most important factor — for example, when you need to get your product to market before the competition.

In most cases, the money is spent to hire more people to perform work in less time. Crashing seems like an obvious solution. If one person needs two weeks to complete a task, then two people could finish it one, right? Well, sometimes. Giving birth is the classic example of why crashing doesn't always work because two women can't join forces to deliver a baby in 4.5 months.

Even with unlimited resources, crashing has its limits. There comes a point when adding resources stops shortening the duration and increases it instead. Suppose one person is assigned to build a brick wall and you estimate that it will take 20 days. Adding another person to help might shorten the duration to 10 days. You might even shorten the duration to 5 days by assigning 4 people to the task. But you can imagine what would happen if you tried to assign 100 people to build the wall in a couple of hours.

Which Tasks Should You Crash?

As with fast-tracking, you should target tasks on the critical path for the best candidates for crashing. However, some tasks cost more to crash per time unit than others. Management might want the schedule shorter but they don't want to spend more money than necessary. To shorten the project duration for the least amount of money, you crash the most cost-effective tasks first and you stop crashing when the finish date is back where it needs to be.

To determine which tasks to crash, you put together a crash table, such as the one in Table 19-1. Here is how each column in a crash table helps you choose the best tasks to crash:

- **Current task duration:** Evaluate the longest tasks on the critical path first. By doing so, you can shorten the schedule crashing the fewest tasks.

- **Cost to crash the task:** Determine how much it will cost to shorten the task duration. You might think that crashing a task is free, for example, because you cut the time in half by adding a second resource. While that might be true for some tasks such as loading a truck, most tasks end up with some overhead. For example, if you add an additional programmer to a development task, the two people have to plan how to allocate the work and then integrate the code they both write. In this example, the task might end up 40 percent shorter instead of 50 percent of the original duration, because the interaction and integration adds 10 percent.

- **Crash reduction:** Determine how much you can shorten the task in a time unit such as days or weeks.

- **Crash cost per time unit:** Divide the cost to crash the task by the crash reduction (cost to crash÷crash reduction) to determine the most cost-effective tasks to crash. For example, one task might cost $2,000 per week whereas another task costs $4,000 per week.

- **Total reduction:** If you sort the table from the most to least cost-effective tasks, the total reduction in weeks shows when you've shortened the project by the amount you need. For example, if you need to shorten your project schedule by 2 weeks, Table 19-1 shows that the first four tasks in the table provide the reduction you need.

- **Total crash cost:** This shows how much you pay to shorten the schedule. In this example, the lowest cost to shorten the project by 2 weeks is $3,250.

TIP If you can bring on additional less expensive resources, consider using them to offload the resources you really need on the critical path. For example, you can focus your most experienced resources on the critical path. Then, assign less experienced resources to the noncritical tasks that had been assigned to your experts.

Table 19-1: A Crash Table Helps You Choose the Tasks to Crash to Shorten a Project.

TASK NAME	DURATION IN WEEKS	COST TO CRASH	CRASH REDUCTION IN WEEKS	CRASH COST PER TIME UNIT	TOTAL REDUCTION IN WEEKS	TOTAL CRASH COST
Candidate 3	4	$500	0.5	$1,000	0.5	$500
Candidate 4	3	$250	0.25	$1,000	0.75	$750
Candidate 2	4	$2,000	1.0	$2,000	1.75	$2,750
Candidate 5	2	$500	0.25	$2,000	2.00	$3,250
Candidate 1	5	$4,000	1.0	$4,000	3.00	$7,250

Other Crashing Considerations

Shortening the duration of a task can change the critical path. After you crash the first task, review the critical path to make sure that the tasks you've selected are still on the critical path. Otherwise, you will spend money without shortening the project duration.

Before you make your final decision on tasks, consider the resources that are available to pitch in. In many cases, the resources offered don't have the skills that the work requires. Or they might be less experienced than the people you already have. In both of those situations, your existing team members might spend time helping the new people get up to speed. And that means you're paying for new people, while reducing the productivity of the people you already have. Be sure to take the new resources' capabilities into account when you calculate the crash cost and reduction.

Using Different Resources

Changes to resource assignments can solve any number of problems. Maybe you have to replace a resource that's been reassigned to another project. Or you're trying to cut costs or shorten the schedule. Resource assignments have the power to affect all of these issues. Keep in mind that resources are usually in short supply, so this technique can be the hardest one to implement. However, here are some resource options to consider:

- **Outsourcing work:** If you're trying to shorten duration, using third-party resources might be the answer. Outsourcing can shorten a schedule because the outside resources might be more experienced than people within your organization or have more time available for your work. On the other hand, hiring outside resources can be time-consuming, as you learn in the section "Procuring Resources from Vendors" in Chapter 13.

- **Using less expensive resources:** You might reduce the cost of a project by hiring people who cost less. However, if those folks are less experienced, they could take longer to complete their assignments, and that could lengthen your project. In addition, if they take a lot longer to finish work, they might cost more than more expensive workers.

- **Assigning more experienced resources:** Sometimes, people who are more experienced can complete work in less time. These people might actually cost less per hour than less-experienced colleagues. In addition, they often deliver a high level of quality. Although these benefits sound attractive, resources like this are usually in high demand and hard to acquire for your project.

- **Using customer resources:** If you are performing a project for an external customer, you might be able to acquire resources from the customer. This approach is akin to homeowners taking over some remodeling tasks to stay within their budget. This option works only if the customer's people have the skills you need.

Asking People to Work Overtime

Instead of bringing new people onto a project, you might consider asking the people on your team to work longer hours for a period of time. By working more hours each day, team members can finish their assignments earlier and deliver the project in less time.

Use overtime sparingly because it has several disadvantages:

- **People can't work long hours forever.** While salaried employees aren't paid for overtime, you can't fall back on overtime to solve all your schedule problems. Although some people have bigger appetites for work than others, even the most energetic workers get tired working long hours. When that happens, people become less productive; they might get sick or make more mistakes. Employee turnover might increase, which means you have to find new people for your project. If you do assign overtime, consider it a last and temporary resort.

- **Project cost increases when people are paid overtime.** If people are paid a premium for overtime hours, your project cost increases because you pay a higher rate for the overtime hours worked. Of course, a higher cost might be acceptable if you're trying to shorten the schedule.

- **Overtime might take time away from better opportunities.** Even if people are willing to work overtime, that doesn't guarantee that the work is the best use of their time. If your organization has other projects under way, the overtime you assigned might prevent your team members from working on other, more beneficial assignments.

WARNING   Don't assign resources to work overtime while you're still in the planning stage. If the project falls behind schedule once work begins, you won't be able to assign more overtime to get the schedule back on track.

Reducing Scope

If you're trying to shorten the schedule and cut costs, reducing scope will do the trick. However, it isn't a popular choice with stakeholders because it also means the project doesn't deliver all the benefits that were projected.

When scope reduction is under consideration, you can work with stakeholders to identify and eliminate the scope items. In many cases, you might find scope items that don't add value. In other projects, you can identify less important scope. In effect, you remove the nice-to-have items from the list and focus on delivering the must-haves. Either way, you might discover that the customer is happy to reduce scope in exchange for lower cost or a shorter schedule.

Because scope reduction negatively affects the success of a project, stakeholders are likely to want to put scope back in if at all possible. If you remove scope from the project, it could reappear if more money, time, or resources become available. However, if you remove scope carefully, the reappearance doesn't occur very often.

Another way to manage scope reductions is to break your project into waves or deliveries. You can include must-have scope in the first wave and save additional scope for later waves. If the project runs out of time or money, the later waves are cancelled.

Your quality management plan defines the required level of quality for your project. If you reduce quality without approval from the customer or sponsor, the project won't make it through acceptance. Even if the decision-makers consider reducing quality, it isn't an attractive solution. You might end up spending time and money on redoing work, fixing problems, making repairs, and trying to salvage your reputation.

Who Approves Course Corrections

Most of the time, the changes you make to get your project back on track require approval from the project sponsor or management team. For small projects or the occasional wayward task, you might be able to straighten things out without anyone's approval.

NOTE Although the project charter describes your authority as a project manager (see "Publicizing the Project Charter" in Chapter 3), it rarely goes into detail. Most of the time, you will have to decide whether or not you can implement project changes without asking for permission. For example, you might have authority to dip into contingency funds or approve budget increases up to a limit.

Extending the project schedule, increasing the budget, or reducing the project scope usually affect the project's objectives and the benefits it delivers. For that reason, changes such as these require stakeholder approval.

If you decide you need approval after evaluating your options, don't go to the decision makers empty-handed. Determine which approaches make the most sense based on what's important for the project. Document the pros and cons of the alternatives you propose. And be prepared to answer questions and back up your recommendations. For example, you might recommend using contingency funds or management reserve to shorten a project schedule if beating the competition to market is a crucial goal. If your organization has several projects under way, you might ask the management team (or portfolio manager if one exists) whether you can obtain resources from other projects. Alternatively, if reducing scope is the answer, you can suggest which scope items to eliminate.

RESETTING BASELINES

When your project plan is approved, you save a baseline for that approved plan as described in the section "Saving Project Baselines" in Chapter 13. That baseline is important as a historical record of what you originally forecast for the project. However, it might lose its value as a reference point if the stakeholders approve a significant increase to the budget, a new finish date, or a significant change in the project scope.

If your plan has changed significantly, a new baseline may be the answer. For example, you can save a new baseline with the new approved schedule or cost.

If substantial change requests are approved, you might save a baseline showing the impact they make on the schedule and cost. On the other hand, you can track change requests outside of the baseline if you obtain additional budget and resources to perform them.

Getting a Project Out of Trouble

Many projects run into trouble — sometimes, very serious trouble. Whether you're a project manager, customer, stakeholder, or team member, troubled projects are stressful and scary. As a project manager, pulling a project back from the brink might sound like an intimidating assignment. In reality, this challenge uses the same project management processes you apply to any project. The main difference with a project intervention is that your people skills are called into action at a higher level.

Recognizing the Problem

Similar to a patient in critical condition, a troubled project needs fast action or it could expire. As project manager, your job is to recognize the problems and initiate steps to get the project on the road to recovery.

The symptoms of a troubled project aren't as varied as those of disease in humans. Here are a few of the most common:

- **Ongoing scope changes:** Scope that continues to grow or that changes direction frequently makes it almost impossible to complete a project successfully.

- **Missed commitments:** If the project continually misses schedule, budget, and other objectives, your plan doesn't reflect what's really going on in the project.

- **Frequent issues, problems, and surprises:** All of these are signs that the project was not defined properly the first time around.

- **People problems:** If the customer, sponsor, or stakeholders are unhappy, the project isn't living up to their expectations. Another red flag is people problems within the project team, such as confusion over roles and responsibilities, low morale, or poor performance.

Evaluating the Situation

When a project is in serious trouble, the overwhelming temptation (and pressure from management) is to jump in and fix it right away. However, if you don't know what the problem is, your treatment attempts could make the problems even worse.

Similar to treating a medical emergency, your first step is to stabilize the project so you can identify the problems and develop a plan. The actions you need to take to apply this project first aid are determined by the crises you face. For example, you might have to reassure your customer or sponsor that you are working to resolve the issues. Or you might identify an interim deliverable to keep the project going until you can prepare your plan.

The best alternative is to not only apply first aid but also start working on identifying the problem at the same time. Because everyone involved with the project is on edge and the clock is ticking, it's important to set expectations up front. Determine how much time the team needs to evaluate the problems and prepare a plan. Then, communicate that time frame to the customer, sponsor, management team, and other key stakeholders. Be prepared to fight for that time, because the decision makers are likely to apply a lot of pressure to start taking action.

Work with everyone involved in the project, management and team members alike, to determine what went wrong. This is the time to practice your best communication skills. Ask questions without blaming anyone.

CROSS-REFERENCE See the section "Minimizing the Fear of Lessons Learned" in Chapter 22 for tips on how to ask questions without blame.

Preparing a Recovery Plan

Most of the time, projects get into trouble because effective project management practices weren't used initially. You might meet resistance about implementing these processes now that the project is in crisis mode. Stand firm so you can plan and implement the recovery successfully.

CROSS-REFERENCE The project purpose and scope are discussed in Chapter 3, "Getting a Project Off the Ground." To review the components of a project plan, refer to Chapter 4, "Getting to Know a Project Plan."

Here are some actions you can take to prepare an effective recovery:

1. Start by revisiting the purpose of the project. Make sure everyone is clear on what the project is supposed to achieve.

2. Re-evaluate the project scope and obtain agreement on what is included in the scope and what isn't. Get approval for the revised scope.

3. Update the project plan for the recovery. You might have to start over if the project is in deep trouble.

TIP When a project is in trouble, it might require drastic action to correct course. Now is the time to work with the powers that be to make tough decisions about the scope, schedule, budget, resources, quality, and other project factors. In addition, you can soothe people's nerves by planning for a few quick fixes so you can show some progress soon after implementing the plan. Or you might decide to make those quick fixes while you're planning to ease the push for action.

Monitoring the Recovery

After you obtain approval for your recovery plan, you implement the plan as you would a regular project plan. For a troubled project, you monitor progress more frequently than you would for one that is on track.

You also communicate more. Publicize progress and positive results. By doing so, you can reassure management and rebuild your team's confidence at the same time.

Similar to closing any project, be sure to gather lessons learned from the troubled project and its recovery. That way, you can help prevent the same problems from reoccurring in the future.

Summary

Projects rarely stay true to the original plan you put together, so as a project manager, you'll probably need to get the projects you manage back on course. You can evaluate methods for getting the project back on track based on whether the schedule, budget, scope, or other aspects of the project are most important. Although you can make some changes on your own, most course corrections require approval from the sponsor, management team, or other decision-makers. When you need approval, you can help the powers that be make their decisions by recommending options and explaining your reasoning.

For projects that are in serious trouble, you go back to the basics. First, you take action quickly to prevent the situation from growing worse. Then, you step through the same processes you used the first time around: Prepare a plan (this time it's one for recovery), monitor and control the recovery, and analyze lessons learned to prevent the problem from reoccurring.

Coach's Review

Use this section to assess what you've learned in this chapter and to apply it to a real-life project you're currently working on.

Test Your Knowledge

Test your knowledge of the material in this chapter by answering the following questions. See Appendix A for the answers.

1. If your project is struggling with many tasks behind schedule, over budget, or both, what is the first thing to look at?

2. If you want to shorten a schedule without incurring much if any additional cost, which technique would you choose? What is the drawback of the technique you select?

3. If the project sponsor asks you to crash the project to shorten the schedule, which tasks would you choose to crash?

4. Name two reasons that overtime should be the last resource method to consider.

Project Challenge

Select a project that you're working on or have worked on in the past. Using the goals for the project you select, evaluate various methods for bringing the project back on track.

1. Make a list of the techniques described in this chapter.

2. For each technique, write an evaluation of whether the technique would help bring the project back on track based on the project objectives.

3. Select the techniques that you would recommend to the project customer, sponsor, and other key stakeholders.

4. Prepare a presentation that you would deliver to the decision makers to obtain their approval for a course of action.

Part

V

Closing the Project

Chapter 20: Obtaining Acceptance and Other Wrap-Up Tasks
Chapter 21: Documenting a Project for Posterity
Chapter 22: Don't Forget Lessons Learned

Obtaining Acceptance and Other Wrap-Up Tasks

When your project deliverables live up to their name and are delivered, congratulations are in order. You've reached the final chapter of the project management life cycle. The closing process group might be short but it's still important.

The first step to closing a project is obtaining formal acceptance from your project customer. Using acceptance tests or other techniques, you demonstrate that the deliverables are complete and the success criteria have been satisfied. Once the customer and project sponsor sign a formal acceptance document, you can perform the rest of the closing tasks and wrap up the project.

You produced reports while your project was underway, so it's no surprise that a report is in order now that the project is complete. A closeout report summarizes a project's achievements, what you did to accomplish them, and how well things went. All this information can be a valuable guide for project managers and teams working on similar projects in the future.

In addition to closing out any contracts you set up for the project, you also make sure any end-of-project transitions go smoothly, whether you're transitioning your team members back to their departments or handing off a product, process, or information to groups such as manufacturing, marketing, and customer support.

Determining Whether the Project Is a Success

Obtaining formal acceptance from the project customer is a crucial step in closing a project. If you allow your project to coast quietly to a stop, you run the risk of the project coming back to life — when someone realizes that a deliverable is missing or not quite what was requested. To obtain unshakable customer acceptance, you had better be able to prove that the project has achieved what it's supposed to. During the initiating and planning of a project, you define the project's deliverables and success criteria, which you use to guide team members as they work on project tasks. During closing, the deliverables and success criteria help you validate that your aim was true. This section describes several methods for demonstrating that you have piloted the project to a successful conclusion.

CROSS-REFERENCE The sections "What Constitutes Success?" and "Specifying the Deliverables" in Chapter 3 describe success criteria and deliverables in detail.

Developing Acceptance Tests

Acceptance tests are one way to show that the project has accomplished what it's supposed to. During project planning, you identify the criteria your project must meet to be considered a success. While work progresses, you and the team might employ several methods to check intermediate results. But during closing, you can run a comprehensive set of acceptance tests so the customer can see that every objective, requirement, and deliverable has been met.

CROSS-REFERENCE The information in this section relates to the PMP Exam's Domain V: Closing the Project, Task 1, "Obtain final acceptance of the project deliverables by working with the sponsor and/or customer, in order to confirm that project scope and deliverables were met."

The acceptance tests you develop depend on the project and its success criteria. Consider a mission-critical financial system that must perform several dozen financial and administrative functions. It must be available 99.999 percent of the time and must not corrupt data in any way. For this example, acceptance tests can determine whether the functions do what they're supposed to and deliver the correct results. You can use a sample set of data or test cases, perform a specific set of tasks, and then compare the results to what's expected. You also need a realistic test environment, such as hardware and network infrastructure, a typical transaction load, and so on. For availability, you have to run the test for a period of time to determine the percentage of time the system is available.

With criteria such as customer feedback ratings or reduced numbers of customer support calls, acceptance tests take a different form. Your tests specify how you will collect the data you need and steps to process or analyze the results. For example, an acceptance test for reduction in support calls might specify the timeframe for the test, such as two months. During the acceptance test, you might record the number of calls, call length, number of callbacks or reopened calls, and categories or topics. In this example, you also need customer support data prior to your project's implementation.

THE SUCCESS CRITERIA ARE SATISFIED, BUT WHAT ABOUT THE CUSTOMER?

The PMP exam's Domain V: Closing the Project, Task 7 is "Measure customer satisfaction at the end of the project by capturing customer feedback, in order to assist in project evaluation and enhance customer relationships." Perhaps you check off success criteria as being met, but only after lengthy negotiations. Or the customer admits that the results meet the specifications, but aren't really what he was looking for.

In addition to asking the sponsor, customer, and other stakeholders to sign that they accept the project, you can survey them to get their opinions about the project. Ask them what they liked, disliked, or would like to see improved. What you do in response depends on the feedback you receive. However, you can add what they tell you to your list of lessons learned and include that information in your closeout reports.

You might develop acceptance tests at different stages of a project. Some straightforward tests spring fully formed from the success criteria you identify. For deliverables with no room for interpretation, such as a certificate of occupancy for a newly constructed building, you either have the deliverable or you don't. As with the customer support measures, you might develop your acceptance tests during planning so you can measure before and after results. Functional tests could evolve over time. For instance, you use a variety of tests as work is performed and then assemble those tests (along with any revisions based on change requests that were incorporated) into a set of acceptance tests to perform during closing.

Running Acceptance Tests

Similar to the tests you perform during a project, acceptance tests follow a cycle. You perform the acceptance tests that you've put together. If they don't complete successfully, you jump back to rework the deliverables until the problems are resolved. Then you run the acceptance tests again.

CHECKING OFF OBJECTIVES, DELIVERABLES, AND REQUIREMENTS

People pay attention when they're actively participating. For example, you are more likely to remember how to get somewhere if you're the person driving the car. Getting the customer involved in checking off completed objectives, deliverables, and requirements is an effective way to drive home the message that the project is a success.

Let's say you have a customer, Doubting Darren, who tends to be skeptical until he sees for himself that something works. The project has a high profile, so Pam, the project manager, wants to ensure that Darren is totally convinced that the project has succeeded.

Pam asks team members to build a checklist that maps the project's objectives, deliverables, and requirements to items in the acceptance tests. She invites Darren to observe the tests. He arrives and is surprised when Pam hands him a pen and a clipboard. She explains that she would like Darren to mark the Pass boxes as the team demonstrates that a test item has passed.

At the end of the test, Darren hands the checklist back to Pam with all the boxes filled in. He wiggles his fingers to get rid of his writer's cramp and congratulates the team on a job well done.

Obtaining Sign-Off

At the end of a project, you ask the sponsor, customer, and other stakeholders to sign off that they accept the project as complete — just as you did when you presented them with the project plan a while ago. A face-to-face meeting with all the players reinforces the accomplishment. Each person signs the acceptance form and passes it to the next stakeholder for signature. If meeting in person isn't feasible, you can hold a conference call to obtain verbal acceptance. In this situation, follow up by sending the acceptance form to the appropriate stakeholders for their signature. When you receive the signed forms, you add them to your project register or notebook.

Documenting the Project: The Project Closeout Report

What happened in your project can act as a guide for project managers and team members working on future projects. They don't have to reinvent effective techniques and they can avoid repeating mistakes made on previous projects.

In addition, data for the actual schedule, cost, and effort helps to improve estimates for future projects.

CROSS-REFERENCE This section relates to the PMP Exam's Domain V: Closing the Project, Task 4, "Distribute the final project report including all project closure-related information, project variances, and any issues, in order to provide the final project status to all stakeholders."

A project closeout report is like a status report on steroids. It summarizes the final status of the project, qualitatively and quantitatively, as described in the following sections.

Summarizing the Project

The first part of a closeout report is a high-level summary of how the project went. This section answers the big questions about the project:

- **Is the project a success?** Did the project achieve its goals and objectives? Did the project complete on schedule, within budget, and to the required level of quality? Is the customer satisfied?

- **What worked well? What didn't work? What would you do differently?** Include a summary of things that worked well, problems and issues you encountered, and your suggestions for improvement.

- **Was risk management effective?** Document risks that occurred during the project, the risk response you chose, and whether the risk response reduced the impact of the issue. Be sure to flag risks you didn't identify initially in the risk management plan that turned out to be issues for your project, so that project managers in the future know to include them.

- **Was project management effective?** Describe the results of the project management processes you used. Suggest any changes you would make in planning and managing the project.

CROSS-REFERENCE To learn about different measures of project performance, see Chapter 18, "Evaluating Progress and Performance."

Quantifying Results

A closeout report includes a summary of quantitative results for the project. The information you include depends on the project, how big it is, and the success criteria you defined. You might include standard measures, such as schedule and cost variance or you might include measures like the reduction in telephone calls to customer support. Figure 20-1 provides a sample closeout report with a summary of the cost and schedule results.

Some of the quantitative results you might include in your closeout reports are:

▪ **Cost:** In the closeout report, you include the total cost for the project and the variance between the final and estimated cost. For large projects, you might break the cost down by phase or high-level summary tasks, or in other ways, such as labor and material costs. Depending on the measures the stakeholders want to see, you might include financial results, such as return on investment (ROI).

CROSS-REFERENCE To learn more about financial measures used to evaluate projects, see the section "Evaluating Financials" in Chapter 18.

Mobile Web Eyeglasses Project   *Closeout Report*

Project manager: Vic Specs.

Project Summary
The mobile web eyeglasses project is complete and unanimously voted a success by all stakeholders. The delivery was delayed 2 months, because the project sponsor and customer had requested several changes to improve the quality of the results.

Quality and Customer Satisfaction
The project customer is ecstatic and was last seen exploring New York City with the help of her web-enabled eyeglasses. Manhattanites did not seem to notice that she was pointing in every direction excitedly to no one in particular.

Issues
The only issue was that research took longer than estimated, exceeding the buffer added for the risks of using experimental technology.

Lessons Learned
Although we anticipated delays due to the new technology and added buffers to the schedule, research exceeded those buffers. Untried technology requires a very flexible schedule and budget.

Risks
New technology and materials were identified as risks. The schedule included a four-month buffer. In addition, we negotiated contracts with three vendors providing the materials for the lenses. That response was successful, because one vendor went out of business and another ran into supply problems. The remaining vendor delivered only two weeks late.

Project Management Processes
We opted to re-estimate the project at the beginning of each phase, which was a good decision. Because of the unknowns in this project, our estimates changed significantly as we obtained more information.

Cost

Estimated cost	$1,400,000
Final cost	$1,875,000
Variance	$325,000
Variance %	23%

Schedule

Estimated finish date	08/26/12
Actual finish date	10/28/12
Variance	2 months

Variances in cost and schedule were both due to approved change requests submitted by the customer.

Figure 20-1: A project closeout report

- **Schedule:** Include the actual final delivery date and the variance from the estimated completion date. You can also include dates and variances for significant milestones compared to the forecast completion dates. Be sure to identify dates that were revised due to approved change orders.

- **Scope:** Start with the deliverables that the project produced. If the scope expanded or shrank, include the scope items that were added or eliminated.

- **Changes:** Summarize significant changes made to the scope, deliverables, and requirements.

- **Quality:** Include quality metrics you used to measure project performance.

Financial, Legal, and Administrative Closeout

Another step in closing a project is to close out contracts you set up, accounts used to charge expenses to the project, and other administrative items, such as time tracking. Once your project is finished, you want to complete and close the contracts you set up. You also don't want anyone charging additional time or expenses to the project.

CROSS-REFERENCE The PMP Exam's Domain V: Closing the Project, Task 3 is "Obtain financial, legal, and administrative closure using generally accepted practices, in order to communicate formal project closure and ensure no further liability."

If your project included a contract with the customer, obtaining acceptance is usually the key to completing contractual obligations. Sometimes, contracts extend beyond the end of the project — for example, when your company commits to supporting the deliverables for several months. You also close contracts you set up with vendors and contractors. Bottom line: you must identify the steps to close every project contract and then complete those steps.

In most cases, you keep the financial accounts open for a few months after the project is complete so that the last few expenses can be processed. For example, if you provide support or product warranties, those expenses occur after project acceptance. If you have approval processes for project charges, you might notice expenses that don't belong to your project. If that happens, you can talk to the person who submitted the charge or the accounting department to correct the records. Another way to prevent erroneous charges is to close most of the accounting codes to new charges, keeping open only the ones that apply to expenses that occur after the project is officially complete.

Finally, you close out any other administrative tasks related to your project. For example, you typically close codes used to assign people's time to the project.

Consider writing short summaries (one or two paragraphs each) of each team member's contributions to the project. For people you didn't interact with directly, you might ask team leads to write summaries for you. These summaries not only recognize and acknowledge people's work, they help resource managers with performance evaluations and future plans for their staff members.

Project Transitions

The end of a project usually marks the beginning of something else. A new team might pick up ownership of and responsibility for what your project delivered while the people on your project team go back to their departments or onto new assignments. As project manager, you can strengthen your relationships in your organization by making sure these transitions go smoothly.

Handing Off Information

The end of a project is the end of a temporary endeavor, but the deliverables from the project live on. You might hand off a new product to several groups: manufacturing, sales, marketing, and technical support to name a few. With construction projects, the owner receives as-built drawings, which show the structure as it was constructed — in effect, the structure with all the change requests that were made. For instance, as-built drawings might show rerouted wiring or upgraded windows.

CROSS-REFERENCE This section relates to the PMP Exam's Domain V: Closing the Project, Task 2, "Transfer the ownership of deliverables to the assigned stakeholders in accordance with the project plan, in order to facilitate project closure."

The information you provide depends on the project and the groups who are taking over. Here are examples of project information you might hand off to other groups:

- **The closeout report:** As you learned in the section "Documenting the Project: The Project Closeout Report," this report summarizes your project so people can quickly scan what was done, and as important, what wasn't.

- **Scope that was eliminated or added:** Make sure that your successors know about any scope changes so they don't do unnecessary work or miss tasks they should be doing.

- **Final specifications:** This documentation goes by different names, such as *product documentation* and *as-built drawings*.

- **Test results:** Projects might be accepted despite a few unresolved defects floating around. Test results give other groups an idea of the work they have to do or the level of support they can expect to provide.

- **Tasks that are incomplete:** Explain the status of incomplete tasks and the reasons they weren't finished. That way, the follow-on groups can decide whether to complete the tasks or take other action.

- **Unresolved issues, workarounds, suggestions:** During the course of a project, you identify issues, discover better ways to do things, and become familiar with a plethora of small details that the next group in line needs to know.

- **The location of the project archives:** The project archives include detailed information about your project so other groups know where to look when they need to dig deeper.

CROSS-REFERENCE Chapter 21, "Documenting a Project for Posterity," describes techniques for organizing and storing project archives so information about completed projects is easy to find.

Transitioning Resources

When your project is complete, your team and other resources move on to their next adventure. As the end of the project approaches, you plan resource transitions to help everyone remain productive through those unsettling times. You ensure that the work on your project is complete. At the same time, the functional managers can line up new assignments without worrying about erratic workloads. As a side benefit, you might earn a reputation as someone who runs a tight and respectful ship. Functional managers and team members will like working with you, which makes it easier to obtain resources the next time you manage a project. Then, when you actually close the project, you confirm your transition plans and bid your resources a fond farewell.

Summary

The first step in closing a project is to confirm the project is truly complete — in other words, its scope and deliverables have been completed successfully. After you obtain written acceptance from the sponsor, customer, and stakeholders, you document the project performance and final status and distribute the reports to all stakeholders. Finally, you close contracts and accounting you set up for the project. Other activities in the closing process group are discussed in Chapter 21, "Documenting a Project for Posterity," and Chapter 22, "Don't Forget Lessons Learned."

Coach's Review

Use this section to assess what you've learned in this chapter and to apply it to a real-life project you're currently working on.

Test Your Knowledge

Test your knowledge of the material in this chapter by answering the following questions. See Appendix A for the answers.

1. What is the purpose of obtaining final acceptance for a project?
2. Name three types of information you would include in a project closeout report.
3. Why do you close contracts and accounts at the end of a project?
4. Name two types of transitions you might manage at the end of a project.

Project Challenge

For a project you're working on, perform the following exercises:

- Develop several tests that demonstrate that the project has fulfilled its objectives, deliverables, and requirements.
- Prepare a closeout report based on the project performance to date.
- Identify the steps you would take to close the legal, financial, and administrative aspects of your project.
- Identify the groups you would transition ownership to at the end of the project.

CHAPTER 21

Documenting a Project for Posterity

Are you a project management trailblazer in your organization? If so, you may be the first one who has managed a project in a structured manner. Because of this, you have history and hard data to offer to project managers coming after you.

Or, perhaps you're the latest in a long line of professional project managers. You've been able to leverage the considerable project archives to help initiate and plan your latest project.

It's likely, however, that you're somewhere in the middle. You leverage the project work of others who came before you, and others coming later will be able to build off your project work. It's rather like the classic cheerleading pyramid, where you're standing on some shoulders, and others are standing on yours.

Providing project managers with metaphorical shoulders on which to stand is the purpose of the *project archives*. By collecting and storing important project files, you're capturing the institutional knowledge you've acquired working on your project and making sure this knowledge is readily accessible for others. Through this archiving of institutional knowledge, which is truly an organizational asset, you're recording hard-won data, capturing effective processes, and taking your organization to a higher level of efficiency.

TIP Project archives are also essential for regulatory compliance and audits. You can turn to your archives if the project or your organization is subject to internal or external audits that ensure that certain processes were followed, the project or product met specific standards, or the project accounting conformed with appropriate financial procedures.

This chapter describes what information belongs in your project archives, how to organize and build your archives, and how to store them and make them accessible to others.

CROSS-REFERENCE The information in this chapter relates to the PMP Exam's Domain V: Closing the Project, Task 6, "Archive project documents and material in order to retain organizational knowledge, comply with statutory requirements, and ensure availability of data for potential use in future projects and internal/external audits."

Gathering Information

So what needs to be in your project archive? Most project managers will tell you that your best bet is to save most or all the contents of your project notebook. If you recall from "Assembling the Project Notebook" in Chapter 3, the term "notebook" is often little more than a polite nod to the three-ring binders of the days of yore. These binders ostensibly contained everything you ever wanted to know about the project.

Nowadays, of course, while the three-ring binder certainly has its place, your project "notebook" might be a bookcase full of multiple binders, a shared drive containing electronic folders and files on the organization's server, or an organizational intranet designed especially for the project.

TIP If the projects in your organization are regulated by a project management office (PMO), be sure to follow its established processes and standards for archiving your project. The PMO or portfolio manager can offer assistance regarding the contents of the project archives, where they should be stored, and what specific techniques should be employed in building the archives.

Whether or not you work with a PMO, you should make yourself aware of any regulatory, certification, or audit requirements regarding your project and its resulting product or service. These requirements will drive the assembly and content of your archives.

CROSS-REFERENCE For more information about how a PMO can ensure that your project meets standards and requirements, see Chapter 23, "Running a Project Management Office."

The following is a laundry list of items that could be included in your project archives. Depending on the nature of your project, you might include just a fraction of these items, or you might have everything in this list and then some. This list is categorized according to the processes from which the content items are produced:

- From the initiating processes
  - Project problem
  - Project goal and objectives
  - Requirements
  - Success criteria
  - Strategy
  - Scope statement, including risks, assumptions, and constraints
  - The stakeholder registry or contact list
  - Project proposal or signoff document
  - Project charter

- From the planning processes
  - List of deliverables
  - Work breakdown structure
  - Responsibility matrix
  - Resource plan
  - Project organization chart
  - Work estimates
  - Cost estimates and project budget
  - Project schedule
  - Quality plan
  - Communication plan
  - Change management plan
  - Risk management plan

- From the executing processes
  - Project register
  - Project baselines and baseline resets
  - Deliverable acceptance log and forms
  - Evidence of completed deliverables

- From the monitoring and controlling processes
  - Change request log
  - Risk management documents
  - Issues log
  - Status reports
  - Schedule updates to progress and costs

- From the closing processes
  - As-delivered project plan
  - Project signoff or project closeout report
  - Project summary and results
  - Lessons learned report or knowledge base

CROSS-REFERENCE For more information about conducting the project final review meeting and documenting the results, see Chapter 22, "Don't Forget Lessons Learned."

Remember that the content of your project archives is as unique as the project itself. Consider any other plans, processes, forms, and logs used throughout the course of the project. If something would be useful to future project managers or auditors to provide a clear picture of your project, then include it.

After you determine the information you need to include in the archives, pull it all together. This can often be accomplished without too much difficulty, as long as you do it as part of the closing processes and you don't put it off as an "optional" task for "when you have time." While creating the project archives is typically not considered an urgent activity (unless it's put off too long), it's definitely important.

As mentioned, you probably already have most of the information in your project notebook. It should all be there as a result of you and your team actually carrying out the project. Be sure to add the acceptance documents, the project summary, and any other closing documents, including the lessons learned report or knowledge base. Obtain any information needed from team members and vendor companies. Also gather necessary information from support departments such as accounting or purchasing. The actual signed-off documents, or at least copies or scans of those signed documents, should be included in the archives for accountability and audit purposes.

Organizing the Project Archives

With all the information now gathered, you can organize it in a manner that will be useful to a future project manager, an auditor, or anyone else who needs to know how this project was conducted. Organizing project archives can seem straightforward, but you might encounter certain challenges, which can be compounded for the larger or more complex projects.

Beware of Too Much Information

You know the feeling when you're at a dinner party and someone "over-shares"? It's awkward, and you find yourself wishing you could "un-hear" what you just heard.

While "TMI" (too much information) in the context of the project archives is not socially unsettling, it can seriously hamper the effectiveness of the archives. It's freeing to have gigabytes of storage easily available for your project files. However, the associated problem is that you can save anything and everything . . . whether you should or not. The tendency during a project can be to just collect every last bit of data and worry about it later.

While saving everything might (or might not) be okay during the course of the project, it's probably not best for the archives. Do the necessary weeding now. Do you really need every email message pertaining to the project? Every brainstorming note? Every draft of every deliverable? Probably not.

Put yourself in the shoes of the future project manager (who might be you). What information would you want to see, and what information would just get in your way?

Categorize Wisely

After you've gathered and weeded until you have the right information for the archives, you need to organize it. Figure out the best organizational scheme for this mountain of data.

If the three-ring binder, electronic project notebook, shared drive, or document library already has a good organizational scheme, just stick with what works. Keep in mind that the organizational scheme that you and your team found helpful in the day-to-day execution of the project might not necessarily be the best scheme for the project archives.

Accordingly, tweak the organization as necessary. Rearrange, add, or remove items as appropriate to make the archives easy for someone else to learn about or leverage your project as efficiently as possible.

Do It Today

One of the biggest challenges about project archives is making sure you actually take the time to create them. More often than not, you and your team members have one foot in another project while you're finishing the current one. You encounter heavy pressure from above to close the current project and move on immediately to the new one.

Resist the temptation to put off assembling the archives. Do it within a few days of closing the project, while your memory (and that of the team members, vendors, and support functions) of the important details is still fresh. You'll be so glad you did it right away when you or someone else is doing a similar project.

Offer a Roadmap

Those reviewing your project archives will be well served by the existence of some kind of index that guides them through the contents of the archives. For smaller projects, the organizational structure of the archives might be index enough. This is true whether you're looking at tab dividers in a three-ring binder or folder names in a shared drive or document library.

However, for the archives of larger projects that have multiple levels of information, an index is essential. This is basically a table of contents that lists the document titles and where they're located. If the index and the documents are digitally accessible, the location field can be a hyperlink that takes the user straight to the file and opens it. If the document titles are not self-explanatory, you can add a short description to each title. Figure 21-1 shows an example of a project archives index.

HyperNet Strategies - Web Training Project Archives
Submitted by Monique Sherman, project manager, 3/7/12.

Item	Description	Location
Project goal and objectives		T:/HyperNet/2012/WebTraining/Initiating/G&O.docx
Requirements document	Detailed requirements from the customer.	T:/HyperNet/2012/WebTraining/Initiating/requirements.xlsx
Success criteria		T:/HyperNet/2012/WebTraining/Initiating/success.docx
Scope statement	Includes scope, objectives, strategy, constraints, assumptions, risks, and rough order of magnitude budget.	T:/HyperNet/2012/WebTraining/Initiating/scope.docx
Proposal	Includes the customer signoff and contract.	T:/HyperNet/2012/WebTraining/Initiating/proposal.docx
Project charter		T:/HyperNet/2012/WebTraining/Initiating/charter.docx
Deliverables		T:/HyperNet/2012/WebTraining/Planning/deliverables.xlsx
Work breakdown structure		T:/HyperNet/2012/WebTraining/Planning/wbs.vsd
Resource plan		T:/HyperNet/2012/WebTraining/Planning/ResourcePlan.xlsx
Project organization chart	Includes responsibility matrix.	T:/HyperNet/2012/WebTraining/Planning/OrgChart.vsd
Work estimates		T:/HyperNet/2012/WebTraining/Planning/WorkEstimates.xlsx
Project budget	Includes cost estimates and resulting budget.	T:/HyperNet/2012/WebTraining/Planning/Budget.xlsx
Communication plan	Includes ground rules, issues handling, and sample reports.	T:/HyperNet/2012/WebTraining/Planning/CommunicationPlan.docx
Change management plan	Includes roster of change management board, procedure, forms, and log.	T:/HyperNet/2012/WebTraining/Planning/ChangeMgmtPlan.docx
Project baseline #1	First baseline, from 10/1/2011.	T:/HyperNet/2012/WebTraining/Executing/Baseline1.xlsx
Project baseline #2	Second baseline, from 11/1/2011.	T:/HyperNet/2012/WebTraining/Executing/Baseline2.xlsx

Figure 21-1: Project archives index

CROSS-REFERENCE A template for a project archives index is available in the companion files for this book. You can download it at `www.wiley.com/go/ProjMgmtCoach`.

If your PMO or portfolio manager has established guidelines for indexing and keywording your project archives, they probably apply regardless of the size of the project.

Storing the Project Archives

As with the project notebook, your project archives can be as manually low-tech or electronically high-tech as the project and your organization's requirements warrant. The project archives can take any of the following forms:

- Three-ring binder(s)
- Electronic folders and files copied onto a compact disc or flash drive and included with the printed project summary notebook
- A project wiki
- A shared drive on the organization's server
- A document library on the organization's intranet
- Part of the organization's document control or document management system

Whichever form the project archives take, be sure you have good answers to the following questions:

- How much space (either physical or electronic) is available?
- Where will they be stored?
- How long will they be stored there?
- How do others access the archives?
- Do any confidential files need to be protected?
- Are files editable or locked?

The storage of project archives should be consistent for all projects. If you have a PMO or portfolio manager, then the archiving process and guidelines have probably been established. If not, confer with the other project managers in your organization as to how and where you'll store your archives. No matter the form of the project archives, be sure that there is at least one backup in a different location in case of data loss or other disaster.

As you and others in your organization archive more and more projects, it becomes increasingly important to establish an index of all the completed project archives. More information is needed beyond just the names on the spines of binders or electronic folder names. Develop this index of completed projects, including the form it will take, how it's accessed, and how it is to be updated and maintained. Figure 21-2 shows an example of an index of completed projects. Include an ID, keyword, or hyperlink to help users find the project archives they need.

Index of Completed Projects

Project Name	Project Summary	Project Manager	Sponsor / Customer	Completed
Live-action software demos	Create a series of 20 live-action videos demonstrating features of the HyperNet Strategies 2011 app for integration with the app and use at trade shows.	Monique Sherman	Lyle Ketman/ HyperNet Strategies	9/30/2011
Staff kitchen remodel	Remodel the staff kitchen in Building A, second floor.	Carrie Paul	John Sparks	10/15/2011
Training program development tools	Design and develop a suite of training program development tools for use by our internal curriculum development specialists.	Barry Melendez	Enrico Tafoya	11/17/2011
Software trade show coordination	Coordinate the vendor booth, demos, workshop, and collateral materials for the 2012 software trade show in New York.	Robert Whiting	Yunie Chai/ Padme Development	1/20/2012
Web training modules	Create series of five self-paced Web training modules for customer service representatives of HyperNet Strategies.	Monique Sherman	Lyle Ketman HyperNet Strategies	3/12/2012

Figure 21-2: Index of completed projects

CROSS-REFERENCE **A template for an index of completed projects is available in the companion files for this book. You can download it at** `www.wiley.com/go/ProjMgmtCoach`.

Summary

Project managers can use archived files from past projects to leverage and build new projects, ever expanding the organization's experience and knowledge base of projects. Project archives are also vital for regulatory or certification requirements, as well as internal and external audits of processes, projects, or products.

Just about everything in your project notebook, whether it's print or electronic, can be part of your project archives. Make sure you have all the information needed from a variety of sources.

Store the project archives in accordance with your organization's standards, making sure that other project managers, including yourself, will be able to find the project information needed for starting a future project.

Coach's Review

Use this section to assess what you've learned in this chapter and to apply it to a real-life project you're currently working on.

Test Your Knowledge

Test your knowledge of the material in this chapter by answering the following questions. See Appendix A for the answers.

1. Name at least two reasons why project archives are important to an organization.

2. Why is the project notebook so important in the development of the project archives?

3. Name at least ten items that can be a part of the project archives.

4. Why is it important to create the project archives as soon as possible after the project is finished?

5. Name at least three methods (printed or electronic) for storing the project archives.

Project Challenge

Practice the knowledge you've gained in this chapter by working through one or more of the following challenges using a real-life project you're working on, or one similar to the types of projects you might work on.

1. With your project notebook as a guide, make a list of all the items you want to include in your project archives. Refer to the bulleted list of possible contents of project archives under "Gathering Information" and see if anything else should be added to your list. Note which items you already have. Note the items you need to create or obtain from someone else.

2. Using your project notebook and your list of contents for the project archives, gather any additional information you need, weed out information not needed, and create your project archives.

3. Organize and store the project archives as appropriate.

Don't Forget Lessons Learned

Learning a lesson, particularly in a group critique setting, might sound like a bitter pill to swallow for project managers and team members alike. If I'm an expert, the thinking goes: "Why should I have lessons to learn? And even if I do have more to learn, do I want others to know that? After all, I have my reputation to consider."

The truth is that the wisest and most skilled project managers recognize that there's always more to discover about project management. Also, whether a project has to do with developing software, rolling out a training program, or constructing a building, there's always more to know about that type of project and its subject matter.

Every project is intended to add to the overall value of your organization or provide benefits in some way. The project might exist for the purpose of increasing profits, reducing costs, improving customer service, ensuring regulatory compliance, or what have you.

In addition, consider the increased skill and knowledge you and your team members gain with each project, even (perhaps especially) if a project fails or is canceled. Regardless of the project outcome, you all will have learned to work as a team, developed processes and efficiencies, tracked progress, and solved problems.

Whether the results are positive or negative, capturing this knowledge is essential to the growth and development of your organization and its ability to successfully execute projects. This knowledge base is a valuable asset to the organization, which goes beyond the stated purpose of the project.

As the project manager, you set the tone for your project, which is like an organization within your organization. For the world of your project, you can develop a culture of learning and continuous improvement that can not only be infectious to the organization as a whole, but can also add significantly to the organization's resulting maturity.

In this chapter, you learn how to gather and document the lessons learned from your project. These lessons learned become part of the project's historical record and can benefit others in the future as they initiate similar projects.

CROSS-REFERENCE The information in this chapter relates to the PMP Exam's Domain V: Closing the Project, Task 5, "Collate lessons learned through comprehensive project review, in order to create and/or update the organization's knowledge base."

How Lessons Learned Help

The more projects you do, the more experience you have to draw on. In many cases, the time the initiating and planning processes take can be streamlined by leveraging the work that you and other project teams have done with projects throughout the organization.

Lessons learned is the concept of reviewing the project in such a way that aspects that were unsuccessful can be constructively resolved and aspects that were successful can be repeated or improved upon in future projects. Some people call it the *project post mortem*, which seems to imply that the project has died and you're examining what went wrong.

A more innocuous and less-threatening term is *project review*, a good description especially when lessons learned are being collected at certain points along the project life cycle. A variation on the review theme are the *project implementation review* and *post-implementation review (PIR)*. These reviews tend to be focused after project completion or even further out, after enough time has passed to ascertain the results of the completed project.

Whatever it's called, it's all about capturing those "teaching moments" that happen throughout a project. The lessons learned are indeed lessons, or even initiations, which usher you into the next level of your development. You receive valuable feedback for yourself. Your team members receive feedback, not only about their own performance, but also about what can be improved in a team and on a project. Lessons learned are a valuable commodity to you, your team, and for the organization itself.

THE CANDID COACH: DON'T USE LESSONS LEARNED TO THINK SMALL

As vital as lessons learned are, don't let them snap your mind shut. Suppose your organization decides to launch a new technology or product line or to expand into a new business area. In this case, relying on the good old familiar processes can actually be counterproductive, even if those processes seem reasonable. The problem is that assumptions can be made about the new product or business environment that are not accurate and that are actually detrimental.

The point of lessons learned is to continue to do things better, and part of doing things better is keeping an open mind to new possibilities.

You and your team members can make personal observations and draw your own conclusions about how the project went. But you and your team gain a deeper and more valuable experience by stopping, taking the time to evaluate, and articulating how the project went.

Lessons learned are particularly valuable for those projects that fail to add the intended value to the organization (increased profits, reduced costs, or whatever). They're also highly valuable for those projects that just unequivocally fail.

By documenting lessons learned, others can also profit from your hard-won wisdom. These others might be looking at your project archives because they're going to do a similar project. Even those doing a dissimilar project can benefit. All projects deal with teams, processes, knowledge areas, and project management methodology. Any experiences you have to share about those more general factors can be valuable to other project managers.

CROSS-REFERENCE For information about assembling the project archives, see Chapter 21, "Documenting a Project for Posterity."

The following are some specific ways that lessons learned can help your organization:

- **Save time:** There always seems to be that point in a project when you desperately wish you could get back time you wasted. With lessons learned, you can share proven techniques, strategies, processes, and shortcuts so you and other project teams can save time in future projects.

- **Save money:** Organizations continually strive to lower costs and increase profit. Time and effort spent on a project more often than not equates to money spent. By sharing the lessons from past projects, you're helping others improve, which often saves time and therefore money.

- **Apply realism:** There's something about project planning that turns some of the most grounded stakeholders into starry-eyed dreamers, and project managers are not exempt. Their hopes for the amount of effort they want a task to take collide with the cold, hard facts of how much time it actually will take, based on history. The same applies to the amount of effort, resource requirements, and cost. By pointing out discrepancies between the estimates in a new project plan against the actuals in a finished project, lessons learned help model a project that more accurately reflects real life. This works on overly optimistic team members, as well as on managing stakeholders applying unrealistic pressure for a shorter time frame or a smaller budget.

■ **Prove it:** Lessons learned, as well as the actual performance you archive, provide the uncompromising data you often need to demonstrate why certain tasks need to be done, or done in a particular way. These solid facts can also help you justify schedule, costs, resource demands, and processes to managing stakeholders.

■ **Validate methodology:** Perhaps your organization is on the fence about professional project management. Lessons learned from a project that ran according to a project management methodology can show how the project resulted in a superior outcome to other projects that did not. Lessons learned can also help your organization determine the most appropriate methodology (traditional project management versus agile or iterative project management) for different types of projects.

■ **Share methodology:** Novice project managers can study lessons learned to deepen their knowledge about the project management methodology, giving them a head start in their "apprenticeship" and continuing efforts.

Gathering Lessons Learned

For many team members, the prospect of discussing lessons learned with colleagues can produce a knot of dread in the belly — even in the smoothest and most successful projects. If the project was awash with problems, personality conflicts, or outright failures, the anxiety level is exponential. Even you as the project manager might feel apprehensive about how team members view your leadership of the project.

It can be difficult for people to acknowledge, especially in front of their peers, that they could have done a better job or that they have more to learn, even as experts in the field. However, there are ways to make the sharing and collecting of lessons learned positive and less threatening for everyone involved. The process becomes more palatable when people acknowledge that it contributes to individual professional development, efficiency and effectiveness of future projects, and the success of the overall organization. When there's a constructive and structured process amid a project culture of openness and respect, sharing lessons learned can make people feel validated, even as they acknowledge that improvements can be made.

THE CANDID COACH: LESSONS LEARNED IN A BLAMING ENVIRONMENT

The realities of the organization can sometimes be at odds with the culture a project manager creates within the sphere of the project. This can manifest itself during lessons learned exercises. If a staff member knows she'll get "dinged" on her next performance review for a project misstep she made, she'll be less likely to bring it up and instead will hope no one else knows about it. An atmosphere of blame and retribution makes it difficult to draw people out and prevent them from pointing fingers.

In such an atmosphere, you can take steps to try and gain the trust of team members and discover the valuable lessons learned. Here are some ideas:

■ Meet with team members one on one.

■ Allow lessons learned questionnaires to be submitted anonymously. Still, be aware that anonymous comments often still telegraph the identities of the team members involved.

■ Have lessons learned meetings conducted among peers, without managers present.

■ Don't include names, titles, or other identifiers in the lessons learned report; rather include the feedback with solutions and recommendations.

Collecting Feedback

Many project managers don't think to gather lessons learned until after the project is completed — if at all. Instead, make collecting lessons learned an ongoing process throughout the life of the project, ideally as part of every status meeting. Short and frequent attention to lessons learned throughout the project is the most effective approach. People remember the details of the issue more clearly and the resulting recommendations can be put into practice sooner. The regular emphasis on sharing this information can be instrumental in establishing a culture of openness and continuous process improvement.

Although you'll gather lessons learned during status meetings and dedicated lesson-oriented sessions, as the project manager, you can always be on the lookout for successes and opportunities for improvement. These are not only sources in and of themselves, but they can prove to be the launching pad for deeper discussions in the lessons learned meeting.

Potential sources for lessons learned include the following:

■ **Periodic team meetings:** Don't wait for a lessons learned meeting. Go ahead and launch into "lessons learned mode" with every issue or success. In fact, you can include lessons learned as a standing agenda item at every team or status meeting, perhaps the final two minutes of each meeting.

- **Status reports:** In addition to updating information on actual work and completion of tasks, you can ask team members to include issues or roadblocks in their status reports. You can also ask them to note any "wins" they've experienced.

- **Issues tracking:** You probably have established a process for tracking and resolving issues as part of your project communication plan. Your issues tracking system is a great source for identifying problems and solutions.

- **Quality management:** As part of your project quality plan, you might have a structure in place for monitoring project or product quality, for identifying variances with the quality specifications, and for developing the associated corrective actions. The variances and corrective actions are another excellent source for problems and solutions that can be captured as lessons learned.

- **Your observation:** As project manager, keep your eyes and ears open for successes and failures that have long-term impact for projects in the organization.

CROSS-REFERENCE For information about quality management, see Chapter 9, "Planning for Quality." For details about status reporting and tracking issues, see the section "What Do You Communicate?" in Chapter 10. For tips about effective team meetings, see "Project Status Meetings" in Chapter 15.

Preparing for Lessons Learned Meetings

Regardless of when you gather lessons learned, do what you can to make the discussions as productive and constructive as possible. Here are some suggestions for preparing for these sessions:

- **Meeting logistics:** If you hold dedicated lessons learned sessions, find a good meeting location, set the start and end times, establish the agenda, and invite the team members. Choosing a different place from the routine meetings can be beneficial — for example, a different building, someplace offsite, even a banquet room or someone's living room or deck. A new atmosphere generates new thought.

- **Facilitator:** Decide who will facilitate the meeting, which quite often will be you, the project manager. However, you might prefer that someone else, perhaps a neutral person not associated with the project, facilitate the meeting.

- **Scribe:** You won't have time to take notes so ask someone to act as the meeting scribe or recorder — a team member or a neutral person from outside the project. A team member will be more familiar with the terms, acronyms, and nuances of the project than an outsider. The disadvantage is that the team member/scribe might be too busy recording everyone else's comments to fully participate. The scribe might record on flip chart sheets, a white board, or projected computer screen. Posting the feedback for all to see fosters the generation of more constructive feedback.

▪ **Open-ended questions:** Develop a series of open-ended questions for the participants to consider. Remember that open-ended questions are those that cannot be answered with a single word, such as "yes," "no," or "fine" (see the sidebar). Be prepared with a detailed series of questions in case you need to coax the team into talking.

STOKE THE CONVERSATION

Here are some examples of open-ended questions for lessons learned sessions, although you will want to adapt them to your project:

■ Name one thing in your own area of responsibility that went particularly well with this project.

■ Name one thing in your own area of responsibility that could have been improved with this project.

■ For something that didn't go so well, what would you suggest as an improvement?

■ For something that went well, how can it be improved even further?

■ How do you feel about our completed deliverables? Are you proud of them, and if so, why? Are you unhappy with them, and if so, why?

■ Can you share a technique or process you discovered that improved results or prevented problems?

■ What was the most difficult problem you encountered during the project, and how did you solve it?

■ What was the most satisfying or fulfilling part of the project?

■ What was the most frustrating part of our project? What would you recommend for avoiding this frustration in the future?

■ Which of our project's processes worked particularly well? Which were not so useful or were difficult to use?

■ What did you think about the participation of our managing stakeholders? If their participation was effective, why? If not, how could we have improved their participation?

■ What would you recommend for future projects?

If you hold lessons learned sessions regularly, you can focus the discussion on a portion of the project each time. For example, you might ask about a particular phase or milestone. Another way to break the project down is to reflect on the different knowledge areas (scope, time/schedule, cost, quality, communication, human resources, risk, and procurement) one at a time.

■ **Provide a questionnaire in advance:** Compile the questions you want the team to consider and distribute them about a week before the meeting. Although you might have a longer list to help jump-start discussion at the meeting, keep the advance list you send to the team relatively short, perhaps three to seven questions on a single page (see Figure 22-1 for a sample). The questions shouldn't feel like busy work. They should get team members thinking about the strengths and weaknesses of the project to help them prepare for the meeting.

Trade Show Project Review Questionnaire

Please answer these questions. Bring the completed questionnaire to our Project Review meeting next Tuesday at 3 pm in the Siskiyou Room.

1. Name one thing that went particularly well with this project.

2. Name one thing that could have been improved with this project.

3. Can you share a technique or process you discovered that saved time, money, or aggravation?

4. What was the most difficult problem you encountered during the project, and how did you solve it?

Figure 22-1: Lessons learned questionnaire

CROSS-REFERENCE A sample of a lessons learned questionnaire is available in the companion files for this book. You can download the file at www.wiley.com/go/ProjMgmtCoach.

Conducting Lessons Learned Meetings

Conduct the lessons learned meeting(s) in a way that suits the culture and geography of your team. Ideally, the entire team gathers in a single meeting room. If it's a very large team, or a project with quite different components, you can have different lessons learned meetings for different aspects of the project. If the team is distributed across various locations, consider the best ways to include all members of the team — for example, by videoconferencing, using a speaker phone, or traveling to a central location.

CROSS-REFERENCE For general guidelines for facilitating a productive and positive lessons learned meeting, see Chapter 15, "The Keys to Successful Meetings."

A LESSONS LEARNED NON-MEETING

Although not the optimum method, you can conceivably gather lessons learned entirely in writing rather than in meetings. The focus would be the lessons learned questionnaire that the team members complete and submit. Because it's a solitary exercise, you would not experience the dynamism you do in a meeting. However, in some situations, it's better than nothing.

In such a questionnaire, include pointed and specific questions. Have the team members answer them and turn in the questionnaire. Be sure to give them a deadline.

Another idea is to set up an online forum to gather lessons learned. The forum would include your questions and the team members' answers. All team members can read one another's feedback, add comments, and continue the discussion.

QUESTIONS FOR THE MANAGING STAKEHOLDERS

Although you're the project manager and possibly the lessons learned meeting facilitator, you have to answer the same questions about the project, as well as a few more.

In addition, you might hold a lessons learned meeting with managing stakeholders, such as the project sponsor or portfolio manager.

- How well did the project realize its stated goal?
- To what extent were the project objectives achieved?
- Were there variances in the finish date, the budget, or the scope? What were the reasons for these variances? Could we have anticipated and avoided these variances?
- What did you learn about your project management methodology? Was it the right methodology to use? What would you do differently?
- How well did the team follow the methodology?
- Was the customer satisfied with the project results?

Some project results aren't known until some time after the project finishes. Schedule a session later on to answer the following questions:

- Was the business value, as defined in the success criteria, realized?
- Given the original problem that engendered the project, was this the right solution? Was the problem solved?

Minimizing the Fear of Lessons Learned

Do all you can to make the gathering of lessons learned less threatening. At the start of the lessons learned meeting, review the ground rules for all participants to ensure that feedback is useful and the tone is constructive and positive. See Figure 22-2 for an example of ground rules you might post on the wall during a lessons learned meeting or include on the agenda.

Lessons Learned Meeting
Ground Rules

Keep it positive.

Be respectful.

Be constructive.

Use "I" statements.

Practice active listening.

Let the speaker finish.

Develop recommendations.

Figure 22-2: Lessons learned meeting ground rules

CROSS-REFERENCE An example of ground rules that you can print and post at your lessons learned meeting is available in the companion files for this book. You can download it at www.wiley.com/go/ProjMgmtCoach.

The following are suggested ground rules for lessons learned meeting participants and information about how you as a facilitator can keep the meeting productive.

■ **Establish the structure of the meeting.** You might allow the discussion to be completely open about any question or aspect of the project. Or, you might discuss one aspect of the project at a time — for example, a phase or milestone. You could cover each question on the team questionnaire in sequence. Communicate the structure and stay on that track.

■ **Keep it positive.** The team has worked hard and built professional relationships. Don't let negativity tear those relationships apart. Alternate positively and negatively phrased questions and issues. When participants describe a problem, an excellent guideline is to have them include the statement: "and my contribution to this shortcoming was . . ." Start and end the discussion on a positive note.

- **Be respectful.** Maintain a respectful tone throughout, especially when discussing difficult issues. As the facilitator, anticipate clashing personalities, difficult topics, and potential conflicts and direct the discussion to get the information you need.

- **Be constructive.** Keep the focus on learning and continuous improvement. The goal is to make the organization better and move forward. Don't let the discussion degenerate into blame or retribution. For example, frame the discussion constructively by saying "These issues are in the past. The point now is to see how we can avoid this situation in the future." Or, "What have we learned? How can we build on this situation so we have a better outcome next time?"

- **Use "I" statements.** Review the value of "I" statements rather than "You" statements to ensure that participants can express their feedback without putting others on the defensive (see the examples in the following sidebar). Participants should avoid "You" statements, which can be blaming or accusatory. Examples of "you" statements can start with "You need," "He always," or "They never."

EXAMPLES OF EFFECTIVE "I" STATEMENTS

Examples of ineffective "you" statements are:

- "You always went over budget on your tasks."
- "Jane didn't inspect the roofing material properly."
- "Management was consistently late providing feedback on the reports."

These same thoughts, recast into "I" statements, can still be thinly disguised "you" statement, as follows:

- "I feel like there was a disregard for the budget."
- "I thought the quality of the roofing material was below our standards."
- "I would have liked feedback on the reports to come in sooner."

More effective "I" statements would be:

- "I don't understand what led to these tasks going over budget."
- "The customer had issues with the roofing materials. I would like to know what we can do to avoid that problem in the future."
- "I couldn't update reports by the deadline because of the amount of feedback and when I received it."

- **Practice active listening.** Remind the group about active listening, especially if you want dialog among two or more participants. In active listening, listeners are expected to focus, understand, interpret, and evaluate what they are hearing. The listener hears what is said and paraphrases back what he just heard. Examples of such a paraphrasing statement can start with "I hear you saying that . . ." or "What I'm getting from this conversation is . . ."

- **Let the speaker finish.** The facilitator must ensure that everyone is free to speak without being interrupted. At the same time, the facilitator must ensure that no individual is monopolizing the conversation and that there is a balance of voices.

- **Be sure each team member has his or her say.** You might go around the table one by one, or call on those who have not spoken much.

- **Develop recommendations.** Whether discussing project strengths or challenges, ask the participants to suggest solutions or recommendations for future projects. This keeps the group focused on being proactive about continuous improvement, rather than allowing them to sink into a morass of negativity.

If a lessons learned session goes awry, participants can walk away feeling frustrated, demoralized, or abused. So be sure to end the meeting on a positive note. You want participants to leave feeling upbeat rather than beat up.

Ensure that the final question is something like "What did we do that we should not consider changing, because it worked?" or "What did we do well?" Remind the group of the great work that was done, along with the close-knit teaming and the positive results for the organization. If appropriate, discuss opportunities for the team to work together again in the future. Figure out how the team can stay in touch.

Consider something rather festive at the end of the lessons learned session, even if there's a separate end-of-project celebration. Fun food (like chocolate, or pizza, or even chocolate pizza!) is always good.

Documenting Lessons Learned

Gather the notes that the scribe recorded and questionnaires you received and assemble a coherent report or knowledge base from which future project managers will be able to learn. A knowledge base is particularly advantageous for documenting lessons learned, especially if you're collecting them throughout the life of the project. A knowledge base can be maintained in a spreadsheet, database, or shared list. Readers can search for a topic or keyword without having to dig through numerous reports.

Deciding on the Information to Include

If you want to keep the report or knowledge base format as simple as possible, you can have a section for what went well (or strengths) and another section for suggested improvements (or challenges). See Figure 22-3 for a simple lessons learned report template.

```
Lessons Learned Report

Project Name:
Project Completed Date:
Project Manager:

Overview of the Project



Overview of the Lessons Learned Process



Successes and Strengths of the Project
   •
   •
   •
   •
   •

Challenges and Weaknesses of the Project
   •
   •
   •
   •
   •
```

Figure 22-3: Simple lessons learned report template

CROSS-REFERENCE A template for the simple lessons learned report is available in the companion files for this book. You can download it at `www.wiley.com/go/ProjMgmtCoach`.

If you have a large volume of information, format the report or knowledge base into logical subheadings, such as project phases, subsystems, functions, or teams. Under those subheadings, document the strengths and challenges.

If you conduct multiple lessons learned meetings throughout the project life cycle, be sure to add to the knowledge base for each meeting, or at least include them in a report or the minutes. Include the outcomes of any suggestions adopted from previous lessons learned discussions and whether those changes were an improvement. The smaller the scope of the lessons learned meeting, the simpler the documentation can be.

Presenting Lessons Learned

Because the lessons learned will become a part of the project archives, most people can easily obtain detail about the project. If the lessons learned will go to audiences who won't have the context of the project, you can provide some background by attaching the project goal and objectives or the scope statement.

For the project's strengths, be sure to emphasize what can and should be repeated in a future project, as well as what strengths can be improved upon. You're not bragging; you're laying a helpful foundation for someone else's successful project.

Likewise, for the project's challenges, stress what can and should be done better in future projects. Maintain a professional, straightforward attitude focused on continuous improvement in the organization.

Include the specifics and recommendations about strengths, challenges, and improvements that will make the information valuable to another project manager, keeping in mind that that future project manager could be someone who has never done a project like this. Use keywords to make the information in your knowledge base or report easier to find.

THE CANDID COACH: USE PASSIVE VOICE TO PROTECT THE GUILTY

Everyone from our ninth grade composition teacher to our computer's grammar checker has admonished us to write in active voice. However, sometimes passive voice is more effective, especially when you want to express a problem diplomatically without assigning blame.

For example, suppose you want to say, "The management team consistently delayed its review of the marketing materials." Using passive voice, you could express it instead as "The review of marketing materials was consistently delayed."

With passive voice, you're still being specific about the challenge without placing blame. The reader concludes that attention should be paid to ensuring that reviews take place in a timely manner.

Using passive voice to express successes can also be effective if you're concerned about coming across as overly boastful. For example, you would probably feel uncomfortable saying "The project manager effectively tracked and resolved issues." The passive voice version sounds less arrogant: "Issues were effectively tracked and resolved."

Use passive voice sparingly, however, as it can make for really dry reading. Use it only when you need to avoid problems of direct blaming or boasting.

You probably cannot avoid department or function names, as those are pertinent in lessons learned documentation. But consider whether you want to use people's names or titles. This isn't an employee performance review; it's a project review with an eye toward improving the performance of future projects. If the documentation emphasizes solutions and recommendations, it might not even occur to you to use names or titles.

FOCUS ON SOLUTIONS AND RECOMMENDATIONS

A lessons learned report or knowledge base that highlights solutions and recommendations for future projects based on the experiences of the current project takes on an entirely different character.

Consider the following comment, which indicates only what happened: "The review of marketing materials was consistently delayed." To get to the correct recommendation, the lessons learned process would need to ferret out the cause. Was the marketing copy unclear and contradictory? Or did the reviewing managers consider the reviews a lower priority for their time? All effective lessons learned suggest some form of cause and a remedy. Once you know the true cause of the problem, you can articulate the recommendation for future projects, such as, "Obtain a commitment from management for turnaround time for reviews, and then enforce that time frame."

Likewise, recommendations can stress what went well with the current project and provide the appropriate details. The statement "The issues tracking system was extremely effective" could become "The issues tracking system can be used as is in future projects. Team members report that information about issues was easy to find. They also liked the ability to add comments or suggestions."

It's best to offer only those recommendations that are a result of the lessons learned meeting. If you decide to include recommendations that were not discussed as a group, make this clear.

The best lessons learned documentation includes both the review of what happened in the current project as well as solutions and recommendations for future projects. A knowledge base in a spreadsheet format is shown in Figure 22-4. If you're creating a report, you can use a table format showing the successes or challenges in one column and recommendations in another column.

CROSS-REFERENCE A template for a lessons learned knowledge base in which the current project feedback is coupled with recommendations for future similar projects is available in the companion files for this book. You can download it at www.wiley.com/go/ProjMgmtCoach.

The nature of the feedback, the quantity and level of consensus or diversity of the comments, and the amount of detail you wish to provide can all dictate the form the documentation takes. At the quick and easy end of the spectrum, you can have bulleted lists of strengths and challenges, along with their corresponding recommendations, taken directly from the scribe's notes. Such documentation records the raw data so you leave it to readers to reach their own conclusions.

	A	B
1	Mobile Web Eyeglasses Product Launch	
2	Lessons Learned Database	
3		
4	**Lesson** (success, strength, challenge, weakness, improvement)	**Recommendation for Future Projects** (be specific)
5	Management review of marketing materials consistently took twice as long as scheduled.	Obtain a commitment from management for turnaround time for reviews, and then enforce that timeframe.
6	Information about issues was easy to find, and they liked the ability to add comments and suggestions.	The issues tracking system can be used as is for future projects.
7	The scripts for the app testing were comprehensive. Bugs were discovered in enough time to be fixed and tested.	Adapt these test scripts as appropriate, but add refinements for testing on different platforms.

Figure 22-4: Lessons learned knowledge base sample highlighting recommendations

At the other end of the spectrum, you might summarize the major themes of feedback and provide an analysis of the results. For example, you can specify the number of occurrences of specific feedback. With an analytical summary, it's good to indicate where there was major consensus, minor consensus, lone wolf dissenters, or no consensus at all. Although this type of documentation is more thorough and often more useful, it will take more time to synthesize and write.

Disseminating Lessons Learned

The lessons learned documentation becomes part of the project archives, whether that's a hard-copy binder, files on a shared drive, or on an organizational intranet. However, you don't want this information to languish in some dusty file cabinet. As you collect lessons learned, distribute them (or a link to the location) to the team, other stakeholders, and anyone else you think might benefit.

Consider creating different versions of lessons learned for different audiences. Team members might get the entire set of information, for example, or just information that has to do with the piece they worked on. Managing stakeholders might receive all the information as well or just an executive summary.

NOTE Be sure to consider any organizational politics when deciding who should receive or have access to your report. All stakeholders deserve to see the lessons learned, as no improvement can be realized if the issues and solutions are not communicated. But the manner in which the lessons learned are presented can be finessed.

Using Past Lessons Learned

Lessons learned should not be relegated to a remote shelf or buried folder. The point is for the lessons learned to become a part of your organization's knowledge base, for project management and beyond. Therefore, as you start new projects, be sure to consult the available lessons learned, either from projects that you've managed or that others have managed.

As you hear of projects that others are initiating, tell your colleagues about existing lessons learned for related projects. The more everyone can leverage each other's knowledge and experience, the stronger and more successful your projects and your organization will be.

Summary

Lessons learned throughout the project life cycle are essential to the project review process and the expansion of the organization's knowledge base. As project manager, you collect feedback from your team members about the strengths and challenges experienced in the project, along with associated recommendations. You compile the lessons learned based on this feedback. The finished documentation becomes an essential component of the permanent historical project archives.

Coach's Review

Use this section to assess what you've learned in this chapter and to apply it to a real-life project you're currently working on.

Test Your Knowledge

Test your knowledge of the material in this chapter by answering the following questions. See Appendix A for the answers.

1. What are at least two other names for "lessons learned"? What are the pros and cons of using these different names?

2. Name at least three ways that project lessons learned can help an organization.

3. In addition to the team members, what are the two roles that must be present for an effective lessons learned meeting?

4. What are the three key types of feedback you are trying to get out of the lessons learned process?

5. Name at least three ground rules for a constructive lessons learned meeting.

6. Where should lessons learned documentation reside?

Project Challenge

Practice the knowledge you've gained in this chapter with the following challenge. Use the project you've been managing as you've worked through the chapters in this book.

1. With information in your project workbook as a guide, including team meeting agendas, status reports, issues tracking, quality management plan, and more, list the successes and challenges that your project has experienced.

2. Plan the lessons learned meeting for your team, using the guidelines in the section "Preparing for Lessons Learned Meetings" earlier in this chapter.

3. Develop at least 15 open-ended questions that will help open a constructive discussion with your team.

4. Develop a project review questionnaire including three to seven questions to provide to team members in advance of the lessons learned meeting. Adapt the questions from those you developed in Step 3, or create new questions. Provide the questionnaire and the agenda to your team members to help them prepare for the meeting.

5. Conduct the lessons learned meeting with your team. Be sure that your appointed scribe records the feedback and discussion of the group as to the project's strengths, challenges, and recommendations.

6. Answer the questions in the "Questions for the Managing Stakeholder" feature, and add it to the team feedback.

7. Using all team feedback, write your lessons learned report or knowledge base. Add it to the project archives, and provide it to your team members and any other stakeholders who should see it.

Taking the Next Steps in
Project Management

Chapter 23: Running a Project Management Office
Chapter 24: Managing a Portfolio of Projects
Chapter 25: Selecting the Right Projects

Running a Project Management Office

A *project management office (PMO)* is responsible for centralizing and coordinating project management within an organization. Often set up as a board or department, the intent of a PMO is to improve project success rates by standardizing and supporting project management practices in the organization.

In this chapter, you learn how a PMO can help an organization standardize and improve project management efforts. You also learn how to determine whether a PMO might be appropriate for your organization, and if so, how to determine the type of PMO needed and plan for its implementation.

CROSS-REFERENCE The information in this chapter relates to the PMP Exam's Domain III: Executing the Project, Task 6, "Maximize team performance through leading, mentoring, training, and motivating team members."

Defining PMO Functions

Your organization might decide that a PMO is needed to help improve its project success rates. This means not only helping more of your projects finish on time and under budget, but also helping more projects achieve their success criteria.

A PMO can help achieve these goals by defining and developing project manager support systems that deal with some or all of the following functions:

- **Standards, processes, and best practices:** The PMO can define and facilitate project management protocols, procedures, and templates to foster consistency in activities common to all projects, such as project proposals, change management, and project closure.

- **Certification and regulatory requirements:** The PMO can support and monitor project compliance with relevant requirements in support of organizational or customer goals and specifications.

- **Methodology:** The PMO can provide support and coaching regarding specific project management techniques, such as critical path method, critical chain project management, agile project management, and so on.

- **Tools and infrastructure:** The PMO can acquire and roll out project scheduling software, develop and disseminate document templates and forms, or just facilitate the availability of space on the organization's network for storing project notebooks and archives.

- **Shared resources and communication:** The PMO can staff a corps of project managers who are assigned to projects throughout the organization. The PMO might facilitate the assignment of resources to projects and coordinate cross-project communication.

- **Mentoring and training:** The PMO might mentor, coach, and train project managers in the organization to increase project success rates and facilitate the project management support systems.

While a PMO can take many forms, it is often directed by a senior-level project manager. The PMO can be staffed by project managers who are assigned to projects throughout the organization, or it can provide support services to project managers who work for various departments. Either way, the PMO has a defined area of responsibility regarding the departments or the types of projects it supports and oversees. For example, a PMO might influence all projects in an organization, or it might be set up to support the projects within a particular program.

Facilitating Standards and Best Practices

One of the best ways your PMO can increase project management efficiency in your organization is through setting up and enforcing project management standards, establishing processes, and implementing project management best practices. This effort fosters consistency and a kind of automation to common project management activities.

For example, your PMO might establish processes and procedures for the following:

- Project proposal
- Project selection
- Work breakdown structure development
- Resource management
- Change management
- Communication management
- Status definitions and reporting
- Project closure
- File management

Target those processes in which project-to-project consistency is needed, that have been problematic and could benefit from a standard workflow, or the ones for which project managers want more guidance.

CROSS-REFERENCE For information about creating good processes and weeding out poor ones, see "Defining Project Processes" in Chapter 14.

The PMO can facilitate the adherence to processes, standards, and best practices by setting up and disseminating templates for associated documents, many of which make up the project plan itself. Examples of such templates include the following:

- Project proposal
- Goal and objectives
- Scope statement
- Project charter
- Budget
- WBS format and numbering scheme
- Responsibility matrix
- Project organization chart
- Project schedule
- Quality plan
- Risk management plan
- Issues log

- Meeting agenda and follow-up templates
- Team status and management status reports
- Change request form and change management log
- Project closeout report
- Project archives contents
- Lessons learned report

CROSS-REFERENCE The chapters throughout this book present many of these project management forms and documents. All samples and templates discussed are available in the companion files for this book. You can download them at www.wiley.com/go/ProjMgmtCoach.

Ensuring Compliance Requirements

The PMO can provide support and monitoring to ensure the fulfillment of certification or regulatory requirements that affect how projects are managed or that govern project results. For example, a project customer might require that the project results conform to the ISO 9000 Quality Management standard. Your own organization might have a mandate to adhere to regulatory requirements such as the Sarbanes-Oxley Act regarding accounting practices. The PMO can even implement audits on projects and project results to ensure compliance.

Supporting Project Methodologies

Different project management methodologies fit different types of projects and organizations. The PMO can investigate techniques such as critical path method, critical chain project management, agile or iterative project management, and others to determine which methods work best for specific types of projects. As a certain methodology is adopted, the PMO can provide project managers with support such as training, standards, best practices, processes, forms, and tools.

Providing Project Management Tools

Project management tools and infrastructure resources can make life easier for your project managers and their teams. These tools and resources can also help enforce the organization's standards, methodologies, and processes.

Your PMO — in cooperation with the project manager, managing stakeholders, and support departments such as IT — can obtain, set up, and customize project management tools. Depending on your requirements, such tools and infrastructure might include the following:

- **Shared space on the organization's network:** You need space to store project documents, including processes, templates, formats, and forms.

- **Project intranet or closed Internet websites:** By using a tool such as a wiki or a Microsoft SharePoint site, your PMO can store templates and documents for access by all project stakeholders, maintain group calendars, and post discussions and announcements.

- **Project management software applications:** The PMO can evaluate, select, and roll out software for estimating and planning, scheduling, resource management, collaboration, and/or documentation. Examples include Microsoft Project, Open Workbench, and Primavera. Such an application can be customized to reflect many of your organizational standards for project management.

When deciding that a tool, infrastructure item, or software application is needed for project management, the PMO first identifies the needs of the project managers, their teams, and other stakeholders. The PMO considers the problems to be solved or prevented, the working styles of the project managers and other users, and the expected benefits. This ensures the PMO obtains the right tools and sets them up in an appropriate manner.

The PMO can inform the project managers of the availability of the infrastructure resource. In the case of new software, the PMO can provide the necessary training.

Managing Resources and Communication

Your organization's PMO might include a corps of dedicated professional project managers. In such a centralized structure, departments request project management support from the PMO, which then assigns a project manager.

Some PMOs, especially in larger organizations, might maintain information about the project *resource pool*. These are the people within the organization who are available for project work. The resource pool information can include job titles, skill sets, home departments, and availability information.

A PMO might also mediate the assignment of scarce, in-demand resources to projects, especially in the case of multiple high-priority projects. The PMO might also keep a watchful eye on the allocation of resources across the projects, to see where resources might be overallocated or underutilized.

If your PMO does not manage and allocate project managers in a centralized fashion, it can still maintain a resource list of project managers throughout the organization. As needed, the PMO can help facilitate the loaning of project managers between departments.

The PMO can also help coordinate cross-project communication, particularly among project managers and possibly among managing stakeholders of different projects. For example, when a new project is being proposed or initiated, the PMO might point the project manager and sponsor to resources about another similar project that has just completed.

Or, if the PMO sees that one project is having success in implementing agile project management techniques, for example, it can connect the project manager and key resources with another project that's struggling with that same technique. In these ways, institutional knowledge about project management is offered in a more responsive manner to help solve problems and improve processes.

Mentoring and Training Project Managers

Through mentoring and coaching, the PMO can work one on one with project managers to guide them through specific challenges they're encountering on their current projects.

The PMO can also sponsor training on project management topics for the organization. Examples of training workshops might include the implementation of a project management methodology such as critical chain or best practices such as project meeting management. The PMO might also sponsor training to advance project management standards, processes, and templates for consistency and cohesion throughout the organization.

If the PMO is responsible for monitoring and oversight of project adherence to specific standards or regulations, it can conduct audits against those standards. If the audit reveals any compliance problems, the PMO can consult with the project manager on appropriate corrective actions and follow up to ensure that those actions are completed and the issues resolved.

Audits can also result in discovering new and better processes and procedures. The PMO can collect such improvements and share them with the other project managers, thereby continuing to develop and upgrade project management processes throughout the organization.

Setting Up a PMO

A PMO is certainly not a one-size-fits-all proposition. Not every organization needs one. Furthermore, the type of PMO varies depending on particular needs. You need to assess your issues and goals regarding projects and project management. Then you can determine whether you need a PMO, what form it should take, and what services it should offer.

When Do You Need a PMO?

An organization typically decides to establish a PMO as a response to a problem. As with any problem, be sure that the problem is properly identified and that the PMO is the appropriate solution.

CROSS-REFERENCE For more information about problem identification, see the section "Discovering the Problem or Opportunity" in Chapter 3.

Think about your current project management challenges. With your answers, you can start to determine whether a PMO is appropriate for your organization. Consider the following questions:

- How many projects does your organization run at the same time? How many project managers are used?

- Is the organization struggling with too many problem projects? In the past two years, how many projects finished late? How many projects fail to achieve their business objectives or success criteria? How many went over budget? How many were canceled before finishing?

- Which certification standards or regulatory requirements must be met by your projects or project results (the product or service produced)? What kinds of difficulties are you having in meeting these requirements?

- Is there any belief or evidence in the organization that implementing a particular standard would make a significant difference in project success rates?

- Which project management processes and practices would you like to see standardized or streamlined throughout your organization?

- Is your organization using any particular project management technique, such as agile or critical path methodology? What problems are you experiencing and what improvements would you like to see in the use of this technique?

- Is the number of different standards or methodologies getting in the way of project progress and impacting project success rates?

- Could most or all project managers in the organization benefit from the adoption of a particular project scheduling software application or a set of project management tools? What's the application? What are the tools?

- Does your organization want to centralize and coordinate the allocation of project managers?

- Are there difficulties with sharing resources across multiple projects throughout the organization?

- What is the structure and matrix of the organization? How much authority do project managers have with their project team members?

- How could your project managers benefit from mentoring, coaching, and cross-project information sharing regarding project management challenges? What kinds of training courses might be beneficial to project managers and other project team members?

After considering these details, also reflect on the following questions about the general state of projects and project management in your organization:

- What is the condition of projects and project management in your organization?

- What is your ideal for projects and project management in your organization?

- How can you achieve this ideal?

- How will you know you have achieved this ideal?

Your answers to all of these questions can not only clarify whether your organization can benefit from a PMO but also point to the ideal PMO structure, objectives, and services.

Understanding PMO Types

Based on the assessment of projects and project management in the organization, your organization can decide on the ideal type of PMO and then design it to fit. The following are three variations of PMO types:

- **The PMO for a specific program or project:** Also known as a program office or project office, this is a temporary function dedicated to managing a program of projects or a single large project throughout its life cycle. This function provides general management support, coordination, and administrative services to the project managers assigned in the program or project.

- **The PMO board or committee:** An entity made up typically of senior-level project managers from various departments who volunteer their time and expertise to serve on the board. The board meets on an as-needed basis to provide support for projects and project managers. The board can set up standards, processes, and procedures for project managers but does not provide ongoing routine support.

- **The PMO department:** A permanent function in the organization, usually led by a senior-level project manager and staffed by several more project managers. In most cases, the centralized project managers are assigned to projects throughout the organization. In this way, the PMO department supports the projects and project managers within its sphere, while also providing ongoing routine support such as training.

If you're not certain of the value of a PMO in your situation, consider implementing the PMO in a limited manner. For example, you might start by forming a PMO for a specific project or a PMO board. After some time, evaluate its value and decide whether a wider implementation would be beneficial.

THE ROLE OF THE PMO IN PORTFOLIO MANAGEMENT

The *portfolio manager* is the person or group that selects and prioritizes projects in a portfolio. The portfolio manager evaluates project ideas, launches new projects, and evaluates current projects at defined checkpoints to assess the project's value to the organization's strategic goals and to reflect changes in the business environment.

Often the PMO tracks project ideas and proposals, and prepares them for consideration by the portfolio manager. Sometimes the PMO manager is a member of a portfolio management committee. The portfolio manager makes final decisions on project prioritization.

For more information about portfolio management, see Chapter 24, "Managing a Portfolio of Projects."

Specifying PMO Objectives and Services

After you've decided that your organization can benefit from a PMO and decided on the type of structure the PMO should have, it's time to establish the PMO's objectives, the services to be provided, and the action plan. In fact, consider the PMO implementation as the PMO's first project. Just like any other project, go through the project initiating processes:

- Articulate the PMO goal and objectives.
- Identify the requirements of the PMO.
- Determine success criteria for the PMO.
- Document the scope of the PMO.
- Identify risks, assumptions, and constraints.

CROSS-REFERENCE For more information about the project initiating processes, see the section "Defining a Project" in Chapter 3.

As you define the objectives and requirements of your PMO, keep in mind the following possible services and determine which of these apply to your situation, and specifically, how you might implement them.

- Define and maintain project management standards, processes, and best practices.

- Facilitate and monitor compliance with certification and regulatory requirements of projects and project results.

- Support implementation of appropriate project management methodologies.

- Evaluate, implement, and support project management tools, including software and network resources.

- Assign project managers to organizational projects.

- Oversee resource assignment and allocation across projects.

- Coordinate communication across projects.

- Mentor and coach project managers on specific project management challenges.

- Offer training on project management topics.

Summary

A PMO is a centralized function or entity that seeks to improve project success rates and ensure that projects serve the organization's strategic goals. To do this, the PMO coordinates project management standards, processes, best practices, and tools. It can help manage shared resources, coordinate cross-project communication, and assign project managers to projects throughout the organization. It can also provide mentoring, coaching, and training on project management topics.

An organization should assess the condition of its projects and project management to determine whether it can benefit from a PMO, and if so, which type of PMO structure would be ideal. The organization can then define the PMO's objectives, services, and action plan.

Coach's Review

Use this section to assess what you've learned in this chapter and to apply it to a real-life project you're currently working on.

Test Your Knowledge

Test your knowledge of the material in this chapter by answering the following questions. See Appendix A for the answers.

1. What is a project management organization and what is its purpose?
2. Name at least four activities that a PMO might be responsible for.
3. How might a PMO help an organization improve its implementation of a project management methodology?
4. Name the three variations of PMO structures.

Project Challenge

Practice the knowledge you've gained in this chapter with the following challenge.

1. Imagine that your manager has asked you to assess the value of a PMO in your organization. Carry out your evaluation based on the material in this chapter, including both sets of questions in the "When Do You Need a PMO?" section. Write the reasons why a PMO would or would not be beneficial in your situation.

2. Suppose you've been assigned to lead the implementation of a PMO in your organization. Based on your assessment in Step 1 of this exercise and with guidance from the "Understanding PMO Types" section, design the structure of your organization's PMO.

3. Based on the PMO structure you've designed in Step 2 of this exercise, identify the goal, objectives, requirements, success criteria, scope, risks, assumptions, and constraints of the PMO.

CHAPTER 24

Managing a Portfolio of Projects

Many financial investors maintain a balanced investment portfolio — a collection of different financial assets such as stocks, bonds, and cash. The assets in a portfolio work in their unique ways to help investors meet their ultimate goals, whether it's finally shipping the kids off to a prestigious college, building a dream home in the mountains, or swimming and golfing every day in a comfortable retirement.

Just like the multiple types of assets in a financial investment portfolio, organizations often undertake multiple projects at one time. These projects might advance different strategic goals. One project might work to optimize and reduce costs in the delivery of a current service, another might strive to develop a product to meet a new market opportunity, and another might endeavor to develop strategic partnerships with key customers. Even though the three projects are focused on very different aspects of the business, they're all working together for the organization's success.

Furthermore, those three projects are indeed an investment: in money, resources, and time. The expectation is that the investment in these projects will return substantial benefits. It makes sense that an organization would want to proactively examine, evaluate, and carefully select the projects that are to become part of the organization's focused *project portfolio*.

This chapter defines project portfolio management and how it can benefit an organization. You learn the role that the portfolio manager plays in evaluating and prioritizing projects for inclusion in the portfolio.

What Is Project Portfolio Management?

A project portfolio is a collection of projects in an organization. The projects that make up the portfolio (a *portfolio project*) have some point in common with one another. It can be as tight a connection as projects within a particular program or department. Or, the projects might have nothing else in common but the fact that they all benefit the company that's running them.

Project portfolio management (PPM) involves evaluation, support, and oversight of the projects in the portfolio. It sets the portfolio strategy to begin with, and then the *portfolio manager* works with executive management to evaluate, prioritize, and select the projects that should be part of the portfolio. Figure 24-1 provides an example of project portfolio allocation within an organization.

Project Allocation

- Strategic Goal 1. Increase profits from sales of existing products.

- Strategic Goal 2. Develop new products to take advantage of emerging market opportunities.

- Strategic Goal 3. Improve customer service to grow brand loyalty.

- Strategic Goal 4. Operate in accordance with principles of social responsibility.

Figure 24-1: Sample project portfolio allocation

Once the project portfolio mix is established, the portfolio manager typically tracks and manages the portfolio. The portfolio manager can be a committee of senior executives or it can be a single executive who keeps the rest of the executive team informed.

Although typically thought of as being the domain of large enterprises, project portfolio management is scalable to all organization sizes. A project portfolio might consist of dozens of projects in a larger organization or a handful of projects in a smaller one.

Instead of treating projects as one-off ad hoc endeavors, project portfolio management takes a strategic perspective toward projects, measuring and calculating them as the investments they are. Because significant money, resources, and time are devoted to each project, an organization can use project portfolio management to ensure not only that more projects are successful but also that the projects are successful in a way that adds value and benefit to the organization.

Specifically, project portfolio management:

- Identifies the portfolio strategy.

- Evaluates and analyzes project proposals against established criteria.

- Prioritizes and sequences projects based on overall business value as well as availability of funding and resources, maintaining an optimal pipeline flow of projects from concept to completion.

- Selects, maintains, and periodically rebalances the appropriate mix of projects in support of the organization's strategic goals as well as the relationship with other projects in the portfolio.

- Tracks overall schedule and cost performance, as well as resource utilization and scope management of the projects in the portfolio.

- Evaluates overall performance of ongoing projects and decides whether projects continue to the next checkpoint or are postponed or canceled.

Continued

PROJECTS, PROGRAMS, AND PORTFOLIOS   (CONTINUED)

A *program* is an overarching endeavor within an organization to produce a specific outcome delivering long-term benefits to the organization. Within the program there are typically several projects that serve the program goals. Those projects can be considered the program's project portfolio. In addition, programs often include operations and other non-project activities (see Figure 24-2).

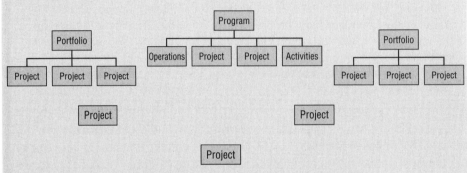

Figure 24-2: Projects, programs, and portfolios in an organization

So the hierarchy of projects, programs, and portfolios can be structured in a variety of ways according to the organization's needs. Projects and programs can be part of the organization's entire project portfolio. Projects can also exist independent of any program or portfolio.

Evaluating and Prioritizing Projects for the Portfolio

With the development of the portfolio strategy, you're ready to create project selection criteria. Alignment with the organization's strategic goals, the cost of the project and the expected return on investment, resource availability, and the relationship with other projects in the portfolio pipeline are typical examples of project selection criteria.

After you have those criteria in place, the portfolio manager can start to build the portfolio.

CROSS-REFERENCE The information in this section relates to the PMP Exam's Domain I: Initiating the Project, Task 1, "Perform project assessment based upon available information and meetings with the sponsor, customer, and other subject matter experts, in order to evaluate the feasibility of new products or services within the given assumptions and/or constraints."

Typically a project review board, which includes the portfolio manager, is the entity that assesses new project proposals. This board evaluates each project idea or proposal that's submitted for inclusion in the portfolio against the project selection criteria.

CROSS-REFERENCE For details about developing selection criteria and evaluating projects against those criteria, see the section "Selecting Projects" in Chapter 25. For more about the project review board, see the section "Succeeding with a Project Review Board," also in Chapter 25.

If the project review board uses objective scoring against the criteria, it has a basis for prioritizing the project proposals. The projects with the highest scores have a shot at being prioritized higher. However, a high score doesn't guarantee that the project will be approved.

The portfolio manager or the project review board must consider these additional factors when determining the fate of a project proposal:

- What is the overall business value of the project? Business value is typically identified as part of the project selection criteria, but there might be other factors related to business value that are not necessarily reflected in the criteria. Such factors can result in a greater or lesser weight for a project.

- How much will the project cost, and when will this funding be available?

- When will the necessary resources be available to work on the project? In fact, there are some methods of project selection that use resource availability as a front-line measurement.

- When is the best timing for the start and finish of this project? Looking at the other projects currently taking place and on deck to start soon, the portfolio manager needs to manage the project pipeline, that is, the timing of all projects from their start to finish. This *pipeline management* ensures proper timing and pacing of projects so that costs and resources flow steadily over time and that benefits realized from successful projects also flow with the appropriate pacing over time.

- Does this project help fulfill one of the strategic goals that is otherwise neglected? Sometimes one or two of an organization's strategic goals get most of the attention from hot new projects, while the other goals languish on the sidelines. Achieving a balanced mix of projects that enable an organization to work toward all of its strategic goals is a good reason to give a higher priority to a lower scoring project idea. For example, a strategic goal to implement green manufacturing techniques might receive a lower score if it's competing with other goals that concern profitability and customer service. But if the organization is philosophically committed to the goal, it'll bump up the priority on related project ideas.

When a project evaluates well and prioritizes high, it's likely to be approved. Upon approval, the project obtains funding and a start date is set according to the constraints imposed by the pipeline management.

FROM THE FIELD: THE DANGER OF NEGLECTING A STRATEGIC GOAL

A West Coast consulting company was prospering with a certain robust portfolio of projects. The portfolio consisted of user interface design, online help development, curriculum development, and training delivery projects for a customer service call center system in the insurance industry.

With this portfolio, the company was fulfilling its strategic goal of providing value-added design and development services to existing clients. The portfolio proved very profitable for the company, and all of its time and resources were spent in fulfilling these projects.

However, another strategic goal — concerning promoting the business to potential new clients — was ignored because there was just not enough time or energy for it.

The insurance project portfolio was completed with great success. The client was very pleased with the outcome and went on its merry way. After the celebrations were over, the executives of the consulting company looked around and saw they had nothing else in the pipeline.

With plenty of money in the bank, and a great reputation to boot, they knew they had ample time. They worked hard to court new clients but came up empty. They scrambled, but employees were laid off one by one. The executives despaired as they were forced to reduce their office space. They panicked as the cash reserves evaporated. No new opportunities emerged in time, and this once-successful company had to close its doors for good.

Moral of the story: Keep a good mix of projects in your pipeline, and balance the projects that fulfill different business needs.

Evaluation of a project continues even after the project has been approved for implementation. To ensure that the project is living up to expectations, the portfolio manager and project review board will continue to assess project performance and benefits as the project moves through its phases, milestones, or other checkpoints. They'll also assess changes and emerging realities in their industry and their business environment.

Tracking and Managing the Project Portfolio

As portfolio projects are approved and implemented by the individual project managers and their teams, the portfolio manager keeps a macro-level eye on all of them. Project managers are expected to keep the portfolio manager apprised of overall schedule and cost performance as well as overall resource utilization and scope management of each project. The more standardized this information is, the better the portfolio manager can compare project performance on an apples-to-apples basis.

CROSS-REFERENCE The information in this section relates to the PMP Exam's Domain IV: Monitoring and Controlling the Project, Task 1, "Measure project performance using appropriate tools and techniques, in order to identify and quantify any variances, perform approved corrective actions, and communicate with relevant stakeholders."

Tracking Portfolio Projects

The project manager is responsible for tracking all the task details of the project, which he obtains from his team members on a regular schedule. He's the keeper of the details for every aspect of his project.

The portfolio manager, on the other hand, doesn't track projects at this level. In most cases, the portfolio manager examines portfolio projects, getting answers to the following types of questions:

- How far ahead or behind the overall project finish date is the project expected to be?

- How far above or below the overall budget is the project estimated to cost?

- How well are portfolio project resources being utilized? Are there any large instances of overutilization or underutilization of team members?

- Can or should resources be shifted from one portfolio project to another? If so, when? How much would such a shift impact schedules?

- Has project scope changed? If so, how much? Will any large scope changes affect the project finish date or final cost?

While resource utilization and scope changes are more qualitative in nature, the finish date and cost are quantitative and easier to measure and compare. Because of this, project finish date and cost projections tend to be the data most closely tracked by portfolio managers.

The earned value schedule performance indicator (SPI) and cost performance indicator (CPI) provide comparable measurements of schedule and cost for a project. In fact, periodically comparing the SPI and CPI of all portfolio projects can provide an excellent analysis.

CROSS-REFERENCE For more information about SPI and CPI, see the section "Analyzing Performance with Earned Value" in Chapter 18.

Conducting Checkpoint Evaluations

In addition to the periodic check-in of schedule, cost, resources, and scope, the portfolio manager (possibly along with the project review board) is responsible for evaluating the project at certain checkpoints. These checkpoints might be milestones or *stage gates*. The purpose of this evaluation is to determine whether the project is still on track to deliver the expected benefits to the organization.

Recall that when a project is in the idea or proposal form, it is ideally evaluated against specific criteria to determine whether it should move on to the project planning processes. Even after elaborate work is done to develop the project plan, another evaluation takes place to determine whether the project should be implemented.

With such careful assessments during the early initiating and planning processes, it makes sense that this philosophy would carry through to the executing processes. The fact that a project plan has been approved for implementation doesn't mean it should not be evaluated again.

Quite the contrary — as a project is executed, it can go in a number of different directions. New information is uncovered and unforeseen events occur, which might produce project results that aren't as rosy as originally anticipated. This information — in addition to facts about schedule, cost, resources, and scope — can help the portfolio manager evaluate whether the project is on target, off target, or beyond hope. The project might be in danger of finishing too late to meet a make-or-break market window. Or the project might be costing too much to provide the required return on investment.

Even a project that's performing beautifully in terms of schedule and cost might have other red flags. For example, a newly introduced technology might indicate that a product under development will be obsolete before it hits the market. Or, a shift in consumer spending patterns might indicate that a service you've been developing won't be profitable after all.

As with an investment portfolio, the project portfolio needs to be reviewed periodically for its mix and balance. The portfolio manager needs to be sure that the portfolio that was properly balanced six months ago is still in position to deliver the expected benefits.

One or more of the portfolio projects might need to be adjusted in some way to bring them back in alignment with the portfolio strategy. One project might need to be put on hold and another one canceled, with their funding and resources transferred to another project that has more promise to actually deliver the goods.

So each evaluation checkpoint is an opportunity for the portfolio manager to objectively review the project and determine whether it is still on track to deliver the expected benefits and meet the success criteria. If it is, the project passes the evaluation and is allowed to continue executing to the next checkpoint. If it is not, one choice is to scale back by cutting resources, reducing funding, or putting the project on hold. Another option is to cancel the project altogether.

As dire as this might sound, defunding or canceling a project can actually be a positive move. Not only does the organization cut its losses on a project that will not produce the expected benefits, but it frees up resources and funding for other projects that are likely to be more productive and profitable.

Reporting on Portfolio Projects

The portfolio manager needs to report portfolio status to the other members of the executive team. They need to know the high-level performance status of the portfolio projects. SPI and CPI of the portfolio projects can be very helpful here. If any projects are falling significantly behind schedule or spending too much money, they'll want to know corrective actions and the prognosis for the projects. Most of all, they'll want to know that the projects are on track to realize the expected benefits for the expected cost.

CROSS-REFERENCE For more information about project reports appropriate for upper management, see the section "Status for Management" in Chapter 10.

Managing Portfolio Details

In addition to tracking, evaluating, and reporting on the portfolio, the following are additional portfolio management responsibilities:

- **Accessing portfolio project information:** The portfolio manager needs access to all high-level project information. This information is readily available in the project notebook. Such information might include the project goal and objectives, success criteria, scope statement, stakeholder registry or contact list, project charter, and list of deliverables. The portfolio manager might also want additional detail, such as the work breakdown structure and project schedule.

- **Resolving portfolio problems:** The portfolio manager should keep an ear to the ground regarding issues and red flags about portfolio projects. If there's a change that might affect project prioritization, the portfolio manager should get involved.

- **Assisting with post-implementation review:** At the appropriate time after a portfolio project ends, the portfolio manager might participate in a *post-implementation review* (PIR) that helps determine whether success criteria were met. Information gained from post-implementation reviews can shed light on future decisions about new project ideas, and how such proposals should be evaluated and measured.

Summary

When an organization carries out multiple projects, it can benefit from project portfolio management (PPM). Project portfolio management starts with a project portfolio strategy. It serves to evaluate, prioritize, and select the right projects for the portfolio, striving for balance among a mix of project types to achieve the organization's strategic goals.

During project execution, portfolio management tracks the high-level aspects of the portfolio projects, including forecasted project finish dates and budget performance, as well as resource utilization and scope management.

Coach's Review

Use this section to assess what you've learned in this chapter and to apply it to a real-life project you're currently working on.

Test Your Knowledge

Test your knowledge of the material in this chapter by answering the following questions. See Appendix A for the answers.

1. Define the term "project portfolio."

2. Name at least four major functions of project portfolio management.

3. What is pipeline management?

4. What two pieces of quantitative data are most useful for gauging the health of portfolio projects?

Project Challenge

Practice the knowledge you've gained in this chapter with the following challenge.

1. Considering your organization and the type of project you've created and have managed through the challenges in this book, what type of portfolio do you think would work for your organization and/or your type of project?

2. Suppose you are pitching the idea of implementing project portfolio management in your organization. What would be your key points to justify the idea?

3. Imagine that you have been selected as your organization's project portfolio manager. List the first five things you would do to start implementing project portfolio management.

Selecting the Right Projects

You've probably heard of those free-spirited travelers who open a map, cover their eyes, and point to a random place to decide where they're going on their next trip. Maybe they'll get lucky and have a fabulous time, but their destination could instead be a disaster. If they were hoping for a tropical vacation but end up in the tundra in the midst of winter, bitter disappointment will likely follow.

Just as travelers have many destination choices, an organization can choose from many projects and initiatives. Even though your organization might have the resources to do several projects at once, some projects are mutually exclusive, and you have to definitively pick one direction or another. Furthermore, regardless of your organization's capacity for project work, you always need to know that the projects chosen support the organization's overall mission.

So choosing the right projects is a delicate exercise in creative judgment. Energy is finite and resources are scarce or already overcommitted. Your organization must apply its collective intellect to develop the right ideas and choose the right projects to run. The good news is that you can systematically collect and evaluate your ideas to determine which ones are worth further development.

This chapter covers the best methods for capturing, evaluating, and selecting the right ideas for further development into projects.

CROSS-REFERENCE   The information in this section relates to the PMP Exam's Domain I: Initiating the Project, Task 1, "Perform project assessment based upon available information and meetings with the sponsor, customer, and other subject matter experts, in order to evaluate the feasibility of new products or services within the given assumptions and/or constraints."

Capturing Ideas for Projects

Inventive ideas are the lifeblood for any organization. Regardless of its core business, every company must innovate to stay competitive and viable in its field.

Idea generation usually is not a problem. Ideas can sprout like wildflowers in the springtime, especially in a culture that fosters a fertile ground of creativity. If, for whatever reason, there is a dearth of new ideas, you can employ techniques to get the creative juices flowing.

Because bright new ideas have a roguish way of popping up at odd times and places, your organization can benefit from a systematic method for documenting and tracking ideas. That way, you won't lose any inspired suggestions that could turn into worthwhile projects that foster success for your organization.

FROM THE FIELD: DARE TO BE CREATIVE

An electronics components manufacturing company had signs made and posted on walls throughout the building: "Dare To Be Creative."

However, whenever any employee took up the gauntlet and offered a new idea or suggestion, upper management invariably shot down the idea with "It can't be done," or "We can't afford it," or "We must follow the established process."

So the "Dare To Be Creative" signs were only lip service. Not only was there no system in place to capture ideas, but those who had the audacity to voice their suggestions were immediately criticized and silenced. Instead of being recognized for developing solutions to existing problems, employees felt as if they were making unwelcome waves and that they were perceived negatively by their managers.

Employees just gave up and concluded that they were not being paid to think, but only to blindly and obediently follow existing procedures.

This demoralizing atmosphere became so pervasive that eventually someone altered the signs to read "We Dare You To Be Creative."

Mining the Organization's Strategic Goals

If one of your organization's strategic goals is to cut operational costs, a project idea to add staff and implement a training program for product support is probably not going to see the light of day. However, if another strategic goal is to improve customer service, the project might get the go-ahead.

Strategic goals are the litmus test for whether a project idea has "the right stuff" for further exploration and development. Whether you're determining the worthiness of an existing idea or developing new ideas, the strategic goals are the first and best place to start looking for the most relevant ideas for achieving organizational success.

CROSS-REFERENCE For information about using the strategic goals to analyze the suitability of an existing project idea, see "Selecting Projects" later in this chapter.

NOTE Sometimes new ideas are generated by the execution of an existing project. If the idea constitutes a change to the current project, it should be handled by your change management board. For more information, see Chapter 11, "Setting Up a Change Management Plan."

When your organization is grounded in its vision, mission, and strategic goals, all projects take on that central focus. There's a cohesiveness and direction to everything that's done, whether it's a project having to do with new product development, a new employee benefits system rollout, or a customer service specialist training program.

Evaluating strategic goals can be the job of the research and development group, the executive management team, or a select group pulled from various disciplines. The idea is to give people the time and space to think creatively about how to best implement the strategic goals. In fact, you can conduct a brainstorming session to unearth project ideas for each strategic goal, one at a time. You might be amazed at the ideas you collectively generate.

At this point, remember that you are focused on idea creation. Leave evaluation, feasibility, analysis, and selection for later. As in all brainstorming processes, remember to do what you can to generate as many ideas as possible. There will be bad ideas, crazy ideas, boring ideas . . . as well as great ideas. Let them all out. Bad or boring ideas can lead to winning ones.

REALITY CHECK: YOUR STRATEGIC PLAN

Your organization might have just developed your strategic goals for the first time or updated them for the year. Either way, the logical next step is to develop the action plan or work plan associated with each of the strategic goals.

The elements in the action plan can, in effect, be your project ideas.

Suppose yours is a technology device company. Table 25-1 shows possible project ideas that can be generated from careful consideration of your strategic goals.

Table 25-1: Ideas Generated from Strategic Goals

STRATEGIC GOAL	POSSIBLE PROJECT IDEA
Increase profits from the sales of existing products.	Participate in application developer and consumer electronics trade shows to promote existing products.
Develop new products to take advantage of emerging market opportunities.	Develop mobile Web eyeglasses as the next new product offering.
Improve customer service to grow brand loyalty.	Develop product support training and documentation for existing products.
Operate in accordance with principles of social responsibility.	Implement an employee volunteer and corporate giving program for local non-profit organizations.

Documenting a Project Idea

Project ideas are an organizational asset, whether you act on them now, later, or never. Because of this, your organization should have a method for capturing those ideas. If no such method currently exists, create one for the area under your control. At least you'll be able to capture ideas from your group. At most, your method might be adopted for wider use, perhaps by the project management office (PMO) or portfolio manager.

The method can be very simple, from a single page or even just a paragraph or two. In fact, keeping the documentation of a project idea simple is ideal because you don't want staff spending too much time on ideas that might never turn into projects. On the other hand, you do need enough information for the management team to decide whether the idea is worth further development.

To achieve this balance, the best approach is to have a series of hurdles for a project idea to clear. Such a process, representing gradually increasing detail and commitment, could be as follows:

1. **Idea description:** A simple one-page or even one-paragraph idea description provides enough information for the reviewers to determine whether they want to explore further. (See Figure 25-1 for a sample project idea form.) If approved, the idea can move on to the proposal stage.

Idea

Please complete this form with information about your idea.

Name: Date:

Phone: Email:

Describe your idea and any process:

Please answer the following questions the best you can:

- How much do you think it would cost (order of magnitude) to carry out this project?

- How much staff time do you think would be needed?

- What special skills or expertise would be needed for this project?

- How would this project further the organization's goals?

- What benefit would this project bring to our organization?

- What would happen if we do not do this project?

Figure 25-1: Project idea form

2. **Project proposal:** The proposal includes further research into the details, including the project goal and objectives, requirements, scope, risks, and preliminary costs. These activities constitute the project initiating processes. If the proposal is approved, the proposal moves on to project planning.

CROSS-REFERENCE **For more information about the project initiating processes, see the sections "Defining a Project" and "Preparing the Project Proposal" in Chapter 3.**

3. **Project plan:** The project plan would include development of the work breakdown structure, the schedule, resource requirements, and budget. If the plan is approved, it moves on to project execution. These activities constitute the project planning processes.

4. **Project execution:** At this stage, you're finally implementing the details of the original idea. There should be checkpoints throughout the project — for example, upon achievement of key milestones, submission of deliverables, or ends of phases. These activities constitute the project executing processes.

CROSS-REFERENCE For more information about the project planning processes, see Chapter 4, "Getting to Know a Project Plan." For more information about project executing processes, see Chapter 13, "Kicking Off a Project."

CROSS-REFERENCE A sample of a project idea form is available in the companion files for this book. You can download it at www.wiley.com/go/ ProjMgmtCoach.

Tracking Project Ideas

With project ideas documented, develop a method for seeing all ideas at a glance and getting more detail as needed. One very simple technique is to set up a "Project Ideas" folder in your computer's filing system and add all the project idea form files to that folder. With enough detail in the filename, you can just browse the folder to see all the ideas.

Another method is to create a spreadsheet for collecting all project ideas. The spreadsheet can include the project idea name, a short description, and the name of the idea sponsor or "champion." You can include the date when the idea is presented to management for consideration and possibly include the current status of the idea, that is, whether it has moved on to project proposal development or beyond. You can link the idea name to the idea form to make the spreadsheet more interactive.

You can have a rating system for the feasibility of project ideas. There can be a comment field explaining what conditions would need to change for the idea to become more viable. For projects that are denied, you can include categories of reasons for the denial.

Ideas have a way of resurrecting themselves on a cyclical basis. The point of having a tracking method is to prevent revisiting the same ground over and over. There's no point in having people re-create the idea form or project proposal every time a seemingly obvious idea surfaces yet again. You can pull out the old idea form and see where the idea is — it might have been implemented as a project by another department by now. Or, you can discover why the idea was tabled so the new idea sponsor can try to make the idea more practicable this time around.

A tracking method can also store an idea until the time is right. Market conditions change along with return on investment and other benefits. A key resource who was previously impossible to get might now be available. Something that was once considered a "nice to have" has suddenly become a certification or regulatory requirement.

Visit your tracking mechanism periodically, maybe toward the end of the fiscal year. Your idea tracker can help you with plans and budget for the new fiscal year.

Selecting Projects

An idea picked for "projecthood" might be the CEO's whim of the month. It might be the product of an executive team that boldly shoots from the hip. It might be the result of a group of department heads that operates on a do-it-if-it-feels-right attitude. Without careful thought or questioning of authority, the project manager and team hurtle on, only to find later that the whim had no staying power as a project. With too many unchallenged assumptions and without judicious consideration of the business case for an idea, the project is headed for failure.

A more mature and clear-thinking organization institutes a systematic process for determining which of the many available ideas are worth pursuing for the best long-term benefits and ultimate success. An astute project selection process is based on objective analysis and data rather than random caprices and emotions. It includes selection criteria and established exceptions to those criteria. Instead of leaving the decisions to a few people who have a certain cult of leadership or persuasive ability, a project review board judiciously and impartially evaluates project ideas and proposals every step of the way. This kind of evaluation ensures that the right ideas become project proposals, that the right proposals become projects, and that executed projects are monitored appropriately throughout their life cycle.

Developing a Selection Process

Consider the following steps for a structured selection process that helps you consistently determine which ideas to develop further:

1. **Justify the reasons for a selection process:** The most common reason is the need for impartial judgment using a set of agreed-upon criteria. Other reasons might include the overabundance of ideas, or the more productive use of time or resources. As you start to think about the right project selection process, be sure you know the problems you're addressing.

2. **Identify stakeholders and gain their input:** Stakeholders for a project selection process might include the top management team, the portfolio manager, a representative of the PMO, program managers, project managers, and others who sponsor projects in your organization. By soliciting input about the best selection process from these stakeholders, you'll enjoy a higher level of buy-in and enforcement.

3. **Draft the process:** A complete project selection process includes selection criteria, exceptions to the criteria, and identification of an entity such as a project review board who will be responsible for project selection.

4. **Review the process:** Have the stakeholders review the drafted process. Obtain more input from those who will be affected.

5. **Document the process:** Keeping it simple and straightforward, document and publish the process for project selection, along with any necessary attachments such as an idea form or a project proposal form. The publication can be an email to all stakeholders, a posting on a shared drive or intranet site, or both.

6. **Launch and enforce the process:** Make sure that everyone involved has the necessary information and tools. Provide assistance as needed. Continue to refine the process to work out any bugs.

The project selection process should be scalable to the organization. For example, a large company might have an elaborate methodology with forms and a project review board that meets monthly to vet ideas. A small company might ask a group of people to discuss new ideas as needed. A small department within a large company with a specific methodology might adapt it further. Ensure that the process makes sense for the needs of your organization.

The key is to have a specific process, with consistent criteria, applied in an impartial manner. These three ingredients ensure that you choose the right projects that help advance your organization's strategic goals.

Criteria for Selecting Projects

Establishing the evaluation criteria for discretionary project ideas is the heart of your project selection process. These criteria are the basis for the business case that justifies project implementation.

One organization might consider benefits, costs, feasibility, and alignment with strategic goals as its criteria. Another organization might consider these items plus resource availability, risks, and timing. Whatever criteria an organization chooses, the criteria should be applied uniformly to all proposed project ideas.

Anyone proposing a new project idea will have a better chance of having the idea considered and approved if the proposal speaks to each criteria item.

NOTE Keep in mind that *nondiscretionary projects* must be done regardless of how they meet (or more typically, don't meet) criteria for benefit, cost, or feasibility. Examples of nondiscretionary projects are often those required for regulatory compliance or to maintain necessary certifications.

What Benefits?

When examining potential projects, often the first questions are "Why should we do this?" and "What's in it for us?" Consider the following benefits:

- **Alignment with business strategy:** How will this project further the mission of the organization? Which of the organization's strategic goals would the project fulfill, and how will it do it? Strategic goals often speak to achievement in the field, increased profits through greater market share or lower operating costs, fulfillment of customer requests, and improved customer service. Other strategic goals might address organizational need, technological advancement, legal requirements, environmental impacts, and social responsibility.

- **Return on investment (ROI):** The revenue gained from doing the project is another large consideration when deciding to move forward with a project. What will the ROI be if you do this project? If you spend $100,000 on resources and other costs of this project, and if you net $150,000 in profits in the first 12 months, is that enough? It's up to the organization to decide what its ROI must be to make a project worthwhile in terms of cost benefits.

- **Impact and other benefits:** Money isn't everything in a project. Sometimes the criteria for project approval transcend monetary measures. Examples of nonmonetary benefits of doing a project can include advancing a new strategy, exposure, certification, compliance, and social responsibility. Whether you're looking at ROI or other benefits, be sure you've done a cost-benefit analysis so that it's clear what impact and other benefits you're getting out of this project.

- **Opportunity:** Does the project idea represent an opportunity that the organization must take advantage of? What's the impact if you don't take on this project? Will there be a lost opportunity that might never come again?

What Cost?

The next category of questions about a potential project has to do with the costs associated with the project. Costs involve money, of course, but can also include time, resources, and risk. You want to know if the project is worth doing and if your organization can afford to take it on.

- **Cost expenditure:** At the project idea or proposal stage, not much research is typically done to pin down costs. However, a rough order of magnitude (ROM) estimate can provide enough information about cost for the evaluators to determine whether there's potential value in pursuing the idea.

- **Time and resource expenditure:** In addition to hard cash, valuable resources and time would be used for the project, which would otherwise be spent on other projects. Is this project the highest and best use of these resources and this time?

- **Risk:** What can go wrong with this project? Do the benefits of doing the project outweigh the potential negative risks? At the idea stage of a proposal, you can articulate the high-level risks. If an idea moves on to the proposal stage, you can identify further details about risks. If the idea moves ahead again to project planning, you and your team can develop the full risk management plan.

Can It Be Done?

The third category of project selection criteria has to do with feasibility. Can you actually carry out this project? Do you have (or can you get) everything you need to implement this project successfully? This includes resource availability, timing, the existence of other projects, and more.

- **Resource availability:** What kinds of resources are needed to carry out this project, and will they be available if you decide to move ahead? If you do not have access to a specific type of programmer, engineer, or designer for the project to be a success, it doesn't matter how well the project scores with the other criteria; you won't be able to do it until that resource becomes available.

- **Timing:** Is there a market window, a product season, an event date, or other fixed deadline that this project must meet to be successful? If you move forward with this project, will you be able to meet that date? If not, the project should be denied or tabled until the timing is right. Another timing consideration is whether the project is ahead of its time. For example, you might want to wait on broader acceptance of a new technological development before marketing a new product based on that technology.

- **Relationship with other projects:** Look at the big picture of projects in the organization when choosing new project ideas. Are there existing or past projects whose work you can leverage? Might this project hamper the efforts of other projects happening simultaneously? Might this project prevent better projects from starting?

Scoring and Prioritizing Project Ideas

When you've established the project selection criteria, consider whether you want to apply scores to each criterion. The criteria scores indicate how important each criteria item is to your organization. You can then apply a score relevant to the project under consideration that indicates how well the project fulfills that criterion.

Scoring aids in the objective analysis of each project idea by providing a concrete basis for discussion among the members of the project review board. Scoring also helps rank project ideas against one another, which not only helps the project review board come to go/no-go decisions but also helps them prioritize projects based on the strength of their scores.

See Figure 25-2 for an example of project scoring. In this example, with the criteria, weights, and scores that have been established, the project results in a score of 26. Of course, if you decide to create such a scorecard, be sure to do so with the criteria, weights, scores, and method of calculation that make sense for your organization. There are a variety of methods for objective evaluation and selection. The important thing is to score all project ideas against the criteria consistently.

New Project Idea Evaluation

Project: Develop mobile Web eyeglasses.

LEGEND
Criteria weight: 3=Mission Critical 2=Very Important 1=Philosophical Priority
Project score: 3=Completely Meets Criteria 2=Often Meets Criteria
1=Occasionally Meets Criteria 0=Never Meets Criteria or Not Applicable

Project Evaluation Criteria	Criteria Weight	Project Score	Weighted Score
Strategic Goal 1. Increase profits from sales of existing products.	3	0	0
Strategic Goal 2. Develop new products to take advantage of emerging market opportunities.	3	3	9
Strategic Goal 3. Improve customer service to grow brand loyalty.	2	1	2
Strategic Goal 4. Operate in accordance with principles of social responsibility.	1	1	1
Return on Investment above 20% in 12 months.	2	2	4
Critical resources are expected to be available.	2	3	6
Benefits outweigh high-level risks identified so far.	2	2	4
Overall Score			26

Figure 25-2: Scoring a project against established criteria

CROSS-REFERENCE A sample of a project idea scorecard is available in the companion files for this book. You can download it at www.wiley.com/ go/ProjMgmtCoach.

You might have a range of project scores that help you decide whether a project idea should be approved. For example:

- **20+:** No brainer. Do the project as a high priority.
- **15–19:** Probably do the project as a low to medium priority.

- ▪ **10–15:** Do more research to see if the project is feasible.

- ▪ **5–9:** Probably not feasible at this time.

- ▪ **Below 5:** No brainer. Don't do the project.

With consistent application of the criteria to all project ideas, you can more easily compare projects. The comparative scores help the project review board decide when a project should be scheduled and to what extent it should be funded.

THE CANDID COACH: THE SCORING SYSTEM IS NOT A CRYSTAL BALL

Develop a scoring system that makes sense for your organization. It's a useful tool and guide for making educated decisions about projects.

However, be aware that project prioritization and approval by management is often based on qualitative factors that can't be accommodated by a strictly quantitative scoring matrix.

No scoring system is a foolproof crystal ball and it should not try to be. There are those who have made it their life's work to create the perfect scoring system only to learn that the world changes around them, and just when they think they've got it right, they need to start over again.

Exceptions to Selection Criteria

Some project ideas might prove to be exceptions to your selection criteria. That is, a particular project has a low score according to your selection criteria, but you need to do the project anyway.

The most compelling reasons to implement such projects are legal, regulatory, and certification requirements. These nondiscretionary projects are often associated with a nonnegotiable deadline that you must be able maneuver within the existing project workload. The fulfillment of these requirements might not align with any of your business strategic goals or give you any return on investment or other benefit. (See Figure 25-3 for an example of how low such a project might score against your established criteria.) But the fact remains that you have to do the project. You might think of such projects as the cost of doing business.

Another exception might be caused by a highly placed project sponsor who insists that you carry out this project, regardless of its score. Or, you might have made a commitment to a customer, and you are compelled to follow through in spite of the cost to your business. Such exceptions are management prerogative and account for other factors that a scoring tool doesn't always accommodate.

When you develop your project criteria scorecard or other tool, understand that there will be cases when the project is so compulsory that you won't even bother to score them — you already know they absolutely must be done. The reverse of this situation is when a project has a very high score, putting it in the category of a "no-brainer, do it." Sometimes, because of factors beyond the scorecard's criteria, you cannot do what seems to be a perfectly good project. Use the scorecard as a guideline, not a rule maker, and you'll be well grounded in reality.

New Project Idea Evaluation **Project:** Remodel manufacturing area to updated OSHA standards.			*LEGEND* *Criteria weight: 3=Mission Critical 2=Very Important 1=Philosophical Priority* *Project score: 3=Completely Meets Criteria 2=Often Meets Criteria* *1=Occasionally Meets Criteria 0=Never Meets Criteria or Not Applicable*
Project Evaluation Criteria	Criteria Weight	Project Score	Weighted Score
Strategic Goal 1. Increase profits from sales of existing products.	3	0	0
Strategic Goal 2. Develop new products to take advantage of emerging market opportunities.	3	0	0
Strategic Goal 3. Improve customer service to grow brand loyalty.	2	0	0
Strategic Goal 4. Operate in accordance with principles of social responsibility.	1	3	3
Return on Investment above 20% in 12 months.	2	0	0
Critical resources are expected to be available.	2	2	4
Benefits outweigh high-level risks identified so far.	2	3	6
Overall Score			13

Figure 25-3: Low project score exception

Succeeding with a Project Review Board

The *project review board* is made up of stakeholders who serve as a gatekeeper, reviewing incoming project ideas for your organization. This group might set the criteria and develop the scorecard or other selection tool. It certainly evaluates new ideas against the criteria, and authorizes or kills new ideas based on this analysis. It probably has the authority to fund approved ideas as they become projects.

The project review board might meet regularly or only as needed. Project review board members ensure that submitted ideas and proposals include the necessary data, and they might ask for additional information to help them decide.

Ideally, the project review board evaluates projects at their various stages of development: original idea, project proposal, project plan, project execution. The board might also assess executed projects at established checkpoints to ensure that the project is still adhering to the organization's criteria. Having the project review board serve these functions — rather than someone more closely connected with the project — is more effective for the organization. Because it's made up of individuals beyond the project stakeholders, the project review board is more likely to be impartial and objective about its findings.

If your organization has a *project portfolio manager* — a person with an eye on all your organization's projects — this person belongs on the project review board, and should probably be the one heading it up.

The project review board can also include a representative from your PMO, if it exists, as well as executives from different functions in the organization. If the board reviews projects for the entire company, board members might need to be the directors of R&D, operations, marketing, accounting, and so on. If the board reviews projects for a functional group or business unit, board members might be the managers of each of the subgroups, for example, program management, development, testing, marketing, user assistance, and product support. In short, stakeholders who would be involved in or affected by all or most projects undertaken by the organization should be represented.

THE CANDID COACH: A WORD TO THE PROJECT MANAGER

As a project manager, it's essential that you understand the selection process for the project to which you're assigned. Familiarize yourself with the scoring tool used. Know the criteria and other factors the project review board considered as they made their decision to move forward with this project idea.

Knowing this background creates a meaningful basis for your initial discussions with your managing stakeholders. Perceiving the primary motivations and priorities that led to the approval of the project idea will help you manage this project more effectively.

Your understanding of the project's context within the organization's strategic goals and priorities will ground you as you deftly lead your project through the stages and phases of its lifecycle.

Summary

Among many suggested project ideas, it's vital for an organization to choose the right projects that are aligned with its strategic goals and offer sufficient benefits. There should be a method for capturing, documenting, and tracking all ideas, whether they're viable at this time or not.

Organizations should develop a project selection method that includes objective criteria and perhaps a scoring system. The majority of the selected projects would be those that meet the most criteria in the most advantageous way, although exceptions do exist. A broad-based and impartial project review board is an effective vehicle for evaluating and selecting the best projects.

Coach's Review

Use this section to assess what you've learned in this chapter and to apply it to a real-life project you're currently working on.

Test Your Knowledge

Test your knowledge of the material in this chapter by answering the following questions. See Appendix A for the answers.

1. What are the four stages of approval that a project idea should go through during its life cycle?

2. What are the three categories for project selection criteria?

3. Name at least three project selection criteria.

4. What are at least two reasons why a project that doesn't meet selection criteria would still be approved for implementation?

Project Challenge

Practice the knowledge you've gained in this chapter with the following challenge.

1. Obtain the list of your organization's strategic goals. Pick one of the goals and generate ideas for projects that could help further that goal. Record those ideas on the page.

2. Draft a project selection process, including selection criteria, exceptions to the criteria, and who in your organization will be responsible for project selection.

3. Evaluate the ideas you generated in Step 1 against the criteria you developed in Step 2.

Part

VII

Reference

Appendix A: Answers
Appendix B: Forms
Glossary

Answers

Each chapter of this book ends with a "Coach's Review" section in which you were challenged with a number of "Test Your Knowledge" questions. This appendix presents the answers to those questions.

Chapter 1: Getting to Know Projects

1. What is the key characteristic that differentiates projects from other types of work?

   A. Uniqueness. Each project has aspects that make it unique.

2. Describe two ways that clearly defined objectives help a team complete a project successfully.

   A.

   - Clearly defined objectives provide targets that the team can use to remain focused on what it is supposed to accomplish.
   - The team can compare the project results to the objectives to evaluate whether the project achieved those objectives.

Chapter 2: Getting to Know Project Management

1. What are the five process groups?

   A.

   - Initiating
   - Planning
   - Executing
   - Monitoring and controlling
   - Closing

2. Which process group uses all nine knowledge areas?

   A. Planning

3. Which knowledge area spans all five process groups?

   A. Integration management

4. When would you want to use an iterative approach to project management?

   A. When the details of the project solution are not clearly defined.

Chapter 3: Getting a Project Off the Ground

1. Name at least three factors that can figure into whether an idea or project proposal is appropriate for your organization.

   A.

   - The organization's strategic goals
   - Return on investment
   - Availability of resources
   - Likelihood of potential risks
   - Strong support of an influential sponsor

2. List at least five elements that should be part of a solid project definition.

   A.

   - Problem or opportunity statement
   - Goal
   - Objectives

- Strategy
- Requirements
- Success criteria
- Project scope
- High-level deliverables
- Risks
- Assumptions
- Constraints

3. Describe at least two negative results that can happen if the project definition processes are skipped.

   A.

   - The outcome of the project does not solve the problem.
   - The project outcome does not meet the requirements of the sponsor or customer.
   - The project outcome does not help meet any of the organization's business goals.
   - The project scope grows out of control.

4. What is the 5-why analysis and how is it helpful in problem definition?

   A. The 5-why analysis is the method of continually asking why a situation is a problem until the root problem is uncovered. It is helpful in distinguishing solutions from the actual problem.

5. Define project goal.

   A. The broad description of what the project is supposed to achieve.

6. What is a "SMART" objective?

   A. A breakdown or component of the project goal that is specific, measurable, assignable, realistic, and time-based.

7. Name at least three techniques for gathering project requirements.

   A.

   - Interviewing
   - Reusing existing requirements
   - Conducting a group requirements meeting or focus group
   - Creating a business process model or use case

- Observing or job-shadowing
- Building a prototype

8. What's the difference between project scope and product scope?

A. Project scope is the definition of work to be done as part of a particular project. Product scope defines the features and functions of the product, service, or other outcome.

9. Define stakeholder.

A. A stakeholder is anyone with a vested interest in the project. Stakeholders include the project sponsor or customer, end users, team members, affected departments, and more.

10. What is the purpose of the project charter?

A. The project charter announces and publicizes the existence of the project and the authority of the project manager as sanctioned by the named project sponsor.

Chapter 4: What Goes into a Project Plan

1. Name at least five components of a typical project plan.

A.

- Work definition
- Resource list
- Cost estimate
- Budget
- Schedule
- Project processes

2. Name the knowledge areas associated with the five components of a typical project plan.

A.

- Scope management
- Resource management and procurement management
- Cost management
- Time management
- Integration management

3. Name three categories of project resources that could be assigned in any typical project.

   A.

   - People
   - Equipment
   - Consumable materials

4. What is a rough order of magnitude (ROM) estimate?

   A. An early cost estimate with an accuracy of plus or minus 50 to 75 percent, typically used for project proposal and selection purposes.

5. What information is a detailed cost estimate based on?

   A. Costs for resources as well as other costs incurred by carrying out tasks such as travel, printing, and facilities.

6. Name the four items that help establish your project schedule.

   A.

   - Durations
   - Task dependencies
   - Resource schedules
   - Deadlines

7. Define task dependency and give an example.

   A. A task dependency is a relationship between two tasks that indicates that one task must finish or start before the other task can start or finish. For example, the task "Prep wall" must be completed before the task "Paint wall" can begin, so these two tasks are linked with a task dependency.

8. How can you prevent problems that have been encountered in the past or take advantage of tips and techniques that worked particularly well?

   A. Refer to lessons learned reports from past similar projects.

9. What project processes could be part of your project plan?

   A.

   - Quality plan
   - Communication plan
   - Risk management plan

Chapter 5: Identifying the Work to Be Completed

1. What is the primary purpose of the work breakdown structure?

    A. It is the document or tool used to identify activities and tasks to be done to satisfy the requirements and scope of the project.

2. What is the ideal method for identifying the work and building the work breakdown structure?

    A. The group project planning process.

3. What documents are the key inputs to the WBS?

    A. The requirements document and scope statement. Other documents created in the initiating processes can also help.

4. Explain the top-down method for identifying work.

    A. You deconstruct the major categories that will fulfill the project goal or scope summary. You deconstruct the categories or activities under those major categories. You continue in this manner until you arrive at the work package level, which is the task level.

5. How do you know you have a good work package with the right level of detail?

    A. When it's manageable, trackable, and assignable to a team member.

6. Name the two typically used WBS formats.

    A. Hierarchical flowchart and outline.

7. What does the WBS number 3.1.2 signify?

    A. Under the third major (first-level) category, under the first second-level category, this is the second activity.

8. What is the purpose of the work package document?

    A. To collect the task details associated with the work packages in such a way that the assigned resources have the information they need to carry out the tasks.

Chapter 6: Estimating Work and Cost

1. What is the advantage to estimating the hours of effort rather than task duration?

   A. Many factors can affect the task duration for tasks with the same number of work hours, such as resource availability, interruptions, non-project work, and the number of people assigned to a task.

2. How does the Delphi technique help eliminate bias in estimates?

   A. The original Delphi technique keeps the participants anonymous and shares only the results. That way, each person produces estimates independent of one another.

3. How do you estimate labor costs when you don't know who will be assigned to your project?

   A. Use average rates for each type of resource you need. In addition, for employees, you can obtain burdened labor costs from your organization's HR department to account for salaries, benefits, and overhead.

4. What numbers do you include in the project budget?

   A.

   ▪ Estimated task costs

   ▪ Costs for materials and equipment

   ▪ Contingency funds

   ▪ Management reserve

Chapter 7: Planning Project Resources

1. Why is it important to have one group (and a specific person from within that group) accountable for each portion of a project?

   A. Having a group accountable for each part of the project means that someone has a stake in making sure that part of the project moves forward and completes successfully. In addition, by naming an individual within the group as accountable, you know to whom to turn if you require a decision or need an issue resolved. Having more than one group accountable could lead to delays and tension if different groups argue over who is in charge or what should be done.

2. How can you use the WBS to determine the resources you need?

A. The work packages that you define for your project include the detail you need to specify the skills people need to have and the other resources needed to complete the work. You can also use higher levels of the WBS to identify broader categories of skills needed for the project and then let team leads or departments select specific individuals.

3. What are at least three components you might include in a resource plan?

A.

- A responsibility matrix
- Resource breakdown structure
- WBS with skills identified
- Project organization chart
- Staffing plan

4. How does a project organization chart differ from a regular organization chart?

A. A project organization chart is the same as a regular organization chart except that it reflects the hierarchy in the project. Working with outside vendors is one potential exception. In that case, you might include the employee within the vendor organization who is responsible for managing the vendor resources assigned to the project.

Chapter 8: Building a Schedule

1. What's the difference between a Gantt chart and a network diagram?

A. A Gantt chart represents each task as a horizontal bar along a timeline. A network diagram represents each task as a box or node. Both charts show links and associated project information.

2. Why would you create a task dependency between tasks?

A. Tasks should be linked when one task cannot start or finish until another task finishes or starts.

3. What is the most commonly used task dependency?

A. The finish-to-start dependency, which specifies that the first task must finish before the second task can begin.

4. What makes the critical path so critical?

A. The critical path determines the finish date of the project. It's the longest sequence of tasks across the project schedule. If any tasks along the critical path are delayed, the project as a whole will be delayed.

5. Why is it important to avoid date constraints?

   A. Because a date constraint imposes a fixed date that the schedule must achieve, it reduces the flexibility in your project that would otherwise use task dependencies, work estimates, and resource availability to determine the schedule.

6. Why is there a distinction between the work estimate and task duration?

   A. The work estimate indicates the amount of time, in terms of person-hours or person-days, that a task will take. The duration is the time span of the task from start to finish. When multiple resources or part-time resources are assigned to a task, the work estimate and task duration are quite different.

7. Name at least two ways that assigned resources can affect the project schedule.

   A.

   ▪ Availability such as vacations and training time

   ▪ The amount of time resources are available for project work each day

   ▪ Whether a resource can work faster or slower than was estimated

   ▪ Whether a resource is part time or full time on the project

Chapter 9: Planning for Quality

1. Name at least two possible sources of quality specifications.

   A.

   ▪ Project objectives

   ▪ Scope statement

   ▪ Requirements document

2. Define quality management.

   A. The ongoing process of assessing, anticipating, and fulfilling stated and implied needs, with an emphasis on customer satisfaction, defect or error prevention, continuous improvement, and management responsibility.

3. What is the difference between quality assurance (QA) and quality control (QC)?

   A. QA focuses on avoiding or minimizing defects or errors throughout the project, whereas QC focuses on finding defects through measurement and testing.

4. Name at least two widely used quality methodologies.

   A.

   - Continuous Improvement (CI)
   - ISO 9000 Quality Management
   - Six Sigma
   - Total Quality Management (TQM)

5. List at least three elements of a project's quality management plan.

   A.

   - Quality standard or specifications
   - Quality methodology
   - QA processes
   - QC processes
   - Cost-benefit analysis
   - Cost of quality (COQ)

Chapter 10: Setting Up a Communication Plan

1. What three things are a minimum for successful communication?

   A.

   - Transmitting information
   - Receiving information
   - Understanding information

2. How can you determine whether you understand what someone else is saying?

   A. By paraphrasing what the person said and asking if you understood.

3. What aspects of communication does the communication plan address?

   A.

   - Audience
   - Information
   - Communication method

- Who is responsible
- Schedule

4. Why are meetings the best communication method for topics that require interaction?

   A. Because you can see nonverbal communication such as body language and facial expressions, which represent a significant part of someone's message.

Chapter 11: Setting Up a Change Management Plan

1. What is the goal of a change management process?

   A. To assess change requests and approve the requests that make sense.

2. What do you need in order to manage changes?

   A.

   - The baseline documents so you can identify the changes that are approved and implemented
   - A change request form to document requests
   - An evaluation process to determine whether requests will be approved and added to the project or rejected

3. What information does an evaluator provide?

   A.

   - Is the change needed?
   - Is the description or design of the change accurate?
   - What's the estimated effort and cost?
   - How does the change affect the project?
   - Are there any risks or side effects?

4. Identify at least three ways to keep change management from becoming bureaucratic.

   A.

   - Handle changes that don't affect the schedule or budget without involving the change review board.
   - Combine small changes into bundles of work.

- Set thresholds for who can approve change requests under various circumstances.

- Identify an emergency change request procedure.

Chapter 12: Managing Risk

1. What is project risk?

   A. An uncertain event or condition — negative or positive — that could happen in the future, which, if it occurs, will have an effect on the project's scope, schedule, cost, or quality.

2. Name at least three methods for identifying risks in the project.

   A.

   - Brainstorm with the project team.

   - Review the project notebook.

   - Review lessons learned from similar past projects.

   - Interview experts.

   - Complete a cause and effect diagram.

   - Examine a system or process flowchart.

   - Do a SWOT analysis on the project.

3. Name the four commonly recognized project risk categories.

   A.

   - Technical

   - External

   - Organizational

   - Project management

4. What are some characteristics of a technical risk category? Name an example from your experience.

   A. A technical risk is often related to requirements, technology, complexity, interfaces, performance, and reliability.

5. Name the two key factors for analyzing risks.

A.

- Probability or likelihood
- Impact or effect

6. List the five response strategies for negative risks.

A.

- Mitigation
- Contingency planning
- Transference
- Avoidance
- Acceptance

7. What does it mean to mitigate a risk?

A. To take action that lessens the probability or the impact of the risk.

8. What is an issue, and how do risks relate to issues?

A. An issue is an event, condition, or problem that affects the project scope, time, money, resources, or quality. A risk that becomes reality is an issue.

Chapter 13: Kicking Off a Project

1. Why must you obtain approval for your project plan before beginning the executing process?

A. So that key stakeholders formally approve the plan and commit funds and resources.

2. Why do you set a baseline for your project before beginning work?

A. So you can compare actual results to the plan to determine project performance. In addition, you set baselines for documents so you can track changes made during execution.

3. What are the main steps in a procurement process?

A.

- Soliciting vendors
- Selecting vendors
- Setting up contracts
- Managing vendor relationships

4. Name at least three things you can accomplish with a kickoff meeting.

   A.

   ■ Introduce team members.

   ■ Build enthusiasm.

   ■ Reinforce the project purpose.

   ■ Review the project plan so team members understand their roles.

   ■ Explain the ground rules you want team members to follow as part of your project.

   ■ Review processes so team members understand the administrative aspects of the project.

Chapter 14: Taming Processes, Problems, and Conflicts

1. What steps can you take so that your team uses a process?

   A.

   ■ Design the process to solve the true problem.

   ■ Test the process in a small area within your project. Correct any issues with the process.

   ■ Publicize the process.

   ■ Make it easy to use.

2. What is the most important thing you can do to solve problems and make decisions more effectively?

   A. Focus on what's important.

3. Describe three steps for making decisions.

   A.

   ■ Identify the underlying problems that decisions are meant to solve.

   ■ Prioritize the decisions you need to make.

   ■ Evaluate your options.

Chapter 15: The Keys to Successful Meetings

1. Name at least four key techniques for effective meetings.

   A.

   - Good preparation
   - Using an agenda
   - Starting on time
   - Stating the goal and outcome of the meeting
   - Skillful facilitation
   - Ending on time

2. How does good facilitation contribute to an effective meeting?

   A. Time is used efficiently, the meeting stays focused, and everyone has the opportunity to contribute.

3. Name at least one thing you can do if a participant consistently takes too much time in meetings.

   A.

   - Enforce a time limit for each agenda item.
   - Enforce a time limit for each speaker.
   - Use a timer.
   - Employ a talking stick or other type of token.

4. What type of meeting might you hold if you need to design a solution to a problem? How would you conduct such a meeting?

   A. A solution planning meeting, conducted as collaboration among the appropriate team members and other experts.

5. In a brainstorming session, what are the advantages of refraining from judgment and encouraging quantity over quality of ideas?

   A. This allows participants more freedom to be creative, to have silly or implausible ideas as well as good and workable ones, because a winning idea could be sparked by an outlandish one.

6. What must be documented after each meeting?

A. Decisions and action items, in a meeting summary.

Chapter 16: Transforming People into a Team

1. What four stages does a team go through during its development?

A.

- Forming
- Storming
- Norming
- Performing

2. When is it most likely that you'll need to help a team?

A. During the forming and storming phases. During forming, teams need guidance and clear instructions. During storming, teams typically need help making decisions and focusing on what they are supposed to accomplish.

3. Name at least three ways to build relationships with team members.

A.

- Clarify roles, responsibility, and authority.
- Set specific, challenging, yet attainable goals.
- Be a good role model.
- Provide assistance.
- Provide feedback.
- Remove obstacles.
- Get to know people personally.
- Introduce fun into the workday.

4. How does evaluation of people performance vary from evaluation of project performance?

A. People performance is more qualitative. In addition to reviewing how assignments go, you also have to see how people work within the project environment, interact with others, solve problems, make decisions, and so on.

Chapter 17: Gathering Progress Information

1. What data should you collect to get an accurate picture of project status?

   A.

   - Actual start date
   - Hours worked
   - Estimated remaining hours
   - Estimated finish date
   - Nonlabor costs incurred
   - Cost associated with fixed-price vendor contracts
   - Quality measures
   - Issues
   - Risks

2. How often should you collect data about project status?

   A. Set a status update frequency so that you receive updates at least once or twice during the most common work package duration.

3. Identify four sources for project data.

   A.

   - Timesheets developed specifically for the project
   - Status reports
   - Reports produced based on project plans, such as risk management and quality management
   - Accounting system

Chapter 18: Evaluating Progress and Performance

1. How do you determine schedule variance?

   A. Compare the actual date to the baseline date. If the actual date is earlier than the baseline date, the schedule variance is positive.

2. Explain one reason why a positive cost variance might not be a good thing for a project.

   A. A positive cost variance means the actual cost is less than the baseline cost. If team members have worked fewer hours than you planned, the labor cost is less than the baseline cost. The cost variance is positive, but the project is probably behind schedule.

3. What is earned value?

   A. Earned value is the monetary value for the project work that is complete.

4. If earned value is less than planned value, what do you know about the project?

   A. The project is behind schedule.

5. If earned value is less than actual cost, what do you know about the project?

   A. The project is over budget.

6. What are the pros and cons of using the payback period to evaluate project financial performance?

   A. The payback period is easy to understand and calculate. However, it doesn't take time value of money into account. The project might not earn income or save money for the full length of the payback period. It also penalizes projects that earn money later rather than earlier.

Chapter 19: Getting a Plan Back on Track

1. If your project is struggling with many tasks behind schedule, over budget, or both, what is the first thing to look at?

   A. Revisit the project definition, including the project goal, objectives, requirements, and scope. If the project wasn't defined correctly, the plan you built around that definition won't be a success.

2. If you want to shorten a schedule without incurring much if any additional cost, which technique would you choose? What is the drawback of the technique you select?

   A. Fast-tracking shortens a schedule without incurring additional cost. However, it increases risk because you start tasks before their predecessors are complete.

3. If the project sponsor asks you to crash the project to shorten the schedule, which tasks would you choose to crash?

   A.

   ■ Tasks on the critical path

   ■ Tasks that reduce the duration for the least amount of money

- Only the tasks needed to achieve the reduction in duration you need
- Tasks that can be shortened with resources that are available

4. Name at least two reasons that overtime should be the last resource method to consider.

A.

- People can work longer hours for only so long before they become less productive and begin to make mistakes.
- Overtime might increase project cost if people are paid a premium for overtime hours.
- The people you assign to work overtime might be able to work on more beneficial assignments with that time.

Chapter 20: Obtaining Acceptance and Other Wrap-Up Tasks

1. What is the purpose of obtaining final acceptance for a project?

A. To confirm that the project objectives, deliverables, and requirements have been met.

2. Name at least three types of information you would include in a project closeout report.

A.

- Cost
- Schedule
- Effort
- Completed scope
- Variances
- Quality
- Analysis of project management processes
- Lessons learned
- Risks that occurred and the effectiveness of risk management
- Change requests incorporated into the project

3. Why do you close contracts and accounts at the end of a project?

   A. To ensure that the project does not incur additional charges or liability.

4. Name two types of transitions you might manage at the end of a project.

   A.

   ▪ Transitioning resources to their next assignments or back to their functional departments.

   ▪ Transitioning ownership of deliverables to the appropriate groups, such as manufacturing and customer support.

Chapter 21: Documenting a Project for Posterity

1. Name at least two reasons why project archives are important to an organization.

   A.

   ▪ For future projects of the same type to leverage information
   ▪ Audit purposes
   ▪ Regulatory purposes
   ▪ Certification purposes
   ▪ To help new project managers learn processes

2. Why is the project notebook so important in the development of the project archives?

   A. Because most of the content of the project notebook makes up the content of the project archives.

3. Name at least 10 of the items that can be a part of the project archives.

   A. From the initiating processes:

   ▪ Project problem
   ▪ Project goal and objectives
   ▪ Requirements
   ▪ Success criteria
   ▪ Strategy
   ▪ Scope statement, including risks, assumptions, and constraints
   ▪ The stakeholder registry or contact list

- Project proposal or signoff document
- Project charter

B. From the planning processes:

- List of deliverables
- Work breakdown structure
- Responsibility matrix
- Resource plan
- Project organization chart
- Work estimates
- Cost estimates and project budget
- Project schedule
- Quality plan
- Communication plan
- Change management plan
- Risk management plan

C. From the executing processes:

- Project register
- Project baselines and baseline resets
- Deliverable acceptance log and forms
- Evidence of completed deliverables

D. From the monitoring and controlling processes:

- Change request log
- Risk management documents
- Issues log
- Status reports
- Schedule updates to progress and costs

E. From the closing processes:

- As-delivered project plan
- Project signoff or project closeout report
- Project summary and results

4. Why is it important to create the project archives as soon as possible after the project is finished?

   A. Because that's when the project details are fresh in your mind and when the information is easiest to collect.

5. Name at least three of the methods (printed or electronic) for storing the project archives.

   A.

   - Three-ring binder(s)
   - Compact disc
   - Flash drive
   - Project wiki
   - Shared drive
   - Document library on the intranet
   - Document control
   - Document management system

Chapter 22: Don't Forget Lessons Learned

1. What are at least two other names for "lessons learned"? What are the pros and cons of using these different names?

   A.

   - Post mortem
   - Project review
   - Project implementation review
   - Post-implementation review

2. Name at least three ways that project lessons learned can help an organization.

   A.

   - Save time.
   - Save money.
   - Create a realistic project plan.
   - Provide history about how a project should be conducted.

- Validate project management methodology.
- Help train novice project managers.
- Improve results.

3. In addition to the team members, what are the two roles that must be present for an effective lessons learned meeting?

   A.

   - Facilitator
   - Scribe

4. What are the three key types of feedback you are trying to get out of the lessons learned process?

   A.

   - What went well and what were the successes and strengths of the project?
   - What didn't go well or were the failures, weaknesses, or challenges of the project?
   - What can be improved?

5. Name at least three ground rules for a constructive lessons learned meeting.

   A.

   - Be positive.
   - Be respectful.
   - Be constructive.
   - Use "I" statements.
   - Practice active listening.
   - Let the speaker finish.
   - Develop recommendations.

6. Where should lessons learned documentation reside?

   A. It should go into the project archives. It should also be provided to the participating team members and managing stakeholders. *Optional additional answers*: It can also be provided to other key stakeholders and to project managers about to initiate a similar project.

Chapter 23: Running a Project Management Office

1. What is a project management organization and what is its purpose?

   A. A committee, board, or centralized department that seeks to improve project success rates and ensure that projects serve the organization's strategic goals.

2. Name at least four of the activities that a PMO might be responsible for.

   A.

   ▪ Coordinate project management standards and processes.

   ▪ Facilitate and monitor compliance with certification and regulatory requirements.

   ▪ Evaluate and support project scheduling software and other tools.

   ▪ Support implementation of project management methodologies.

   ▪ Assign project managers to projects.

   ▪ Coordinate cross-project communication.

   ▪ Mentor and coach project managers.

   ▪ Provide training on project management topics.

3. How might a PMO help an organization improve its implementation of a project management methodology?

   A. The PMO can evaluate the proper uses of a specific methodology to a project, it can standardize processes and practices associated with the methodology, it can provide tools and templates to support the methodology, and it can provide coaching and training regarding the methodology.

4. Name the three variations of PMO structures.

   A.

   ▪ A PMO for a specific program or project

   ▪ A PMO board or committee

   ▪ A permanent and centralized PMO department

Chapter 24: Managing a Portfolio of Projects

1. Define the term "project portfolio."

   A. A project portfolio is a collection of projects in an organization.

2. Name at least four major functions of project portfolio management.

   A.

   - Set portfolio strategy.
   - Evaluate project proposals.
   - Prioritize projects.
   - Select projects for inclusion in the portfolio.
   - Track portfolio project status.
   - Manage the portfolio.

3. What is pipeline management?

   A. Pipeline management is the pacing of the start and finish of selected projects so that costs, resources, and realized benefits flow optimally over time.

4. What two pieces of quantitative data are most useful for gauging the health of portfolio projects?

   A.

   - Projected finish date
   - Projected budget performance

Chapter 25: Selecting the Right Projects

1. What are the four stages of approval that a project idea should go through during its life cycle?

   A.

   - Idea description
   - Project proposal

- Project plan
- Project execution

2. What are the three categories for project selection criteria?
   A.

   - Benefit
   - Cost
   - Feasibility

3. Name at least three project selection criteria.
   A.

   - Alignment with business strategy
   - Return on investment
   - Impact and other benefits
   - Opportunity
   - Cost
   - Risk
   - Time and resource expenditure
   - Resource availability
   - Timing
   - Relationship with other projects

4. What are at least two reasons why a project that doesn't meet selection criteria would still be approved for implementation?
   A.

   - Legal requirements
   - Regulatory requirements
   - Certification requirements
   - Project sponsor demand
   - Customer commitment

This appendix presents the project management forms discussed throughout the book and available for download at www.wiley.com/go/ProjMgmtCoach.

Chapter 3: Getting a Project Off the Ground

Solution Rating Matrix

Problem: We have no historical data on customer complaints, so we have no way to identify and resolve systemic problems.
Goal: Develop a system for tracking and analyzing customer complaints.

		Solution rating: How well does the solution satisfy the criteria? (0=not at all, 5=very well)							
Criteria	Weight: How important is the criteria? 5=required	Solution 1 rating: Paper form with hardcopy file	Solution 1 score	Solution 2 rating: Computer form with hardcopy file	Solution 2 score	Solution 3 rating: Customer database including complaint fields	Solution 3 score	Solution 4 rating: Add complaint fields to existing customer tracking system	Solution 4 score
Track customer complaints.	5	5	25	5	25	5	25	5	25
Compile customer complaints.	4	5	20	5	20	5	20	5	20
Easy to record complaints.	4	4	16	5	20	5	20	5	20
Easy to compile complaints.	3	1	3	1	3	4	12	4	12
Generates reports.	2	0	0	0	0	5	10	3	6
Quick to develop.	2	5	10	5	10	2	4	4	8
Inexpensive.	2	5	10	5	10	1	2	4	8
TOTAL SCORE			84		88		93		99

Form 3-1: Solution Rating Matrix

Project Name:
Scope Statement

Scope Description
The characteristics of the product, service, or result that the project is to achieve.

User Acceptance Criteria
The process and criteria for accepting completed products, services, or other results.

Success Criteria
The business goal(s) to be achieved by the project: what, how much, by when.

Project Deliverables
The tangible items being produced through the execution of the project.

Project Boundaries
What is being excluded from the project.

Project Constraints
Limitations on the project that constrain project options, such as time, budget, etc.

Project Assumptions
Identification of any information that is unknown at the time.

Form 3-2: Project Scope Statement

Project Proposal for _____

Problem or Opportunity Statement
Scope Statement, Project Description, or Statement of Work
Project Goal
Project Objectives
Success Criteria
Risks
Assumptions
Constraints
High-Level Project Costs

Form 3-3: Project Proposal

Chapter 6: Estimating Work and Cost

	Hours	Labor cost	Materials, equipment, and facilities	Other costs	Total cost
Mobile Web eyeglasses project	1885	$232,500	$55,000	$25,500	$313,000
Lenses and frames	830	$100,500	$27,000	$10,000	$137,500
Develop feasibility study	200	$20,000	$1,000	$1,000	$22,000
Perform market research	280	$28,000	$1,000	$3,000	$32,000
Create eyeglass prototype	350	$52,500	$25,000	$6,000	$83,500
User Interface and mobile apps	1055	$132,000	$28,000	$15,500	$175,500
Research functionality and write specs	325	$32,500	$2,000	$3,000	$37,500
Research feasibility of top apps	200	$20,000	$1,000	$4,000	$25,000
Build and test prototype	350	$52,500	$25,000	$8,000	$85,500
Write app development guidelines	180	$27,000	$0	$500	$27,500
Total mobile Web eyeglasses estimate					$313,000
Contingency funds (15%)					$46,950
Project cost					$359,950
Management reserve (5%)					$15,650
Project budget					$375,600

Form 6-1: Estimate Work Book

Chapter 7: Planning Project Resources

	Materials research team	User interface design team	Information architecture team	Software development team	Manufacturing lab	Software testing	Product testing	Marketing	Customer	Sponsor
Lens and frame feasibility	R,A				C		I		I	C
User interface and mobile apps feasibility		R,A	R,C	R		I			I	C
Lens and frame development	C				R,A		I		C	C
User interface and mobile apps development		R	R,C	R,A	C,I	C	I	I	I	C
Build prototype					R,A		C	I	I	I
Test prototype		C		C	R	R,A			I	I
Market test prototype					R	R	A	I	I

Form 7-1: Responsibility Matrix

Chapter 10: Setting Up a Communication Plan

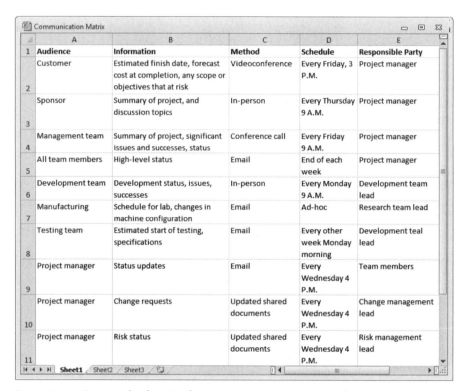

	A	B	C	D	E
1	**Audience**	**Information**	**Method**	**Schedule**	**Responsible Party**
2	Customer	Estimated finish date, forecast cost at completion, any scope or objectives that at risk	Videoconference	Every Friday, 3 P.M.	Project manager
3	Sponsor	Summary of project, and discussion topics	In-person	Every Thursday 9 A.M.	Project manager
4	Management team	Summary of project, significant issues and successes, status	Conference call	Every Friday 9 A.M.	Project manager
5	All team members	High-level status	Email	End of each week	Project manager
6	Development team	Development status, issues, successes	In-person	Every Monday 9 A.M.	Development team lead
7	Manufacturing	Schedule for lab, changes in machine configuration	Email	Ad-hoc	Research team lead
8	Testing team	Estimated start of testing, specifications	Email	Every other week Monday morning	Development teal lead
9	Project manager	Status updates	Email	Every Wednesday 4 P.M.	Team members
10	Project manager	Change requests	Updated shared documents	Every Wednesday 4 P.M.	Change management lead
11	Project manager	Risk status	Updated shared documents	Every Wednesday 4 P.M.	Risk management lead

Form 10-1: Communication Matrix

Team Member:	Julia		Time Period:	5/5/12 - 5/11/12						
			Scheduled Start	Scheduled Hours	Scheduled Finish	Actual Start	Hours Prior to This Period	Hours This Period	Est. Remaining Hours	Est. Finish Date
Assigned Tasks:	Task 1		5/2	40	5/8	5/4	8	24	8	5/15
	Task 2		5/8	8	5/11	5/2	0	8	0	
	Task 3		5/10	40	5/18	5/10	0	8	24	5/18

Form 10-2: Status Update Form

Chapter 11: Setting Up a Change Management Plan

Change Request

Project:
Project manager:
Submitted by:
Date submitted:

Submitter fills in:
Business justification:

Connection to project goal and objectives:

Description of change, design, and deliverables:

Project manager fills in:
Change request number:
Evaluation:
Estimate:

Hours	Cost	Duration	Effect on project

Recommendation and analysis:

Approved	Denied

Signature: _____   Date: _____

Print name: _____

Form 11-1: Change Request Form

A	B	F	G	H	I	J	K	L	M	N	O	P	Q	R	S
CR	Description	Addl. Docs	Est. Hours	Est. Cost	Est. End Date	Est. Proj. End Date		Approved /Rejected	By	Appr. Date		Assigned To	Act. Hours	Act. Cost	Act. End Date
1															
2															
3															
4															
5															
6															
7															
8															
9															
10															
			Total Est. Hours	Total Est. Cost		Est. Proj. End Date							Total Actual Hours	Total Actual Cost	Act. Proj. End Date
			-	-									-	-	

Form 11-2: Change Request Log

Chapter 12: Managing Risk

Risk Log											
Risk ID	Risk Statement	Probability	Impact	Priority Score	Response	Scope Impact	Schedule Impact	Cost Impact	Resource Impact	Quality Impact
1	Vague requirements can cause scope creep.									
2	The product depends on new technology that's not fully tested, which can increase R&D time.									
3	Design might take longer to determine how the technology will interact.									
4	The new technology could integrate more easily than expected.									
5	The product speed and reliability are unknown and might not satisfy requirements.									
6	Delays in shipments might delay the schedule.									
7	Materials could be delivered in half the time scheduled.									
8	Legal requirements could change, increasing project scope and cost.									
9	The regulations under review could not change after all.									
10	An unknown competitor could get their version to market first, which would impact our return									
11	A key competitor could drop out of the market.									
12	The customer could change the project direction.									
13	Construction will continue into hurricane season, which could mean delays.									
14	A light hurricane season could result in less downtime than planned.									
15	A critical task depends on a deliverable from another project, which has been delayed									
16	Another high-profile project could take resources our project depends on.									
17	Our project budget could be cut due to a drop in sales.									
18	Management is more focused on new development than on projects like ours, which									

Form 12-1: Risk Log

Risk Detail Sheet

Risk ID #	Risk Statement
Owner	Risk Description

Probability Rating:　　**X　Impact Rating:**　　**=　Priority Score:**

Response Strategy (mark one)

　　Mitigate　　　Plan Contingency　　　Transfer　　　Avoid　　　Accept

Response Description (include trigger if applicable)

Action Plan

Relevant Dates

Scope Impact	Schedule Impact	Cost Impact	Resource Impact	Quality Impact

Status (mark one)　　Inactive　　　Active　　　Resolved　　　Closed

Form 12-2: Risk Detail Sheet

Chapter 15: The Keys to Successful Meetings

<Project Name>	**Meeting Agenda**		
Project Goal *Research and develop the new* *mobile Web eyeglasses product.*	**Meeting Name:** **Meeting Date and Time:**		
Meeting Goal or Outcome:			

Topic	Responsible	Time Limit	Decision, Action Item, Due Date, Owner, Notes

Form 15-1: Meeting Agenda

Mobile Web Eyeglasses
Development Project

Meeting Agenda

Project Goal
Research and develop the new
mobile Web eyeglasses product.

Weekly Status Meeting

November 14, 2014, 1-1:30 pm

Meeting Goal:
Weekly check-in from each team member about accomplishments, goals, and obstacles.

Topic	Time Limit	Notes

Weekly check-in, round robin
 	
  Tasks accomplished since last week
 	
  Tasks in progress
 	
  Tasks being completed in the next week
 	
  Obstacles to completing tasks
	1-2 min each
	
	15 min total	

Other risks or issues	5 min	
Problems solved	5 min	
Lessons learned	5 min	

Form 15-2: Status Meeting Agenda

Chapter 17: Gathering Progress Information

Status for:	<Resource name>					
Tasks	Actual start date	Hours worked	Estimated remaining hours	Estimated completion date	Issues	Other comments
Assigned task 1						
Assigned task 2						
Assigned task 3						

Form 17-1: Progress Update Form

Chapter 18: Evaluating Progress and Performance

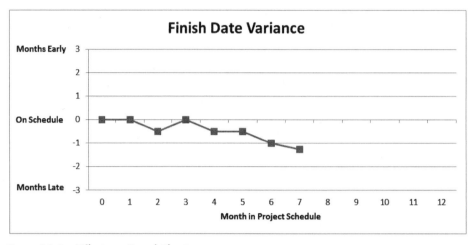

Form 18-1: Milestone Trend Chart

Chapter 20: Obtaining Acceptance and Other Wrap-Up Tasks

Mobile Web Eyeglasses Project   *Closeout Report*

Project manager: Vic Specs

Project Summary

The mobile web eyeglasses project is complete and unanimously voted a success by all stakeholders. The delivery was delayed 2 months, because the project sponsor and customer had requested several changes to improve the quality of the results.

Quality and Customer Satisfaction

The project customer is ecstatic and was last seen exploring New York City with the help of her web-enabled eyeglasses. Manhattanites did not seem to notice that she was pointing in every direction excitedly to no one in particular.

Issues

The only issue was that research took longer than estimated, exceeding the buffer added for the risks of using experimental technology.

Lessons Learned

Although we anticipated delays due to the new technology and added buffers to the schedule, research exceeded those buffers. Untried technology requires a very flexible schedule and budget.

Risks

New technology and materials were identified as risks. The schedule included a four-month buffer. In addition, we negotiated contracts with three vendors providing the materials for the lenses. That response was successful, because one vendor went out of business and another ran into supply problems. The remaining vendor delivered only two weeks late.

Project Management Processes

We opted to re-estimate the project at the beginning of each phase, which was a good decision. Because of the unknowns in this project, our estimates changed significantly as we obtained more information.

Cost

Estimated cost	$1,400,000
Final cost	$1,875,000
Variance	$325,000
Variance %	23%

Schedule

Estimated finish date	08/26/12
Actual finish date	10/28/12
Variance	2 months

Variances in cost and schedule were both due to approved change requests submitted by the customer.

Form 20-1: Project Closeout Report

Chapter 21: Documenting a Project for Posterity

HyperNet Strategies - Web Training Project Archives		
Submitted by Monique Sherman, project manager, 3/7/12.		
Item	**Description**	**Location**
Project goal and objectives		T:/HyperNet/2012/WebTraining/Initiating/G&O.docx
Requirements document	Detailed requirements from the customer.	T:/HyperNet/2012/WebTraining/Initiating/requirements.xlsx
Success criteria		T:/HyperNet/2012/WebTraining/Initiating/success.docx
Scope statement	Includes scope, objectives, strategy, constraints, assumptions, risks, and rough order of magnitude budget.	T:/HyperNet/2012/WebTraining/Initiating/scope.docx
Proposal	Includes the customer signoff and contract.	T:/HyperNet/2012/WebTraining/Initiating/proposal.docx
Project charter		T:/HyperNet/2012/WebTraining/Initiating/charter.docx
Deliverables		T:/HyperNet/2012/WebTraining/Planning/deliverables.xlsx
Work breakdown structure		T:/HyperNet/2012/WebTraining/Planning/wbs.vsd
Resource plan		T:/HyperNet/2012/WebTraining/Planning/ResourcePlan.xlsx
Project organization chart	Includes responsibility matrix.	T:/HyperNet/2012/WebTraining/Planning/OrgChart.vsd
Work estimates		T:/HyperNet/2012/WebTraining/Planning/WorkEstimates.xlsx
Project budget	Includes cost estimates and resulting budget	T:/HyperNet/2012/WebTraining/Planning/Budget.xlsx
Communication plan	Includes ground rules, issues handling, and sample reports.	T:/HyperNet/2012/WebTraining/Planning/CommunicationPlan.docx
Change management plan	Includes roster of change management board, procedure, forms, and log.	T:/HyperNet/2012/WebTraining/Planning/ChangeMgmtPlan.docx
Project baseline #1	First baseline, from 10/1/2011.	T:/HyperNet/2012/WebTraining/Executing/Baseline1.xlsx
Project baseline #2	Second baseline, from 11/1/2011.	T:/HyperNet/2012/WebTraining/Executing/Baseline2.xlsx

Form 21-1: Archive Contents

Index of Completed Projects					
Project Name	**Project Summary**	**Project Manager**	**Sponsor / Customer**	**Completed**	**Keywords**
Live-action software demos	Create a series of 20 live-action videos demonstrating features of the HyperNet Strategies 2011 app for integration with the app and use at trade shows.	Monique Sherman	Lyle Ketman/ HyperNet Strategies	9/30/2011	video, demonstration, HyperNet Strategies, trade
Staff kitchen remodel	Remodel the staff kitchen in Building A, second floor.	Carrie Paul	John Sparks	10/15/2011	kitchen, remodel, construction
Training program development tools	Design and develop a suite of training program development tools for use by our internal curriculum development specialists.	Barry Melendez	Enrico Tafoya	11/17/2011	tools, training, R&D
Software trade show coordination	Coordinate the vendor booth, demos, workshop, and collateral materials for the 2012 software trade show in New York.	Robert Whiting	Yunie Chai/ Padme Development	1/20/2012	trade show, workshop, booth, trade show demo,
Web training modules	Create series of five self-paced Web training modules for customer service representatives of HyperNet Strategies.	Monique Sherman	Lyle Ketman HyperNet Strategies	3/12/2012	training, HyperNet Strategies

Form 21-2: Completed Projects

Chapter 22: Don't Forget Lessons Learned

Trade Show Project Review Questionnaire

Please answer these questions. Bring the completed questionnaire to our Project Review meeting next Tuesday at 3 pm in the Siskiyou Room.

1. Name one thing that went particularly well with this project.

2. Name one thing that could have been improved with this project.

3. Can you share a technique or process you discovered that saved time, money, or aggravation?

4. What was the most difficult problem you encountered during the project, and how did you solve it?

5. What did you find to be the most satisfying or fulfilling part of the project?

6. What was the most frustrating part of our project for you? What would you recommend for avoiding this frustration in the future?

Form 22-1: Lessons Learned Questionnaire

Lessons Learned Meeting
Ground Rules

Keep it positive.

Be respectful.

Be constructive.

Use "I" statements.

Practice active listening.

Let the speaker finish.

Develop recommendations.

Form 22-2: Ground Rules

Lessons Learned Report

Project Name:
Project Completed Date:
Project Manager:

Overview of the Project

Overview of the Lessons Learned Process

Successes and Strengths of the Project
-
-
-
-
-
-

Challenges and Weaknesses of the Project
-
-
-
-
-

Form 22-3: Simple Lessons Learned Report Template

Lessons Learned Report

Project Name:
Project Completed Date:
Project Manager:

Overview of the Project

Overview of the Lessons Learned Process

Successes and Strengths of the Project

Successes and Strengths	Recommendations for Future Projects

Challenges and Weaknesses of the Project

Challenges and Weaknesses	Recommendations for Future Projects

Form 22-4: Recommended Lessons Learned

Chapter 25: Selecting the Right Projects

Idea
Please complete this form with information about your idea.

Name: **Date:**

Phone: **Email:**

Describe your idea and any process:

Please answer the following questions the best you can:

- How much do you think it would cost (order of magnitude) to carry out this project?

- How much staff time do you think would be needed?

- What special skills or expertise would be needed for this project?

- How would this project further the organization's goals?

- What benefit would this project bring to our organization?

- What would happen if we do not do this project?

Please submit this form to your department manager for further consideration. You may be contacted for more information. Thank you!

Form 25-1: Idea Form

New Project Idea Evaluation				LEGEND				
Project: Develop mobile Web eyeglasses.				*Criteria weight: 3=Mission Critical 2=Very Important 1=Philosophical Priority*				
				Project score: 3=Completely Meets Criteria 2=Often Meets Criteria				
				1=Occasionally Meets Criteria 0=Never Meets Criteria or Not Applicable				
Project Evaluation Criteria	Criteria Weight	Project Score	Weighted Score					
Strategic Goal 1. Increase profits from sales of existing products.	3	0	0					
Strategic Goal 2. Develop new products to take advantage of emerging market opportunities.	3	3	9					
Strategic Goal 3. Improve customer service to grow brand loyalty.	2	1	2					
Strategic Goal 4. Operate in accordance with principles of social responsibility.	1	1	1					
Return on Investment above 20% in 12 months.	2	2	4					
Critical resources are expected to be available.	2	3	6					
Benefits outweigh high-level risks identified so far.	2	2	4					
Overall Score			26					

Form 25-2: Idea Score Sheet

Glossary

Activity — Work identified at levels higher than the work package in the work breakdown structure — for example, summary tasks describing phases or subsystems. In some organizations, however, "activity" is synonymous with task or work package.

Actual cost (AC) — How much has been spent for the work completed up to the status date.

Agile project management — A variation of iterative project management in which the solution is gradually identified over successive rotations throughout the project. Partial yet production-quality solutions are completed with each iteration, allowing for quicker realization of customer benefits and feedback.

Assumption — A condition that will affect the project, although the specifics of the condition are not yet known. For the purposes of planning, the specifics are assumed and called out as an assumption.

Baseline documents — Items such as the project plan, requirements, schedule, and budget that the managing stakeholders have approved. After approval, any changes are controlled by the change management process. In addition, numeric data such as planned start and finish dates, as well as work and cost estimates, are available for later comparison against actual values.

Benefits realization — Outcomes of a project or the success criteria that indicate how a project achieved its goal. Benefits realization often happens well after project completion and is often expressed in terms of strategic business goals such as increased revenue, decreased costs, increased customer satisfaction, and so on.

Buffer — Time added to the project schedule as a safety measure against delays due to issues, unknown conditions, or unexpected events. Also known as schedule buffer, contingency reserve, or time reserve.

Cause and effect diagram — A chart associated with a technique for identifying factors linked to potential problems, risks, or effects. Factors can include time, machinery, methods, material, energy, measurements, personnel, and environment. Also known as the Ishikawa diagram or fishbone diagram.

Change management plan — The document that outlines a project's process for handling requested changes to the project. This process typically includes defining the baseline documents, documenting change requests, evaluating and deciding on change requests, updating baseline documents to reflect changes, and monitoring the changes.

Change request — An appeal to the change review board for a modification to the project by any stakeholder. The request typically includes the justification, relationship of the change to the project goal and objectives, description of the change and deliverables, and effect on project risk.

Change review board — The primary group that decides whether or not change requests become a part of the project. A change review board is typically made up of key project stakeholders.

Closeout report — The final summary document indicating the final status and results of the project. The closeout report includes a qualitative summary of how effective and successful the project was. It also includes quantitative results such as standard measures, variances, scope, schedule, cost, and more.

Closing process group — The set of activities performed to conclude a completed project, including final acceptance, documenting final performance and lessons learned, closing contracts, releasing resources, and evaluating success.

Communication plan — The document that identifies the processes for communicating with project stakeholders. Includes facts about the types of information needed by different audiences, status reporting, and meetings.

Constraint — Any limitation that places boundaries on the project. Common examples include a finish date or budget imposed by the project sponsor or contractual conditions imposed by the customer.

Contingency funds — Money set aside for the project to respond to risks or resolve issues, established as a safety measure against going over budget. Also known as contingency reserve, contingency allowance, or management reserve.

Contingency reserve — Time or money added to the project schedule to respond to risks or resolve issues, established as a safety measure against delays or going over budget. Also known as schedule buffer, contingency reserve, or time reserve.

Continuous improvement (CI) — The ongoing effort to improve products, services, or processes in every facet of an organization's operations. CI is characterized by involvement of the entire organization at all levels, often in teams. CI is also known as Kaizen.

Corrective action — The response, such as defect repair or preventive action, to any shortcoming found in a quality audit.

Cost of quality (COQ) — Money spent during the project to avoid failures, including prevention and testing costs. COQ operates on the premise that costs for meeting quality requirements are less than those for dealing with nonconformance to requirements.

Cost performance index (CPI) — The ratio of earned value to actual cost, indicating how close the planned cost for completed work is to the actual cost. A CPI greater than 1 means the project is under budget. A CPI less than 1 means the project is over budget.

Cost variance (CV) — The baseline cost of completed work minus the actual cost of completed work. That is, earned value minus actual cost. If the earned value is greater than the actual cost, less was spent than planned for the completed work, resulting in a positive cost variance.

Crashing — Adding money and resources to a project to shorten the schedule.

Critical chain — The resource-constrained critical path that results when resource availability is applied to the schedule. The critical chain is often different from the critical path because of the effect of scarce resources on a schedule.

Critical chain project management — The variation of traditional project management, which focuses on the ways that assigned resources — particularly overallocated resources — affect the schedule's critical path. This approach also adds shared time buffers to the project, task sequences, and resources.

Critical path — The longest task sequence of dependent tasks through the schedule. If any task along the critical path is delayed, the project finish date will also be delayed. By definition, the critical path has no slack.

Critical path method (CPM) — The variation of traditional project management in which the critical path is established by the work estimates, task dependencies, and fixed date constraints of tasks in their sequences. Uses slack to determine the scheduling flexibility and the project time span.

Critical task — A task that's part of a project's critical path. A critical task has no slack, and if any critical task is delayed, the project finish date will also be delayed.

Date constraint — A fixed, imposed date that dictates when a project task can be scheduled. A date constraint often specifies a day when a task must start or finish, start or finish no later than, or start or finish no earlier than.

Deliverable — A unique and tangible outcome of a task or series of tasks. The item being produced indicates or proves that the project scope and product scope are being fulfilled. Deliverables are verifiable and often complete a process, phase, or project.

Dependency — The logical relationship or link between two tasks that indicates that one task must finish or start before another task can start or finish. The series of task dependencies creates task sequences through the project time span.

Duration — The time span of a task from start to finish. The time span often assumes the number of resources assigned but does not include weekends, holidays, or other nonworking time.

Earned value (EV) — Earned value is the value (in dollars) that the project has, in effect, earned because of the work that is complete up to the status date. This is the same as the baseline cost for completed work.

Earned value analysis (EVA) — Measures that use planned value, earned value, and actual cost to provide a complete assessment of project status to date in terms of schedule and budget.

Effort — The amount of time, typically in hours, for a task to be accomplished, regardless of the number of resources assigned. Also known as work or person-hours. Contrast with duration.

Equipment resource — A machine that helps accomplish project tasks — for example, a computer-aided manufacturing system or a construction crane.

Estimate to complete (ETC) — The approximate cost to complete the project, using the cost performance index (CPI). The baseline cost for the project's incomplete work is divided by the CPI. If the CPI is greater than 1, the estimate to complete will be lower than the baseline cost.

Executing process group — The set of activities performed to launch the work of the project, such as gaining approval and holding a kick-off meeting.

Fast-tracking — The technique for shortening the schedule in which adjustments are made where possible to overlap tasks, execute tasks in parallel rather than in sequence, or shorten lag time.

Final specifications — The final document that indicates how the product was actually delivered — for example, product documentation or as-built drawings. Final specifications are part of the project closeout report.

Finish-to-finish (FF) dependency — The task relationship in which the two linked tasks must finish at the same time — that is, the predecessor's finish triggers the successor's finish. The FF dependency is typically associated with at least a short period of lag time.

Finish-to-start (FS) dependency — The task relationship in which the preceding task (or predecessor) must finish before the succeeding task (successor) can start. This is the most common type of task relationship.

Float — The amount of time a task can be delayed without delaying other tasks. Also known as *slack*.

Free slack — The amount of time a task can be delayed without delaying the start of any successors. Also known as free float.

Gantt chart — A project scheduling diagram in which each task is represented as a horizontal bar along a timeline. The length and position of the bar indicates the task's duration, start date, and finish date. A table shows more task information in corresponding rows. Connecting lines between the bars represent the links between tasks.

Generic resource — A placeholder representing the type of resource needed to be assigned to a task, for example, "Engineer," "Trainer," or "Plumber." Using generic resources helps define resource requirements.

Human resources — Individuals who are assigned, have responsibility, and perform the tasks in a project. These resources, who make up the project team, can be employees, vendors, contractors, and consultants.

Initiating process group — The set of activities in which the project is defined in terms of the business case, goal, objectives, requirements, scope, and success criteria. Also known as scoping or pre-planning.

Integration management — Processes and activities that bring together all the other knowledge areas for successful project management. This includes developing the project plan and managing changes because these activities affect the scope, schedule, cost, and other aspects of the project.

Internal rate of return (IRR) — The annual return that the project's cash flows deliver, with the time value of money considered. Typically, an organization sets a minimum IRR that projects must achieve in order for the project to be approved.

Issue — An issue is an event, condition, realized risk, or problem that affects the project in some way, typically in terms of one or more project constraints — scope, time, money, resources, or quality.

Iterative project management — The methodology for managing projects in which the solution is gradually identified over successive rotations throughout the project. Partial, yet production-quality, solutions are completed with each iteration, allowing for quicker realization of customer benefits and progressive feedback. Also known as rolling wave and agile project management.

Knowledge area — A collection of related management processes and activities that are required for successful project management. The project management knowledge areas deal with project scope, time, cost, quality, human resources, communications, risk, procurement, and integration management.

Lag time — A delay between two linked tasks in which the successor task starts later than the dependency type (such as finish-to-start) would otherwise dictate.

Lead time — A partial overlap between two linked tasks, in which the successor task starts earlier than the dependency type (such as finish-to-start) would otherwise dictate. This is a common method for fast-tracking the schedule.

Lessons learned — Information provided by team members and other stakeholders about how aspects of the project can be repeated or enhanced and how problems and issues can be prevented or resolved. This information can be used to improve the performance of future projects. Lessons learned are collected in a knowledge base or report.

Management reserve — Time and money beyond the project's normal schedule buffers or contingency funds, which management can allocate to respond to an unanticipated problem that causes a schedule delay or increased cost.

Managing stakeholder — A project stakeholder with management or executive oversight. Managing stakeholders can include the project sponsor, the customer, the portfolio manager, and other members of an organization's leadership team.

Material resource — Goods or supplies consumed as part of fulfilling project tasks — for example, lumber for a construction project or binders for a training project.

Milestone — A significant event within the schedule that marks progress. A milestone can represent the completion of a deliverable, the beginning or ending of a phase, a decision, or a handoff to another team.

Monitoring and controlling process group — The set of activities performed to gather project status information, evaluate progress, and make adjustments and corrections to keep the project on target.

Net present value (NPV) — The measure of the value the project provides, with money spent, the amount earned or saved, and the time value of money taken into consideration. Inflation, money borrowed, and annual rate of return can make this value vary over time.

Network diagram — A project scheduling flowchart in which each task is represented as a box, or node. Each box includes the task name, start and finish dates, work amount, assigned resources, and other schedule information. Task dependencies are shown with connecting lines between boxes.

Order of magnitude estimate — An early and rough cost estimate developed for project proposal and selection purposes. Based on the cost for similar projects in the past, the order of magnitude estimate approximates the order of magnitude for the project cost, for example, $10,000, $100,000, or $1,000,000.

Overallocated — The condition in which resources are scheduled beyond what their availability allows during a time period.

Payback period — The length of time the project requires to earn back the money spent to perform the project. This analysis is based on the cost and duration of the project as well as how much the project is expected to earn or save per time period when benefits are realized.

People resources — Individuals who are assigned, have responsibility, and perform the tasks in a project. These resources, who make up the project team, can be employees, vendors, contractors, and consultants.

Planned value (PV) — The baseline cost for work originally scheduled to occur before the status date.

Planning process group — The set of activities that defines the work to be done to fulfill the project's goal and objectives. Also includes estimating project effort and cost as well as developing the schedule, resource, quality, risk, and other plans for implementing the project.

Portfolio manager — A person or group that evaluates and prioritizes project ideas, launches new projects, and evaluates current projects to assess the project's value to the organization's strategic goals.

Portfolio project — A project that's a component of an organization's project portfolio.

Post-implementation review (PIR) — A project review meeting with project stakeholders after project completion, or later, after success criteria and other project results are known. Also known as project implementation review.

Predecessor — A task that must finish or start before a dependent task can start or finish.

Product scope — The definition of features and functions of a product or service, often in the context of the project that's producing the product or service. Compare with *project scope*.

Program — An overarching endeavor to produce a specific outcome delivering long-term benefits to the organization. Within the program, there are typically several projects that serve the program goals. In addition, programs often include operations and other non-project activities.

Program Evaluation and Review Technique (PERT) — A statistical approach to estimating that uses a weighted average of three values: optimistic, pessimistic, and most likely.

Project — A unique endeavor with clearly defined objectives and deliverables, clear-cut starting and ending dates, and, most of the time, a budget.

Project archives — The collection of all plans, results, and other project documentation associated with the project for historical purposes. The project archives capture the institutional knowledge acquired during the course of the project.

Project charter — A document officially announcing an approved project. Distributed by the project sponsor, the charter identifies the project manager and the extent of the project manager's authority.

Project goal — The broad description of what the project intends to achieve, expressing the desired state of affairs.

Project management office (PMO) — A department, committee, or board responsible for centralizing and coordinating project management, with the intent of improving project success rates by standardizing and supporting project management practices in the organization.

Project notebook — The collection of all documentation associated with the project, including requirements, scope statement, work breakdown structure, project schedule, quality plan, spreadsheets, communication, and so on. The project notebook, also known as the project register, can be maintained in print or electronic formats.

Project portfolio — A collection of projects in an organization, which may or may not have some point in common with one another.

Project portfolio management (PPM) — The practice of taking a strategic perspective toward projects, measuring them as business investments rather than as ad hoc endeavors. PPM seeks to ensure that the projects undertaken add benefit to the organization.

Project post mortem — A meeting with team members after project completion to review how aspects of the project should be repeated, improved upon, or constructively resolved as necessary in future projects. Results are compiled in a report and maintained with the project archives. Also known as project review.

Project review board — A group of stakeholders who evaluate incoming project ideas for the organization, often based on set criteria, a scorecard, or other selection tool. The board has the authority to approve, fund, hold, cancel, or reject project ideas and proposals.

Project scope — The definition of activities to be done as part of the project. The project scope identifies the boundaries of a project, indicating not only what will be done, but what will not be done. Compare with *product scope*.

Quality assurance (QA) — The practice of improving, auditing, and stabilizing a product, service, or other result based on quality requirements and the results of quality control measurements. The focus of QA is to avoid or minimize defects or errors.

Quality audit — A structured, independent review of the project to determine whether and how well the project is adhering to organizational and project policies, processes, and procedures.

Quality control (QC) — The practice of testing or measuring and recording results at checkpoints to assess performance and ensure that the project performance meets the standard within appropriate parameters.

Quality management plan — The document that identifies the processes for implementing quality for the project and its results. Includes the quality standard, methodology, quality assurance procedures, and quality control metrics.

Quality methodology — A system of practices, techniques, and procedures for improving quality in a project or organization. Examples of formal quality methodologies include Total Quality Management and ISO 9000.

Quality standard — A set of specifications or requirements for a product or service. A project can be governed by a quality standard developed by an international or national standards organization or one specified by the project customer or sponsor.

RACI — The code that refers to the levels of involvement on a project as specified in a responsibility matrix. RACI stands for responsible, accountable, consult, and inform.

Requirements — Detailed specifications for the product, service, or other result that the project will produce, given the project goal and objectives. Requirements are developed from an analysis of the needs and expectations of the sponsor, customer, and other stakeholders.

Residual risk — The remaining possibility and impact of a future uncertain event or condition after response to the original risk has been planned.

Resource — The people, equipment, materials, and other items needed to complete the tasks in a project plan.

Resource leveling — The technique that schedules tasks so that the assigned resources are not overallocated. Resource leveling often uses available slack between tasks.

Resource pool — People within the organization available for project work. Resource pool information can include job titles, skill sets, home departments, and availability information.

Resource plan — A document that includes the staffing plan (skill sets or job titles, quantity, and dates) for team members needed for a project. The resource plan also includes the responsibility matrix and project organization chart.

Responsibility matrix — A document that specifies the groups and their levels of accountability and communication with the different aspects of a project. Typically uses the "RACI" levels of involvement. Also known as the responsibility assignment matrix.

Risk — An uncertain event or condition that has a possibility of occurring in the future, which, if it occurs, will affect the success of the project in some way, either negatively or positively.

Risk management — The process of identifying negative and positive risks to a project, analyzing the likelihood and impact of those risks, planning responses to higher priority risks, and tracking risks.

Risk management plan — The document that identifies the risk management processes for a project, including risk categories, risk identification and analysis, risk response strategies, risk assignments, and risk tracking.

Rolling wave project management — A variation of iterative project management in which detailed planning for an upcoming time period is added to the plan after the most recent period has ended so that there is always a detailed plan for the same amount of time, such as the next four weeks.

Schedule buffer — Time added to the project schedule to respond to risks or resolve issues, established as a safety measure against delays due to unknown conditions or events. Also known as schedule buffer, contingency reserve, or time reserve.

Schedule performance index (SPI) — The ratio of earned value to planned value, indicating how close the actual project schedule is to the baseline schedule. An SPI greater than 1 means the project is ahead of schedule. An SPI less than 1 indicates the project is behind schedule.

Schedule variance (SV) — The baseline cost of completed work minus the baseline cost of the work that was supposed to be completed. That is, schedule variance is earned value minus planned value. If more work was completed than planned, the earned value would be greater than the planned value, resulting in a positive schedule variance.

Scope creep — The addition of tasks to the project scope — typically reflecting functions and features — without examining the effects of those additions on the project schedule, budget, or resources, and without obtaining approval from the customer or the change review board.

Slack — The amount of time a task can be delayed without delaying other tasks. Also known as *float*.

Specifications — Detailed requirements for the product, service, or other result that the project will produce, given the project goal and objectives. Specifications are developed from an analysis of the needs and expectations of the sponsor, customer, and other stakeholders.

Stakeholder — Any person with a vested interest in the project. Project stakeholders include the project sponsor, project manager, team members, and end users of the project result.

Start-to-finish (SF) dependency — The task relationship in which the successor cannot finish until its predecessor has started. That is, the start of the predecessor triggers the successor's finish. This dependency is the most rare.

Start-to-start (SS) dependency — The task relationship in which the start of the successor task is triggered by the start of its predecessor. The SS dependency is typically associated with at least a short period of lag time.

Success criteria — Specific and unequivocal statements that indicate how the project manager or project sponsor will know that a project achieved its goal, often reflecting strategic business goals.

Successor — A task waiting for a dependent task to finish or start before it can start or finish.

SWOT analysis — A problem-solving or decision analysis technique in which strengths, weaknesses, opportunities, and threats to the project or organization are examined.

Task — The smallest unit of work in a project and often synonymous with the work package in a work breakdown structure. A task is a project activity that's finite enough to be estimated, scheduled, assigned, tracked, and managed.

Task relationship — The logical dependency or link between two tasks that indicates that one task must finish or start before another task can start or finish. The series of task relationships creates task sequences through the project time span.

Total Quality Management (TQM) — A management philosophy based on the premise that the quality of products and processes can be continuously improved.

Total slack — The amount of time a task can be delayed without also delaying the finish date of the project. Also known as total float.

Traditional project management — The methodology for managing projects in which process groups flow one after another, in waterfall fashion, from initiating, to planning, to executing, to monitoring and controlling, to closing. This methodology is characterized by the ability to take a single pass through each process group from start to finish, as contrasted with agile or iterative project management. Also called waterfall project management.

Variance — The difference between planned or baseline schedule or cost data and the actual schedule or cost data.

Work breakdown structure (WBS) — The framework in which the project goal is deconstructed into manageable, task-sized details called work packages to identify all work to be done to complete the project.

Work — The amount of time, typically in hours, for a task to be accomplished, regardless of the number of resources assigned. Also known as effort or person-hours. Contrast with *duration*.

Work package — The task defined at the lowest level of the work breakdown structure. The work package is a project component that's finite enough to be estimated, scheduled, assigned, tracked, and managed. Often synonymous with *task*.

Work package document — A document that identifies the work the assigned resources are to perform and any specifications associated with the work. This can range from a simple to-do list to a full page of notes and supporting documents such as specifications, blueprints, and guidelines. Also known as the WBS dictionary.

Index

22-minute meeting, 253

A

AC (actual cost), 437
acceptance tests
  developing, 318–319
  running, 319–320
accountability, responsibility
    matrix, 124
activity, 437
administrative closeout, 323–324
agile project management, 22–23,
    437
ancillary plans, 16
approval, 65–66
  obtaining, 228–229
approval *versus* sign-off, 62–63
approved projects, 69
archive contents form, 433
archives, 327
  information gathering, 328–330
assumptions, 59, 437
  scope statement, 54

audience
  communication plan and, 175
    functional managers, 180
    management stakeholders,
        178–179
    team members, 180
  external, 177
  project sponsor, 177
  stakeholders and, 176
    management stakeholders, 177
  team members, 177
audit, quality audit, 162–163

B

backyard deck construction, 5
baselines
  documents, 437
    defining, 195
    updates, 200–201
  resetting, 310–311
  saving, 229–230
benefits realization, 52, 438

blaming environments, 341

body language, communication
    and, 174

bottom up estimating approach,
    115

bottom up work identification,
    92–93

bottom-up thinkers, 93

boundaries, scope statement, 54

brainstorming, 46–47
    meetings, 261–262

broad requirements, 49

budget, building, 75–76, 117

buffers, 438
    CCPM and, 149

C

categories, 74

cause and effect diagram, 43, 166,
    438

CCPM (critical chain project
    management)
    buffers, 149
    schedule building and, 148–149

certification, PMO and, 358

change management plan, 16,
    191–192, 438
    baseline documents
        defining, 195
        updates, 200–201
    change requests
        decision making, 199–200
        documentation, 195–198
        evaluation, 198–199
        monitoring, 201
        tracking, 197–198
    change review board, members,
        193–194

delay prevention and, 198
    exceptions, 200
    not managing changes, 192–193
    notebook and, 230

change requests, 438
    decision making, 199–200
    documentation, change request
        form,
        195–196
    evaluation, 198–199
    form, 195–196, 427
    information needed,
        196–197
    log, 427
    monitoring, 201
    tracking, 197–198

change review board, 438
    members, 193–194

channels, communication plan
    and, 175

charter, 66–67
    distribution, 68
    elements, 67

charts
    control chart, 165
    Gantt chart, 441
    run chart, 165

CI (continuous improvement),
    159, 439

closeout report, 320–321, 438
    quantifying results, 321–323
    summarization, 321

closing process group, 19, 438

code of conduct, 24

communication
    body language and, 174
    conference calls, 184–185
    content, audience needs, 178–180
    description, 170–171

e-mail, 185–186
frequency, 188
importance, 170
in-person meetings, 184
listening, importance of, 174
methods, 184–188
notebook, 231
overview, 169–170
paraphrasing, 174
PMO and, 358, 361–362
positive/negative balance, 173
process, 171
responsible parties, 187–188
stakeholder groups and, 122
successful, 172–173
teleconferencing, 184–185
telephone, 187
timing, 188
videoconferencing, 184–185
written, 187
communication management, 26
communication matrix,
        176, 426
communication plan, 16, 438
    audiences, 175
    channel, 175
    content, 175
        status reports, 180–184
    method, 175
    responsible party, 175
    schedule, 175
completed projects form, 433
compliance, PMO and, 360
conference calls, 184–185
conflict resolution, 248–249
constraints, 59–60, 438
    date constraint, 140–141,
            141–142, 440
        deadlines, 142

milestones, 142–143
    specific dates, 142
identifying, 47–48
quality, 158
resources, CCPM and, 149
scope statement, 54
consultation, responsibility
        matrix, 124
content, communication plan
    and, 175
    audience needs, 178–180
contingency allowance, 218
contingency funds, 110, 218, 439
contingency plan
    approval, 217
    schedule buffer,
            217–218
    triggers, 219
contingency reserve,
        217, 218, 439
contracts
    cost plus, 234
    fixed price, 234
    retainers, 234
    time and materials, 234
control chart, 165
COQ (cost of quality), 161, 439
core planning team, estimates
        and, 106–107
corrective action, 439
cost
    budget, building, 75–76
    data collection, 280–282
    earned value analysis and, 295
    estimates, 16
        ROM (rough order of
                magnitude), 64, 75
        WBS and, 87
    lessons learned and, 339

management, 25
overtime and, 309
reducing in schedule, 151–152
cost of quality (COQ), 161
CPI (cost performance index), 296, 439
CPM (critical path method), 440
crashing, 150, 305, 439
critical chain, 22, 439
critical path, 138–139, 439
critical task, 440
culture, 242
customer tracking system case study, 41–42
CV (cost variance), 439

D
daily Scrum, 253
data collection
  accounting system, 286
  cost data, 280–282
  detail level, 283
  issues and risks, 282–283
  quality data, 282
  schedule data, 280–282
  sources, 284–286
  update frequency, 283–284
date constraints, 140–141, 440
  deadlines, 142
  flexibility, 141–142
  milestones, 142–143
  specific dates, 142
deadlines, 80, 142
decision making, effectiveness and, 244–247

defining projects. *See* project definition
delegation, 30
deliverables, 5–6, 440
  defined, 5–6
  scope statement, 54
  specifying, 57–58
  WBS and, 97
Delphi technique of estimating, 113
denied projects, 69
dependency, 440
  task dependencies, 78–79
diagrams
  cause and effect, 43, 166, 438
  fishbone, 43, 166
  Ishikawa, 43, 166
  scatter diagram, 165
discovery process, 40–41
documentation
  baseline documents, 437
    defining, 195
    updates, 200–201
  change request form, 195–196
    tracking requests, 197–198
  closeout report, 320–321
    summarization, 321
  lessons learned, 348–353
  meetings, 264
  notebook and, 230
  project ideas, 382–384
  project scope, 52–53
    scope statement, 53–54
  responsibilities, 122–125
  roles, 122–125
  work package document, 101, 448

duration, 440
  estimate, 78
  tasks, 145
  versus effort in estimates,
      110–111

E

e-mail
  content flow, 186
  scheduling, 186
  subject lines, 185–186
earned value analysis
  actual cost, 294
  CPI (cost performance index),
      296
  earned value, 293–294
  ETC (estimate to complete),
      296–297
  graphs, 295–296
  performance evaluation, 295–297
  SPI (schedule performance
      index), 296
effectiveness guidelines
  decision making, 244–247
  defining problem, 246
  help, 247
  options, 246–247
  prioritization, 246
  problem solving, 244–247
effort, 440
  versus duration in estimates,
      110–111
end users, 61
equipment resource, 77, 125–126,
  440
estimates, 75, 105–106. *See also*
  cost

bottom up, 115
budget, building, 117
contingency funds, 110
Delphi technique, 113
levels of estimates, 108–109
management reserve, 110
methods for, 111–115
Monte Carlo method,
    114–115
order of magnitude, 108
padded estimates, 109–110
PERT (Program Evaluation and
    Review Technique), 114–115
preparing estimates
  duration *versus* effort, 110–111
  estimating tools, 112–113
  experts and, 112
  information reuse, 112
  parametric models,
      112–113
project costs, 115
  equipment costs, 116
  facility costs, 116
  labor costs, 116
  material costs, 116
project life cycle and, 108
recording values, 112
task duration and, 145
team, core, 106–107
top down, 115
uncertainty, 107–110
work book, 425
ETC (estimate to complete), 296–
  297, 440
ethics, 24
EV (earned value), 440
EVA (earned value analysis), 440
executing process group, 17, 440

executing project
  approval, 228–229
  kickoff meeting, 235
  project notebook, updating,
    230–231
  resources
    in-house, 231–232
    vendors, 232–234
external audience, 177
external risks, 205

F
facilities, 77, 126
fast-tracking, 150, 441
  off track projects, 304–305
fault tree analysis, 42–43
feedback, 182
  gathering, lessons learned and,
    341–342
  issues tracking, 342
  quality management, 342
  status reports, 342
feeding buffers, 149
FF (finish-to-finish) dependency,
  441
final specifications, 441
financial closeout, 323–324
financial evaluation
  IRR (internal rate of return),
    300
  NPV (net present value),
    298–300
  payback period, 297–298
fishbone diagram, 43, 166
float, 152, 441
follow up meetings, 263

documentation, 264
  project plan adjustment, 264
forming, team development
  and, 268
forms
  archive contents, 433
  change request, 195–196, 427
  change request log, 427
  communication matrix, 426
  completed projects, 433
  estimate work book, 425
  idea form, 436
  idea score sheet, 436
  lessons learned questionnaire,
    434
  meeting agenda, 429
  milestone trend chart, 431
  progress update form, 431
  project closeout report, 432
  project proposal, 423
  project scope statement, 424
  proposal template, 63
  recommended lessons
    learned, 435
  responsibility matrix, 425
  risk detail sheet, 428
  risk log, 429
  solution rating
    matrix, 424
  status meeting
    agenda, 430
  status update form, 426
free slack, 441
frequency of status updates,
  283–284
FS (finish-to-start) dependency,
  136–137, 441

G

Gantt chart, 441
  schedule building and,
      132, 134
generic resource, 441
  assigning to tasks, 143–144
goal setting, team development
      and, 271
goal statements, problem
      statements and, 45
goals
  developing, 44–45
  neglecting, 374
ground rules, 81
group planning, 89–90

H

human resource management,
      25–26
human resources, 125, 441

I

idea form, 436
idea score sheet, 436
ideas for projects
  documentation, 382–384
  organization goals and,
      380–385
  tracking, 384
identifying work
  bottom up, 92–93
  team members and, 88
  top down approach and, 90–92
implementation review, 338
in-house resources,
      231–232
in-person meetings, 184

information
  gathering, project archives,
      328–330
  hand off, 324–325
  responsibility matrix, 125
infrastructure, PMO and, 358
inherited projects, validation, 40
initiating process group, 14–15,
      441
  business case, describing, 15
  project charter and, 15
  project definition, 15
initiation processes. See project
      initiation
integration management, 27–28,
      441
IRR (internal rate of return), 300,
      441
Ishikawa diagram, 43, 166
ISO 9000 Quality Management,
      159
issues, 442
  data collection, 282–283
  tracking, 221–222, 342
iterative project management,
      22–23, 442

K

kickoff meeting, 235, 258
knowledge areas, 23–24, 442
  communication management, 26
  cost management, 25
  human resource management,
      25–26
  integration management,
      27–28
  process groups and, 24

procurement management, 25–26
quality management, 26–27
risk management, 27
scope management, 24–25
time management, 25

L

labor costs, 116
lag time, 139, 442
  shortening in off track projects, 305
lead time, 139, 305, 442
legal closeout, 323–324
lessons learned, 442
  benefits, 338–340
  blaming environment and, 341
  dissemination, 352–353
  documenting, 348–353
  fear, minimizing, 346–348
  feedback, gathering, 341–342
  knowledge base, 352
  meetings
    conducting, 344–345
    managing stakeholders, 345
    preparation, 342–344
  passive voice use, 350
  past, 353
  planning and, 82
  presenting, 350–352
  questionnaire, 434
  recommended lessons learned form, 435
  report template, 349

solutions and recommendations, 351
  team information, 183
levels of estimates, 108–109
life cycle, estimates and, 108
line managers, team develoment and, 274
listening, importance of, 174
low-medium-high risk matrix, 209

M

management
  meetings, 260–261
  processes, 81–82
  status reports, 183–184
management reserve, 110, 217, 218, 442
managing stakeholder, 442
  lessons learned meeting, 345
material resource, 77, 126, 442
meetings
  22-minute meeting, 253
  agenda, 253–254, 429
    status meetings, 259–260
  brainstorming, 261–262
  contributors, 257
  ending, 258
  expectation setting, 256
  facilitating, 257
  feedback and, 341–342
  focus, 257
  follow up, 263
    documentation, 264
    project plan adjustment, 264
  in-person, 184
  inviting participants, 254–255

kickoff meetings, 258
lessons learned
   conducting, 344–345
   managing stakeholders, 345
   preparation, 342–344
management meetings, 260–261
planning, 252–253
planning meetings,
      262–263
project status, 259–260
schedule and, 255
Scrum huddle, 253
speakers, 257
starting, 256
teleconferencing, 256
time limits, 257
troubleshooting, 257
video conferencing, 256
Web conferencing, 256
methodologies
agile approach, 22–23
communication plan and, 175
critical chain, 22
iterative approach, 22–23
lessons learned and, 340
PMO and, 358, 360
quality management, 160
risk identification, 204
waterfall approach, 21–22
methods of communication,
   184–188
Microsoft Project, 134
milestones, 442
marking, 142–143
milestone trend chart, 431
progress tracking and, 290–291
money, 77
lessons learned and, 339

monitoring and controlling
      process group, 18, 443
Monte Carlo method of
      estimating, 114–115
multitaskers, scheduling and,
   147–148

N

narrative status reports,
      285–286
negative risks, response
      planning, 212–214, 219
network diagram, 443
   scheduling building and, 132,
      133
non-project time, scheduling and,
   146–147
nonworking time, scheduling
   and, 146
norming, team development and,
   268–269
notebook
   approved projects, 69
   assembling, 68
   change management and,
      230
   communication and, 231
   denied projects, 69
   documentation, 230
   format, 69–70
   quality management and, 230
   risk management and, 230
   tabled projects, 69
   updating, 230–231
NPV (net present value), 298–300,
      443
numeric risk rating, 209–210

O

objectives, 5–6
  creating, 45–46
  defined, 5–6
off track projects
  correcting course, 304–310
    approval, 310–311
    overtime work, 308–309
    resource options, 308
    schedule, fast-tracking, 304–305
    scope, reducing, 309–310
Open Workbench, 134
opportunities triggering projects, 42
order of magnitude estimate, 108, 443
organization chart, 127
organizational risks, 205
outsourcing, 308
over-allocated, 443
overlapping tasks, 305
overtime work, 308–309
ownership, conflicts, 122

P

padded estimates, 109–110
parametric models for estimating, 112–113
Pareto analysis, 43, 166
part-timers, scheduling and, 147–148
passive voice use, 350
payback period, 297–298, 443
people resources, 76–77, 443
perceived stakeholders, 61
performance, earned value analysis and, 295–297

performing, team development and, 269
PERT (Program Evaluation and Review Technique), 114–115, 444
phone communication, 187
PIR (post-implementation review), 338, 443
planning
  budget, building, 75–76
  categories and, 74
  groud rules, 81
  group, 89–90
  implementing plan, 235–236
  lessons learned, 82
  management processes, 81–82
  meetings, 262–263
  post mortems, 82
  process group, 15–17, 443
  resources, 76–77
  schedule, building, 78–79
  team, estimates and, 106–107
  WBS (work breakdown structure), 74
PMBOK (Project Management Body of Knowledge), 13
PMI (Project Management Institute)
  Code of Ethics and Professional Conduct, 24
  PMBOK (Project Management Body of Knowledge), 13
PMO (project management office), 444
  best practices, 358–360

certification and, 358
communication and, 361–362
compliance and, 360
compliance requirements, 360
document templates, 359–360
functions, 357–358
mentoring and training, 362
methodologies, 360
methodologies and, 360
need for, 363–364
objectives, 365–366
procedures, 359
processes, 359
regulatory requirements and,
    360
resources and, 361–362
services, 365–366
standards, 358–360
training and, 358
types, 364–365
portfolio manager, 443
portfolio project, 370, 443
positive risks, response planning,
    214–215, 219
post mortems, 82, 338
post-implementation review,
    52
PPM (project portfolio
    management), 444
allocation sample, 370
detail management, 377
evaluating, 372–374
evaluations, 375–376
overview, 370–372
prioritizing projects,
    372–374
project reporting, 377
project tracking, 375

tasks, 371
predecessors, 444
    task dependencies and, 135–136
prioritization, effectiveness and,
    246
problem solving, effectiveness
    and, 244–247
problem statements, 43
    goal statements and, 45
    strategies, 47
process flowchart, 166
process groups, 13–14
    closing, 19
    executing, 17
    initiating, 14–15
    knowledge areas and, 24
    monitoring and controlling, 18
    planning, 15–17
procurement management, 26
product development, 5
product scope, 444
programs, 444
    definition, 371–372
progress
    tracking
        earned value analysis, 293–297
        milestones, 290–291
        stoplight reports, 293
        variances, 291–292
        WBS and, 88
    update form, 431
project archives, 327, 444
    included items, 329–330
    index, 332
    information gathering, 328–330
    organization, 330–332
    storage, 333–334
project baselines, saving, 229–230

project buffers, 149
project charter, 444
  development, 14–15
  initiating process and, 15
project closeout
  administrative, 323–324
  financial, 323–324
  legal, 323–324
  report, 320–321, 432
    quantifying results,
      321–323
    summarization, 321
project costs, labor
  costs, 116
project culture, 242
project definition, 4, 37
  initial, 15
  questions to ask, 38
project elements, 4
project goal, 444
project initiation, 35
  discovery process, 40–41
  overview, 36–37
project management
  basics, 12–13
  risks, 206
project managers
  appointing, 14
  characteristics, 28–30
project notebook, 444
  change management and, 230
  communication and, 231
  documentation, 230
  quality management and, 230
  risk management and, 230
  updating, 230–231
project organization chart, 127

project portfolio, 444
  managing (*See* PPM (project
    portfolio management))
project post mortem, 445
project processes
  conflict resolution, 248–249
  defining, 240–244
  effectiveness guidelines, 244–247
  poor, 243–244
  results, 247–248
  success, 241–242
project proposal form, 423
project results, quantifying,
  321–323
project review board, 445
  idea success, 391–392
project reviews, 338
project scope, 445
  documentation, 52–57
    scope statement, 53–54
  scope creep, controlling, 55–57
project scope statement, 424
project sponsor, 177
project success
  acceptance tests
    developing, 318–319
    running, 319–320
  determining, 318–320
  sign-off, 320
  success criteria, 318–319
project transitions
  information hand off,
    324–325
  resources transition, 325
project website, 70
projects, 444
  complete projects form, 433

deliverables, 5–6
example projects, 4
ideas, 380
  documentation, 382–384
  organization goals,
    380–382
  project review board, 391–392
  tracking, 384
objectives, 5–6
off track (*See* off track projects)
overview, 3–4
selecting
  criteria, 386–390
  process, 385–386
troubled
  evaluating, 312
  recovery plan, 312–313
  symptoms, 311
uniqueness, 5
proposal
  finalizing, 65
  preparing, 62–65
  quick and dirty, 64
  template, 63
PV (planned value), 443

Q
QA (quality assurance), 156, 445
  audits, corrective actions, 163–
    164
  QC and, 162–163
  quality management plan and,
    160
QC (quality control),
  156, 445
  inspection, 164

purpose, 164
QA and, 162–163
quality management plan and,
  160
testing, 164
quality
  cause and effect diagram, 166
  CI (continuous improvement),
    159
  constraints, 158
  COQ (cost of quality), 161
  data collection, 282
  defects, 156
  inspection, 156
  ISO 9000 Quality Management,
    159
  management, 156
  measuring, 165
    run chart, 165
    scatter diagram, 165
    statistical sampling, 165
  overview, 156
  Pareto chart, 166
  prevention, 156
  problem discovery, 166
  process flowchart, 166
  recording, 165
    control chart, 165
  requirements
    identification, 157–158
    specifications, 157–158
  requirements document,
    157–158
  responsibility,
    161–162
  scope statement, 157
  Six Sigma, 159

standards organizations,
158–159
TQM (Total Quality
Management), 159
quality audit, 162–163
corrective actions, 163–164
quality credit, 445
quality management, 26–27
feedback and, 342
notebook and, 230
plan, 16, 445
integration, 161
methodology, 160
QA (quality assurance), 160
QC (quality control), 160
standard, 160
quality methodology, 445
quality standard, 445
quantifying project results,
321–323
questions to ask at project
definition, 38

R

RACI, 445
recommended lessons learned
form, 435
records, control chart, 165
recovery plan, 312–313
regulatory requirements, PMO
and, 358, 360
relationship building with team,
269–270
reports
closeout report, 438
lessons learned, 349
PPM and, 377
project closeout report, 432

status reports
management, 183–184
risks, 220
team members, 181–183
stoplight reports, 293
requirements, 445
broad, 49
differentiating, 50–51
document, 157–158
jump starting project and, 88–89
mining for, 49–50
prioritizing, 50–51
updating, 95
residual risk, 213, 446
resource leveling, 446
resource plan, 446
resource pool, 446
resources, 446
assigning to tasks, 143
generic resources,
143–144
multiple resources,
144–145
specific resources, 144
buffers, 149
CCPM and, 149
equipment resource, 77, 440
executing process group and, 17
expenses, 308
generic resource, 441
assigning to tasks, 143–144
human resources, 441
identifying, 77
in-house, 231–232
material resource, 77, 442
money, 77
needs breakdown, 126–127
off track projects, 308
outsourcing, 308

overallocated, 152
people resources, 76–77, 443
plan preparation, 127–128
planning, 121
PMO and, 358, 361–362
productivity, scheduling and, 147
resource leveling, 446
resource plan, 446
resource pool, 446
responsibilities
  documenting, 122–125
  responsibility matrix, 123–125
roles, documenting, 122–125
schedule optimization and, 152–153
transitioning, 325
types
  equipment, 125–126
  facilities, 126
  materials, 126
  people, 125
vendors, 232–234
work space facilities, 77
response planning, 211–212
negative risks, 212–214
positive risks, 214–215
residual risk, 213
risk detail sheet, 214
risk log, 213
responsibilities, 122–125
responsibility matrix, 122–123, 123–124, 425, 446
levels of involvement, 124–125
responsible party, communication plan and, 175
results, quantifying, 321–323

retainers, 234
risk, 58–59, 203–204, 446
analysis
  low/medium/high, 208–209
  numeric, 209–210
as opportunities, 207
categories, 204–206
data collection, 282–283
identifying, 204–208
low-medium-high risk matrix, 209
lower priority, 219
new, 219
plan response, 209
reality, 219, 220
status report, 220
tracking, 218–220
risk detail sheet, 214, 216, 428
risk log, 207, 216, 429
prioritizing risks, 211
ratings, 210
response plan and, 213
scores, 210
risk management, 27, 82, 446
contingencies, 216–217
  contingency funds, 218
  schedule buffer, 217–218
notebook and, 230
plan, 16, 446
  identified risks, 216
  key elements, 215–216
  monitoring plan, 216
  risk analysis tool, 216
  risk categories, 215
  risk detail sheet, 216
  risk log, 216
prioritizing, 210–211
residual risk, 213
response planning, 211–212

negative risks, 212–214
positive risks, 214–215
risk detail sheet, 214
risk log, 213
tracking risks, 218–220
roles, documenting, 122–125
rolling wave project
    management, 446
ROM (rough order of magnitude),
    64, 75
run chart, 165

S

sampling, 165
scatter diagram, 165
schedule, 92
  buffer, 446
    contingency plan, 217–218
  building, 16, 78–79
  communication plan and, 175
  crashing, 305–307
  data collection, 280–282
  deadlines, 80
  dependencies, task, 78–79
  duration estimate, 78
  earned value analysis and, 295
  fast tracking, 304–305
  meeting time, 255
  soft date targets, 80
  work estimate, 78
schedule building
  CCPM (critical chain project
      management), 148–149
    buffers, 149
  contingencies, 153
  crasing, 150
  date constraints, 140–141
    flexibility, 141–142

milestones, 142–143
deadlines, 142
fast-tracking, 150
from finish date, 140
  CCPM and, 148
from start date, 140
Gantt chart, 132, 134
interactive software application,
    132–133
  Microsoft Project, 134
  Open Workbench, 134
lag time, 139
lead time, 139
multitaskers, 147–148
network diagram, 132, 133
non-project time, 146–147
nonworking time, 146
optimization, 149–150
  cost reduction and,
      151–152
  resource assignments, 1
    52–153
  shortening schedule,
      150–151
part-timers, 147–148
specific dates, 142
starting, 137–138
task dependencies, 135–136
  critical path, 138–139
  FF (finish-to-finish), 137
  FS (finish-to-start), 136
  SF (start-to-finish), 137
  SS (start-to-start),
      136–137
tasks
  float, 152
  linked, 138
  resource productivity, 147
  slack, 152

scope, reducing in off track projects, 309–310

scope creep, 447
  controlling, 55–57

scope management, 24–25

scope statement, 53–54, 157
  assumptions, 54
  boundaries, 54
  constraints, 54
  deliverables, 54
  example, 54–55
  jump starting project and, 88–89

Scrum huddle, 253

sequencing, 92

SF (start-to-finish) dependency, 447

SharePoint, risk tracking, 220

sign-off, 65–66, 320
  versus approval, 62–63

Six Sigma, 159

slack, 152, 447

SMART objectives, 45–46

soft date targets, 80

soft skills of project manager, 29–30

software, schedule building, 132–134

solution rating matrix, 48–49, 424

specifications, 447

SPI (schedule performance index), 296, 446

SS (start-to-start) dependency, 136–137, 447

stakeholders, 447
  as audience, 176
  change review board, 194
  communication, 122
  customer representatives, 61

end user representatives, 61
  identifying, 14–15, 60–62
  lessons learned meeting, 345
  management, communication needs, 178–179
  management meetings, 261
  managing stakeholders, 60, 81
  perceived, 61
  support function representatives, 61
  team members, 60

status
  assignment status, 183
  meetings, 183, 259–260
    agenda, 430
  update form, 426
  update frequency, 283–284

status reports, 180
  feedback gathering and, 342
  management, 183–184
  narrative, 285–286
  risks, 220
  stoplight reports, 293
  task status forms, 285
  team members, 181–183

stoplight reports, 293

storage, project archives, 333–334

storming, team development and, 268

strategies
  brainstorming, 46–47
  problem statements and, 47
  selection tips, 48–49

success criteria, 51–52, 318–319, 447
  benefits realization, 52
  post-implementation review, 52
  scope statement, 54

successors, 447
  task dependencies and, 135–136
summarizing project, 321
support functions, 61
SV (schedule variance), 447
SWOT analysis, 46, 447

T

tabled projects, 69
task relationship, 78–79, 447
tasks, 447. *See also* work package
  assigning resources, 143
    generic resources, 143–144
    multiple resources,
        144–145
    specific resources, 144
  crashing schedule and, 306–307
  dependencies, 78–79
    critical path, 138–139
    FF (finish-to-finish), 137
    FS (finish-to-start), 136
    predecessors and, 135–136
    SF (start-to-finish), 137
    SS (start-to-start), 136–137
    successors and, 135–136
  duration, 145
  fast-tracking, 150
  overlapping, 305
  progress reports, 181–182
  resource productivity, 147
  status forms, 285
team
  as audience, 177
  assignment status, 183
  core, estimates and, 106–107
  decision information, 182
  development, 267–268
    assistance, 271

authority, 270
example setting, 270
expertise and, 272
feedback, 271
forming, 268
fun, 272
goal setting, 271
influence, 272
information gathering
    questions, 273
leadership and, 272
line managers, 274
norming, 268–269
people problems, 275
performance evaluation, 273–
    275
performing, 269
relationship building, 269–270
relationships and, 272
responsibilities, 270
roles, 270
storming, 268
feedback, 182
lessons learned, 183
related tasks status, 183
status reports, 181–183
work identification and, 88
technical risks, 205
technical skills, project managers
    and, 28
teleconferencing, 184–185, 256
telephone communication, 187
templates. *See also* forms
lessons learned, 349
PMO and, 359–360
time management, 25
time reserve, 217
time saving, lessons learned and,
    339

top down estimating approach, 115

top down work identification, 90–92

top-down thinkers, 93

total slack, 448

TQM (Total Quality Management), 159, 448

tracking, ideas, 384

trade show exhibits, 5

traditional project management, 448

training
  PMO and, 358
  program development, 5

trasitioning resources, 325

troubled projects
  evaluating, 312
  recovery plan, 312–313
  symptoms, 311

U

urgency, 244–245

user acceptance criteria (scope statement), 54

V

variance, 448
  earned value analysis and, 295
  progress tracking and, 291–292

vendors
  contracting, 233–234
  selecting, 233
  soliciting, 232–233

videoconferencing, 184–185, 256

W

waterfall project management, 21–22

WBS (work breakdown structure), 85, 448
  agile and, 90
  deliverables, 97
  dictionary, 101 (*See also* work package document)
  example, 87
  format, 97–99
  group planning and, 89–90
  multiple branches, 91
  multiple levels, 91
  naming, 99
  need for, 87–88
  numbering, 99–100
  organization chart format, 98
  outline format, 98
  planning and, 74
  rolling wave and, 90
  validating, 95
  work identification
    bottom up, 92–93
    team members and, 88
    top down, 90–92
  work organization and, 96–100
  work package and, 86

Web conferencing, 256

website, 70

work
  definition, 448
  estimate, 78
    WBS and, 87
  identification
    bottom up, 92–93
    team members and, 88

top down, 90–92
package, 86, 448
  detail level, 94
  document, 101, 448 (*See also*
    WBS dictionary)
  proportionality, 94

work breakdown
  structure, 16
work space facilities, 77
working overtime,
  308–309
written documentation, 187